Religions in Practice

FOURTH EDITION

Religions in Practice

An Approach to the Anthropology of Religion

John R. Bowen

Washington University in St. Louis

Boston ■ New York ■ San Francisco
Mexico City ■ Montreal ■ Toronto ■ London ■ Madrid ■ Munich ■ Paris
Hong Kong ■ Singapore ■ Tokyo ■ Cape Town ■ Sydney

Senior Series Editor/Series Editor: Dave Repetto
Series Editorial Assistant: Jack Cashman
Marketing Manager: Kelly May
Production Editor: Patrick Cash-Peterson
Editorial Production Service: TexTech International
Composition Buyer: Linda Cox
Manufacturing Buyer: Debbie Rossi
Electronic Composition: TexTech International
Cover Administrator: Kristina Mose-Libon

For related titles and support materials, visit our online catalog at www.ablongman.com.

Between the time website information is gathered and then published, it is not unusual for some sites to have closed. Also, the transcription or URLs can result in typographical errors. The publisher would appreciate notification where these errors occur so that they may be corrected in subsequent editions.

ISBN 13: 978-0-205-57861-0
ISBN 10:   0-205-57861-6

Library of Congress Cataloging-in-Publication Data

Bowen, John Richard, 1951–
    Religions in practice : an approach to the anthropology of religion / John R.
Bowen.—4th ed.
        p. cm.
    ISBN-13: 978-0-205-57861-0
    ISBN-10: 0-205-57861-6
    1. Religion.   2. Religions.   3. Ethnology–Religious aspects.   I. Title.
    BL48.B625 2009
    200—dc22   2007042089

Printed in the United States of America

10 9 8 7 6 5 4 3 2 1   11 10 09 08 07

To Vicki,
for love and support

Contents

11 ᔐ *Sacred Speech and Divine Power*   151

12 ᔐ *Transnational and Diaspora Religions*   177

Preface

*A*s in the previous editions of this book, I have tried to write about religion from my own perspective for as wide an audience as possible. As an anthropologist, I emphasize the ways in which people engage in religious activities. I take a broad view of "religion," including in its domain those activities that, in one way or another, invoke realities and powers beyond the reach of ordinary senses. Religion thus includes healing through spirit possession, sacrificing to appease gods, uttering spells, reciting scripture, and many more things.

In each chapter, I consider a specific dimension of religion and draw examples from both small-scale religions and large-scale ones. In my discussions of large-scale religious traditions, such as Islam, Hinduism, and Catholicism, I focus on one or more emphases within that tradition rather than attempting to survey all its dimensions and branches. For example, I examine the importance of sacred speech in Navajo, Islamic, and Protestant traditions in Chapter 11, with extended examples drawn from Quaker and Baptist churches as well as from Luther's writings. A study devoted to Protestantism per se would have included material from Lutheran, Presbyterian, Methodist, and other denominations. This book, concerned with comparisons across religions, has to be more selective.

The book is intended to be read on its own by any interested reader. As a course text it can be supplemented in various ways. In an anthropology course it might be combined with ethnographic case studies, either those referred to in the chapters or others. In a course on comparative religions it could be used together with some of the many excellent introductions to Islam, Hinduism, religions of China, and other large-scale religions. Also very effective are video clips and films on pilgrimage, church singing, sacrifice, and other practices. For additional suggestions of teaching materials check the Allyn & Bacon Web site *www.ablongman.com/anthropology*, and my own site: *www.artsci.wustl.edu/~anthro/blurb/b_bowen.html*.

New to the Fourth Edition

*I*n each new edition of this text I write new chapters, update previous ones, and change sections according to reader comments. Here are some of the major changes in the fourth edition:

- A new Chapter 12 on Transnational and Diaspora Religions emphasizes the complex flows of ideas and practices across continents and over centuries.

- Three additional chapters each provide a focus on one religious tradition and emphasize global or transnational dimensions. Chapter 9 on Hinduism combines new and old material to discuss this worship tradition from ethnographic, historical, and political perspectives. Chapter 10 on Catholicism emphasizes the importance of imagery in carrying Catholicism into new lands. A new Chapter 13 on Muslims in Europe examines the distinct patterns of Islamic adaptation across European countries.

- A new Chapter 5, "Transforming Selves," engages religion on a personal level by asking how people engaged in prayer, initiation, or conversion in effect change their ideas of who they are. I focus on gender as a particularly central category of religious transformation.

- A new Chapter 7, "Science and Religion," combines new and previous material, adding discussions of what science has to say about religion and how religious believers can teach science.

- Chapter 14 adds new discussions of why cross-religious violence occurs in some places and not others, and emphasizes the importance of looking for social and political factors to explain these patterns of conflict.

- A new Chapter 15 looks at the ways in which secular states govern religious diversity through political and legal structures. Here, we consider the United States in a broader comparative context.

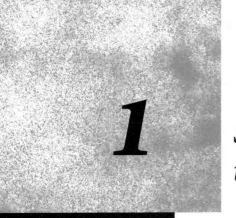

1

Studying Religion through Practice

*I*n September of 2003 I was on my way to Washington, D.C., to discuss Islam with people engaged in public policy discussions. On the flight I found myself seated next to a congressman. An evangelical Christian about to embark on a fact-finding mission to Iraq, he knew little about Islam but thought I might bring him up to date. Since the entire purpose of my trip was to enlighten Washington people about the complexities of contemporary debates among Muslims, I was eager to oblige.

I began by asking him about his own understandings of Christianity. He related the story of his early days in college and the family business, his search for a more meaningful path, the decision to devote himself to the Lord's work through public service, and then his efforts to understand U.S. history in terms of religion. "The founding fathers thought religion should inform public life and government, but that religion should not itself govern," he explained, contrasting the theocratic Puritans with the Pilgrims, in whose civic religion and politics he saw the model for the United States today. He sought guidance for his own politics in scripture, but thought little of Bible literalists who refused to see that scripture was fitted to its place and time. We must adapt the lessons of scripture to the conditions of today's world, he argued.

Much as I disagreed with the idea that political deliberation ought to draw on religious texts, I saw in his thoughtful approach to scripture a fine way to begin learning about Islam. I explained that many Muslim public intellectuals advocated not a theocracy, but a democratic political structure in which Islamic scripture would provide moral touchstones. Muslims, too, debated among themselves about how best to view scripture. As with Protestant Christians, some Muslims take verses of the Qur'ân to be immediately clear and universal commands, whereas others see some of the verses as historically limited, as the most appropriate way for God to deliver a message to a particular group of people in seventh-century Arabia. What the congressman saw as God's "dispensations" to humans—historical eras marked by divine gifts—Muslims saw as periods of revelation. While I explained that Muslims recognized several distinct schools of jurisprudence as legitimate, as several possible interpretations of God's will that are made by fallible humans, he saw parallels with his own acceptance of differences in religious views among Protestants.

I think we both learned something about religion during our flight. The conversation succeeded because we never floundered among the generalities of what "Islam says" or "Christianity teaches" that produce only confusion or, worse, muddled hostility. Instead we discussed practices, how real Muslims and Christians try to work out what scripture might have to say about their lives, and how they differ among themselves regarding those views. We both understood that neither Islamic nor Christian doctrines explain why people have attacked, killed, or saved one another, but that people have drawn on those doctrines for various reasons, reasons that required sophisticated analyses of struggles for resources and recognition in Palestine, Iraq, Saudi Arabia, and in the United States itself. At arrival we parted, not in agreement about religion and politics, but in at least partial agreement about how to understand other people's religions and politics.

I begin with this story because of a sense of immediacy I have about the importance of correctly understanding the roles religion does and does not play in modern public life, and the contributions the anthropology of religion can make to this understanding. The issue arises most pressingly with regard to contemporary armed conflicts, from those in the Balkans in the 1990s, through the continuing struggles in parts of the former Soviet Union, Kashmir, Iran, and Palestine, to the post–9/11 security debates about Islam in the United States and Europe. Are people fighting because of their religion? Does their religion shape how they think and act? Or is it just a way of mobilizing support? How far can religions be stretched to adapt to new ways of life?

These basic questions are less often posed than are the answers to them simply assumed. In less dramatic ways, many people living in Europe and North America continue to search for new forms of religiosity within or alongside established religious organizations. The fast-rising Christian churches in Melanesia, Africa, and Latin America are posing new challenges to indigenous religions. Muslims are engaging in internal deliberations about how to rethink issues of gender, of the public sphere, and of their religion's place in European and North American societies. Practitioners of smaller-scale religions throughout the world find themselves struggling for recognition or survival.

What Is "Religion"?

*D*iscussions of religion are often based on knowledge of only a few familiar religions. Many U.S. politicians and school officials who support a moment of silence for prayer in schools, for example, assume that all religions include the practice of silent individual prayer to a god; and some people find the Islamic practice of five daily prostrations before God disruptive. German officials have declared that Scientology is not a religion. Indonesian officials exclude animist beliefs and practices from the category of religion.

What then is "religion"? I view religious traditions as ever-changing complexes of beliefs (including those authoritative beliefs called "doctrine"), practices (including formalized rituals), and social institutions. But how do we decide which beliefs, practices, and institutions are to be called "religious"?

In most Western traditions one finds two very common definitions. One emphasizes an individual's beliefs; the other, his or her emotions. The first defines religion as a set of shared beliefs in spirits or gods. The second identifies religion in terms of a sentiment of awe and wonder toward the unknown. For me there is no hard and fast definition of religion. This book examines a wide variety of ways in which people in different societies and times have thought about the world beyond the immediate sense-world. Some posit a set of deities; others do not. Some have a distinct sphere of life called "religion"; others do not distinguish religion from the rest of life.

Sufficient for our purposes is that the collection of phenomena we will study— prayer to God, uses of magic, death rituals—all involve the idea that there is something more to the world than meets the eye. This definition is much broader than standard Western usage. What if we said that religion was whatever involves a stated belief in spirits or gods? In those cultures strongly shaped by modern Christianity, people do indeed tend to think of religion in these terms. The idea of a separate religious sphere is recent, even in Western history. In other societies people define the world in different ways, treating as a natural part of everyday life actions and ideas that we would want to include in a cross-cultural category of religion.

Consider the practices of the Azande people of the southern Sudan that ethnographers have labeled "Witchcraft." According to the Azande, some people carry in their bodies a substance called *mangu*. This substance is inherited, and it sends out emanations when the person feels jealousy, anger, or other negative emotions toward another person. The substance causes things to happen, and it fits into everyday ways of explaining misfortune. "I tripped at a place where I never trip; it must be witchcraft that caused me to trip."

When the person causing a particular misfortune is discovered (by using oracles) the person is asked to blow water from his or her mouth and to say: "If I was doing harm, I certainly did not mean to, let it be gone." And that is the end of the matter. The Azande do not concentrate on blame or intentions, but on the particular problem at hand and how to solve it. Indeed, they believe the substance sometimes acts on its own without the person's knowledge.

What do we make of these practices? From a Western point of view they refer to a reality beyond the immediately verifiable, and thus we legitimately may include them in a comparative study of religions. The Azande, on the other hand, see mangu and oracles as everyday, ordinary aspects of reality. Some of the Azande who have converted to Christianity continue their use of oracles and accusations of mangu precisely because they do not see those activities as part of a separate religion, but more as an American Baptist or Catholic might regard the use of an astrological chart.

The diversity of ideas about what constitutes a particular religion places any student of religion in a difficult position. If I write about a particular religion as the symbols, statements, and practices of a particular group of people, I will almost inevitably differ with some of them as to what their religion is. The perspective of an outside observer, who wishes to include a wide array of opinions and activities, may be much broader than that of a practitioner, who may insist on his or her own view of what properly lies within the boundaries of the religion in question.

I have frequently met with objections to the way I define "Islam" when describing certain Sumatran village practices to students in Indonesian Islamic colleges. For example, many villagers gather at ritual meals to ask ancestral spirits for help in healing the sick or in ensuring a good rice crop. These practices may have their origins in pre-Islamic times, but villagers view them as consistent with their understandings of Islam, and they explain them in terms of prophets and angels. For this reason I include them in my own writings about Sumatran Islam. But for the Islamic college students these practices conflict with proper understandings of Islam. "Those practices are what we try to teach them to throw aside," the students say. For some of them, my own writing could become part of the very problem they are trying to solve, that is, an overly broad idea of Islam.

How do we respond to these challenges? My own response has been to realize that definitions of religion are not just academic matters, but part of the very social reality we are studying. I thus refrain from giving too precise a definition for religion or Islam, and instead look at issues and debates among practitioners over the boundaries of religion, recording what they say and what is at stake for them.

People in the United States have not worked out definitive answers to these questions either. Some people would consider modern forms of witchcraft practiced in the United States to be a religion; indeed, the Rhode Island state legislature passed a law making it so in 1989. What limits the state should place on religious freedom is also a matter of continued debate, no more so than in cases of Christian Scientists denying medical treatment to their children. (Until August 1996, treatment given by Christian Science practitioners was considered "medical" for purposes of Medicare and Medicaid reimbursements, on grounds that to deny them that category would be to violate their religious freedom.)

I propose to define religion in two stages. First, we can use an extremely broad definition, such as "ideas and practices that postulate reality beyond that which is immediately available to the senses." This broad definition allows us to look at a very wide range of things. Second, for each society we study, we ask how *these* people construct their world. They may have a shared set of beliefs in spirits and deities and thus fit squarely into Western definitions of religion. Or they may speak about impersonal forces, such as the East Asian idea of a life force or *chi* that permeates the natural and social world. Or, they may not focus on describing beliefs at all, but rather, concentrate on carrying out rituals correctly, with a general understanding that the rituals are important. (This description fits the practitioners of Jain religion in India [Humphrey and Laidlaw 1994].)

What we call *religion* may look quite different from one society to another—in the relative importance of a shared belief system, in the degree to which religious practice involves strong emotions, and in the social functions and contexts associated with religious practices.

An Anthropological Approach to Religion

What is the peculiarly anthropological approach to the study of religion? These days, most of us reach across disciplinary boundaries to engage with colleagues in other disciplines. As I work on my own current questions, which in 2008 revolve around debates in Europe about religion and politics,

I consult the work of specialists from sociology, history, politics, law, and so forth. And yet I find that multidisciplinary research highlights rather than hides the distinctive contributions made by anthropologists. Three closely connected features guide an anthropologist's study of any topic.

First, anthropology is based on a *long-term relationship with people* through fieldwork. We live for a fairly long time, more than one year and sometimes many years, in a particular place. During that time we develop close friendships with some people and gain, we hope, the trust and respect of many more. I spent about six years in Indonesia, about four of them with Gayo people in Sumatra. My experience is not unusual. I developed a very close and continuing friendship with a Gayo family. The eldest daughter now lives in the United States. She began a career with Procter & Gamble in Jakarta, moved to Cincinnati, changed her career to pursue interests in consulting and Islamic fashion design, and now works for a California mosque. My children call her "Cousin Evi."

Close relationships help us to interpret social life. We trust certain people to report what they think truthfully, and we know enough such people to be able to check our interpretations with people who might be expected to disagree in their views on things. For example, I know people who have very different perspectives on religious rituals from my own, and I can depend on them to disagree with whatever I see. One can compare this source of reliability to that which psychologists obtain by repeating experiments.

Second, anthropologists pursue their study initially through *local perspectives.* Rather than studying the economy by creating a model of what people might do and then seeing whether they do it, or studying religion by reading scripture and then seeing what they believe, we begin with the ideas and practices we learn about in the field. Then we follow the connections to larger institutions like government agencies, religious schools, or national banks—but we always start from local views of those institutions.

When I studied Islamic law in Indonesia, for example, I began with how Gayo village and townspeople talk about law, how and whether they refer to it when resolving conflicts, and to what extent they make use of courts or religious authorities. Then I study the courts, the universities that educate the authorities, and the national institutions that seek to shape what happens locally, including the Supreme Court and the National Council of Islamic scholars. I learn about colonial law, contemporary civil law, and Islamic codes, but only after studying everyday social life, in order to anchor these codes and institutions in local practices. This feature distinguishes anthropology from disciplines that usually begin with historical, religious, or legal texts, or with national political institutions.

Finally, anthropologists study *connections across social domains.* Rarely do we look only at the economy, or at literature, or at religion. We might wish to focus on one of these domains (indeed it is required when writing a doctoral dissertation), but when we do, we usually discover that our chosen domain is connected to other domains. Suppose I want to learn about rice cultivation and discover that the planting and harvesting is tied to the performance of elaborate religious rituals, and that work on the irrigation system depends on local political structures. I have to investigate religion and politics, then, in order to understand how rice is cultivated.

Conversely, my study of Islam in Gayo society also involved learning about how rice is grown, how the major rice-growing regions were allocated among villages, how healing takes place, the origins of political parties, and the short history of a poetic genre written in Arabic script—all because they were part of local practices that people explained by referring to Islam. Indeed, I focused on Islam only as a third project; I was brought to it because the topics I came to study—social structure and oral literature— were interwoven with Islamic ideas about society and history. Even when we work in new kinds of sites we retain these features in our work. My current research on Islam in France finds me sitting in religious schools along with Muslim students, interviewing French political actors, and analyzing newspaper stories and law review articles. I don't work in a village, or even in a single neighborhood. (Other anthropologists are carrying out that sort of work alongside of mine.) How is what I am doing different from the work of a political scientist? Well, it comes close to the approach of some of my French colleagues in political science—the French version of that discipline having developed more attention to everyday life than has its more behaviorist American cousin—but it retains a critical difference. I focus on how a wide range of Muslims and non-Muslims talk about matters of importance to them—schools, mosques, political coalitions—in private and public contexts. The "local" setting in which I work is multiple: a set of institutions and events across France in which people deliberate and debate. Starting from these deliberations and debates leads me to look at law, politics, jurisprudence, ethics, the history of immigration, and the perspectives of French social scientists on their own society—in other words, the connections across domains. As one political science friend said to me recently, her eyebrows slightly raised, "you're studying us, too, aren't you?" That it was so more intrigued than troubled her; it was a way of marking our disciplinary differences, and transoceanic differences in perspective, alongside our shared interests in French Islam.

Differences across Disciplines

Consider how scholars in different disciplines approach a question about why people believe the (religious) things they do. As I said before, most anthropologists approach the question through fieldwork. Susan Harding (2000), for example, set out to under- stand how it is that people become "convicted" (that is, convinced) followers of the Reverend Jerry Falwell's Fundamental Baptist community. Her ethnographic approach was to spend a lot of time in the community, listening to what people said and how they said it. She worked to counteract her basic skepticism toward Falwell by "bracketing," as the phenomenologist Husserl put it, her preconceptions, and trying to accept his state- ments as true. This approach allowed her to perceive the complexity and the force of the arguments made by the Baptists. It also gave her a strong, personal sense of what it meant to have a soul and to know that Satan is real. She did not convert but she gained a felt sense of conviction.

Harding's work fits the overall account of the anthropological approach that I offered earlier. She got to know people well enough to be able to discuss a wide range of topics with them and to grasp how they saw the world. She tried to start with their concerns, rather than bringing her own categories and ideas to the field. And she did not limit her study to one specific domain, but investigated ritual, schooling, gender issues, and politics.

Most anthropologists of religion teaching in North America or Europe carry out at least their initial fieldwork outside those areas, reflecting the general anthropological emphasis on grasping the widest possible range of human experiences, practices, and ideas. This centrifugal tendency also means that they must study and explain to their readers the social and cultural context within which one finds religion: kinship and marriage systems, local and national political structures, and broad cosmologies and ideologies. One could limit one's reading to the subfield of the anthropology of religion and nevertheless gain a good understanding of all of social anthropology.

Even though many sociologists carry out fieldwork, the fundamental orientation of their discipline is different from that of anthropology, with a greater interest in developing general propositions about social life, but (one might say ironically) less of a concern with broad-based comparative studies. Most sociologists of religion teaching in the United States study the organization of religions, changes in religious attitudes and beliefs, or new religious movements, usually focusing on people and institutions found in the United States. This focus means that they can assume general knowledge of institutions and ideas on the part of their readers, and that they often pitch their writings to generally held concerns, such as the decline in attendance at mainstream churches or the rise in New Age religions.

Penny Edgell Becker's (1999) study of congregations illustrates one sociological approach. She asked how congregations in the United States manage internal conflict. Her concern thus was primarily organizational. She selected a sample of churches in Chicago, choosing her sample to have variation in size, organizational structure, and liberal–conservative orientation. Her concerns were primarily to develop a general model consisting of types of church organizations and concomitant types of conflict resolution. These goals were motivated by a broader theoretical literature in sociology concerning institutions and their cultures in the United States. Along the way she discovered interesting histories of each church and ways of preaching and worshipping, but each of these mini-ethnographies was inevitably partial, useful only to the extent that it contributed to her particular question.

Psychologists more rarely study religion, but a few anthropologists have taken up the methods of experimental psychology to pursue research into why people believe certain religious propositions. Pascal Boyer (2000, 2001), for example, observed that people around the world have a strikingly small number of basic ideas about supernatural beings: that they behave much as ordinary beings or objects do except for a slight variation in their properties. Thus one has supernatural agents who are very much like people except that they can go through walls, be invisible, hear everything, or live forever. We do not find gods who exist only every other day, or who exist in six dimensions, or who think about everything in the world at once, including the contents of all our refrigerators. Why is this? Boyer and others hypothesized that the more limited set of limited god-concepts were conceptually easier to work with for humans. They then tested this idea through experiments with children and adults, and found that it held across a number of different cultures. This work resembles that of other psychologists in that it is carried out through controlled experiments and tests some universal propositions about human minds (see Chapter 7).

Practices, Contexts, Diversity

*I*n the chapters that follow I examine religious life from different perspectives: the relations of doctrines to rituals; the role of religions in explaining misfortune, overcoming grief, and extending human powers; the ways that rituals of prayer, preaching, and sacrificing shape religious belief and experience; the ways that images and taboos can be used to organize religious life or change it; and the role of religions in public life.

The emphasis on practice includes the study of doctrines, but focuses on how doctrines are embodied in texts or other forms and how they are understood; this relation of doctrine to practice is examined in greater detail in Chapter 3. Religious practices often invoke texts: someone reads, chants, recites, or sings a text. These textual practices are critical in linking local practices to broader religious traditions. Certain practices are especially characteristic of one or more religious traditions, and in some chapters I analyze at length those traditions. For example, images are particularly central to Catholicism, and in Chapter 10 I focus on imagery in worldwide Catholicism.

The particular contribution of ethnographic and social historical studies to knowledge of religion lies in the attention to interconnections among domains of social life, among religion, economy, marriage, politics, and so forth and to the ways that cultural ideas and social institutions shape activities in many of these domains. The importance of such cross-domain connections was underscored by Durkheim and Marx, who continue to have a strong influence on many anthropologists (see Chapter 2). A particular religious practice such as worship may structure communities in particular ways, or lend a religious interpretation to existing social divisions, as when a Hindu priest distributes consecrated foods according to caste standing, or when men and women worship separately in a Muslim mosque, or when church pews are reserved for those who have contributed to the church.

The interpretation of texts and doctrines is strongly shaped by local factors, as Clifford Geertz (1968) showed in contrasting Islam in Morocco to Islam in Java, a contrast I revisit in Chapter 4. Comparing two or more cases of a practice can help to highlight these shaping processes, and in each of the following chapters I engage in such comparisons. In Chapter 4, for example, I contrast treatments of death in Japan, New Guinea, and Bali; in Chapter 8, patterns of sorcery in different societies of Africa; in Chapter 5, ways of becoming pious in Mexico and Egypt; in Chapter 15, the relationship of religion and state in Germany, France, Britain, and the United States.

Finally, I consider the diversity of religious understandings and practices even within small-scale societies. Diversity includes both questions of how knowledge and ideas are distributed in the society—between men and women, or adults and children, or across other social groupings—and the debates among people about how best to understand the norms and forms of religious culture. Anthropology has often been insufficiently attentive to diversity. This insufficiency has been due in part to the idea that a "culture" is an integrated whole, an idea inherited from German nineteenth-century cultural studies, and in part due to ways of carrying out research by concentrating on a small number of "key informants"—or even, in some cases, one such informant.

We know that the same practice may be interpreted in myriad and diverse ways. Beginning from particular religious practices and then examining diverse interpretations allows us to capture these diversities, and in some cases explain them in terms of accompanying social differences and changes. Certain religious traditions allow a particularly broad diversity of practices to flourish—the case of Japan is explored in Chapter 3. Debates within Islam are explored at several points in this book. I draw on my own fieldwork with the Muslim Gayo of Sumatra and on Islam in France in some of these chapters. I also examine debates within Christianity: concerning the role of the Virgin Mary in Chapter 10, and the nature of divine election in Chapter 11.

The final chapter returns us to the broad debates concerning the place of religion in public life with which I began this chapter. It is with an eye to these debates that I write this book. A great deal of misunderstanding and, to my mind, wrong-headed public policy in many countries, but certainly in the United States, has been based on ideas about religion that ignore diversities, debates, and possibilities. For example, particular features of certain strata of Middle Eastern societies (the role of women, views on Islam law) are frequently confused with Islam in general. Religious beliefs are all open to debate and transformation; attending to those debates reminds us of a sense of the open-ended nature of religious ideas.

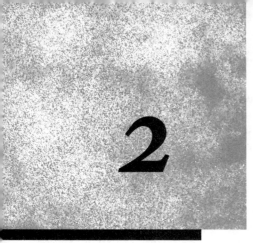

Social Theory in the Anthropology of Religion

*A*nthropology is not only a general approach and a set of fieldwork methods; anthropologists studying religion also draw from one or more bodies of social theory. Rarely in anthropology does theory become a set of propositions to prove or disprove. Instead, theory serves to suggest questions and guide research. Theoretical choices also predispose researchers to follow certain initial questions, study certain dimensions of religion, and engage in certain kinds of scholarly activities rather than others.

In what follows I make distinctions among several general sets of questions and approaches to studying religion anthropologically, all which have continued to provide guidance for research. We continue to read major works in social theory because they set out those questions and approaches for us. E. B. Tylor asked why people hold certain religious ideas and not others, and this question has retained its importance. Émile Durkheim asked how it is that social norms have such a hold on us, and we continue to pose this question, albeit in new ways. Karl Marx and Max Weber asked how modern capitalism came to dominate the world, and gave very different answers; their work continues to provide starting points for contemporary social scientists. I prefer to distinguish in this way "social theory" as a body of work from which social scientists draw questions and guidance, from specific "theories of society," which may prove more or less perceptive and appealing.

Religion as Intellectual Activity

*O*ne dimension of religion is the intellectual: what do people think exists, and why do they think those things? These questions can survive the rise and fall of specific answers to the question.

In the mid-nineteenth century, the early years of anthropology as a formal discipline, scholars in most disciplines tried to explain the diversity and complexity of today's religions by postulating a process of religious evolution. They were strongly influenced by German idealist philosophers, who saw human history as the development of a set of human essences. These philosophers understood religion as a unity of thought and feeling, intellect and emotion, that had developed historically from initial germs. The philosopher Hegel postulated a universal idea of religion that preceded its particular historical manifestations. As it developed over time from an initial germ, it became increasingly complex. This idea of development or evolution did not concern the history of a particular religion or a particular people, but the evolution across time and space of an idea, independent of particular cultures.

This theory of general human cultural evolution provided the intellectual framework for the early anthropology of religion, as well as for social anthropology generally. The comparative study of religion in the late nineteenth century was based on two assumptions: that religion progressed from the simple to the complex, and that one could reconstruct the origins of religion by studying "primitive peoples" in the world today. Many students of the origins of religion did not subscribe to the universal truths offered by their churches, and their accounts were more or less subtle ways of discrediting the absolute truth of Christianity. If Catholic or Anglican beliefs evolved from something very simple then they looked much less absolute than if they had been delivered through divine revelation.

E. B. Tylor and the Origins of Religious Ideas

The most famous study along these lines was *Primitive Culture* (1970 [1871]) by Edward B. Tylor (1832–1917). Tylor was the first person to be appointed to a university position in anthropology in England, in 1884 at Oxford. Tylor argued that primitive people acted as proto-scientists when they created religion, constructing concepts to explain what they perceived through their senses. Tylor (1970, vol. 2) asked: "What is true of all religions?" He looked around him and saw that all religions employed a belief in spiritual beings. The higher ones had souls, gods, angels, and so on, while the more primitive ones had spirits and ghosts. The primitive form of this belief he called animism. He saw this belief as basic to religious development.

"Why do people come to hold such a belief?" he then asked. Well, he answered, they perceive things that lead them to suppose these spiritual entities. They perceive different states of consciousness (wakefulness, sleep, death), dreams (and the appearance in them of places and persons), and shadows. Then they think up things to explain these appearances. "Soul" explains the different states of consciousness, because as soul sleeps, or leaves the body, we lose consciousness or life. "Ghost" explains the phenomenon of dreams, because as we sleep, our ghost or spirit leaves the body and travels to other places, and we vaguely remember these wandering perceptions when we wake. Finally, shadows are one form taken by souls and ghosts. Tylor was able to amass a large body of evidence to support his claims. (Indeed, the ways many people today speak about sleep, dreams, death, and shadows do sound very much like Tylor's account.)

Religion is therefore due to "the plain evidence of men's senses" for Tylor. As it develops it continues to build on perceptions and logic. People reasoned that because animals, too, have life, then they must have souls. If they are killed, then their souls can follow those of their masters to the world of the beyond, and there do work for them. Burial practices from such diverse civilizations as Egypt and China attest to this belief.

Furthermore, because plants also live and die, they must have souls as well. All living things, concludes Tylor's primitive thinker, thus have souls; such is the origin of "animism," the belief that all living things are "animated" by souls.

But how is it, asks Tylor, that such ideas have survived until today? One way is through psychological development. As children, we have the very same experiences, and make the very same inferences, as did primitive people: we have dreams and we attribute life to things and play with them as if they were alive. When we grow up we are thus prepared to accept as true, because in some sense natural, the claims of the religions we are taught. We do so because—and here is the second way the early ideas survived—the ideas of advanced religions are merely further elaborations of the primitive ideas. Tylor offers the example of the Eucharist, the Christian ritual wherein bread and wine become, or symbolize, Christ's body and blood. This ritual might appear to be far from primitive religion. But, he argues, it is a development of the idea of sacrifice, which itself was based on the notion that the soul of the sacrificed animal or person would travel to the world beyond.

Tylor's account of religion captures elements that one does, indeed, find throughout the world. The ideas of soul, spirit, dreams that he described as basic or primitive do indeed animate many religious systems. Tylor's weakness, from our contemporary perspective, is that he emphasized an essential commonality to all religious beliefs and thus played down what most anthropologists emphasize today, namely, the diversity of ways in which humans have constructed their religious beliefs and practices. But by analyzing the logic of a set of beliefs, Tylor did inspire his successors to analyze the different ways people have constructed their understandings of the cosmos, their "world views."

An eminent successor to Tylor in this enterprise was James Frazer (1854–1951), whose massive compendium of religion and myth, *The Golden Bough* (1981 [1890]), first issued in two volumes and later expanded to twelve, brought together in a readable style much of the knowledge of the day about comparative religion. Frazer followed Tylor in sharply distinguishing among science, magic, and religion as distinct modes of thought. Religion, in their view, involves acts intended to appease deities; magic, like science, assumes impersonal relationships between certain actions and their outcomes. Magic rests on two basic, albeit mistaken, ideas. The first is the idea of similarity, that like causes like (a green stone will cure jaundice). The second is that of contagion, that contact between two objects allows someone to control one through manipulating the other (a person's hair-clippings can be burned, thereby harming the person). Magic is thus pseudoscience; religion proper involves a qualitatively different kind of activity.

Tylor and Frazer's intellectualist legacy has been to focus anthropological energies on understanding how particular people view the world, taking their world view seriously as an intellectual or philosophical enterprise. Most anthropologists continued to pose these questions thereafter.

In the United States, and in reaction to the evolutionary approach of Tylor and others, Franz Boas and his students developed cultural anthropology around a twofold approach to studying small-scale societies. On the one hand, they sought to discern the patterns of each culture as they were reflected in art, myth, kinship, and everyday ways of speaking. On the other hand, they traced the historical processes through which people transmit cultural ideas across societies and also change them. This dual focus on both ideas and empirical processes reflects Boas's own German training in both empirical sciences and idealist philosophy.

Claude Lévi-Strauss and the Structure of Mythic Thinking

Boas's complex approach to myths probably was best continued by the French anthropologist Claude Lévi-Strauss. Lévi-Strauss drew from Tylor's analysis of the intellectual operations detectable in myth-making, but he also, following Boas, sought to trace transformations of myths as they have passed from one society to another. Myths, in his analysis, are composed according to intricate codes, each of which concerns a distinct level of local life and awareness: a code of flora and fauna, one of geography, one of social institutions. These codes are structured as oppositions among categories: cold versus hot, high versus low, mother's versus father's relatives, and so forth. Moreover, neighboring peoples often tell contrasting versions of these myths, and these contrasts across societies indicate that myths reflect differences in local social life, and that they may function to underscore the boundaries between peoples.

In one of his best-known analyses, Lévi-Strauss dissects a myth told among several peoples of the Northwest Coast of North America, the "Story of Asdiwal" (1976). The myth is structured around four distinct codes of geography, economy, society, and cosmology. Events often concern all four codes at once: for example, a marriage involves geographical movement, fishing, a particular kind of marriage institution, and movements between earth and sky. Lévi-Strauss argues that the myth depicts in especially salient ways the contradictions that are at the basis of Tsimshian society. Marriages among families of chiefs, for example, were supposed to create or reaffirm relations of hierarchy among them, but precisely who was superior to whom was debated fiercely at each marriage. The myths depict such chiefly marriages as ending in death and battle, thus representing in heightened form problems inherent in the social structure. The myths also try out alternative realities, such as trying to inherit from one's father and one's mother, "in order to show that they are untenable" (1976, 173).

Differences between two versions of the myth show how myths, as they are transferred from one place to another, are recast in light of local conditions. One version was collected along the coast, from people who make a great seasonal migration from one region to another to catch candlefish in the spring on one river and salmon in the summer on another. In their version of the myth, characters travel great distances and they engage in very different economic pursuits, as do the humans telling the myth. Lévi-Strauss points out that this version of the myth is characterized by strong oppositions between categories along geographical and economic codes. But oppositions are also strong along the social and cosmological codes (for example, featuring people who are distantly related to each other), as if to follow the oppositions generated by the codes of economic life and geographic movement. This priority of some codes, the economic and geographic, over others is mentioned by Lévi-Strauss in referring to himself as a Marxist.

In the versions of the myth that were collected along a river where the residents made fewer movements in the course of the year—they hunted candlefish but not salmon, for example—the oppositions were weaker, again along all four codes. This comparative analysis thus supports Lévi-Strauss's conclusions that codes of a myth are internally integrated, and that they all differ in a systematic way across societies. Others, especially James A. Boon (1990), have used this insight in their own ethnographic analyses of how people structure religious and social life through their use of oppositions and contrasts. In these studies, myths are seen as extended commentaries on the practice of everyday social life.

Religions in Social Life

*A*lthough neither Tylor nor Lévi-Strauss conceived of religious ideas and practices as divorced from society, they underscored the intellectual dimension of religious ideas. Boas, too, and especially his students, emphasized the ways in which religious and other ideas cohere in patterns. As we will see, this emphasis on the cultural patterning of religion has retained a central role in anthropology.

At the same time, social theorists stressed that religious ideas, sentiments, and orientations had developed out of specific social conditions. Each of the three major social theorists of modern Europe—Durkheim, Marx, and Weber—crafted some distinctive ways of understanding religion's relationship to broader social processes. All three theorists were primarily concerned with explaining features of modern life—the rise of modern capitalism, challenges to social solidarity, and the peculiar nature of rational and legal authority. In the process of developing their theories they also tried to explain the role of religion in pre-modern societies.

Émile Durkheim on the Social Origins of Religion

Some scholars continued Tylor's quest for the origins of religion, but sought those origins in social life. The sociologist Émile Durkheim (1858–1917), for example, saw the birth of religion in the ideas and emotions generated out of collective social action. "Religious representations are collective representations that express collective realities," he wrote (1995, 9). Durkheim was not entirely the originator of this general idea. Aristotle, after all, had declared that "men create the gods after their own image." The French historian Fustel de Coulanges (1830–1889) and the Scottish scholar of Semitic societies W. Robertson-Smith (1846–1904) linked social organization to religious ideas in ancient societies. Robertson-Smith had argued that the earliest societies had been totemic, that is, they had been organized into clans, each of which had a special relationship to a species of animal—"my clan is a wolf." Sacrificing this animal was a way to communicate and commune with the deities, and at the same time it was a means to strengthen the emotional bonds among clan members.

Durkheim drew from these earlier writers to argue that knowledge in general, and religious knowledge in particular, has a social foundation. His argument was philosophical, against Kant's idea that humans had innate categories of the understanding. But it was also social and moral, and grew out of the concerns of the day (Lukes 1973).

Durkheim wrote at a time of great social and moral turmoil in France, when older certainties about God and Church had been excised from public and legal life by the Revolution, but no alternative moral certainties had yet replaced them. The country appeared to be polarized between urban agnostics and rural Catholics. Battles were especially sharp over the future of the school system: should it be secular or Catholic, and if secular, what would be its moral content? No wonder that in his first articles, Durkheim was deeply sensitive to the problem of social cohesion in contemporary society: "A society whose members are not bound to one another by some solid and durable link," he wrote in 1886, "would resemble a loose pile of dust which could at any time be dispersed by the slightest wind to the four corners of the world" (quoted in Alexander 1982, 82). But what are these bonds? And how do they unite people in societies that have not undergone the sort of schisms experienced by France?

As one would expect given the evolutionary way of thinking in vogue at the time, Durkheim sought his answer in a study of *The Elementary Forms of the Religious Life,* the title of his 1912 book. The book posits an early type of social consciousness in those societies where everyone is for all important purposes alike: everyone has the same statuses, duties, and roles. In such societies people's feelings are also alike, and thus strongly reinforce each other whenever people gather together. Moral sentiments, religious beliefs, and other cultural ideas are all very strong, and law, religion, and social norms are strong as well.

Durkheim postulated that religious beliefs and sentiments must correspond to something real, and that they could not be purely illusory or mistaken, as Tylor and Frazer had concluded. They clearly were false if taken at face value. The problem then was to go underneath the symbol to the reality that it represents and that gives it its true meaning. What is "religion"? Rather than defining it as the belief in spirits, as did Tylor and Frazer, Durkheim viewed it as involving a fundamental division of the world into sacred versus profane things. Religion is thus a collective reality that concerns how the members of a particular society divide up the world, rather than an individual reality consisting of what a person believes. But *how* the world is divided into sacred and profane varies greatly from one society to the next; what determines this division?

Here Durkheim accepts Robertson-Smith's thesis that totemism was the earliest basis for social organization and that it was the wellspring of religion. He turns to the religions of Australian aborigines to prove his thesis. In these societies specific groups perform rituals at sacred sites that are associated either with ancestral spirits or with mythical beings that lived during the ancient "dream time" that came before the time we know. Each group also has objects made of wood or stone engraved with symbols of these ancestors or mythical beings, and these *churinga* objects themselves have sacred powers.

Each such social group also has a special ritual relationship toward certain species, such as kangaroo, or certain natural phenomena, such as rain or wind. Members of the group may have special rules regulating their activities with respect to these species, the group's *totem,* and the group can carry out rituals that increase the species' numbers. These rituals sometimes involve eating an item of the species, and Durkheim thought that this practice confirmed the theory that sacrifice and communal eating were the earliest, basic forms of religious ritual.

Durkheim argued that the general idea of spiritual force that underlay totemism existed prior to ideas about spirits or souls, and he cited related ideas from other societies, such as the notion of impersonal force or *mana* in Melanesia. (He also could have cited the Chinese idea of life force, or *chi.*) This same force, at later stages of development, gives rise to ideas of souls, ancestral spirits, and God, stated Durkheim.

Durkheim set out his argument on two different levels. First, he explained the variety of religious ideas by arguing that particular features of societies give rise to particular features of their cultures and religions. Religion thus represents society. So, there are "societies in Australia and North America where space is conceived in the form of an immense circle, because the camp has a circular form." The early division of society into two halves or *moieties* gave rise to ideas of the cosmos as dualistic. In societies such as the Australians just discussed, where people were organized into clans, these people often postulated an animal, or sacred place, or force, as the totem of that clan. These totems were the projections onto a spiritual place of a sense of belonging together in the clan. As the society grew and spread over a wider area, giving rise to a sense of a broad social group with shared interests that spilled over the boundaries of the clan, totemic representations synthesized into the idea of one or more gods, "the god being only a figurative expression of the society," Durkheim summarily stated (1995, 227).

This level of argument presumes that there already is a general religious idea that can be shaped by society. So arguing at a second level, Durkheim tried to explain the emergence of general religious ideas and sentiments in the first place. People sense a moral force that is exterior to them, he argued. This idea is given social content in those moments when people come together in social assemblies, such as dances, meetings, or festivals. These assemblies create a social effervescence out of which religious ideas are confirmed and given stronger emotional meaning. A qualitative change takes place, and people began to feel themselves transported to an altered state.

Religion also serves the function of strengthening social solidarity by communicating specific ideas and sentiments, and by regulating and strengthening social relationships. A totem, for instance, reminds you what kind of person you are (a member of a certain clan) and thereby regulates relations among individuals. It also gives you a feeling of strength: speaking of one Australian society, Durkheim wrote: "The Arunta who has properly rubbed himself with his churinga feels stronger; he is stronger" (1995, 229).

This functional perspective on religion gave Durkheim a way of discussing the place of religion in modern society. Religion is no longer a satisfactory *cognitive* solution to the "problem of meaning," in which science is now the master. But religion continues to be *symbolically* important: cult and faith are essential to any society's social solidarity, including our own.

Durkheim emphasized the cognitive, emotional, and social aspects of religious ideas and practices. His *Elementary Forms* focuses on the social origins of religion by way of a theory of collective emotions, but there and in other writings, Durkheim also emphasizes the logical nature of religious classifications. In *Primitive Classification* (1963 [1903]), Durkheim and his nephew Marcel Mauss (1872–1950) compared the symbolic classifications found in Australian, native North American, and Chinese societies. The Zuni Pueblo people of the U.S. Southwest, for example, assign to each of the cardinal directions (plus center, and the zenith and nadir of the sun's apparent motion) a color, a season, and a kind of weather, together with a general force such as creation or destruction, a specific group, and an animal. Durkheim and Mauss claimed that members of these societies have created totalizing religious systems; these systems unite the social, natural, and cosmological realms. Their comparison of logical similarities across these societies inspired later anthropologists to more detailed studies of symbolic classification.

Durkheim's legacy in the field of religious studies was twofold. First, he connected the religious to the social, leading later anthropologists to look for social origins or functions of specific religious practices and ideas. This strain of his legacy was a foundation of British social anthropology, from A. R. Radcliffe-Brown through Edmund Leach and Mary Douglas. For Mary Douglas, for example, the key to understanding food taboos, whether in the Hebrew Bible or in the societies of central Africa she studied in her fieldwork, is to look for the social functions such taboos may have served. She argued that by separating the sacred from the profane, and then by restricting membership in the community to those who observed the rules, food taboos make group membership sacred.

Durkheim also emphasized the ways that participating in collective religious practices confirm faith, and this insight remains compelling. Consider how many European Catholics find visions of Mary to be central events cementing their faith, or perhaps their hope within their faith. In less spectacular ways, the good feelings of participating in something with friends and neighbors may also make the religion particularly "true." Particularly important is the way in which public ritual generates religious commitment. A service, for example, in which many people worship together, can be a wonderfully compelling context, generating a sense of being together and being in the presence of something else. Such feelings, perhaps most startlingly displayed when Christian worshipers speak in tongues, lay behind Durkheim's claim that coming together as a social group gave rise to the earliest ideas of the supernatural. Most people, however, most of the time, experience their activities of carrying out worship, consulting oracles, or avoiding tabooed foods as routine actions. It may indeed be the case that the routine nature of most of religions' demands, the integration of religion into everyday life, provides a social and psychological comfort.

Secondly, Durkheim connected the religious to the intellectual, continuing Tylor's emphasis. "The essential notions of scientific logic are of religious origin," he wrote in *Elementary Forms* (1995, 431). This statement has broadly echoed in cultural anthropology throughout the world, and most notably by Claude Lévi-Strauss, who saw classificatory systems as the product of intense, imaginative intellectual activity. Rather than seeing totems and totemic social organization as a primitive form of identification that then gave rise to higher forms of society and religion, Lévi-Strauss considered them, in his *Totemism* (1963a [1962]), as one among many ways of classifying the world in order to understand it. Particular plants or animals are chosen to be totems not because they have utility or excite awe in themselves, but because they provide a usable symbolic template through which to make distinctions in the natural, social, and cosmological worlds.

Karl Marx on Religion in Capitalist Europe

Durkheim's approach to religion assumed that society, and therefore religion, was an integrated whole. But what if society is not like that, but consists instead of several groups whose interests and ideas are in conflict? How then ought we to understand the social origins and functions of religion?

This question lies behind the work of both Karl Marx and Max Weber. Karl Marx (1818–1883) emphasized the historical process by which different social groups come to dominate social life. The key to this process was the interplay between the material forces of production and the social relations of production: how things were produced and how their production and distribution was organized. Each historical period in European history has thrown up its own distinctive dominant ideology: politics in classical Rome, the Catholic Church in the medieval period, and capitalism as ideology in the modern period. Marx and his collaborator, Friedrich Engels, saw religion as serving ideological functions in all periods, as providing social cement in the face of class divisions, but also as expressing class interests (Marx and Engels 1965 [1946]).

Studies of religion inspired by Marx have looked for the material interests served by movements gathered together under the banner of religion. Engels (1956 [1850]) argued that the religious wars of the fifteenth and sixteenth centuries in Germany, although couched in the language of religious dissent, were motivated by the disparate interests of the nobility, burghers, and peasants. Among these movements were those millenarian Christian movements that prophesied the imminent moment (the "millennium," or thousand years) when the corrupt leaders of the church would face the Day of Judgment. German millenarian prophets combined apocalyptic teachings with calls for the end of the feudal system, supporting Engels's thesis that material interests and religious ideas were intertwined. Engels thus showed the power of religion to subvert as well as to confirm the existing social order. His study launched a distinguished tradition of investigations (for example, Worsley 1968) into the material and religious sources of those radical religious movements whose leaders preach an imminent radical transformation of society, if not the end of the world—"millenarian" in today's general sense of the term.

Max Weber on Religion in Modern Civilizations

Max Weber (1864–1920) also analyzed the relationships between particular interest groups and religious ideas. Weber (1978 [1956]) took the social action of the individual as his unit, distinct from Durkheim's emphasis on social structure and function, and Marx's emphasis on changing modes of production. Weber wrote that one can only come to understand social action by, first, discovering the meaning of the action for the individual and, secondly, explaining it in terms of the social conditions and actions that preceded it. Social science thus involves both interpretation and causal–historical explanation.

Religion provides one major source of ideas and orientations for the actor, and Weber devoted much analysis to the comparative study of religions. His interest was not religious doctrine per se, but the spirit or *ethos* that was produced in individuals by their adherence to one faith versus another, as well as the social conditions that allowed new types of religious orientation to emerge. Weber saw the development of Western society as the progressive *rationalization* of society, a concept that implies both the increasing differentiation of social life into functionally defined domains or spheres—family, economy, religion—and the systematic reorganization of each domain around a single set of values or rules. Economy gradually became reorganized around the maximization of profit; family, around the general solidarity of kin; religion, around the worship of God. In Weber's view of Western world history, religion gradually shed its "magical" character and developed a set of universalistic doctrines about a divine order, and a set of ethical principles that apply to everyone, everywhere.

Weber's theory of religious history is both sociological and universal. Weber carried out separate studies of India, China, Islam, ancient Judaism, and modern Europe. He saw each of these societies as characterized by a distinctive set of religious beliefs, a particular economic ethic, and a specific set of interest groups; his research concerned the interplay of these three elements. In his study of India, for example, Weber argued that the caste system and the doctrine of *karma*—the idea that one's actions in this or a previous life determined the course of one's life—inhibited the development of a rational economic ethic because it led religious energies away from this world and directed them toward the "other world." Only with the development of Calvinist Protestantism in Europe did there arise a religion-driven energy to rationally remold the world; this energy pushed forward modern capitalism.

Weber traced similar developmental processes within each socio-religious system. In the larger-scale societies he studied, prophets arose to challenge an older way of thinking, often in the name of a universal creed and god. But with the demise of the prophet, followers had to "routinize" the movement, creating a religious community or congregation. The eventual development of a rational, differentiated religious system required the parallel development of a bureaucratic state, whether in India, China, or Europe.

Weber's analysis rested on the "ideal types" he created—the other-worldly mystic, the this-worldly prophet. These types give us an initial, clear sense of the contrasts in dominant ideas among large-scale religions. But they are less useful in analyzing the many ways in which people reinterpret and transform those ideas. Weber's ideal types have been questioned by later students of each society. For example, Weber based his claims that the Indian doctrine of karma would retard economic development on the assumption that the doctrine, as contained in religious texts, was also what ordinary people believed. But popular Indian ideas about fate and action in the world are not the same as the textual doctrines (Babb 1983), and they have not prevented people from engaging in modern industrial development (Singer 1964).

Clifford Geertz and the Ethnography of Civilizations

Although a number of anthropologists began to study large-scale societies, or "civilizations," in the 1950s, probably the best-known among them has been Clifford Geertz. In his *Religion of Java* (1960), as well as in other works on Indonesia and Morocco, he analyzes the diversity of religious beliefs in a large Muslim society.

Geertz draws from Weber's emphasis on the answers that large-scale religious doctrines provide for life's key questions, such as: Why is there evil in the world? Who gets to heaven and why? But whereas Weber worked largely from the writings of religious figures and other literate men—those who formed what Robert Redfield (1956) was to call the urban "great traditions"—Geertz relies on the testimonies of ordinary village and townspeople, those people participating in what Redfield called the rural "little tradition." Geertz looks at the diversity of ideas in a single society.

In his study of Java, Geertz defined three "streams" of Islam, each situated in a different institutional context: a set of village understandings that focused on spirits and community rituals; a more scripturally oriented Islam of the religious school and the market; and a focus on status and etiquette among noble Javanese. Although criticized for not emphasizing that people in all three streams were Muslims, and that many read works of Islamic doctrine and spirituality, his analysis was able to capture both the variety of ways Javanese men and women talked about religion and society, and the ways that large-scale institutions of politics, economics, and religion shaped their understandings and their actions.

Geertz's approach has been especially influential in the anthropology of religion. Today many anthropologists place even more emphasis than he did on the ways that villagers and religious experts ("culture brokers") interpret and reshape the texts and ideas of religious traditions in their societies. For example, Stanley Tambiah (1970) studied the uses that monks and other villagers make of Buddhist texts in northeastern Thailand. Dale F. Eickelman (1985) traced the career of a rural Moroccan judge. In these and other studies, anthropologists have situated large-scale changes in specific towns and villages and with respect to specific people.

The Psychology of Religion

Cognitive and social approaches to religion sometimes fail to provide a full account of the psychological dimension. The individual as portrayed in Tylor and Durkheim, for example, is rather one-dimensional: he or she is a would-be scientist, or simply part of a crowd marked by religious euphoria.

Weber and Suffering

Of theorists considered so far, Weber paid the most attention to the psychological dimension of religion. He wished to explain how different religious orientations toward the world would produce different economic ethics, leading to different kinds of economic organization. In particular, he sought to explain how Protestant ideas spurred on modern capitalism in Europe. The key Protestant idea was the doctrine of "unknowable election"—the idea that some people were elected to heaven and others condemned to hell, but that no one could know his or her category nor change what God had preordained. Weber argued that this doctrine, taught by the theologian John Calvin, was so unsettling that people worked hard to succeed in this world, grasping at the idea that the material signs of their success also were signs of God's favor. The "Protestant ethic" was thus the psychological consequence of a specific doctrine, and it, not the doctrine itself, was a key element in the rise of modern capitalism.

Weber thought that the idea of predestination also served to affirm the absolute, transcendent power of God over his creations. The idea explains the presence of evil in the world by stating that God's motives are beyond human understanding. The idea is basic to one of the most powerful and enigmatic of the Bible stories, the story of Job. The story concerns how Job retains his faith in God through a series of terrible tests—he loses his family, health, and wealth. God wagers with Satan, allowing Satan to inflict these sufferings, with Job's faith as the prize. Job has done nothing to deserve his suffering, but suffer he does. Others voice to Job their belief in a rule-bound God: "Does God pervert justice?" asks one. But of course God does do precisely that, or, rather, he stands above human norms of justice. It is human self-righteousness that leads people to challenge God: "Will you condemn me that you may be justified?" answers God out of a whirlwind (40 Job v.8). The point of the story is to show the reader or listener someone who loses everything and yet keeps his faith—and finally understands the total power of God and his demand for total submission to him.

The Book of Job offers to those who read it a sense that their own suffering is not to be argued with but accepted. This acceptance may provide a psychologically powerful, perhaps comforting way to survive suffering. One finds similar narratives in other religions. For many Muslims, the story of the martyrdom of Husain at the Battle of Karbala plays this role. The story concerns how Husain, the grandson of the prophet Muhammad, died through treachery in battle. The story is important to those Muslims who believe that Muhammad's descendants are his rightful successors. Every year, these Muslims, called the *Shi'i*, or "Shiites," celebrate Husain's martyrdom as an enacted narrative of their own suffering, and their position today as a minority within the Muslim world. Processions in which Husain rides his horse through large crowds of celebrants, while some beat themselves bloody with sticks or chains, dramatize and religiously contextualize suffering (Waugh 1977).

Some Christians stage similar reenactments of Christ's suffering on his way to crucifixion. In some societies people volunteer to play the role of the crucified Christ, enduring great suffering as they are hung from crosses. These "Passion plays," public dramatization of suffering and death, remind the faithful of the human drama captured in the phrase, "he died for your sins."

Each of these stories and reenactments represents suffering as part of a broader framework, one that transcends human societies but also adds meaning to human societies. We can see these stories as several responses among many to the general human problem of how to endure suffering. They can enable us to place our own problems "in perspective."

Religion Explained by Emotions

Other social theorists have based their approaches to religion more completely in psychology than did Weber. Although the notion that religion springs from emotions is ancient, an important modern argument along these lines came from David Hume, the philosopher of the Scottish Enlightenment. In his *Natural History of Religion* (1757), Hume argued that religion first came from "the incessant hopes and fears which actuate the human mind." Religion thus offers one way of overcoming anxiety.

This idea was given ethnographic substance by Bronislaw Malinowski (1884–1942), one of the first anthropologists to carry out long-term fieldwork. Malinowski worked in the Trobriand Islands, today part of Papua New Guinea, between 1915 and 1918. He distinguished between the practical, rational knowledge and skills that Trobrianders employ to carry out their everyday tasks and the religion and magic they call on to supplement their knowledge and powers. Ideas about the afterlife help people live despite their knowledge that death awaits them, wrote Malinowski, and funeral rituals add further authority to the idea that something awaits them after death. These rituals and ideas "save man from a surrender to death and destruction" (1954 [1926], 51). Ideas about the powers of spells and prayer to change the world also serve a psychological function; they reduce the anxiety that comes from uncertainty, allowing people to carry on their practical life. Religion and magic are thus not pseudosciences; rather, they arise in response to deep-seated, innate human fears and concerns.

Malinowski was influenced by the psychologist William James (1842–1910) as well as by David Hume. In his *Varieties of Religious Experience* (1972 [1901–1902]), James defined religion in terms of a set of individual human attitudes, as "the feelings, acts, and experiences of individual men in their solitude, so far as they apprehend themselves to stand in relation to whatever they may consider the divine." James advocated *pragmatism* in philosophy and science; in his version of this approach, the experiences one accumulates, whether in the laboratory or in everyday life, are the basis for deciding about truth and falsehood. Since belief in God works toward the general good, it is "true." Religious beliefs are validated when they are shown to have beneficial consequences, such as reducing anxiety and fear.

References today to innate or unconscious psychological impulses usually draw on the writings of Sigmund Freud (1856–1939), the founder of modern psychoanalysis. Freud argued that the psyche was more than the conscious. Powerful drives for self-preservation and pleasure often shape our actions and conscious ideas in ways of which we are only half-aware. These drives in the individual run headlong into societal norms, creating repression and neuroses. Freud's (1930) views on religion were negative. Born of infantile feelings of helplessness and society-caused suffering, religion only keeps us from rationally critiquing and rebuilding our social lives, he wrote. But Freud's ideas about the power of religious symbols have been used by some anthropologists to explain why certain objects—hair, the color white, blood—have the frequent and powerful positions they do in religious ritual.

Other theorists and historians of religion have taken up the issue of how and why certain symbols have widespread power. Among them are theorists who stress the irreducible nature of religious experience. Carl Jung (1875–1961), a student of Freud, saw religion as an experience of awe at the power of the divine, a submission to a superior power that is later codified into doctrines and rituals. Jung followed William James and the theologian Rudolf Otto in finding the truth of religion in these religious experiences. But Jung then postulated a "collective unconscious" of humankind that contains all religious symbols. These symbols stem from "archetypes" that are innate in every human being, and that make possible the translation of religious experiences across persons and cultures. These archetypes—the hero, the earth mother, gods—form the basis of the universal religious experience.

Also viewing religion in terms of archetypes is Mircea Eliade, born in Romania in 1907. Eliade exemplifies the "phenomenological" study of religion, that is, bracketing what we think we know of the external world to focus our study on experience itself as an irreducible phenomenon. For Eliade (1954 [1949]), religious objects, acts, and roles are symbols that have multiple meanings, but that eventually come together in a cosmological unity. This unity is mainly about the primordial creation of the universe. Eliade examines myths and rituals from many societies, interpreting each as fundamentally about the creation of life, order, and the world. The view of religion in terms of universal archetypes has become even more popular through the writings of Joseph Campbell (1949) on myth. As with Tylor's intellectualist approach, however, this approach points to broad patterns but is unable to provide an analytical foundation for understanding specificities: how people have come to create and understand particular religious forms in particular times and places.

Symbols between Society and the Individual

Among anthropologists seeking to integrate sociological and psychological dimensions of religious practices was Victor Turner, whose work has focused on symbols and meanings. Turner is attentive to unconscious meanings and near-universal symbols, but he emphasizes the ways that ritual and social uses of symbolic objects shape their meanings for particular people.

Turner (1967) analyzes the meaning of symbols from three distinct perspectives. He begins by asking how members of the society explain a ritual or unpack the meaning of a statue. He then asks how objects are used in ritual processes and in interpreting their use. Finally, he examines the place of the object in a system of symbols. The meanings he derives from these three perspectives themselves are arrayed between two poles: one around which cluster meanings that relate to general human emotions and desires, especially those of a natural or physiological sort, and a second pole of social norms and values.

Turner's most famous symbolic analysis illustrates this process. His ethnographic work was done among the Ndembu of Zambia, a society organized around matriliny, that is, the continuity between mothers and children. When a girl reaches puberty, the Ndembu hold an initiation ceremony, during which they wrap the girl in a blanket and place her at the foot of a tree, the *mudyi,* known for its white latex. This ritual is thus known as a "white" ritual.

Turner understood the "native symbolic meaning" of the symbols largely from many discussions with one "key informant," a man named Muchona. Based on these discussions, he concluded that the tree stands for human milk, for the ties between the girl and her mother, and for the principle of ties through women more generally. These meanings seem consistent with other Ndembu statements and practices, although discussions with a broader range of Ndembu men and women might have introduced a greater diversity of meanings into the analysis.

These symbolic meanings include both physiological and social poles: aspects of the human body and of social institutions. Turner then considers the way the tree is used in ritual practices, and here he finds several distinct meanings: in one event the tree is the center for all-female activities from which the men are excluded (meaning of women versus men); in other contexts it is associated with the girl undergoing initiation.

Finally, Turner examines the broader system of symbols, and finds this tree to be one among several trees that are used in ritual activities, each associated with white, red, or black. Each color calls forth associations with natural substances: black with putrification and feces, red with blood, white with milk and semen. Although these associations are "natural" in the sense that blood is indeed red, the values placed on these associations are cultural and relatively arbitrary. Is blood good? Powerful? Polluting? The Ndembu highlight certain values and play down others. Red is linked to power and wealth; black is linked to pollution and disease; white is linked to purity and life. They then can interpret the value of various ritual and medicinal objects in terms of this color scheme. Medicines made from the "white" mudyi tree, for example, aid a woman having difficulties breastfeeding.

For the Ndembu, then, the three primary colors provide a template for much of social life, just as do the four cardinal directions for the Zuni. Turner's account of religious ritual situates the ritual in its matrilineal social context, analyzes the Ndembu explanations of rituals and symbols, and considers the emotional power of Ndembu ritual associations. Other anthropologists, for example Gananath Obeyesekere (1981), emphasize the ways that personal, sometimes unconscious meanings of key symbols in a culture shape the lives of individuals. For these and other writers, symbols are studied for their roles in the lives of individuals in particular societies.

3 Ideas and Practices of "Religion" in Europe and Elsewhere

*M*ost people living in Europe or North America are used to thinking about religions as sets of formal beliefs or doctrines. Christian denominational differences, for example, have developed largely from debates about doctrine. A Christian may ask someone who practices another religion: What do you believe?, and not mean, What particular things do you as an individual believe? but, What are the shared beliefs sanctified in your religion? (Many from Muslim and Jewish backgrounds would ask the same question.)

And yet, the relationship between doctrines and religious lives is quite complex in Western as well as in other societies. This chapter considers the genealogy of Western ideas about the nature of religion. Only relatively recently have people in Western societies seen the world as composed of distinct religions, each with its own set of beliefs. The rise of this idea has colored the way Europeans have understood other religions.

We also explore how Japan illustrates very different ideas about religions in practice. People in Japan freely combine elements of more than one religion to resolve problems of everyday life. However, the issue of religion's definition recently has become highly politicized, as people fiercely debate whether Shinto practices form a religion or a state ideology.

Western Ideas of Religion

*F*or most of Western history, religion was regarded as an individual's personal piety or faith. People did not write books about religion, but about faith, on the one hand, and the institutions of the church, on the other.

The word *religion* comes from the Latin word *religio,* whose early meaning appears to have been a power outside the individual, or a feeling relative to such a power. *Religiosus* meant a powerful place and conveyed a sense of mystery. The term also came to refer to the particular pattern of worship, the *religiones,* that was due a certain god (W. C. Smith 1978, 19–31).

The early leaders of the Christian Church adopted these usages from the Romans. Roman authorities forced the early Christians to participate in the traditional Roman cultic ceremonies. If they refused they often were put to death. So, the key issue about religion was how to worship: the Roman way or exclusively the Christian way. This focus on one's own religious rituals as opposed to those of other people gave rise to a new sense of the plural: our way of worship (*nostra religio*) as opposed to the *religiones* of outsiders. In this context the phrase "the Christian religion" was often used to mean the Eucharist, the central ritual performed by people considering themselves Christians.

The concept of religion might then have developed into its current meaning, as a term used to refer to the system of beliefs and practices of each of a number of societies. But it did not develop in this way, and the word religion itself virtually passed out of existence for a thousand years. (An exception is St. Augustine, whose *De Vera Religione* we might translate as "On Proper Piety"; it concerned the bond between an individual and God and not a system of beliefs and practices.)

Despite the general impression, true in many ways, that the European Middle Ages were an age of religion, it appears that no one ever wrote a book using "religion" in the title or as a concept during this period. Not until the fifteenth century, during the Renaissance, was the term taken up again, and then with the sense of a universal capacity for piety and worship common to all human beings. There was to be only one kind of *religio*, but it would exist in different degrees in different people.

The Reformation continued this line of thought; both Martin Luther and John Calvin stressed the importance of individual piety and faith over and against any external religious system, by which they meant the Catholic Church. Luther inveighed against any "false religion," or putting faith in religion rather than in God. Indeed, Luther inaugurated a tradition in the German language of avoiding the term "religion" altogether in favor of *Gottesdienst,* "service to God" (W. C. Smith 1978, 35).

Religion as a Belief System

The idea of religion as a system of beliefs, as opposed to personal piety, did not take hold until the seventeenth century. The change was partly the result of efforts during the Enlightenment to classify and understand the world as a schema, accessible by the intellect. It was also because of a growing diversity of religious claims within Europe and the increased awareness, because of trade and travel, of religious traditions beyond Europe. By the eighteenth century, treatises on religions of the world (introducing religious pluralism) began to appear. The plural "religions" is possible only when we think of religion as a cultural system rather than a personal one. There are no plural forms for piety, reverence, or obedience.

As Europeans began to study other religions, they tended to use the religions most familiar to them, namely Judaism and Christianity, as a general model. They assumed all religions would have three central elements: a central text, exclusivity, and separation. The central text was assumed to be a collection of doctrines or beliefs that all adherents shared, ideally, written in a sacred book that had been inspired by a god or gods. Exclusivity meant that a person was a member of one and only one religion, at least at any one time. Separation indicated that religion constituted an area of social life distinct from politics or economics. The idea of separation developed in modern Western Europe, partly in response to the destructive religious wars of the seventeenth century. John Locke, writing in the late seventeenth century, advocated the separation of state and religion as a way of ensuring toleration and religious freedom. His argument became the basis for the principle of separation of church and state in the United States; nowhere else was it so fully realized.

While this model of religion worked well to describe European practices, it fit poorly with religions of India, China, and Japan. No one book provides a shared creed for practitioners of religion in these societies; instead, each contains a large number of books written on diverse aspects of life and on teachers and organizations of followers. Today we know these collections of texts and teachers under the general rubrics of *Hinduism, Buddhism, Taoism,* or *Shinto,* but these labels are modern inventions.

Nor does the idea of exclusivity fit with norms in these societies. In Japan, for example, people routinely bring offerings to shrines dedicated to local gods (practices associated with the label *Shinto*) and, in the same temple complex, venerate Buddha. The same people may marry in a Christian church. The idea of a separate religious sphere is also alien to many other religious traditions. Muslims, for example, argue that all of life should be conducted in accord with God's commands. Hinduism involves ideas of purity and pollution that permeate all social life.

Other Religions, Other Models

*M*odern attempts to understand these other religions have been based on the European model. By the nineteenth century, books appeared about other religions, introducing for the first time the names that we use today. *Buddhism* was first used in 1801, *Hinduism* in 1829. (Before then writers referred, more accurately, to "the wisdom of the Japanese" or "Hindu teachings.") The term *Islam* also began to be used; previously, Europeans referred to *Muhammadism,* treating Islam not as a religion, but as allegiance to a false prophet (W. C. Smith 1978, 51–79).

The nineteenth-century European notions of what counted as a religion have powerfully shaped how other religions and other countries have viewed religion. For, with few exceptions, the creation of terms for *religion* and for particular religions have been the result of Western, Christian influence.

Take what we often refer to as Hinduism. In India today, religious practice and the precise formulations of doctrine vary from place to place. Indeed, it is a central tenet of religious teaching in India that one should follow the inspiration derived from one's teacher in pursuit of enlightenment. Thus, there is not, nor is there supposed to be, one single formulation of Hindu Religion.

The word *Hindu* itself was not used by ancient Indians to refer to their religion. It is a word meaning "river," and in particular is used as the proper name for the Indus River. Foreigners—Greeks, then Muslim conquerors—came to designate the people living near that river as "Indian" or "Hindu." Under Muslim rule, the term came to be used to refer to all non-Muslims in the country and included Buddhists and Jains. Only recently has *Hindu* been used as a residual term to designate those people, and their beliefs, who are residents of India but who are not Jains, not Sikhs, not Christians, not Muslims, and not animists. But in the 1980s and 1990s some politicians made the creation of a "Hindu India" their party platform, and they succeeded in rallying large numbers of supporters to their cause. Whatever was once the case, today "Hindu" is experienced by many Indians as a unitary social as well as religious category (see Chapter 15).

Consider the Chinese who have traditionally had no word corresponding to the Western idea of religion. They borrowed a word from the Japanese, *Tsung-Chiao,* which the Japanese themselves had created to accommodate the Western concept. Nor did they have words meaning Confucianism, Buddhism, or Taoism in the sense of religions that one joined or left. Instead, people were aware of collections of teachings that could be followed in trying to find a path toward truth; these teachings included the sayings of Confucius, Buddha, and Lao Tse (a possibly mythic figure who urged followers to find the true path, or Tao).

In a rather neat exchange of terms, the Japanese borrowed the word used to refer to indigenous traditions, *shinto,* from the Chinese. In fact the term was first used by foreigners to refer to local practices. The Japanese today use a translation of this term—*kami no michi,* or "the way of the spirits or gods"—to refer to these practices (Reader 1991, 23). The definitions of what is included in "religion" are of much public interest in Japan today. At the end of the nineteenth century, the Japanese government declared that the indigenous, or Shinto, worship at shrines was not a religion. But what came to be called State Shinto, to which the cult of the emperor was central, became an ideological pillar of twentieth-century Japanese efforts to modernize society, and for that reason the cult was abolished under the post–World War II Occupation.

The boundaries of religion were again debated when the new emperor, Akihito, succeeded his father, Hirohito, in January 1989. According to Shinto creed, the emperor is the descendant of the Sun Goddess, and he performs certain rituals at the goddess's shrine when he takes office. Are these rituals to be taken as religious? If so, they imply his claim to be the chief priest of Shinto and the intermediary to the Sun Goddess. But this status was abolished under the occupation, in the Constitution. Are they perhaps just political ritual? There was a fierce debate in Japan over this question, and the matter (which we consider in the next section) remains unsettled.

The names for religions were often provided by outsiders—one can add to the preceding examples that the term *Judaism* is Greek, not Hebrew. The name *Islam,* used from the beginning by the religion's adherents, is the major exception. However, the term means "submission to God," not the set of beliefs and practices themselves. Indeed, the religious scholar Wilfred Cantwell Smith (1978, 114) has argued that if one believes in God as a Jew or Christian, and realizes that from an Islamic perspective Muslims, Christians, and Jews worship the same God, then one cannot truthfully say in Arabic, "I am not a Muslim." One submits to God, after all, in whatever language.

Imposed Definitions of Religion

Even as religions differ in what they include in the definition of "religion," many modern states in Asia, Africa, and Latin America have drawn their ideas of religion from

Western, Christian, and, to some extent, Islamic models. They adhere to a model of religion that does not fit with local beliefs and practices of some peoples within their borders, and may place pressure on them to conform to this model.

Let us turn to Indonesia to consider these problems of state-imposed definitions of religion. Indonesia, the world's fourth largest country, has about 200 million people living on thousands of islands and speaking more than 300 distinct languages. About 85 percent of the people call themselves Muslim, and the remaining 15 percent includes important Christian and Buddhist minorities as well as practitioners of indigenous religions.

The Indonesian government has "belief in one God" as one of the planks of its ideology. The state defines religion as having a sacred book, a monotheistic foundation, exclusive boundaries (such that one person cannot belong to two religions at the same time), and as transcending ethnic boundaries (rather than being essentially an aspect of a hereditary culture).

This model came by way of several large-scale religions. In the early centuries of the present era, rulers adopted the symbols and ideas of Hinduism and Buddhism, sometimes both together. The Indonesian word for religion, *agama*, comes from Sanskrit, and means "text." The agama of a person was the set of texts from which he or she derived teaching and religious direction: the books of Hinduism, Buddhism, Islam, or others. The idea of a central text does not require that the religion have exclusive boundaries; that idea came later, in the fourteenth through sixteenth centuries, when many rulers began converting to Islam. Islam does insist on absolute exclusivity and on the idea of one and only one true foundational text, the Qur'ân. Christianity, brought to Indonesia at about the same time, shares these ideas.

By the time of Indonesian independence, then, the major religions supported this model of religion. The state decreed that everyone should belong to one of five religions: Catholicism, Protestantism, Islam, Hinduism, or Buddhism. (Confucianism has enjoyed an ambiguous status in these decrees.) One might be surprised to hear that Hinduism, with its many, vividly represented deities, stood for monotheism; the Indonesian resolution of this problem—supported by some Hindus—was to declare that the various Hindu gods were all manifestations of a single absolute deity.

Today, Indonesians who practice local religions that do not conform to the official model are pressured to join one of the state-recognized religions, although this pressure has begun to ease since the fall of President Suharto in 1998. Those who do not convert may be accused of being atheists and therefore communists, a dangerous label in this strongly anti-communist state. So defining one's religion is a matter of great concern, and for some a matter of sheer survival (Kipp and Rodgers 1987).

What do people who practice other religions do? Some nominally convert but retain some older practices, such as ways of healing that involve calling on spirits to possess a healer and speak through him or her. Other people work to have their indigenous practices counted as a world religion, usually as Hindu. In one such case, a group of people on the island of Sulawesi did manage to become recognized as Hindus, despite the fact that there were few resemblances, other than a few words of Sanskrit, between their religion and anything practiced in India. A problem arose when one member of this group was elected to the local parliament. Members of parliament need to be sworn in on "their book." So what was this fellow's scripture? Well, because the book had to be Hindu, as the group's practices were called that, the parliament wrote to a Hindu association in Jakarta asking for their book. The association sent along a book in Sanskrit (I could not determine what book it was), and the new member was duly sworn in using it. Appearances were saved, and the religion's credentials established: they had a Book.

Wana Practices and Indonesian Definitions

Some people reshape their indigenous ideas in response to state pressures to convert. The 5,000 Wana people of Sulawesi, described by the anthropologist Jane Monnig Atkinson (1987, 1989), practice forms of divination and shamanism, and their ideas about spirits and possession surface in many domains of everyday life. They do not have a distinct domain called "religion."

Central to Wana efforts at dealing with the spiritual domain are the performances called *mabolong*. These rituals of possession and healing are performed by shamans, ritual experts who are possessed by spirits. Shamans are called on to perform mabolong when someone is ill and requires supernatural assistance. Often many people attend these performances. The shaman is invited to feast from a tray of food, and he in turn invites his "spirit familiars" to join him in enjoying the food. He then asks these spirits to discover what is ailing a patient, to rid the patient of foreign objects, and to go with him on a spirit voyage to recover souls or dream spirits that the patient has lost.

Shamans have greater inner powers, and they draw on these powers to keep people healthy and to increase their own social standing. They are heroes in their community. Indeed, they often create new social communities as people seek to live near them. It is in these rituals performed by shamans that ordinary humans engage the spirit world. The Wana have no written texts that prescribe doctrines or beliefs, and their narratives concerning the spirit world are many and varied. What brings their diverse ideas and stories together is collective attendance at shamanic rituals.

But Wana also face intense pressure from Muslim officials and from Christian missionaries to convert to a state-recognized religion, an agama. Wana come into contact with Muslim peoples living on the coast and serving as local state officials, and, more recently, Christian converts living in other upland regions.

As they have come to understand what is meant by agama, some Wana have constructed their own ideas of what their religion must be. These constructions are not about healing and possession, but about what distinguishes Wana from Muslims and Christians: diet, burial practices, and ties to government among them. Most saliently, Wana are people who, unlike Muslims, do eat pig, and, also unlike Muslims, kill chickens by wringing their necks rather than slaughtering them by knife.

Wana have also constructed a set of beliefs along the lines of Muslim and Christian beliefs, but distinct from them. They claim, for example, that they have a single God and that this God is the same as the Muslim and Christian creator. They recently invented a heaven that corresponds to the images of heaven taught to them by Muslims and Christians but reverses those groups' teachings about the destiny of the Wana. In the Wana notions, Wana lead poor lives on earth and therefore they will have the best

Wana shaman during possession at a healing session, Indonesia. (COURTESY OF JANE ATKINSON.)

places in heaven. Muslims, by contrast, they believe, will live in pig excrement because they avoid it here. Christians will have only scraps of clouds to eat (an idea probably derived from pictures of Jesus in the clouds in Bible schools).

Most Wana have so far resisted conversion, but even in resisting they have transformed their religion in accord with the dominant, ultimately Western, model of proper religion.

Combining Religious Practices in Japan

*J*apan illustrates an orientation toward religion that contrasts with that which developed in the West. Japanese freely blend elements from indigenous practices, state-inspired Shinto, and the traditions of Buddhism, Confucianism, and Taoism. There has been little or no religious inspiration for "purism." One common saying sums up the division of labor as "born Shinto, die Buddhist," referring to the daily appeals to Shinto spirits during one's lifetime, and the Buddhist priest's responsibility for carrying out funeral rites (Reader 1991). Marriages are increasingly conducted in Christian style, and many Japanese consult practitioners of the New Religions for solutions to recurring illnesses. These sects themselves combine ideas and practices from many sources, including Hinduism, Japanese nativist writings about racial superiority, and indigenous healing practices. To take an extreme example: it seemed not at all unusual or striking to Japanese that the Aum Shinrikyo sect responsible for the 1995 nerve gas attack in Tokyo combined Buddhist and Hindu texts.

Practice and Belief

About 65 percent of Japanese people have told survey-takers in repeated surveys that they have no religious beliefs (compared to fewer than 10 percent in the United States). Only 20 percent to 30 percent say they believe in the existence of spirits (*kami*) or in souls of the dead. But 76 percent of these respondents have in their homes either a Shinto altar devoted to kami, or a Buddhist one devoted to the souls of the dead; 45 percent have both. Eighty-nine percent say they visit the graves of their ancestors to pray for them (Reader 1991, 5–12).

These results are very puzzling to Western readers if we assume that people think of their beliefs as governing their practices. One problem is with the word *religion,* which in Japanese is *shukyo,* a word originally devised to answer pesky missionaries who asked Japanese to state what their religion was. It was taken to refer to a separate set of beliefs, removed from everyday life, and not to some everyday activity like stopping for a moment at a shrine to make an offering. Thus, asking someone in Japan if he or she has a religion or religious beliefs is something like asking a person in the United States if he or she is a member of a religious movement, a question that would elicit denials from many churchgoers.

Many students of Japanese culture have also emphasized that ideas about beliefs and morality are more focused on specific events and situations than is true for European cultures. Anecdotes from World War II relate how Japanese prisoners of war, having just been bent on killing Allied troops, suddenly became model prisoners of war. In their eyes, the situation had changed and so had their responsibilities.

Finally, a pragmatic try-it-and-see attitude underlies the approach taken by many Japanese toward religious ritual. This approach emphasizes the importance of sincerity for the ritual to work, but not a general "belief," and certainly not an exclusive commitment to that religion and no other. It is thus relatively easy, within the Japanese religious world view, to try a new healing religion without abandoning offerings to household spirits and Buddhist deities. This willingness to participate in more than one religion lies behind the common practice of declaring oneself to census takers as both Buddhist and Shinto, marrying in a Protestant church, and attending sessions of a healing sect to seek a cure for an illness. And it is evident in figures about religious membership: about 75 percent of the population are classified as Buddhist by the government, 95 percent as Shinto, and over 10 percent as members of new religious movements (Reader 1991, 6). Japanese do affiliate with religious organizations, and usually more than one.

Perhaps, then, answers to surveys underplay the extent to which Japanese assume that there are spirits at work in the world. It would appear that the practices of keeping an altar at home and reciting prayers for one's ancestors at graveside imply such a set of beliefs. And yet haven't we all engaged in practices for which we are unsure of whether we agree with the associated doctrines? Modern Western religious culture emphasizes the importance of believing in the doctrines behind practices, in the paramount importance of creeds of faith, and this emphasis may make it quite difficult for some people in the United States, for example, to deny belief in God to a survey-taker, whatever his or her doubts might be. Japanese religious culture does not make this same emphasis; consequently, denying the belief while going along with the practice may be easier for the Japanese person than for the American.

This religious–cultural emphasis on practices over doctrines makes it easier for Japanese to combine elements from different religious traditions, as we see in later chapters. First we can explore the roles played by two major traditions—Shintoism and Buddhism—and how people's actions may imply their belief in a proposition about the spiritual world without them directly expressing that belief.

Shinto and Spirits

Basic to the Japanese Shinto tradition are spirits, or *kami* (Earhart 1982), which are located in specific places in the empirical world: in a boulder, or a house, or a shrine. One Japanese estimate is that there are "eight million spirits"—meaning they are innumerable. When foreigners asked Japanese to name their religion, in order to distinguish it from Buddhism, they called it "the way of the *kami*," although it came to be called Shinto in the West (Reader 1991).

The term *kami* refers both to the sense of power felt in things of the world, and to particular spirits. A waterfall is a powerful kami; calling it a kami communicates the sense an observer has of its immense power. Space may also contain kami and may be demarcated by rocks, or by a shrine with boundaries and a gateway. One sees these *torii*, Shinto gateways, with two pillars and one or two crossbeams, throughout Japan and in many U.S. cities. A Japanese rock garden works similarly, demarcating a sparsely filled space rather than, as in European-style ornamental gardens, featuring a dense collection of plants. Although kami can be anywhere, they are not everywhere; these boundaries serve to separate the sacred from the profane.

Perhaps the most important spirits are those in the house. They occupy particular places and protect the members of the household when in those places: the god of the kitchen lives in the kitchen, the latrine god in the latrine, and so forth. There is also a guardian deity of the household as a whole; this spirit is made up of many ancestors who have merged to guard the household as a corporate unit that exists over time. The village has a guardian deity, often a fox god or an ancestor of a founding member. The village, like the household, is a corporate group, with control over irrigation, cooperative use of some land, and religious festivals. Villagers will ask the village god for help in their rice harvest or for success in schooling. Village elites once controlled the shrine festivals for the village gods, but today, with many villagers engaged in urban pursuits, their importance has diminished.

Also important to everyday life is the spirit of a rice field. This spirit lives a dual existence, as the figure of Inari, the rice deity, and also as the spirit guarding each particular field. Spirits of the fields and of rice live in the mountains and come down in the spring when the soil is tilled. They guard over the rice, and return to the mountains in the fall after the harvest. They are sometimes represented as fox spirits, probably

Temple complex near Narita, Japan, with Shinto and Buddhist shrines, and shops selling amulets, books, and other items. (COURTESY OF J. BOWEN.)

because foxes, also associated with rice, sexuality, and fertility, were thought to come down from the mountains in spring.

People create new spirits as needed. When the Tennis Players' Association was created in Japan before World War II, someone suggested the creation of a new god, to be named "Heavenly God of Speedy Ball." And in a less individuated way, all equipment, from computer chips to cameras to automobile production machinery, are thought to have a spiritual side. The machines are blessed by a Shinto priest before they are used, and in 1990 engineers met at Tokyo's Chomeiji temple to thank their used-up equipment for the service it had given them. Photographs of the cameras and video recorders were burned as a Buddhist priest chanted verses. Even in the electronics industry Shinto and Buddhism are mixed (Sanger 1990).

Kami can also be the spirits of deceased persons. Sometimes famous people will become deified as kami and have shrines built to them, but for a mixture of reasons. One ninth-century court official, for example, had died at the hands of his rivals for power. As a spirit he wreaked havoc with their lives until they built a shrine to him.

Spirits and Social Change

Japanese relationships to spirits developed in a civilization centered on enduring social units: the household, the village, and the Imperial House. Household spirits stood for the continuity of the household over generations. Households in a village were protected by community spirits. And everyone was under the protection of the unbroken imperial line, itself said to come from the Sun Goddess and dating at least back to the seventh century C.E. Although these continuities have been disrupted by massive migrations to cities, older orientations toward spirits of the collectivity—including the emperor and his temples—continue in Japan.

Many kami are venerated in shrines, and some shrines, such as the great shrine at Ise to the Sun Goddess, are the focus of national veneration. The Ise shrine is rebuilt every 20 years as part of a cycle of national renewal of life and fertility; the last rebuilding, in 1993, was widely publicized by banners erected throughout Japan.

Parents routinely take their newborn babies to the local shrine to be placed under the care of the spirit guarding the local community. An offering is placed on the altar, and the shrine priest says prayers requesting these blessings. In the older, agrarian world in which Japanese religions developed, they also would have carried out rites at this shrine to ensure the fertility of the crops. The shrine also served as the place for community meetings and recreational activities; it was thus the center of social life. Often the community shrine was said to be a branch shrine of a famous national shrine, such as that at Ise. Performing rituals at the shrine thus linked the individual to the community and the nation–state.

Worship at a shrine, Narita temple complex, Japan. (COURTESY OF J. BOWEN.)

Since World War II, Japanese have flooded from country to city and from farming to other occupations. In 1950, 62 percent of all Japanese families lived in rural areas, and fully 50 percent of those rural families were full-time farmers. Just 30 years later, in 1980, only 24 percent of families lived in rural areas, and only 10 percent of these families still engaged in full-time farming. This rapid shift in population has meant that a civilization and a set of religious practices that had developed around stable rural households now had to be modified for urban living. But Shinto shrines have been part of this transformation. People who commute to the city from suburbs or rural areas still visit the shrines to seek blessings for their babies and seek further spirit protection for young children, though now they may dress in Western-style clothes and record the occasions with expensive video cameras.

People living in the cities may return to their ancestral villages for harvest festivals and for the New Year's festival, when they acquire new amulets from the shrines to protect their homes during the coming year. For two years Ian Reader (1991, 61–64) watched proceedings at the Katano shrine midway between the cities of Osaka and Kyoto in what has become a commuter village. He records that on festival days, hundreds of people took trains from both cities to the shrine to seek blessings and purchase amulets. A shrine priest could call on office girls to work as temporary "shrine maidens" on these occasions; at one festival, Reader found himself being blessed by one of his own students who had been engaged to work as such a shrine maiden during the holidays. Businesses sent rice, or sake, to be placed on the altar for blessings (and afterward quickly consumed by visitors). The same priest was called upon to bless a new university building nearby. He had a temporary altar to the shrine spirit constructed inside the new building for the occasion.

Increased ease of transport has meant that Japanese increasingly visit the more famous shrines in larger cities. Several million people visit these shrines each year, while some rural shrines, those not on commuter lines and unable to afford priests, have closed. The social ties affirmed by attending a shrine are less and less local and increasingly national in scope.

Buddhism and Souls

Most of the people frequenting these shrines with their newborns, or at festivals, also participate in rituals drawn from Buddhism (Saunders 1964). The Buddhist religion began in the sixth century B.C.E. in South Asia, when the historical Buddha, Siddhartha of the clan Gautama, found enlightenment after long meditation. The followers of Buddha also seek enlightenment; his teachings provide examples and practices to follow rather than creeds to which followers must adhere.

In South Asia, Buddhism diverged into two major streams. One, called "Theravada" ("the elders") emphasizes the role of the monastic community in mediating between laypersons and Buddha. This stream spread from Sri Lanka to mainland Southeast Asia. The second stream was called "Mahayana," or "Greater Vehicle," for its universalistic approach to salvation. In this stream, individuals are encouraged to engage in practices that lead to their salvation and to enter directly into contact with Buddhas and other deities.

The Mahayana stream of Buddhism spread northward from India through Tibet and China. Japanese scholars learned about Buddhism in China, and for that reason Japanese Buddhism adopts the Mahayana orientation. Mahayana Buddhism emphasizes the illusory character of the world and orients the individual toward a transcendent reality in which he or she might achieve salvation. One sees this emphasis in paintings, where individual Buddhas are depicted floating above the world we live in, transcendent of its specific concreteness. These diverse Buddhas—Fudo, Amida, Maitreya—provide multiple sources of divine aid and multiple paths for individuals to seek salvation.

Each of the several major schools of Buddhism in Japan—Zen, Shingon, Nichiren, and others—combines a set of spiritual disciplines that lead to salvation (Reader 1991). They all evince a special concern for death and treatment of ancestors. Zen Buddhism, the best known of these schools in the West, emphasizes meditation. Indeed, the word *Zen* itself means "meditation." Zen teachers point to the example set by the historical Buddha, Gautama, who achieved enlightenment in this world by sitting and meditating. Zen practitioners may use *koan,* problems that appear unsolvable, as a way of breaking down the barriers that everyday linear thinking places in the path to enlightenment. They practice together in communities of meditators, engaging in strenuous physical labor—scrubbing floors, chopping wood—as additional aids to enlightenment. Laypeople may participate in retreats at Zen temples, and businesses routinely send their employees on special retreats that incorporate some of the austerities of temple life.

Japanese Buddhism's emphasis on individual meditation and enlightenment provides a counterpoint in religious practice to the overall Japanese cultural emphasis on the value and continuity of the group. But Buddhism also adapted itself to those values by assuming responsibility for the care of family ancestors. Even if they have no other contact with Buddhism, and would not state that they believe in Buddha, most Japanese "die Buddhist," that is, their children or other relatives seek out the service of a Buddhist priest to perform a funeral service. The main activity at most temples is in fact not meditation but performing memorial services for the dead. Most Japanese households are affiliated with a particular temple for this purpose.

Before Buddhism, Japanese people considered that each person's soul traveled to a world of the dead, where it continued to watch and intervene in the lives of its relatives. People carried out rituals designed to ease the transition to the other world and to keep the spirits happy. When Buddhism came to Japan, people saw the priests as possessing spiritual powers due to their activities of meditation. They began to call on those priests to perform the funeral ceremonies. Priests added new practices to the rituals, practices designed to guide the spirit toward enlightenment after death. The priest and his associates cremate the body to rid the soul of its impurities, and chant Buddhist texts and prayers to lead the soul toward the state of enlightenment. The word for dead soul, *hotoke,* also means a Buddha.

These ancestors continue to affect the lives of their kin, and both Buddhist priests and practitioners of New Religions are concerned with keeping the ancestors happy and resolving problems that occur when they are not. (See Chapter 6 for an example.)

Buddhism coexists with Shinto in Japan. The temple complex at Nara, which I visited in 1994, contains both Buddhist temples and Shinto shrines, and visitors stop at both.

Temples may include images of kami alongside those of a Buddha, although the former are said to no longer contain spirits but only to represent them. The two kinds of entities are represented in clearly contrasting ways. In paintings, for example, kami are depicted in a realistic manner as specific, human-looking personages, sometimes identifiable as historical figures, and always standing near or on the place with which they are associated. Buddhas and bodhisattvas, by contrast, are abstract in their appearance, and not confined to specific spaces. Often they are painted as floating above the ground or on clouds.

Two other religious traditions have also influenced Japanese ideas and practices. Taoism (from *tao*, the "way" in Chinese) developed in China as an approach to understanding the way of the universe. Taoism includes methods of divining good or bad days by consulting calendars. Japanese adopted some of these practices—there was even a bureau of divination in early Japan—but no Japanese would identify himself or herself as a Taoist.

Confucianism, based on the teachings of the Chinese philosopher Confucius (551–479 B.C.E.), has played an important role in shaping Japanese social and moral values (Smith 1983, 37–67). Confucius taught that social order and welfare depended on maintaining the proper hierarchical relationships between persons, particularly those of father to son and ruler to subject. In Japan, these ideas strengthened the notion of the family as a corporate entity, with succession passing from father to eldest son, and that of the nation as a family-like entity headed by the hereditary emperor.

The State and Religion

Japan's rulers have added to their legitimacy by drawing on Shinto and Buddhism. The state has variously promoted one or the other of these two complexes of religious ideas and practices. In its encounter with outside cultures and in particular with Christianity, the Japanese state has created indigenous alternatives—systems of ideas and practices that looked like religion as defined in the West.

State promotion of religions began between the sixth and ninth centuries with the adoption of Chinese ideas that the emperor is both a divine being and the active ruler of society. Just as village guardians often were thought to be the ancestors of the village elite, the emperor declared himself (or herself) the descendant of the Sun Goddess. (These borrowings were a major source of Confucian influence in Japan.)

Scholars began to teach Buddhism in Japan during the Nara period (710–784 C.E.), named after the capital city of Nara. Emperor Shomu (reigned 724–749) quickly made Buddhism the state religion. Buddhism appealed to the emperor and his advisers because it came from China, along with the writing system and ideas of the divinity of the emperor, and also because it could be made the basis of a state-centered system of religious temples, with scriptures and priests. The preexisting religious practices were decentralized, with local spirits and shrines. Buddhism offered the possibility of constructing a religious hierarchy under imperial control.

In 728, the emperor built the Todai temple in Nara (just south of present-day Kyoto) as the first national temple. The statue of Buddha inside the temple, called "Lochana," still stands as the largest Buddhist statue in the world. Lochana, or Dainichi,

Todai temple, Japan, with statue of the Buddha Nyiori. (COURTESY OF JOHN RENARD.)

is the Sun Buddha. When he was building the statue, the emperor had to seek approval from his ancestress, the Sun Goddess Amaterasu, at her temple in Ise. Reportedly the goddess told the emperor that the Sun Buddha was the same as the Sun Goddess, and approved building the statue.

The emperor then ordered two temples built in each province, one as a monastery and one as a nunnery. Monks and nuns were recruited to these temples to recite Buddhist scriptures and accumulate merit, and then to pass on the merit to the nation as a whole. This form of mediated merit was not part of the Mahayana tradition imported by the state; it was created by the emperor for his own project of state building. By venerating the Sun Buddha, the emperor managed to link Buddha to his own Sun Goddess ancestor. By constructing a national temple system, he linked acts of individual merit-making to the welfare of the nation as a whole, and forged a religious connection between the people and the state. But the temples and their priests, particularly at Todai temple, grew more and more powerful, and the decision to move the Imperial capital to Kyoto in 784 was in part to establish a separate power base away from the temple.

In succeeding centuries the influence of state-sponsored Buddhism waned along with the power of the emperor. But in 1600 the warlord (*shogun*) Tokugawa Ieyasu consolidated power throughout Japan, ending the many centuries of political disorder, and reduced the emperor to a figurehead. Ieyasu once again promoted Buddhism as the state religion, building a new hierarchy of temples. All Japanese were required to register at a temple, proclaim their religion, and use the services of Buddhist priests for funeral services. These state actions were not motivated by religious piety but intended to tighten state control and exclude Christianity, as a disruptive, foreign ideology. Thus, Buddhism was promoted as the best alternative to Christianity, as "not-Christianity."

In 1868 a coalition of warlords and a rising economic elite took power in the name of the Emperor Meiji, and sought to reduce the influence of Buddhism because of its association with the old regime. The Meiji Restoration combined economic restructuring with the creation of a cult of the emperor. A hierarchy of Shinto priests was created, and the result has come to be called State Shinto. Shrines were created to appeal to popular opinion. Foremost among these new shrines were Yasukuni, founded in 1869, where those soldiers who have died for the honor of the state are enshrined and deified, and the Meiji shrine, built in 1920 to honor the deceased emperor. Both produced talismans for people to take home with them, and people were also required to have talismans from Ise in their homes (Hardacre 1989, 79–99).

These efforts were meant to create a religious plane on which individual households would be merged into the state. The Confucian values of filial piety were emphasized as well as the common descent of all Japanese, as in the following section from a teacher's manual used in the 1930s:

The connection between the Imperial House and its subjects is thus: one forms the main house and the others form the branch house, so that from ancient times we have worshiped the founder of the Imperial House and the heavenly gods. Our relationship to this house is sincerely founded on repaying our debt of gratitude to our ancestors. (quoted in Smith 1983, 32)

After World War II, the American forces that occupied Japan insisted that the new Constitution remove the aura of divinity from the emperor. The Constitution states that the emperor is not divine, but only "the symbol of the state and of the unity of the people." The Nobel Prize–winning writer Kenzaburo Oe has written of his and others' astonishment when on August 15, 1945, they heard the emperor speak over the radio. "The Emperor speaking to us in a human voice was beyond imagining in any reverie. The Emperor was a god, the authority of the nation, the organizing principle of reality" (Oe 1995, 103).

The Occupation forces also proclaimed Shinto to be a religion and that because people ought to be able to choose their religion freely it could not be taught in the schools or be supported by state funds. And yet despite this new official ideology, the Sun Goddess Amaterasu continues to be worshiped at the great shrine at Ise. Each time the shrine is rebuilt the ancient mirror that is thought to embody the Sun Goddess's spirit is moved into the new shrine. Six and a half million Japanese visit the shrine each year. Japanese visit Ise the way that Jews visit Israel and Muslims visit Mecca, as a journey to a sacred place.

The precise status of Ise and the nature of the emperor's relationship to the Sun Goddess (if any) became major political issues when Emperor Hirohito died in January 1989. At Hirohito's funeral the following month, the Shinto rites were performed behind curtains, evidently so that visiting dignitaries would not have to acknowledge them. Yet many in Japan criticized these proceedings as tantamount to worship of the emperor and thus a violation of the 1946 Constitution.

Then, in November 1990, Hirohito's son and successor, Akihito, was enthroned. Part of the enthronement procedure is the "great food-offering ritual," in which the new emperor offers special foods to the deities of the heaven and earth and performs a ritual of union of sorts (left ambiguous in official accounts) with the Sun Goddess. The last time this ritual had been performed was in 1928, when the emperor was still considered a god. At Ise he still is thought of as the chief priest of Shinto. There was a great deal of protest from those who considered the ritual to be religious, and thus to violate the Constitution's mandate that state and religion be separated (Weisman 1990).

Similar controversy continues to surround the Yasukuni shrine to the war dead. Prime Ministers regularly visit the shrine, located next to the Imperial Palace in central Tokyo, to venerate the war dead, sometimes in their official capacity. In August 1985, Prime Minister Nakasone with his cabinet made an official visit to the shrine to pay tribute to the war dead. But here Japan's difficulty in facing its wartime history surfaced, because major ("Class A") war criminals executed by judgment of the 1946–1948 Tokyo Trial are among the two and a half million people listed as gods in the shrine's record book. Furthermore, the Rape of Nanking is among the events celebrated, a fact that led China to protest this attendance. Protests by many Japanese led Nakasone to forgo additional state visits to the shrine. But on August 15, 2006, Prime Minister Koizumi prayed at the Yasukuni shrine, choosing the most diplomatically explosive day, the anniversary of the end of World War II, and drawing immediate protest from China and South Korea.

Veterans' groups continue to enshrine and deify the spirits of Japanese soldiers, however. In 1988, the Japanese Supreme Court backed up one such group over the objections of the widow of a soldier about to be deified. She was Protestant and protested that the deification violated her religious beliefs, but the Court claimed that her religion had no bearing on the group's freedom to carry out the ritual. The idea of religious exclusivity—that one religion excludes others—is not part of the Japanese legal tradition (Haberman 1988).

Death practices, indeed, have all along been important elements in the state–religion nexus. The eighth-century ascendancy of Buddhism was accompanied by a change from burial to cremation for emperors and empresses, following Buddhist practice. During the 1600–1868 Tokugawa period, Shinto nationalists were gradually able to reduce Buddhism's official status—after 1654, although burial rites for the imperial family continued to follow Buddhist practices, the bodies were interred rather than cremated. Only at the funeral of Emperor Meiji's father, Komei, in 1867, were all Buddhist elements eliminated from the funeral, and thus one could say that the funeral ushered in the new Shinto-dominated Meiji era. The government prohibited cremation entirely in 1873, as part of its effort to drive out Buddhism, but it was forced to rescind the order as people pointed out that, already, Japan lacked sufficient space to bury intact bodies (*Far Eastern Economic Review,* March 16, 1989, 66–70).

The place of religion in public life, even the definition of what religion is, continues to be the subject of debate in Japan. What *is* clear in Japan is that lines between religions are fuzzy or, rather, that religions are not defined by the individual's exclusive commitment to one set of doctrines as opposed to others. Japan challenges our idea of what religion means for the individual, for the nation, and for the state.

4 *Rituals and the Shaping of Emotions*

*R*eligious practices include those fixed sequences of actions that we often call rituals. People carrying out a religious ritual try to conform to certain rules to get the ritual right. Sometimes they seek a specific end, such as healing, pleasing a deity, or restoring fertility; sometimes they perform rituals out of a general sense of obligation. We will consider these and many other types of rituals in this book, from pilgrimage to prayer to sacrifice. In this chapter we consider rituals that mark transitions of various kinds and explore the way such rituals shape, or are motivated by, emotions.

In most, perhaps all, societies people mark transitions or life stages by carrying out certain transition rituals or rites of passage. These rituals often have a religious dimension, and they tend to cluster around several points in the life cycle: birth, puberty, marriage, and death. Rituals that mark the passage into adulthood may involve changes in name, membership in a new society of initiates, bestowal of new social rights and duties, or, in the case of religiously competent persons, conferral of supernatural powers. Death is also ritually represented as a transition in most societies; death rituals are usually intended to ease the passage of the spirit to another social state and possibly to another world.

Many other kinds of rituals are concerned with transitions. The beginning of an agricultural cycle or the succession to an office may be ritually enacted in ways that resemble life-cycle transition rituals. Anthropologists have long noticed that such rituals are often structured in three parts. Transition rituals shift actors out of their normal social roles, into an intermediate or "liminal" stage, and then reintegrate them into society. The liminal period provides a time for experiencing, sharing, and representing emotions or ideas not usual to social life, as well as a time for accomplishing the tasks of the ritual process.

Transition rituals often emphasize the creation of life: new persons, life after death, or the soil's fertility. Initiation rituals that move people from an immature to a mature state are of course directly concerned with reproduction and biological fertility. But funeral rituals also may tie death to the regeneration of life, refocusing attention and emotions on life and fertility rather than death and loss.

Furthermore, the content and sequence of rituals shape specific emotions in the participants. Feelings of grief are given well-specified forms of expression, sometimes a prescribed period of mourning followed by a break from mourning, sometimes the reverse: stoicism followed by an emotional release. The promise of new life gives hope after loss, and rituals that structure time support the notion that humans can control natural processes of growth, maturation, and death.

Finally, transition rituals represent the social order in a particular way, often an idealized or partial way, and often as if the rituals themselves produce or shape the social order. Relations and differences between men and women, or superiors and inferiors, may be projected onto a cosmic plane, or produced in the ritual itself, especially in initiation rituals that create adolescent or adult males and females. Initiations often reveal secrets, the mere possession of which is the basis for initiates' claims to supremacy over noninitiates. Secrecy creates status and boundaries across a range of social institutions. From members of initiation societies in Africa and New Guinea, to Mormons and Masons, those "in the know" can claim superiority, power, or at least special status. Death rituals often have a different social design, to restore social order after a loss.

Rites of Passage

The sociologist Arnold van Gennep pointed out in 1909 (1960) that transition rituals display a similar sequential structure across cultures. Rites marking birth, puberty, marriage, and death, he remarked, as well as many other rituals of initiation or succession, often are structured temporally as three distinct stages.

The first stage separates the person from the ordinary social environment. It may involve rites to purify the body, seclusion, cutting hair, or simulating death. The separation may be the social recognition of a natural event, such as the onset of menstruation or death, providing a cultural definition for the event. It may create a peer group, such as a group of boys or girls to be initiated. It may define a geographical space, as when Muslims exchange their ordinary identities and clothing for the garb of pilgrims when entering the sacred precincts of Islam in Arabia.

Next comes a stage of marginality, the transitional or *liminal* ("threshold") stage during which the person is outside of normal social life. The liminal person may have to observe certain taboos, or be isolated, or be subjected to beatings and insults, or be elevated to temporary high status. This stage may be as short as a brief baptismal ceremony in a Christian church or as long as certain New Guinea initiation cycles lasting 10 years or more. It is a period of social work, where the liminal person is transformed in bodily or spiritual status.

Finally comes the reaggregation or reincorporation of the individual into society (or into an afterlife society), now possessing a new status. A girl may have become a woman, or a boy a man; a candidate is now a king; the loose soul of a dead man takes up its place in heaven.

The middle or liminal period has key importance to the sequence of events. Consider what happens when a signal event occurs: a girl's menstruation begins; a man dies. The event changes the natural condition of the individual in a way that underscores the limits of society's control over nature. Such events are often thought of as polluting. Ritual removes the person from everyday life and provides time for people to define the event and its consequences; to transform the person in body, mind, and status, and then to define the new state—as a fertile woman, or a soul proceeding to the world of the dead.

Of course, some events that are sequenced as transition rituals are not unplanned acts of nature: the initiation of a group of 10-year-olds, or a baptism, or a pilgrimage. Yet the liminal stage of these rituals, too, provides the setting for a dramatization of the individual's recasting into a new form, a convincing statement that the old has died and the new is born.

Reshaping, Reversing, Communitas

No one kind of process dominates these liminal periods; I mention three here. The first is what Gilbert Herdt (1981, 305) has called the "radical resocialization" of the individual—working the person over until he or she feels and thinks in new ways. Herdt writes of the often violent initiation rituals of Melanesia, which may involve long periods of beatings and abuse of young boys, who emerge shaken, with new psychological and social identities (Poole 1982).

A second process is status reversal, or "ritual of rebellion," when ordinary social relations are turned upside down. An Ndembu chief-to-be is placed in a hut where anyone is free to revile him. "A chief is just like a slave on the night before he succeeds," goes an Ndembu saying (Turner 1969, 101). Such periods may also be part of annual cycles. In fertility rituals held at the beginning of the planting season in some Zulu villages in southern Africa, for example, women reverse their otherwise subordinate roles. Donning men's garments, or singing lewd songs, or milking cows, normally taboo practices. These reversals are thought to increase the chance for a good harvest by appealing to the female spirit associated with the rains and fertility (Gluckman 1963).

Related to these stages are festivals that feature role reversals. In the South Asian festival of Holi, dedicated to the god Krishna, high-caste Brahmans and wealthy people are beaten and chased by low-caste people, such as washermen. Across early modern Europe, rituals held to mark annual feast days frequently featured women (or grotesque female beasts) chasing men, or used floats depicting women dominating their husbands, or had men and women dress in each other's garb. Some of the European rituals, like their African counterparts, were seen as promoting fertility.

Status reversals may have provided an outlet for "unruly" sentiments, as some historians and anthropologists argue, but they also sometimes provided a vehicle for critiques of or even attacks on the ruling order. The historian Natalie Zemon Davis (1965, 121–154) points out that in Europe of the seventeenth and eighteenth centuries, peasants sometimes dressed as women to carry out attacks on government officials, "putting ritual and festive inversion to new uses." Men dressed as women attacked land surveyors and tax collectors, stole the king's deer and tore down his fences. The males were able to distance themselves from their normal roles and responsibilities, but could also exploit the sexual energy dramatized during festival occasions. Ritual thus appears to have fed into politics.

A third, related, characteristic of some middle periods is what Victor Turner (1969, 94–165) called "communitas," a state wherein individuals step outside their normal social roles and experience relative equality and direct sociality with each other, as on pilgrimages or in spontaneous gatherings. (Status reversal may also have this effect.) The Islamic pilgrimage, the hajj, provides an excellent example of equality during the transition stage. The hajj, to be examined more fully in Chapter 11, places all pilgrims in a liminal position once they enter the holy cities of Mecca and Medina. All pilgrims, rich and poor, female and male, wear the same simple white garb as they carry out rituals of submission to God and commemoration of Muhammad's first pilgrimage.

Turner, who wrote prolifically on the subject, argued that communitas was generally associated with liminal stages in transition rituals. (He also saw social life in general as a dialectic of structure and communitas.) But, as the Melanesian initiations mentioned earlier suggest, such an association is not at all a general one. Even some pilgrimages do not support this association, such as that portion of South Asian pilgrimages in which caste distinctions are preserved during the journey. We can best understand the specific form given liminal life in a particular ritual sequence by examining the purpose of the ritual and the cultural context in which it occurs. Liminality does seem to involve the suspension of ordinary sociality, but what replaces that ordinary sociality may vary from a highly regimented, even repressive, order (in Melanesia or in a U.S. Army boot camp) to the spontaneity celebrated by Turner.

Initiation, Secrecy, and Fear

*I*nitiation rites may mark a passage from childhood into adulthood, or celebrate the movement from outside to inside a society or association. In contemporary U.S. society these two kinds of initiation rites seem quite different: joining the Masons is very unlike the celebration of becoming a bar mitzvah, a full male member of the Jewish religious community. One involves joining a volunteer association as an adult; the other is a stage in life for those born into a particular religion.

Yet both processes involve new knowledge and new responsibilities. In many societies, passing from childhood into a condition of full social responsibility also involves entering into a religious association and acquiring new knowledge, sometimes secret knowledge. The rituals that mark this transition often draw out the liminal or middle stage of the transition gradually, and sometimes painfully, revealing knowledge that will forever mark the individual.

Hopi Whipping and Disenchantment

Hopi Pueblo rituals fuse secrets, pain, initiation, and fertility in a way found in many societies. Hopi community rituals designed to make the seasons begin and end, or to ensure a fertile crop, or to guard the welfare of the community involve dances by men dressed as spirits (Gill 1987, 58–75; Parsons 1939, vol. 2, 467–476). In the public portion of these rituals, men don elaborate, colorful masks, paint their bodies, strap on rattles and bells, and dance in the plaza. They represent *kachinas,* spirit beings, whose power is lodged in the dancers' masks. The dances and singing draw on this power and channel it toward accomplishing the ritual's goal.

Each February a ritual is held to encourage the coming growing season to be plentiful. This festival, called *Powamu,* is the occasion for the kachina spirits to return to the Hopi mesas from their winter homes in the mountains. Every several years the festival includes initiation rites, when boys and girls around the age of 10 are inducted into either the Kachina association or the Powamu association. The children are taken to underground rooms called *kivas,* where the secret portions of rituals are held. There they are whipped by the kachinas. They then assume a fetal position and watch the men with their masks entering the kiva.

The children now realize that the masked figures were only men, not spirits. The shock they experience is fearful and traumatic. One Hopi woman said, "I cried and cried into my sheepskin that night, feeling I had been made a fool of. How could I ever watch the Kachinas dance again?" (Gill 1987, 63).

The whipping communicates both a threat against revealing secrets, and the power of the association into which the child has been initiated. (Full initiation requires a second ritual several years later.) Religious historian Sam Gill argues that the initiation is about the disenchantment of the magical world. Gill points out that initiation rites in other societies also disillusion children of their former beliefs that masked dancers are spirits. The child is torn away from his or her naive belief that what is seen is real and set to participating in the kachina cult activities as an adult. The adult begins his or her religious life as a reflective skeptic. The Hopi woman who recalled her weeping went on to say (ibid.): "I know now it was best and the only way to teach the children, but it took me a long time to know that."

New Guinea Traumas and Homosexuality

Much more severe than the whippings inflicted by the kachinas are the long, painful initiation rituals experienced by young boys in some New Guinea societies. John Fitz Porter Poole (1982) relates that the male initiation cycle in Bimin-Kuskusmin society stretches from 10 to 15 years in a boy's life, usually beginning at seven to 10 years of age. One of its stages takes place in a forest house, where the initiates are secluded, beaten, told they are vile (and that women are vile as well), and tormented. Over succeeding days they are rubbed with stinging nettles, forced to vomit, and beaten. Many actions are taken to firm up their bodies and heighten their masculinity, including rubbing boar blood on their chests. They are also told a series of secret myths and ordered not to reveal them.

The initiators explain that they are making the boys into men. One aspect of that process is teaching them how to control anger, an esteemed quality for a warrior. The boys are furious, reports Poole, but must suppress their anger on pain of further beatings. Throughout the ritual they are deceived by men they had trusted, abused by everyone older than they, and denied maternal support. The trauma is great; some boys go into shock. Some of the initiators express concern, but see the beatings as necessary to make the boys mature. The boys themselves suffer afterward from fearful dreams, in which concern for their body parts is evidenced.

Such processes of "radical resocialization" (Herdt 1981, 305) in this and other societies are intended to wrest the boy from his mother, make his body masculine, his sexuality potent, and his emotional makeup that of a brave warrior. Other New Guinea societies emphasize sexuality more than anger. Gilbert Herdt (1981, 1982) describes the ritualized homosexuality among the Sambia that marks the initiation process. Men are produced from boys in part through the ingestion of semen, which is seen to replace the breast milk they ingested as infants and is intended to wean them from women and make them into men. This form of homosexuality is thus a way of replacing an earlier bodily relation to the mother with a relation to other men and fits with the idea, discussed earlier, that men and women have sharply differentiated but parallel relationships to the social and natural world. Herdt (1982) reports that the boys experience fear, maternal loss, and shame when confronted with the initiated men and when they begin to understand what is expected of them. They share their mothers' fears of male aggression and threats, symbolized by secret (phallic) flutes, which stand for male dominance of women and elder male dominance over the young boys.

Female initiation rituals in New Guinea involve less trauma. Girls are separated from younger girls, but not from women. The rituals described by Nancy Lutkehaus (1995) for Manam Island in Papua New Guinea are directed toward cleansing girls of the pollution brought on by first menstrual blood and turning them into fertile women. As practiced generally in the 1930s, and with some girls today, the rites involve a long series of actions intended to isolate the girl from her normal social state and from her bodily state. She is not allowed to touch herself or her food. Once she has bathed in the sea to begin the seven- to 10-day ritual sequence, the young girls who attend her are also forbidden to touch her. Slits are cut in her back with knives and ash rubbed in to raise scars to mark her as a fertile woman. She jokes with other women throughout the process.

Sadness is introduced with mourning songs sung at the start and close of the ritual, signaling that the girl is renouncing the pleasures of childhood and now expects to bear children and to leave her village of birth to marry.

Pain, fear, demands for secrecy—all are strongly remembered experiences that impress the initiate with the seriousness of the social norms and ideas he or she has learned. Strong emotions and newly acquired secrets further serve to reinforce the separation between elders and juniors and between men and women. Children are indeed radically reshaped into new kinds of humans.

Death Ritual and the Social Order

*I*f initiation rituals underscore conceptions of gender, death rituals make especially visible ideas about the individual and the collectivity. If an individual leaves society, is he or she to remain part of it? In the answer to that question people often highlight their picture, real or ideal, of society and of an individual.

In much of China and Taiwan, villagers conceive of the spiritual world as composed of three beings: ghosts, gods, and ancestors. Each is dealt with differently; for example, offered different kinds of food or money. These three beings are also associated with three kinds of humans. Gods are dressed in the garments of officials and they can punish people and be bribed. They keep records; they are clearly bureaucrats. They are worshipped in temples (Wolf 1974). Ghosts, by contrast, are worshiped outside, with large offerings of food or clothing, and they resemble bandits or beggars—strangers, in other words. Ancestors are, well, ancestors. You owe them a debt for your own life and prosperity, and you feed them as you would feed a human visitor to your home.

This close correspondence between society and supernatural beings suggests that in different Chinese settings people would interpret these beings somewhat differently, and they do: the god who is a police official today may have been an influential country gentleman in the past.

From Spirit to Household God in Japan

In rural Japan, where the individual is thought of as a member of a household and of a community, at death a person becomes a spirit (kami) as well as a Buddha (hotoke). Funerals are performed by Buddhist priests, but death ritual also involves pre-Buddhist ideas of pollution and ritual. A long transition stage allows the spirit to progress from an individual's spirit to one element in the household deity. Death ritual thereby reinforces the notion of spirit collectivity (Plath 1964; Smith 1974).

Death begins a three-stage process of transforming the deceased into a part of the spirit collectivity. At death the body may be cremated or buried; urban Japanese inevitably cremate. In either case, bodily death pollutes the spirit (shirei) as well as the close relatives of the deceased. Death ritual helps to separate the spirit from the pollution. The grave receiving the body is located far away from the residential part of a village and is called the "abandoned grave." In some parts of Japan a second, "ritual grave," consisting of a headstone is built nearer the house. This grave may be tended without encountering the pollution of the dead body. Urban Japanese must rely on funeral parlors. (Today the combined expenses of burial, home altar with tablets, and the services of a Buddhist priest can amount to a middle-class family's one-year pretax income!)

The memory of the deceased individual is preserved for the first 49 days after death. The survivors set up a mortuary tablet on the household altar, together with a photo of the deceased, incense, bells, and other objects. Buddhist memorial services are held for the individual every seven days until the 49 days are completed. The soul also wanders near the house during this period, before leaving on the 49th day.

Sometimes the soul takes some action on its own on the 49th day to settle accounts with the living. In an eighteenth-century puppet play called "The Woman Killer and the Hell of Oil," Yohei murders Okichi, but no one knows that he is the murderer. Yohei arrives on the 49th day of the ritual, just after a rat has run along the rafters of the room, dislodging a scrap of paper with evidence of the murderer's guilt; and the husband of the dead woman exclaims that this was a sign from the dead person. "This I owe to Buddha's mercy," he says.

At the end of this initial period the family holds a series of rituals to transform the spirit of the dead into an ancestral spirit (*sorei*). The photo is put away and the temporary tablet disposed of, replaced by a permanent tablet, usually an upright wooden plaque four to six inches high, lacquered in black or gold, and inscribed with a special posthumous name of the deceased and the date of his or her death. (Buddhist temples provide these after-death names.) This tablet is placed with the other tablets on the altar.

The altar and tablets stands for the house's history (Smith 1974, 1978, 152–165). The household (*ié*) is thought of as a corporate group, the headship of which passes from father to son over the generations. The tablets are the first objects to be saved (standard newspaper accounts of fires say that "flames swept through the building so rapidly that the residents only had time to carry out the altar and tablets"). The tablets are even more important than the Buddha image. As one man put it, the ancestors need help like anyone else, whereas the Buddha can take care of himself.

But the tablet itself is impermanent. After either 33 or 50 years (depending on the region of Japan) the tablet is destroyed and the spirit becomes a god. The spirit is sometimes transferred to the household god in a noteworthy ritual in which the tablet is cast into a river and then a pebble is picked up from the river bed and placed on the household god's altar. This collection of pebbles represents the spirits merged into the guardian god of the household as a collectivity.

Thereafter, services are held for the collective dead, without identifying them singly, both with daily offerings of flowers and on seasonal occasions, in particular: New Year's on January first through third, Obon or the Festival of the Dead or of Lanterns on August 13 through 15, and the equinoxes in late March and September.

The Obon festival, when the ancestors come down from where they live to their villages, has been celebrated at least since the year 606 C.E. One dedicates temples and recites Buddhist verses and makes offering to ancestors. One category of ancestor is especially grateful for these offerings: ancestors who committed misdeeds in past lives may end up on the plane of existence called *gaki-do,* or Plane of the Hungry Ghosts. They suffer from hunger and thirst, and they alone out of all one's ancestors may benefit from offerings one makes to a holy or virtuous person.

But Obon is the time to make offerings to the ancestors generally. The ritual grave near the house is cleared and a path is swept leading back to the house. The household altar is cleaned and a dance (today in decline) is held in the village. People return to their ancestral villages to participate in the festival and end the ritual by taking lanterns and small boats to the graveyard or to a mountain or river to see the spirits off on their return to their abode. Japanese overseas also celebrate Obon. In St. Louis, where I live, it is the time for a Japanese festival at the Botanical Gardens, with the lighting of lanterns around the lake in the Japanese garden.

The long transition stage to Japanese death rituals supports the idea of a gradual melding of the individual into the collectivity and thus also supports the general cultural importance of the collectivity.

Regenerating Life from Death

Death rituals also frequently feature images of journeys to new worlds, enactments of rebirth, or the disinterment and reburial of bones (Bloch and Parry 1982).

Images of journeys are sometimes the material focus of religious innovations. As Sumatran Toba Batak people left their ancestral homeland for big cities, they began to use their new wealth to build elaborate family tombs back home. These tombs were carved in the shapes of boats and other images of soul journeys, and the tombs kept alive a sense of attachment to the homeland and a promise of rejoining the family for the journey to the afterworld. In Ghana, a man named Connie Kway began to carve elaborate, painted coffins in the shapes of boats or birds during the 1970s. These coffins sold for the equivalent of a year's average wage and were snatched up by the rich. They were an innovation; Ghanians had not used fancy coffins before, but because they dramatized the comforting and spirit-raising belief that the dead were going to a resting place where loved ones would see them again, they quickly became popular and spawned imitators. (In 1996 a museum tour of the coffins swept the United States, where they were competed for as treasured folk art objects.)

Death is often linked to life and fertility in the transition stages. This linking may take different forms. Bloch and Parry (1982, 7) argue that death rituals tend to revitalize "that resource which is *culturally conceived* to be most essential to the reproduction of the social order." The resource may be the land, or human fertility, or some combination of the two. Thus in four African hunter-gatherer societies compared by James Woodburn (1982), social reproduction was thought to depend most importantly on control over nature, and the ritual response to death was to reawaken the productivity of nature.

For the Merina of Madagascar, studied by Maurice Bloch (1982), reproducing the society requires that members of a descent group have their bones buried together in ancestral tombs. Because these related individuals do not live in the same place, they are initially buried where they die. Their bones later are dug up and moved to the ancestral tomb. The initial burial is attended by sadness and mourning, but the subsequent "regrouping" of the body with the ancestors is full of joy and dancing. During this dancing, women repeatedly throw the brittle bones to the ground, smashing them to bits. These actions merge the physical remains of the individual with the ancestral groups as a whole. The ritual also employs the symbolism of birth, entering into and emerging from the tomb as if it were a womb.

Asmat Headhunting and Birth through Death

Consider in more detail the case of the Asmat, a society of about 50,000 people living in the swampy plains of southwest Irian Jaya, the name for the western half of the island of New Guinea that in 1963 became part of Indonesia. The Asmat are best known in the West for the tall *bis* poles, made out of sago palm, examples of which are to be found in many Western museums (Kuruwaip 1974).

The Asmat (Sudarman 1984) call themselves the "tree people." Their environment is wood; stone or metal for tools must be acquired from elsewhere. Canoes, poles, housing are all from wood. Their staple, sago, is also wood. Every four or five days, the men of a clan will spend an entire day finding a large (45-foot-high) sago palm tree in the forest, cutting it down, removing the pith, and then pounding, washing, drying, and roasting the pith into large cakes of sago to be pounded into sago flour. Sago is regarded as a human being. The sago palm resembles a woman: life comes from within it, and

Drawing of Asmat bis pole, Irian Jaya.

the white, milky sago resembles breast milk. When an Asmat man carves a sago palm into a pole he considers his work as very like what he does to help produce a baby. Asmat hold that the father does not cause conception, but molds the child through frequent intercourse into the shape he or she eventually has at birth (Gerbrands 1967).

Much of the Asmat men's time used to be spent in warfare between clans, fueled partly by their practices and beliefs surrounding death. Asmat believe that deaths are due to malevolent actions by others, that people in other clans kill your own relatives either in an observable way (in a raid, for example) or through sorcery. The spirits of the dead demand retribution or revenge for their deaths (Zegwaard 1959). Asmat once took revenge for a death by taking a head in a raid on another clan, thus continuing the cycle of death and retribution. The relative taking the head would have carved for him a long, 15- to 20-foot *bis* pole. The clan would then drum and dance to entice the spirit into the pole. The relative would dedicate the pole to the deceased, and cry out (for example): "Oh mother, I have killed a man from [place name]." Then the spirit of the dead person, which would have remained in the village until avenged, would begin its journey out of the village and toward a island somewhere off the western coast, later to be reborn as a new human (Kuruwaip 1974).

Today, headhunting is prohibited, and Asmat seem to have abandoned the practice. But they continue to carve images of deceased relatives onto the long poles, to drum the spirit into the pole, and to erect the pole and publicly dedicate it, calling out for the spirit to leave the village.

Through their myths, the Asmat believe the acts of producing sago from palms, carving wood poles, and cutting heads to be situating their lives in the universe. Taking a head reenacts a sacrifice made at the beginning of time. In a widely told story, a being who was both god and man killed his brother and cut off his head, immediately causing the universe to come into existence, and all of culture with it. (In some versions of this story, the god–man cut off the head of a crocodile in order to create non-Asmat people.) Taking a head thus caused life to emerge (Zegwaard 1959).

In practice, the skulls of the dead help to bring about a new birth. In past times the skull used would have come from a headhunting expedition, and thus the same skull would accomplish two important functions: it would allow the spirit to leave the world, and it would bring a new person into it. Today the skull would come from a relative. A young male being initiated into manhood sits for days in the men's house, contemplating a skull between his legs, pressed against his genitals. Then he is carried out toward the setting sun in a canoe, following the journey made by the spirits of the dead. When the canoe has traveled far enough from shore he lies in the bottom of the canoe in imitation of someone who has just died. Then he is thrown into the water, still holding the skull, to resurface as a newly born initiated man.

Cutting the sago is also likened to taking a human head and releasing energy. The palm is thought to have the same spirit as a human. Men attack the palm, throwing spears at it, and butcher the starch. Asmat also draw on these ideas to project human actions onto the animal world. They see an analogy to headhunting in the behavior of the praying mantis. The insect is seen as human in its movements (think of how its stance gave rise to its English name), and the female bites off the head of the male during mating.

Not only is the mantis's cannibalism like taking a head, but it reminds the Asmat observer of the mock, or part-mock aggression enacted by women toward men in everyday life. For when the Asmat men return along the river with the sago palm, women carry out an attack on the canoes from the village shore. The attack is ostensibly to keep malevolent spirits from entering the village along with the palm, but in practice women throw their spears hard and accurately and, not uncommonly, men are injured.

Drumming the spirit of the dead into the *bis* pole also replicates a mythic event. The very first man on earth was called Fumeripits. He drowned in the sea but he was brought back to life by War, the name of the white-tailed eagle, who pressed smoldering bits of wood against his body. Then Fumeripits built a large men's house and carved images of men and women. He began to drum, and they came to life, dancing. The carvers and drummers of today cannot create life, but they can attract spirits through their carving and drumming, thereby reenacting Fumeripits' deed on the spiritual level.

In everyday life, too, Asmat experience the link between heads and the continuity of life. All adults sleep on skulls, usually skulls of close relatives, and report feeling a continued tie to the deceased through this skull-sleeping. Some men will (or did) sleep on the skull of a powerful enemy, claiming that they absorb some of the deceased's power at night. Carving the pole and cutting heads thus not only frees the spirit from the village (and the village from the spirit) but also signifies to the living that the dead will be reborn and life will continue. The ritual also gives the bereaved a concrete way to care for the spirits of their relatives. And since they practice it together as a social group, a single individual's death strengthens the power of their origin myths.

The ritual as it once was carried out allowed the individual to complete a logical and emotional circle: a death, avenged by taking a head, was completed when the skull of the victim was used to release the spirit from the village and then to cause a rebirth. But now the circuit has been shorted at the point of headhunting. The Dutch (when they controlled the territory) had already prohibited headhunting throughout the region, but they had little direct sway over the Asmat. The Indonesian government has been much more direct in its plans to change Asmat lives and religions: it encourages missionaries to promote the adoption of proper religion, with a book, a creed, but no violence. The missionaries offer salvation through communion (which might be interpreted by Asmat as a different kind of cannibalism) and rebirth through baptism (a different path to rebirth through immersion in water).

Secondary Burial

The "regrouping" of bones practiced by the Merina (discussed earlier) is one example of a widespread practice of secondary burial, or the removal and reburial of a corpse. This practice is intended to provide material signs of the transition from life to an afterlife by permitting people to examine the bones of the dead after decomposition has set in. Secondary burial is relatively rare, but it is found in culturally unrelated areas throughout the world—Greece, Africa, Siberia, Indonesia, the Americas, and in early Jewish practice. Medieval Christian burial in Europe often included the display of bones in an ossuary.

Peter Metcalf (1982) provides a detailed description of the practice from the Berawan society in Borneo. In this society, a body is stored in a large jar right after death. After several days the bones are cleaned of flesh and stored in the longhouse or on a platform outside. Months or years later (Metcalf records a range of eight months to five years) the bones of some of the dead, but not others, are removed and placed in a permanent death monument. For the Berawan, the display of bones stands for the passage of the spirit of the dead outside the community. It confirms that the spirit has reached the land of the dead.

Robert Hertz (1960) wrote a comparative essay on the practice in 1907. Hertz used material from Borneo and Indonesia but also made reference to similar practices elsewhere. Based on his reading of available ethnography, Hertz argued that people take the natural fact of bodily decomposition as the basis for thinking about the process of death, the transition from the loss of soul to the passage to another place. Just as the body decomposes, so the spirit gradually leaves the body, transformed to a new state in which the spirit is definitively separated from the body.

The process of decomposition, then, defines three moments in the death process, each of which serves as a sign of the unobservable process through which the spirit leaves the body and the community. At the moment of death the spirit has left the body. During decomposition the spirit is uncertain as to its final home, and during this period it may haunt the living and roam the community. But when the bones are seen to be clean, then the spirit has left for its new home.

Hertz noted that people have a horror of the corpse throughout the world, but that it is not a physical repugnance. The same people fear the corpse but wash it, sit with it, even drink the wash water. The fear is for two reasons. First, the death tears a hole in the community, and the social fabric must be mended and order restored. The more important the person, the more ritual work needs to be done, so only some bones are subjected to secondary burial. Second, the soul remains near the corpse, and until it has left the community it will remain to haunt the living. The rites of secondary burial enact the finality of the passage out of the community.

This analysis explains why Berawan people evinced horror at the practice of embalming when Metcalf described it to them. Embalming for purposes of viewing the body in a "lifelike" state is seen by Berawan as delaying the process of decay and thereby retarding the successful separation of the soul from the community.

Similar concerns are found in the official policy on burial of the Greek Orthodox Church. Bodies must not, commands the church, be buried in airtight caskets lest the natural, and God-ordained, process of decomposition be halted. In rural Greece today, relatives exhume the bones of the deceased five years after the body is buried, and remove the bones to the village ossuary (Danforth 1982). If the bones are clean and white, relatives are assured that the soul has passed to heaven. If decomposition has not been completed, villagers wait an additional two years and then repeat the process. Meanwhile they say prayers for the forgiveness of the person's sins; it is these sins that have retarded the soul's passage and the body's decomposition.

In these and other cases people feel ambivalent about the passage of the soul from the community. People may wish loved ones to remain near them, but they also wish for closure in the process of dying and mourning. Death rituals demonstrate to the living that the dead have left the community, taking danger with them, but also that they remain close by and that they can be called on to help the living. The soul of a Berawan person remains ready to aid the living in times of illness or other need. Asmat send the spirits of the dead away from the community to an island off the coast, but people continue to sleep with the skulls of deceased loved ones and sense that the person continues to remain with them. For people in many societies, death involves desires for both finality and remembrance; death rituals give those desires a material form.

Grief and Ritual Form

Transition rituals marking events such as initiations or death are emotional times. Often the emotions are produced by the rituals themselves. The sociologist Émile Durkheim (1858–1917), stressing the social base for much of religious life, argued that ritual action, especially when in a group, channels and determines emotions.

Durkheim maintained that although there might be natural emotional responses to death, they are highly subject to social shaping. Is this view correct? How culturally different are those emotions? What role does ritual play in the interior lives, the feelings, and the grieving of the survivors? Do rituals create emotions or do emotions determine what kind of rituals people create?

Consider the contrast between the way two Muslim peoples mourn the loss of a close relative. In Java, where people typically value the control of their emotions, Clifford Geertz (1960, 73) reports a man he knew well, distancing himself from the loss of his wife, describing how he kept his emotions inside him. A girl who wept softly after her father died was told she could not participate in the funeral events unless she stopped crying. And yet, in Morocco, another Muslim society, the expected behavior is just the opposite. People in mourning tear their clothes and hair and wail loudly and publicly (Westermarck 1968, vol. II, 34–42).

These marked differences in public behavior are between two peoples with the same religion. Ritual forms, linked to dominant cultural values, prescribe sharply contrasting patterns of mourning behavior.

But we cannot assume from such publicly observed contrasts that the emotions and the grieving process experienced by the individual are correspondingly different (Rosaldo 1984). Many Moroccans may feel indifference; many Javanese, great sorrow. Yet men and women in each society are expected to act in certain standardized ways regardless of their feelings. Many people in the United States report feeling quite different from what their public mourning behavior would suggest. Some feel guilty at the gulf between their mixed emotions and the expressions of grief that they are expected to display. Others adhere to religions that urge their followers in a different direction, to maintain a hopeful attitude consistent with a strong belief in the afterlife. Mormon services reflect this attitude, and Christian Scientists argue that bereaved people can and should lift themselves out of sorrow through the sheer force of the will. Yet many adherents to these faiths do grieve, and may find their social networks not offering the support they need (Palgi and Abramovitch 1984).

Is Grief Universal?

Perhaps the most devastating loss to an American adult is the death of a child, and here cross-cultural variation is striking. Psychologists (Bowlby 1980) argue that parents in all societies develop attachments to their children and experience grief at the loss of children. The attachment and the grief seem to have a basis in the evolution of social relationships. Both features are found in nonhuman primates as well as humans. And yet in many societies the deaths of newborns are not accompanied by the same expressions of loss and grief as are the deaths of older children or adults. In many societies children are not named until some number of days have passed after birth, and a death before that time is treated very differently than later deaths. Do these practices indicate that parents feel the loss less? How strongly does such a cultural practice shape emotions?

Two studies in anthropology have addressed this question but reach distinct conclusions. Nancy Scheper-Hughes (1992) argues that some poor Brazilian parents do feel loss less than do most middle-class parents. She emphasizes the cultural malleability of emotions—cultural practices shape emotional response. Unni Wikan (1990), emphasizing the distance between public expressions and inner emotions, finds that Balinese people feel strong grief emotions, but that they follow culturally prescribed practices of working on their grief through laughter and sociability. These and other studies underscore the emotional importance of rituals and other practices during the transition stage after a death—and also the difficulties in generalizing about "private" emotions.

Nancy Scheper-Hughes lived, worked, and studied in a very poor region in northeastern Brazil in the 1960s and then again in the 1980s. Many in the area had little to eat, and infant death was common. Mothers, fathers, and siblings developed an attitude of "letting go" toward those infants who seemed near death, often drawing on an elaborate catalogue of symptoms that pointed to an inevitable death.

Scheper-Hughes tried to make sense of the families' emotionally flat responses by challenging the Western view about attachment and mourning. In that view, attachment is a basic instinct that structures relationships between all human mothers and their children. The death of a child triggers natural responses of mourning, which must be worked through if the survivors are to be able to carry on in a healthy way. But Scheper-Hughes (1992, 400–445) argues that many mothers in fact have an ambivalent attitude toward their newborns. When the mother–infant experience is positive, and when nurturing all one's children is possible, parents invest emotionally in their children and feel great loss at a death. But in poor Brazil and some other places a "lifeboat" ethic leads parents to choose, reluctantly, to nurture only those who have a chance at surviving. Cultural practices reinforce this survival strategy: parents delay naming their infants and hold them much less often than do middle-class mothers.

Death ritual also plays an important part in this survival strategy. In some parts of Brazil, lower-class men and women treat the death of a very young child as a blessing. The child will be taken to heaven, is already a little angel, they say. The wake held for the little child, who is dressed in a white or blue shirt with curled hair and floral wreaths, includes joyous music and samba dancing. Although much more sober in tone in the community where Scheper-Hughes worked, the "angels" were a "transitional object" for these women, she points out (1992, 421), both because the infant is in transition from life to death, and because the dressed-up corpse and coffin allows the woman to let go of her child by giving her an idealized heaven-child to hold onto. Women told Scheper-Hughes: "I feel free" or "I feel unburdened" after the funeral. Grief seemed absent. For some students of Brazilian society the flat emotional response is a mask, a wall against the unbearable. But Scheper-Hughes takes the responses of these women at face value, arguing that culture and ritual succeed in preventing grief responses. The idea that deaths need to be worked through by a process of open mourning, she says, is applicable only in some societies.

Still, it may be difficult to decide between several possible interpretations of Scheper-Hughes's data—are denials of grief a mask, or are denials accurate reports of feelings? Another study of the same area (Nations and Rebhun 1988) reports very different findings. High rates of infant mortality are found in many parts of the world, and yet women mourn these infants. Finally, we should note that arguments for a universal attachment structure are based on cross-cultural research: the major early empirical work (Ainsworth 1967) was not from the West but from Uganda!

Emotions and Their Expressions

Scheper-Hughes's argument was intended to counter universal theories of death, emotions, and ritual. By contrast, anthropologist Unni Wikan draws on her fieldwork in Bali to oppose culturally relativist theories about the malleability of emotions. In Bali, as in neighboring Java, people are expected to preserve a "face" of equanimity at loss or disaster. Anthropologists had long understood the grace and composure of Balinese as a cultural style that focused on beauty and on distancing oneself from emotions. Balinese selves, wrote the anthropologist Clifford Geertz (1966), are quite different from Western ones; they live in a "dramatistic" world composed of masks, roles, and a stage.

Wikan (1990) argues instead that Balinese think and feel their way through the world in ways that are much closer to European ways than earlier anthropologists believed. She describes several months in the life of one woman, who lost her fiance in an accident. Her friends laughed and joked with her, insisting that she laugh too. During the following months she appeared bright-faced and happy, even to her friend Wikan. After several months Wikan did see her cry, and then the woman began to tell of how devastated she had felt through the whole experience. About the same time her friends began to change their ways of being with her, sympathizing out loud with the distress she must have felt. Her emotions, and their understanding of them, were not all that different after all.

But why did she laugh her way through the first few months, and why did her friends insist that she do so? The key lies in a distinctive set of ideas about the relationship between one's "face"—appearances and behavior—and one's "heart"—emotions and thoughts. For the Balinese with whom Wikan spoke, emotions of sadness and sorrow weaken one's life force. A weak life force opens up the body to all sorts of invasions, but most particularly to attacks from sorcerers. These attacks are always near at hand; half of all deaths are attributed to sorcery. Moreover, these sad feelings can spread from one person to another, endangering the community, so one has a social as well as a personal responsibility to keep sorrow at a distance. How does one do that? Whereas we might think of emotions as having a life of their own—grief inevitably following loss—the Balinese think that behavior, including how one forms one's face and the choice to laugh or cry, shapes the heart and channels emotions. Laughing, then, keeps sadness from welling up, and thereby keeps the person strong against murderous sorcery.

Wikan concludes that Balinese appearances of calm and joy are not due to a theaterlike detachment from the world, but rather to their strong fears of sorcery and their ideas about how best to combat it. During the transition period after death these dangers are at their highest and thus when the practices of laughing together are most required.

Wikan, then, affirms the distinctiveness of Balinese ideas and practices but sees them as responses to a universal emotion of loss and grief. Scheper-Hughes claims that the emotions of the Brazilians she studied are quite different from those experienced by middle-class families, but she does so by way of a general theory about the responses of mothers (and others) to infants and to risk. Both underscore the critical role of culturally sanctioned practices designed to shape the emotions people feel when a loved one dies. Balinese laughing and Brazilian "angel caskets" bridge the transition period between death and the reintegration of the survivors into the ordinary routines of life.

5 *Transforming Selves*

*I*n the previous chapter we focused on ways in which religious rituals shape and mediate the transitions across the life cycle. Each such ritual transforms the self, even as it moves the self from one stage to another: the subject becomes a recognized individual at birth, rather than something less, an adult at marriage, and a post-life spirit after death. Of course, nearly all rituals involve transformations of selves in one way or another, and in this chapter we focus on that quality. We begin by an overview of the "techniques of the self" (Foucault 1978) employed to fashion culturally specific, gendered selves, and then consider, more specifically, how individuals fashion themselves into particular kinds of religious selves. We look in some detail at three cases: the steps nuns take to draw closer to Christ in their own selves, Muslim women's use of prayer and education to fashion ethical Muslim selves, and a look at conversion to a Protestant faith as a process of religious self-transformation. Then, in Chapter 6, we examine a related process whereby a subject is able to heal the self by way of religious practices.

Gender and Anthropology

*O*pen any textbook on anthropology, and without difficulty you will find a section where the authors discuss the universality of gender differences. Since the early days of the discipline, anthropologists have written about ways in which male–female relationships are constructed in different societies. But in the 1970s a new feminist anthropology turned to studying gender and sexuality for answers to pressing political and cultural questions about equality and human rights. They asked big questions about gender and inequality. Michelle Rosaldo (1974), Sherry Ortner (1974), and others observed that wherever one finds inequalities in women's and men's access to resources, it is the men who control more than the women. Why, they asked, should there be such consistent inequality?

Rosaldo, Ortner, and their collaborators argued that the answer lay in a political inequality based on biological differences between women and men. Women, taken up with tasks of raising children, were identified more closely with natural processes than were men. Men, considered relatively more "cultural," were able to grab the public podium and control how social matters were represented and how resources were divided. Although this cross-cultural inequality could be (and, they wrote, ought to be) overcome, because humans are not the prisoners of history, it was nonetheless the general human–historical background against which all such overcoming must take place.

Although these authors were careful to note that they were speaking of the public cultural representations in a society and that they did not believe that only men ever exercised power (Ortner 1996, 139–146), their early formulations were followed by criticisms and reformulations, often made by the same authors. For example, Ortner and Whitehead (1981) pointed out that the earlier approaches had downplayed the wide variation in the ways people think about gender and sexuality. In some societies, people assume that biology strongly determines male–female differences. In other societies, however, biology is subordinated when people believe that practices of nurturing, maturing, or being initiated shape a human into a fully male or female person (see also MacCormack and Strathern 1980).

We can probably safely say that people in all cultures recognize differences between men and women, and, furthermore, that in elaborating their ideas about these differences they point to features of physiology and biology and to different roles in procreation. But that is about as far as we take the idea of physiology and gender, because there are widely differing ideas about gender and sexuality. More precisely, and interestingly, people are not unambiguously sorted into the categories "male" and "female" according to a single set of criteria in every society. The Hua in the highlands of Papua New Guinea, for example, classify people both in terms of their external genitalia and in terms of the amount of male or female substance each person is thought to possess. A person accumulates both kinds of substance through physical contact with others, so one's behavior determines one's substantive sexual identity. Some Hua are considered male in terms of genitalia but female in terms of their substance, or vice versa (Meigs 1990).

These feminist critiques were notably as critical of previous methods of ethnography as they were of commonly held notions of gender. Reinforced by renewed studies of well-known anthropological terrains, feminist anthropology explained why an ethnographer's perceptions may be shaped both by his or her prior assumptions and by the limits placed on the field of action in the society being studied.

Creating Gender through Ritual

*H*ow does religion come into this picture? Religious representations of people add a degree of cultural force to gender ideas, so that people regard them as universal, or cosmic, or God-commanded, or "natural." Each type of representation has a very different consequence, but they all make what appears to be culturally specific seem inevitable because it is ordered by deities, or because it is simply there, in nature. We can call these the *ideological* consequences of religion, when beliefs are linked in some way to the social and political system. Religious ideas also may be sources of strength for both women and men who wish to challenge how society is put together. Religious ritual also contributes to culturally specific ideas of gender because it casts male and female beings in particular cultural terms.

Producing Men and Women

Let us reconsider the Melanesian initiation rituals we studied in Chapter 4 (pages 47–48), this time as ritual means of producing mature and fertile men and women. These initiation rites are understood as creating sexuality; they highlight the distinctions between men and women (Keesing 1982). Men and women are seen as radically different, and the fluids and powers of one are dangerous to the other. Distinctions, separation, and hostility characterize ritual representations of gender in many of these societies.

But men and women are also seen as creating biological parallels to each other. Semen and menstrual blood are polluting to the opposite sex in Melanesia (whereas female pollution of males through menstruation is a widespread belief). Female rites are centered on removing menstrual pollution to create fertility; male rites on separating the boys from women.

Male rites sometimes imitate those female rites that are closely linked to physiological events. Thus, men symbolically "give birth" to canoes in the Manam society of Papua New Guinea (Lutkehaus 1995). In some Melanesian societies men "menstruate" by spilling blood from their slashed penises. This act and other blood-lettings on one's own body strengthen sexual powers. In these cases the female body and processes of biological reproduction serve as symbols of social reproduction of men and women.

The parallels and the sexual segregation also support notions that homosexuality is required for male growth (Herdt 1981, 1982; Poole 1982). Men are required to "grow boys into men" in some societies. Older males bleed and multilitate younger males, reveal secret knowledge, and provide them semen to ingest, all in order to strengthen their bodies and their reproductive and aggressive capacities. In some cases men also use semen to fertilize the crops.

Some of these practices have parallels in Amazon societies. In both places one finds an emphasis on male mysteries and solidarity, on the use of such specific objects as sacred flutes and bull-roarers as emblems of male exclusivity and power over females, and threats of gang rape against women who view these male cult objects (Keesing 1982, 9). In central Africa, too, people speak of "growing a girl" and "growing a boy" into an adult through the initiation rituals (Turner 1967, 101–102).

Ritual, Fertility, and Culture

Drawing on these and similar examples, some feminist anthropologists proposed a general theory of gender differentiation (Rosaldo 1974; Chodorow 1974) that turns on the ways in which boys and girls are socialized. They argued that, across cultures, women and men differ in the degree to which they require active socialization into their respective gender roles. Girls are oriented toward the domestic sphere, these authors claimed, and thus can remain within it as they mature. Boys, who are oriented toward the public sphere, must distance and differentiate themselves actively from their mothers. Male initiation rituals bring about and represent this differentiation of males from females.

The Chodorow–Rosaldo theory does explain the role of negative emotions toward women that characterize teachings central to male initiation rituals in some New Guinea societies. Their theory of the *reproduction* of gender differences in the development of each individual human was later expanded by feminist scholars (Collier and Rosaldo 1981) into a theory of the *origins* of gender differences in the early history of humankind; this theory also explained the ideas about fertility underlying many representations of gender.

Contrary to the received wisdom of an earlier era, these scholars argue, in many societies of simpler technology it is men, not women, who are credited with promoting fertility (Whitehead 1987). Many societies based on hunting and either gathering or horticulture in Australia, the Americas, and Africa feature rituals celebrating men's powers to create life without women. Why should this be? Collier and Rosaldo (1981) argued that ideas of fertility are really ideas about social relationships, and that it is men's power to bring about marriages that these ideas celebrate. And why do men control marriage? Simply put, the story that explains their control starts with their deficiencies: men rely on marriage to eat. Because men do not have automatic access to the foods gathered or cultivated by women, they have a great interest in marriage. Because men must find a spouse, they must secure social ties to potential parents-in-law and brothers-in-law. Men also seek to have their general sociability recognized as both culturally and biologically important, claiming that fertility is the outcome of their social activities. Whitehead (1987) argues that in New Guinea, for instance, male control of intercommunity exchanges of goods and services allows men to claim fertility as their contribution to society and thus justify excluding women from fertility rituals.

This theory uses comparative evidence to suggest origins story similar, in its logical form, to the classic "social contract" theories proposed by John Locke and Thomas Hobbes to account for the origins of society. The feminist theory was proposed at a time when many anthropologists were looking for new origins stories to counter some of the sweeping, male-centered stories such as "man the hunter" (see Conkey and Williams 1991). But like all grand narratives the story can account for only some of the social reality it seeks to explain.

For example, women also undergo initiation, and sometimes the initiation process is intended to make them, not the men, more cultural and fertile. Janice Boddy (1989) describes the practice of infibulation found in many areas of the Middle East and northern Africa, when part or all of a girl's clitoris and labia minora is removed as part of a ritual designed to make her into a woman. Reasons given for these operations include the need to protect a family's honor by preserving its daughters' chastity and to curb women's sexual desire.

Boddy points out that the men and women in northern Sudan both subscribe to the general idea that men acquire more reason or rationality (*aqal*) than women do and that women have more emotions and desires (*nafs*). Men say further that women are less able than men to control their desires, viewing infibulation as part of a larger repertoire of social practices (including seclusion and veiling) designed to control those emotions.

Women take a different view. Although they, too, see women and men as differing in their natures, they make concerns about fertility the most important reason for practicing infibulation. Only by undergoing the practice, they say, can women marry and thus have legitimate children.

Women regard carrying out infibulation as continuing the work that God began by creating humans. Only after circumcision and infibulation do girls and boys become fully gendered. It is then that they are expected to behave as women and men, sleeping and eating separately, and no longer playing together (Boddy 1989, 58–59). In a constricted social world where cousins are one's prime marriage partners, turning kin into potential spouses begins early.

Women see themselves as having the central role in structuring the physical and social reproduction of their community by preparing women for marriage and for giving birth. They consider that their activities make them, and not the men, the guarantors of the cultural order. They see men as marginal to the society, mediators between the village world and the outside world. Women's and men's views of gender and culture start from the same position, then diverge widely. Because men dominate public forums of discussion, women's views are less often heard.

Gender Differentiation and Initiation

It has been demonstrated that initiation rituals represent gender relations and are often seen as producing them. And initiation ceremonies generally underscore ideas of gender found throughout the society or carried by a particular religious tradition in that society.

Hopi society is organized around matrilineal clans, and, as in most such societies, Hopi men and women play complementary roles and enjoy status that is more nearly equal than in many other North American societies. As we have seen (in Chapter 4), the initiations of 10-year-olds include both boys and girls. This is in striking contrast to the New Guinea and Amazon cultures, discussed previously, with strong male–female oppositions in social life and strong ritual symbols of gender distinctiveness such as menstrual blood and semen.

Within any one New Guinea society, rituals construct and represent the male and female orders in different fashion. In Manam Island society (Lutkehaus 1995), boys are initiated in cohorts but girls are initiated individually, attended by other girls. The boys become members of secret male societies, whereas the girls become members of women's networks. In classic Durkheimian fashion, the ritual form depicts the most salient form of sociability toward which each gender is headed. Male domination of women within the society is not only actively promoted during the initiation but is also supported by the very existence of the men's houses. Women and children are excluded from the houses, and this "very fact of exclusivity serve[s] to create and perpetuate the politically dominant position of men" (Lutkehaus 1995, 200).

Strong themes of male–female difference also run through many African societies, where the major focus is on male initiation and where boys and girls are initiated by strictly segregated paths into different secret associations (La Fontaine 1985). Along the western African coast, for example (in much of Liberia, Sierra Leone, and the Ivory

Coast), men are initiated into the Poro association, women into the Sande. Each association has internal grades along which an individual may advance. Most people do not pass beyond the first grade, but at higher grades men or women gain new secret knowledge. Those in the highest grades of the men's Poro wield considerable power in the society; their control of spirits legitimates their overruling the chief. The main theme of initiation and of the associations themselves is hierarchy: between occupants of different grades, and by the Poro over the rest of the society.

Each society has numerous lodges, so called after the example of Freemason lodges. Indeed, Poro members remark on the similarity of their society to that of the Masons. A Liberian man told one European ethnographer: "It is a pity you are not a Mason, for then I could tell you more. The Poro is just like Freemasonry" (quoted in La Fontaine 1985, 94). Creoles in Sierra Leone, ineligible to join a Poro society because they were not tribal members, indeed became attracted to Masonry because it provided them with the equivalent of the Poro. The association, structured around grades and secrets, had become a cultural type, to which Masonry was assimilated.

In Sierra Leone, initiation into the women's society takes girls and women away from villages and into the bush, where they stay for a week or two at a time, dancing, feasting, and acquiring new knowledge. But the girls also undergo infibulation. Although the operation is always painful and often dangerous, and it leads to health problems later in life, many women reject calls for an end to the practice. They point to the value of the camaraderie they enjoy in the women's society. "This is a happy time for us," said one just-initiated 16-year-old girl, pointing to the freedom the women and girls feel among themselves (French 1997). The future of the initiation has become the focus for debate in the country about how religion and custom ought to be understood and changed.

Producing a Pious Female Self

The religious traditions of Judaism, Christianity, and Islam have developed precise technologies of crafting new, pious selves. These technologies, to borrow Foucault's (1978) term, lead the individual to take on a new set of self-definitions. She or he is directed and constrained, but the process involves *self*-transformation. Lis Harris (1985) has traced one Jewish woman's journey from the "mainstream" American way of life to the constraints of a religious Hasidic life. Harris shows the sense of purpose and fulfillment that this woman derives from her refashioning of herself, through gender segregation, observance of strict dietary rules, and purification through ritual baths.

The Nun's Surrender to Christ

A more personal sort of surrender defines a nun's progress from postulant to taking perpetual vows. Rebecca Lester (2005) followed first-year nuns in the Siervas congregation in Puebla, Mexico, to trace their processes of self-transformation.

The Siervas was founded in 1885 by Father Muro, a Mexican priest who combined service to humanity with a strong critique of modernity—a critique that nuns read in his writings and in biographies of his life. The original convent, Central House, contains his sainted remains. Father Muro intended the convent to develop femininity in the service of Christ, and this training of religious feminine selves would serve as an antidote to the individualism and materialism that he saw as associated with modernity. By the late 1990s, when Lester spent 18 months in the original house in Puebla, the Central House, the congregation had 78 houses on four continents, with over 600 sisters in Mexico alone.

Lester (2005) worked closely with the 20 young women who had just entered for their first year of training in Central House. These women, called postulants, remained free to come and go, allowing them to decide at the end of the year if they wished to continue to the second stage, that of the novice. Most did. The novice takes the habit and lives in seclusion. After two years of this life of intense self-study, she may proceed to five years of working with older nuns in any of the order's countries, until, at the end of nine years, she takes perpetual vows.

As this timetable makes clear, a nun undergoes a very long process of learning, working, and changing, before she is asked whether she has become fully ready to embrace Christ. At the center of this process is a struggle to remake her own bodily and mental self into the ideal self, one which has surrendered completely to Christ. Lester's study gives us a detailed account of how that struggle proceeds in the first year, and she does so by drawing on the three-stage model of rites of passage that we saw in the preceding chapter. The postulants are separated from their everyday ways of being, undergo a long stage of "liminality," and then reincorporate a new sense of self.

That separation begins long before they enter the convent, as they come to recognize a sense of "brokenness," meaning that something is missing in their lives, and to give that vague feeling the concrete image of a call from Christ. Often dreams provide the clues, as when one soon-to-be postulant dreamed of standing with Mother Josephine from the Siervas looking at a painting of Jesus knocking at a door and hearing a voice say "Jesus is knocking . . ." In case she failed to realize the message, shortly thereafter she found herself standing with Mother Josephine at the convent in front of just this door, and the superior uttered the same words heard in the dream (Lester 2005, 96). As the woman develops a sense of being called to the convent, she tries out her feelings by attending retreats and interviews, until she decides to enter the convent.

Much of what postulants must accomplish is to adjust to a new social architecture of daily life. They are encouraged—through role-playing games and in the constant proximity to one another—to develop a sense of belonging to the postulant group as a whole. Beyond the predictable cliques—one "gang of five" was taller, lighter-skinned, and better-educated—is the challenge of adjusting to a new kind of shared intimacy with the object of their religious affections: "We want to please Jesus . . . but we have to share our boyfriend with so many other women" (Lester 2005, 111). Postulants share a dormitory, and have only their bed-stand to themselves. This social intimacy characterizes only the first year (higher-level sisters have private rooms) and is intended to build bonds among them, and to emphasize their break with the outside world.

If solidarity is fashioned within the group, cross-group interaction is carefully regulated. The convent is divided into sections, each occupied by women at different levels of training. This separation is asymmetric, in that higher-level sisters may enter the postulants' area but not vice versa. Interaction across levels itself is discouraged, lest it break the forward progress of the more advanced women.

Nuns must learn new ways to use their bodies as well: to reduce laughter and noise, avoid staring at others, and to move and work with new kinds of clothing, particularly their head-coverings. (One of the key arts is to avoid moving quickly and sending the veils flying across the room.) Watching their diets, prostrating, engaging in manual labor, and subjecting themselves to penance all emphasize the importance of controlling and reliving the body as part of transforming the spirit.

Rules, taboos, and boundaries are essential tools for many religions in mapping out the social world into the sacred and the profane, the permissible and the impermissible, and we versus they. These take the form of sacred spaces, food taboos, or rules for who may greet, or eat with, or marry whom. The detailed rules regulating conduct in the convent do much more, however. Lester shows that these rules not only teach about hierarchy and solidarity, and induce the proper attitudes of humility and piety, but also focus the nun's attention on their interior worlds as the domain to be worked and refashioned during their stay.

These strivings are all in the service of helping the postulant open herself to *entrega*, or sacrifice and surrender to God. This attitude is bodily and mental: prayer, indeed, should be part of physical labor, and physical labor rethought as a kind of service to God. Many of the women experience moments of entrega as passivity, becoming "an instrument of God," as when Magda, finding herself inadequate as she leads villagers through the stations of the cross, suddenly experiences God speaking through her so that her words come out in a way that amazes the villagers. (You might compare a moment when you let a learned skill, in sports, or speaking, or art, come through without exerting yourself to direct your own body.) The sisters experience these moments as constituting their "conversion" to their true orientation to God (Lester 2005, 207–209).

Finally, the women learn to reconstruct the narratives of their own lives so as to see God in them. She comes to see that God was guiding her life from the very beginning, even if she did not realize it. Celeste now saw the two rape attempts she had suffered as a girl as ways in which God had strengthened her so that she would be able to help others. He did not wish that they happened, but he allowed them to happen because he knew what the outcome would be (Lester 2005, 225–226). By recollecting the events of her life into a new narrative of God's purpose, each woman does not make her life into a story of God's justice or punishment, but one of ultimate purpose.

Most importantly, in Lester's argument (2005, 252), is the way that these processes of religious formation not only create women who successfully surrender to and engage with God, but also, perhaps primarily, teach them new ideas of gender. The women speak much as Father Muro wrote over a century before, about the dilemma posed to women by the twin images of domesticity and modernity. These women reject that choice, and find in the convent a way to develop a meaningful femininity, one that does good in the world without renouncing the values they see as Mexican, Catholic, and ultimately necessary to save the world.

Crafting an Ethical Self through Islamic Worship

A parallel process of fashioning religious selves takes place in Egypt, where Muslim women gather in a mosque to listen to lessons given by women teachers. Saba Mahmood (2005) examines how women learn to cultivate values of sincerity, humility, and awe, ethical elements of Islamic conduct. These elements must be part of one's worship and prayer, and these women learn to cultivate them in their everyday moments so as to be able to properly worship at moments of prayer.

Among these emotions, the fear and awe of God is critical in building an awareness of sins, and women try to cultivate that sense of fear and awe; one woman explained why she attended mosque lessons given by a woman who preached the torment of hell and the wrath of God, because this sharp style "startles us and keeps us from getting lost in the attractions of the world" (Mahmood 2005, 144). This form of fear emerges in the act of worship itself and leads some women to cry during prayer. Fear or awe motivates these women to pray and emerges as a commendable dimension of their prayer.

Beyond the worship context, many of the women with whom Mahmood worked discussed religious conventions as forms of behavior that helped them to modify their feelings in the proper direction. One woman once had thought of the emotion of shyness as being something that had to come of itself, until she read a Qur'ânic verse that listed shyness among the good deeds. As a deed, shyness becomes something to cultivate purposefully, rather than to simply let emerge on its own, and "once you do this, the sense of shyness eventually imprints itself on your inside." Another woman followed the same logic regarding wearing head covering, the *hijâb*: "You must wear the veil first, because it is God's command, and then, with time, because your inside learns to feel shy without the veil, and if you take it off, your entire being feels uncomfortable about it" (Mahmood 2005, 157).

Both cases point out in ethnographic detail how women embrace the delimitation of their autonomy and their subordination to formal religious structures (of the convent, the mosque) as a way of developing their selves in a socioreligious framework. The objects of emotional recrafting differ—the absorption of Christ in the one case, the awe at God's power in the other—but both involve an appropriation of an external force to redefine the fulfilling self.

These and other studies challenge the liberal political–theoretic assumption that maximal freedom from constraint is best for developing the subject. In Mahmood's terms (2005, 14), these works uncouple "the notion of self-realization from that of the autonomous will." In other words, these anthropologists no longer assume that the only pathway to a productive and satisfying development of a self, and in particular a religious and ethical self, is by throwing off the social norms and values that constrain one's actions. For some women and men, self-realization takes place precisely by immersing oneself in a set of constraining institutions, such as the convent, or social norms embedded in the larger society, whether Islamic, Protestant, orthodox Jewish, or, to leave the religious domain, those of a law firm or corporation that highly regulates the lives of its associates.

These issues have arisen most pointedly for feminist anthropologists, because women in most societies experience male control. Anthropologists have looked for ways in which women nonetheless can realize satisfying senses of "agency," meaning the ability to form oneself and to act effectively in the world. One strategy of this search is to seek those reserved spaces or spheres where women can exercise autonomy. For example, Janice Boddy (1989) shows how women in northern Sudan organize and lead healing *zar* cults, and through their activities both articulate current social problems and weave inter-village social networks. The strategy exemplified here is to see how, in other instances, women incorporate hierarchy and constraint into their projects of fashioning selfhood and agency.

Converting to a New Faith

Converting to a new religion clearly involves a transformation of the self as well, although cultures of conversion differ more than we might think. The following examples all involve Protestant religions and show the range of these cultures.

Calvinists in Sumba

As we move from the Catholic nuns' focus on reshaping their material and ethical selves, to the parallel endeavors by Cairene Muslim women in prayer circles, to the missionary activities of Calvinists, we also shift across very distinctive ideas about the role of materiality in religion. As Webb Keane (2007) writes in his study of Calvinism and missions in eastern Indonesia, the desire of Calvin and others was to purify the direct relationship of the human worshipper to God. The Calvinist strains of Protestantism—today reflected across a great deal of Protestantism—emphasized the sincere intentions of the Christian in prayer and in action, and the grace given by God to that Christian, or withheld by Him. Calvin objected to Martin Luther's acceptance of the Catholic idea of transubstantiation, whereby the body and blood of Christ exist in the wafer and wine given at Communion. For Calvin, we only employ such symbols as the bread and wine because we, weak humans, are so incapable of directly grasping the will and nature of God.

The Protestant impulse was to stress the faith and belief of the Christian and the grace of God, and not the ritual practices or material objects as such. In this view, people speak of beliefs already held, rather than submit to the objective consequences of a ritual performed by a priest, as in the mystery of transubstantiation. Keane argues that this emphasis led to a cycle of reactions against the inevitable routinization of practices and creation of material objects—statues, churches, robes. He makes the broader argument that reform of religion, from this perspective, is shared across faiths, including Judaism and Islam, and is part of a modern striving to "purify" our human world of domination by things, to make ourselves free to act as we wish, unburdened by material constraints. This idea that purification characterizes modernity was formulated by Bruno Latour (1993), but Keane argues that the religious ideas of the immediacy of meaning in human intention gave a historical push to purification.

When Dutch Calvinist missionaries came to eastern Indonesia to convert the people on Sumba island, they brought their ideas about meaning with them. They took local practices and expressions to be ways of talking about religious concepts, which then could be allied with Christian concepts. So the blessing with "cool water" that was part of local ritual was rendered as a metaphor: the water stands for God's blessing, and so can be replaced by it (Keane 2007, 111). The material form, in this case flowing water, was immaterial, so to speak, to reaching the higher goal of realizing God's purpose. In similar fashion, missionaries scoured the world for evidence of God's revelations, degraded though they might now seem. Ideas of a "high God," or of salvation, all were read for their deep, ultimately Christian meaning.

But even if there are traces of revelation in local "pagan" religions, some saw conversion as requiring a sharp break with the past. Ironically, in Sumba, when Dutch missionaries urged Sumbanese converts to preserve the songs and gongs from their traditional culture in their Protestant liturgy, the converts refused to do so lest these tokens of the past bring older deities back to mind (Keane 2007, 134). Keeping certain key terms of the new religion, and in particular the name for God, in a foreign tongue can resist assimilating the new God to the old deity. Many Indonesian Muslims were scandalized when, in the 1990s, a leading theologian proposed to translate Allah with the Indonesian word for God, *Tuhan*. The problem was that he then had to distinguish between that word and the word for mere deity, as in "false gods," particularly in the Islamic confession of faith, "there is no deity but God." In Arabic, this distinction is accomplished through a difference in pronunciation, between different forms of a shared root, but Indonesian only has the one word *tuhan*. The theologian thought he had solved the problem by capitalizing the one and leaving the other in lower case, but in a largely oral aural culture, this solution was a failure.

When a local Sumbanese notable converted to Calvinism, he tried to solve the problem of continuity vis-à-vis rupture by delivering a ritual speech about his conversion, in which he placed himself in the pathways set out by the ancestors, even as he also began a new pathway, to the future as a Christian. The imagery of pathways dominates public ritual speaking in many eastern Indonesian societies; these paths link today's people back to original centers. But the notable refused to carry out the ritual sacrifices that normally provide the material support for such speeches to communicate to ancestral spirits, and so he left himself open for attacks, which did indeed follow. The attack pinpointed the contrast in how Calvinists and the traditional ritual practitioners communicate with spirits: the Calvinist claims immediate contact with God; the traditional practitioner uses the ritual couplets provided by the ancestor, the material of religious ritual. The contrast and debate that took place about religion in Sumba mirrors that between Calvinist and Catholic theories of communication, as directly with God through faith and belief, or as mediated by the priest and his objectively efficacious rituals.

Conversion also makes the individual the lone agent of worship. The structure of the church emphasizes individuality. One aristocratic Sumbanese woman told

Keane that she feels embarrassment when she attends church, which she does every Sunday, because she finds herself among strangers. Social life in this society is for the most part among those you know. Conversion thrusts you as an individual not only before God, but also among other people with whom you share nothing but a presumed common faith.

Commitment to a religion may require, or indeed may itself be, a kind of conversion. The interdependence of conversion and commitment may be understood most easily with regard to children, who are not expected to become adherents and practitioners of a religion without effort. Children are usually required to study in order to become fully accepted members of a religious community, when they may undergo a ritual of acceptance that includes commitment to the religion of their parents. The acts of commitment required of a child are often the same as those required of an adult convert: learning a text by heart, reciting a statement of commitment, undergoing an initiation ritual.

Adult Baptism among the Amish

Consider the Amish, one of several Protestant religions that underwent persecution in Europe beginning in the sixteenth century (others include Hutterites and Mennonites). They were persecuted mainly because they practiced and preached adult baptism, and thus were called Anabaptists ("to baptize again"). They did so because they believed that only someone who had reached the "age of reason" could make an informed and conscious decision to become a member of the Church.

Today, Amish communities are found in many parts of North America, concentrated in Pennsylvania, Ohio, and Indiana. Amish people live in villages and towns, close to non-Amish people they call "English." They continue to learn and use a dialect of German within the community. Their major religious values are submission to God, humility, and openness. They live according to their values by wearing simple clothing, renouncing those inventions that would separate them from the land and from work, and preventing the outside world from intruding on family life.

A commitment to the Amish way of life means staying apart from mainstream society. Boys and girls make that commitment at baptism, which occurs between the ages of 16 and 21. Candidates take a series of classes that stress the strict nature of the Amish social code, the Ordnung. They are told that it is better to not join the order than to join and then break the code. The baptism itself takes place in front of the congregation after a regular Sunday service. Kneeling, the candidate agrees to obey God and his church, and the presiding bishop drips water over his or her head.

The idea of active commitment, of the seriousness of the vows taken, explains a puzzle in their lives. On the one hand, the Amish more than any religious group in America try to keep themselves cut off from the broader society. Electricity, telephones, automobiles, public schools are all suspect because they plug the community in (literally or figuratively) to the wider sociocultural grid. Telephones are one of many subjects of intense controversy because they provide safety and comfort but they also disrupt family and social life. (One solution is to have telephones in separate buildings, so that they can be used if needed but cannot break up, for example, dinner conversations.) On the other hand, the Amish also permit their teenagers to "flirt with the world" (Kraybill 1989, 138). Indeed, although the Amish churches exercise strict control over the lives of adults, with sanctions that include being shunned by the community, the churches have no direct authority over children and adolescents. Until they are baptized, Amish boys and girls are supposed to be under the authority of their parents.

Amish teenagers typically join one of the several "crowds" of youths in the community (Kraybill 1989, 138–140). A crowd plays sports together, attends films, and travels to cities and to the beach. For their outings they buy and wear clothes similar to those worn by "English" youth. The boys often drive cars and are sometimes arrested for drunken driving or have serious accidents. In the late 1990s several youths were arrested for drug trafficking.

A student of the Amish, Donald Kraybill (1989, 139), writes that this liminal period and tolerated rowdiness serves as a "social immunization" against the subsequent temptations young people face. Having experienced something of the world, they can reject it with knowledge. And though they would find it difficult to leave the Amish world they have been educated for and where their friends live, they believe that they have a choice because they are presented with one. About 80 percent of Amish youth do choose to undergo baptism and remain in the church. There is a psychological soundness to the Amish idea that you can knowingly reject only what you know. For an example of the problem faced by a group of people who have never known such temptation, and are thereby unable to face it with strength when it arrives, one could do no better than to read Mark Twain's classic story, "The Man Who Corrupted Hadleyburg." Hadleyburgians, naive believers in their own goodness, could not withstand the temptation of some easy money to be made through telling a simple lie.

Conversion as Total Social Change

What does conversion entail? It may appear to be merely a matter of changing one's religious allegiance—going to a different place of worship, perhaps wearing different clothes or eating different foods or making different friends. It is, then, an individual choice, accomplished fairly quickly, perhaps with some changes in lifestyle (less likely if the conversion is within Christianity).

This idea of conversion, however, only makes sense for those societies that have an easily detached notion of "religion." If particular spirit beliefs permeate all aspects of one's life, then giving up all those beliefs for some new set will most likely entail leaving the society altogether and changing one's ideas about oneself.

The experience of the Akha people of highland Burma and Thailand offers an example of how, in many societies, conversion can be a process of near-total social change (Kammerer 1990). In the 1960s when their neighbors were converting to Catholicism and Protestantism in droves, the Akha stood out among the peoples of this region for their resistance to conversion. But by the 1980s conversions were occurring with increasing frequency among the Akha. Why this sudden shift?

The answer returns us to our earlier discussion of what the category of religion looks like in different societies. In the Akha language, the word *zah* is the closest to the English *religion*, but it includes much more—the rules for planting crops, holding funerals, healing the sick, and conducting a marriage. For the Akha, their zah defines who they are. Others have their own zah, and those rules define them. One should not, they say, mix zahs from different people. (This sounds rather like the most extreme statements of "cultural wholes" in American anthropology.) Akha have been less likely to marry people of other ethnic groups, and when they do, often they become one of those people, a Lisu, say, rather than an Akha. Custom and culture (including religion) is seen as an all-or-nothing affair.

The Akha were somewhat more insistent than were their neighbors about changing zah, which would logically initially keep them from converting. To change zah would be in effect to change one's overall identity, to become something other than Akha. But we are still left with the task of explaining why, at some point, the balance tipped and the Akha began to convert in large numbers. Here, too, understanding their idea of identity helps us to understand what happened. Akha had begun to attend state schools and learn broader Thai ways, and at some point the intricacies of their older zah became too difficult to learn and practice. Because Akha saw their zah as a unity of practices, and not any better or worse than other people's zahs, it made sense to change zahs entirely, to convert to another kind of people, those who practice "Jesus zah" rather than "Akha zah."

Kammerer (1990) points out that Akha never say they "believe" in new or old zah, Akha-ism or Christianity. For them conversion is a matter of exchanging older practices for new ones, for pragmatic reasons. For the Akha conversion is neither a change of heart nor a sitting on the fence.

External and Internal Conversion

A different case study shows us that conversion may also turn out to be something quite different: not an all-or-nothing choice of social life, but a long-term process of reworking and reinterpreting social practices. John Barker (1993) studied the Uiaku Maisin people of the Oro province in northeast Papua New Guinea. The Maisin people have been Christians since the early 1900s, when they were converted by Australian Anglican missionaries. But Barker observes that conversion continues to take place, and does so in two ways. What he calls "external conversion," associated with the mission station, has to do with trying to acculturate local people to relatively cosmopolitan ways. By contrast, "internal conversion" takes place in villages, where people debate and adapt their ideas to new circumstances. The advantage of Barker's perspective is that it locates distinct conversion processes in two distinct social environments. People have no trouble separating the two, because each addresses distinct concerns.

"From the mission station," writes Barker (1993, 208), "Uiaku appears a Christian community." The church is the center of social life, for sports, women's groups, and for celebrations of saints' days. Bells mark the hours for church and school attendance. Avenues are wide and straight. The church council encourages church attendance, urges people to grow cash crops, and comforts the sick. Councilors fly to other cities in the country to meet with delegates from religious, political, or other organizations.

But village hamlets are organized along quite different lines, one that mark a continuity in social and cultural organization. People build houses near birthplaces. Elders preside over dispute-resolution sessions and have the power to strike through sorcery. Not that things in the village have not changed over the years—villagers added God to the list of powerful spirits in the cosmos, for example. They also stretched older ideas they held to become the equivalents of Christian ideas taught by the missionaries. For example, the term Barker translates as *amity* probably once referred to a peaceful condition that resulted from balance in the exchanges of goods and services between clans. As missionaries taught about Christian "universal brotherhood," people stretched their idea of peace-inducing balance to translate the new idea.

But these stretchings were more than just translations; the new cultural categories, once in place, could serve as moral foundations for criticizing contemporary practices. Barker relates how the extended notion of amity was mobilized by the church deacon (a local man) to condemn some people who allowed the period of mourning to continue too long, so that it was disruptive. In response, some subsequent deaths were met by much shorter periods of mourning than ever before. Villagers understood this change not as an adaptation to Western norms, but as a more consistent pattern of behavior in terms of their own social norms, *their* idea of amity.

This "internal conversion" is thus a kind of moral ironing-out of everyday and ritual practices in terms that are seen as local, but that have been transformed as a result of the process of "external conversion." Villagers participate in both worlds (see Hefner 1993).

Missions and Civilization in South Africa

Another case study of conversion as a long-term process comes from the work of Jean and John Comaroff (1986, 1991, 1997). The Comaroffs study the dual British colonial project of converting "natives" in South Africa to Christianity and creating a socially modern and disciplined colonial society. They describe how Protestant evangelical missionaries failed to realize their dreams of constructing a unified black Protestant church but succeeded in reshaping the way Africans carried out their lives. Their study focuses on the lives of the Tswana people of South Africa and Botswana and on the activities of the Methodist London Missionary Society beginning in the 1820s.

The Comaroffs point out that Methodist missionaries (and, in varying ways, other Christian missionaries) measured their effectiveness not merely by obtaining formal conversions, but by their success in changing natives' ways of behaving. French sociologists, among them Marcel Mauss and Pierre Bourdieu, have termed the ways an individual acts, responds, speaks, walks, and so forth, his or her *habitus*. South African Methodists were bent on teaching the Tswana the "arts of civilization," which included the arts of cultivation. Missionaries urged the adoption of the plow, which, because only men tended cattle, had the effect of raising the value of male labor relative to female labor. They also taught that natives should live in monogamous households arranged in rows and squares rather than in circles and arcs. The church clock and the church calendar now regulated social life. And as the hourly base for figuring wages, time was now used to measure the value of an individual's labor.

But the Methodist message contained the seeds of destruction for the colonial project. Central to the Wesleyan idea of self-perfection preached in the churches was the equality of people and their freedom to perfect their natures. This message was blatantly contradicted by the realities of mining labor in the nineteenth and twentieth centuries. It also gave ammunition to those within particular churches who would resist any kind of central control, leading to the subsequent proliferation of churches, as dissatisfied factions set out to found new denominations (Comaroff 1985).

The Comaroffs present the encounters between missionaries and Tswana as part of an ongoing conversation. Each side incorporated the other's messages into its own way of thinking, and yet also changed its religious practices slightly as a result of the encounter. The control of water was a matter of survival, for example, but also a political and cosmic matter (Comaroff and Comaroff 1991, 206–213). It was the ruler who brought on rains, and the rainmaking rituals, carried out at his direction, that ensured the rains' arrival.

The missionaries regarded these rituals as the height of superstition and thought they should be eradicated. But they themselves were caught in a contradiction, proclaiming that rain was a matter of nature and scientific meteorological detection, while saying that rain was ultimately in God's hands. The Tswana concluded from this missionary double-talk that their scientific instruments were merely their version of rainmaking devices, which worked through their deity.

Consider how the Tswana people's firm grasp of missionary logic shaped the following dialogue between a mission medical doctor (MD) and the rain doctor (RD).

MD: . . . you cannot charm the clouds by medicines. You wait till you see the clouds come, then you use your medicines, and take credit that belongs to God only.

RD: I use my medicines and you employ yours; we are both doctors, and doctors are not deceivers. You give a patient medicine. Sometimes God is pleased to heal him by means of your medicine; sometimes not—he dies. When he is cured, you take the credit for what God does. I do the same.

The rain doctor is simply calling the medical doctor's bluff: if he really believes, as the missionaries did indeed claim, that all is in the hands of God, then how could he or any other European claim that his human science had cured someone or predicted rains?

The Tswana version of how rain arrives was in fact fairly complex. Rainmaking rituals did not work in some automatic, mechanical way; they required that the community be in a state of "moral recitude, of 'coolness' (*tsididi*)" (Comaroff and Comaroff 1991, 210). Therefore, the ritual expert's primary task was to remove social pollution that might be preventing the heavens from unleashing the rain. It was thus fully within Tswana logic when they later blamed the presence of the Europeans for the failure of rainmaking rituals. For their part, Europeans began to include rain services in the church calendar, the more effectively to combat the natives' view. The conversion effort thus became an extended exchange of and change in the views of both sides.

6

Extending our Powers: Magic and Healing

eligion in the very broadest sense includes a variety of ways in which we try to reach out to find new ways of changing the world: predicting the future, finding a partner, or healing a loved one. Using objects and spells to do so often has been termed "magic," but in fact these practices are found at the heat, or at least in the mainstream, of most religious systems. Small statues, written talismans, appeals for intercession: are these not both religious and "magical"?

Magic, Patterns, and Causes

arlier students of religion sought to identify the fundamental features that lay behind beliefs in magic. The nineteenth-century anthropologists Edward Tylor and James Frazer thought of magic as a pseudoscience, what primitive people did instead of science. Magic for them was just like science in that it sought to act directly on the world, in a technical or instrumental way, but it was empirically false in its assumptions. Magic was a set of spells and techniques acquired with more attention to their effects (the practical side) than their principles (the theory).

Likeness and Contact

In his massive work on myth and folklore, *The Golden Bough* (1981), Frazer isolated two ideas that he saw as the basis for magical thinking: like affects like; and things that come into contact affect each other. The first he called "homeopathy," the second, "contagion." Homeopathic magic makes use of similarities, either natural or human-made, to reach its end. One kind of similarity is in the appearance of an object, so dolls or pictures of a person, when altered in some way, will, because like causes like, cause a corresponding alteration in the target person—the proverbial "voodoo doll" with the pins stuck in it. But there are other ways similarities are drawn on for practical ends. One can transfer the properties of any object to someone for a good or ill purpose. Gayo people use leaves that feel cool to the touch to bring down a fever on the assumption that the patient will feel cool because the leaves are cool.

Actions, rather than objects, can also have efficacy through the logic of likeness. Take the *couvade*, for example, a ritual first remarked in native North America wherein a father-to-be imitates the process of giving birth while his wife is experiencing labor pains. By his enactment of the successful birth he is supposed to push the process along and make it easier. (Perhaps this way of thinking underlies Lamaze birthing procedures in which the woman's companion performs blowing and counting exercises along with her.) A more complex logic underlies the "cosmic balance rituals," long called "increase rituals," in native Australia (Swain 1995, 25–28). Aboriginal groups recognize a particular plant, animal, or other object as their protective totem. They act out the birth of their totemic animal or plant and thereby increase its number. The additional special relationship between totem and people then leads to their prosperity.

The second principle is contagion, that contact between two objects means that action upon one of the objects will produce effects on the other. The hair or nails of a person, or clothing, may be used to work magic on the person. During the beginning of my fieldwork, several neighbors were concerned that I might become the victim of illness-causing magic and warned me not to hang up my wash outside. A shirt could be used to work magic on me, they said. Of special interest to societies around the world are discarded body parts, from fingernail clippings to the placenta. Because it is born along with the child, the placenta is treated in some societies as the child's brother, and how it is treated can affect the child's fortune. Some people bury it, to ensure that the child will always return from a trip; others store it away. The history of contact with the person gives the placenta its importance.

But "magic" is not limited to marginal activities or small-scale societies. The history of the Christian Church is inextricably bound up with what, from the perspective we take here, we would call "contagious magic." The power held by relics of saints, after all, derives from the relic's history as a part of the saint or as something that came into contact with the saint. For several centuries new churches had to be founded on a relic. Certain portraits, such as Our Lady of Czestochowa in Poland, draw special power from the contact with a saint (Saint Luke in this case). And of course the Shroud of Turin's special claim is not its likeness of Jesus but the supposed contact with Jesus's face. From the point of view adopted by Frazer, "magic" is less a type of practice than it is a psychological basis for making certain claims about power and efficacy. We find the ideas of likeness and contact compelling, and so we are especially likely to accept claims made on their bases.

Magic and Anxiety

Frazer's view of magic as replacement for science too neatly divided the world into "primitive" and "modern" societies. "Magical thinking" is in fact part of religious life and everyday life in all societies. The anthropologist Bronislaw Malinowski (1954) argued that science and magic are not substitutes for each other, but in that all societies they cooperate to create a psychologically satisfactory life. For all people, argued Malinowski, our ability to control our environments stops at some point, far short of what we would like. At that point magic comes in. It allows us to act on the areas of life filled with uncertainty, thus reducing our anxiety and allowing us to get on with life.

Contrary to what Frazer claimed, Malinowski said that no people in the world confuse technical or scientific knowledge with magic. People everywhere realize that their knowledge and control over the world has limits. Within the limits of that knowledge and control, practical, empirical science and skill is sufficient, and one does not find magic. Malinowski offered examples from his fieldwork in the Trobriand Islands, part of present-day Papua New Guinea. For Trobrianders, most everyday activities are fully under their control and therefore do not involve magic. A Trobriander knows how to make a basket or a pot with little chance of breakage and how to fish in safe areas, within the lagoon, for example, with no danger and little uncertainty. These activities are not accompanied by magic. On the other hand, activities that do have a certain degree of uncertainty, risk, or danger connected with them are likely to have magic. When Trobrianders venture out into the open sea to fish, they must use more chancy methods of fishing and face much more danger; it is then that they use magical spells to ensure a safe and successful venture.

Malinowski's approach gives us clear predictions of when we will find magic and when we will not. To state the argument abstractly: in any particular domain, activities that involve the most uncertainty are also the most likely to be accompanied by magic, that is, by practices that do not have technically or scientifically apparent effects but are believed by the actors to help their chances of success.

George Gmelch (1978) provides an example from American baseball. There is a clear division in baseball between activities in which players are expected to succeed nearly all the time and those in which they are not. Fielding is an example of the first, where failing to catch a pop fly ball will be counted as an error and not as an expected, common failure. Pitching and hitting are clear examples of the second category, where players have much less control over what happens. A player who hits one-third of the time is very successful, as is a pitcher who throws strikes only half the time.

Is Malinowski's prediction right for baseball? It appears so: pitching and hitting, where so many things can go wrong, are accompanied by magic; fielding is not. Players practice magic by experiment and correlation. They try wearing an outfit or eating a certain food; if they do well on that day, then the clothes or food become "lucky" and a required part of their daily preparation. Gmelch himself, a former player, ate pancakes on mornings before games after he had won games on pancake days. Or they may decide to abstain from sex (as did an entire Canadian team during the 1996 Olympics), or the opposite, before game days.

Baseball magic can, as Malinowski stressed, relieve anxiety and build confidence. But once a player starts relying on magic he starts to require his magic to keep up his confidence. Magic can create anxiety as well as resolve it—a point made by a contemporary of Malinowski's, the anthropologist A. R. Radcliffe-Brown (1965).

One might say that for Malinowski, magic was a kind of psychology, not science; it arises out of one's awareness of one's own inability to control a situation but a desire to be able to control it. Magic is close to wish fulfillment or daydreaming. Malinowski's approach is an important corrective to Frazer's in providing a richer portrait of why people make use of magic. For example, the couvade, where the father imitates the birthing process, was explained by Frazer in terms of "like affects like." But why do we find magic for this event, giving birth, and not for many others? What drives people to make use of "like affects like" here? Malinowski would say that the couvade gives the father a feeling of participation and accomplishment in a situation in which he otherwise has little to do. In the United States, at least, the joke used to be that the father would be sent to boil endless pots of water, ostensibly to sterilize equipment but in fact to channel his nervous energy. The couvades-like techniques of Lamaze and other birthing exercises are, from Malinowski's point of view, more refined forms of magic.

Seeing Patterns in Sports

Does Malinowski's insight work for all instances of sports magic? Let us consider the notion of luck, good and bad, how you can change it—and most importantly, how you perceive it. Consider wearing the number 13 on your jersey: does it bring bad luck? It sure looks that way once you start to consider examples of players who did so, as does one popular writer (Morrison 2003). In 1999 baseball pitcher Jeff Fassero wore it for two teams and compiled the worst earned run average since 1937. Reaching back to 1951 one finds pitcher Ralph Branca in number 13 and surrendering "the shot heard round the world" home run by Bobby Thomson. I looked through the list of 13-wearers and saw the former St. Louis Rams quarterback Kurt Warner, who had a few great seasons and then collapsed—unusual for football, and requiring explaining. Hmmm, maybe so?

My reaction is common: once you find a few examples that fit the pattern it is human nature to believe in the pattern. We do look for patterns; we are pleased to find them—in the skies, in our lives, in sports. But what if I had come across Kurt Warner's name in 2001, when he was completing long passes left and right? I probably would have read down the list until I found another name that fit the pattern.

One pattern many players find in their game is "hot hands." Known best in basketball, "hot hands" designates a winning streak, one ball going in the basket after another. The psychologist Gilovich et al. (1985) interviewed players, dedicated fans, and statisticians of basketball, and found that the more deeply they knew their sport the stronger their belief in the reality of "hot hands." And yet when his research team analyzed every shot sequence for all games played by the Philadelphia 76ers over a season and a half, they didn't find that a hit was likely to be followed by another (what the "hot hands hypothesis" would predict) but that a hit was slightly more likely to be followed by a miss! Now, there were strings of hits, as one would predict even if hits and misses occurred randomly, and it probably is the memory of a few of those strings that lead people to believe in the hypothesis. And, of course, strings of hits also are the product of players being alert, in their stride, and so forth—it's just that when we look at the overall picture these strings occur randomly. (See one "hot hands" site at: *www.hs.ttu.edu/hdfs3390/hothand.htm.*)

Many of the most common ideas and practices about luck and rituals in sports depend on perceiving some patterns, like the cases of "hot hands" or truly unfortunate 13-wearing pitchers, and ignoring others, like successful 13-wearers or season-long random patterns of hits and misses. Chicago Cubs fans blame the curse of Murphy the Goat for their long history of losing key games. In 1945, a saloon owner named Billy Goat Sianis tried to bring his billy goat Murphy onto Wrigley Field. P. K. Wrigley denied the goat entrance, saying it stunk, and Sianis replied, "Cubs, they ain't gonna win again." They didn't, and fans have since blamed the curse, forgetting that they hadn't won for 37 years before the curse either!

These are many examples. Does appearing on the cover of *Sports Illustrated* jinx an athlete? Some athletes think so, and they cite the many cases of athletes who suffered disastrous streaks shortly after being featured in the magazine. *Sports Illustrated* editors thought the rumors potentially damaging enough to hire some statisticians to study the subject (Wolff 2003). They found that a *Sports Illustrated* cover appearance did jinx players 37 percent of the time (and therefore did not do so 63 percent of the time) and that the rate was significantly higher for players of individual sports. Did the appearance have an effect? It is, of course, very difficult to simulate non-appearance by these players, but the difference in terms of type of game suggests that some players may get nervous after expectations have been raised by their appearance—a "clutch" phenomenon—or even that worry about the jinx effect itself affected their play, a reverse placebo effect.

Our tendencies to read causality into patterns make sports magic an empirical science of sorts. Players who are doing well often respond by wearing the same clothes, eating the same food, or doing anything that they happened to be doing when their successful streak began, hoping or wishing that this behavior will keep them "hot" on the field. Sometimes they disconfirm their own actions, as when University of Kansas oarswomen Lauren Royall began wearing a black sports bra to every meet, because she had once worn one and won. The first time she lost wearing the black bra she was furious, and swore off magic entirely. "Now I try not to pay attention to what I put on" (McNearney 2002). The search for causality may explain the famous (and illegal) corked bats used by hitters, which got Sammy Sosa into trouble in 2003. The cork seems to add nothing to performance but was likely adopted when some players happened to hit well with such a bat.

Prayer, Faith, and Healing

*N*ow we focus on the ways in which people try to heal themselves or others through religion. In the United States, healing through prayer is widely accepted. A 2003 *Newsweek* poll found that 84 percent of Americans believe that their prayers can help someone else heal, what is known as "intercessory prayer" (Kalb 2003).

Christian Science

Prayer-based healing abounds in Christian denominations, and a belief in the power of prayer made a particularly strong entry into U.S. bookstores and minds in the 1990s. The oldest representative of this approach is the Christian Science Church, founded in 1879 by Mary Baker Eddy. From the enormous Mother Church in Boston emanate the *Christian Science Monitor* and high-quality radio news programs. Adherents are found mainly in the United States and Protestant areas of Europe.

Christian Science healers, called "practitioners," and laypersons can cure themselves and others by appealing to God through prayer and by reading from the religion's two key books: the Christian Gospels and Eddy's book, *Science and Health,* reissued in a new edition in 1996 by the church. This book tells followers that humans are spiritually perfect, though morally far from perfect, and that they only need realize they have the power to abolish sickness. The miracles performed by Jesus are nothing but instances of God's law, available to all humans. Sin, sickness, and death are closely related, and the pure life brings health with it. These beliefs resemble Indian notions of *dharma,* the concept of natural and moral law, where one's moral actions (*karma*) have a direct effect on material events in the world, including one's sickness and health.

Christian Science advocates often relate anecdotes about a recovery through prayer that doctors thought impossible—beginning with Eddy herself, who was inspired by her own recovery from a bad fall on the ice. One writer describes a serious automobile accident in South Dakota, after which he foreswore all medical treatment but called a Christian Scientist practitioner in New York who applied "absent treatment," praying at a distance (Leishman 1958, 127–133).

Science and Health suggests how to pray for health and urges the patient to "mentally contradict every complaint from the body." It contains no secret formulas; but for some practitioners, fixed prayers may take on "magical" qualities. The practitioners studied by Bryan Wilson in England recited the following phrase each morning as a defense against the malevolent forces of "animal magnetism":

Malicious animal magnetism does not know where I am or what I am doing: it does not know God's plan or purpose for me, nor the work that God has given me to do; nor can it perpetuate any lies about me; for I live, move, and have my being in God, in Spirit, in the secret place of the Most High. (Wilson 1961, 130)

Mary Baker Eddy herself once flirted with hypnotism as a remedy for illness, and later strongly denounced it, leaving a trace in this prayer and in the general suspicion of mental suggestion as a source of illness and sin. Practitioners admit that the common cold may afflict people, but argue that it spreads only if we so believe. We must repel the "aggressive mental suggestion" that colds spread, thereby keeping ourselves from catching them.

In theory Christian Scientists oppose trying to mix medicine with prayer, arguing that the two remedies are so different that they cannot be combined. In some cases Christian Science parents have refused medical treatment for their child. A Minnesota couple and practitioner who let an 11-year-old boy, Ian Lundman, die of diabetes in 1989 were successfully sued for 1.5 million dollars in compensatory damages, an award later upheld by the U.S. Supreme Court. But other Christian Scientists do wear glasses, enter hospitals, seek dental treatment, and allow doctors to treat broken bones and infections (Fraser 1996).

Trance, Possession, and Healing

H ealing practices often turn on the idea that a spirit has possessed the patient and is causing the illness. The cure then involves putting the patient (or sometimes a curer) into a trance state, investigating the reasons for the spirit's actions, and driving out the spirit (or *exorcising* the patient).

Afro-Brazilian Trances

In Brazil today, healers draw on Afro-Brazilian religion traditions to carry out their art. Afro-Brazilian religions, variously called "Candomblé," "Umbanda," or "Macumba" (and related to Haitian "Voudun" and Cuban "Santeria"), developed when people living in West Africa were forcibly brought to the Americas as slaves (see Chapter 12). Forced to conceal their own religious ideas and practices, they developed a blend that appeared Catholic but contained elements of West African religion. Today these traditions have changed in various directions, some emphasizing African sources, others Native American elements, still others the ties with Catholicism and with European Spiritism (Brown 1986; Goodman 1988, 42–51).

In the Brazilian trance-healing practices called Macumba (Richeport 1985), trance is employed in varied settings to aid in healing. In sessions involving "professional mediums," specialists sit in a separate, cordoned-off part of a room. They are dressed in white and are already in a trance. They each have special "spirit familiars" with whom they communicate. Patients deliver to the staff slips of paper containing their questions; usually the questions are about their own illnesses. The mediums then ask for answers from their spirit familiars and relay these answers back through the staff. These sessions are calm, although sometimes a supplicant will slip into trance, and in such cases he or she may be approached about becoming a medium.

A second type of session involves mass trances. Dozens or hundreds of people gather together for evenings of trance, dancing and music, and consultation. These large-scale sessions also employ mediums, but they walk and dance around on the floor, mingling with other people who wish to attend. Rather than having personal spirit familiars, all the mediums cycle together through several standard spirit types during the evening. Each type represents both a familiar cultural figure of the Brazilian environment and a kind of emotion. When the mediums are possessed by the "old black slave" spirit, they sit, smoking pipes, and dispense this old man's wisdom to those attending (who are often relatives or friends). When they take on the flashily dressed woman called *Pomba Gira*, they are seductive and loose, enjoying this break from normal behavioral restrictions. When they are the child they scamper about eating candy. (There is also an Amazonian equivalent of these sessions in which Indians act the role of whites, drink champagne, and act terribly refined.)

Use is also made of trances at clinics for the mentally ill. Patients are encouraged to enter a trance state and act out their emotions and frustrations; often they, too, take on stereotyped roles such as those mentioned previously.

Shared Healing in Southern Africa

The Kung people living in southern Africa once lived entirely from gathering and some hunting. The great variability of rainfall and thus food in their lands led them to develop norms of sharing and exchange. Sharing distributes risk and gives people a source of food during periods of drought and scarcity.

Healing follows similar lines of thought. The Kung heal those who have fallen ill by assembling in a group at night around a fire and dancing to reach a trance-like state of transcendence called "kai," reached by tapping into the energy, *num*, that everyone has in the pits of their stomachs. About half of the men tap this energy, and about one-third of the women. (They tend to be people whose parents did so. Larger percentages try, and somewhat smaller percentages become active healers.) Num energy is not a limited good, but is given by God to individuals and benefits everyone in the group when people tap it.

Reaching the state of kai can be dangerous and painful. An older healer described the feeling in terms of death and rebirth.

Your heart stops. You're dead. Your thoughts are nothing. You breathe with difficulty. You see things, num things. You see spirits killing people. You smell burning, rotten flesh. Then you heal, you pull sickness out. You heal, heal, heal. Then you live. Your eyeballs clear and you see people clearly. (Katz 1982, 45)

When your own num has begun to boil others feel it and they, too, begin to dance.

Healing takes place in three stages. The healer, once his or her num is boiling, can see the num in other healers and the spirits causing illness. Then the healer pulls out the sickness, laying hands on the ill person to put num in and draw out illness, and then shaking the illness out into the darkness. The healer begins to sweat as his num boils; this sweat is the num and he or she rubs it into the patient to forcibly expel the illness (Katz 1982, 106–108).

Then the healer, in a heroic confrontation, does battle with spirits and gods. Usually the illness has been caused by spirits of the dead. Sometimes they have specific complaints about the living person they are bothering; sometimes they are just looking

Kung healing dance at dawn, Botswana. (COURTESY OF RICHARD KATZ, *BOILING ENERGY*, p. 33.)

to stir up trouble. But they are also messengers from the great god, Gao Na, a capricious god who may destroy humans should he find them annoying.

Healers may argue with the spirits or even journey to the god's home. Others at the dance hear one side of a dialogue between the healer and the spirits or god, a dialogue of cajoling or threatening. The healer may hurl insults at the spirits or reason gently with them, telling them that they gain nothing from bothering humans.

Kung trance-healing is collective in spirit and in practice because the source of healing power, the num energy, is more powerful the more it is shared.

Modern Magic in Japanese New Religions

*I*n Japan, new forms of healing and worship bring trance mechanisms together with the Japanese cultural heritage to heal patients suffering from what we would call psychosomatic illnesses. These New Religions developed in response to new life situations, particularly in response to the new illnesses and anxieties felt by many newly urban Japanese. Those millions of Japanese who have moved into cities since the 1950s have found themselves cut off from their accustomed places for ritual practice and sources of religious strength. They also found themselves living in a radically new era, with new kinds of pressures on the job and at home.

The New Religions range from the nationally important Soka Gakkai, with its millions of adherents, its own newspaper and university, and its strong ties to a major political party, the Komeito, to smaller sects and cults. Between 10 percent and 30 percent of Japanese are estimated to follow one of the New Religions. But these New Religions and their healing practices draw on elements from Japan's older religious traditions.

One such religion, studied by Winston Davis (1980), is Mahikari, meaning "True Light." It was founded in 1959 when a man of lower-class origins in Tokyo recovered from illness and debt and received a revelation from God that he was to change his name and bring light and health to the people of Japan. This man, now known as Okada Kotama, began to heal people through the use of amulets (a method he had learned from another group), and the sect grew rapidly in popularity. By the late 1970s Mahikari had more than 150 dojos (buildings for practicing spiritual disciplines) and somewhere between 50,000 and 100,000 active members. Close to half a million had received its amulet.

Purification and Apocalypse

The major activity engaged in by people who join Mahikari is called "okiyome" (purification). The process of okiyome is designed to rid the body of spirits that have possessed it. These spirits may be those of ancestors, or of other people, or of animals, especially foxes and badgers. The process involves divination and then exorcism of the spirit.

People generally come to be healed at Mahikari because of a physical complaint, the roots of which are often psychosomatic: cramps, back pains, headaches, and so forth. In their theory of causes of these illnesses, the healers join physical and psychic explanations. Consider one account of illness:

"There is much poison around us," said a Mahikari teacher. *(Indeed, in the main river in the city where Davis studied Mahikari, fish introduced to the river die within 3 minutes from industrial toxins!)* *"We eat poisoned food and the poisons build up inside and cause illnesses. But,"* he then asked, *"why did we eat the poison? Or, given that bacteria can be carried in food and then eaten by us, what led us to eat the infected food?"*

The Mahikari world view offers to supplement the scientific world view by bringing the laws of natural cause and effect down to the level of the individual and his or her suffering.

The answer to our suffering is that we are possessed by spirits. Indeed, according to Mahikari, nearly all illnesses are caused by spirits. Each person has an astral spirit, which must burn off its impurities on the astral plane. (Here we see echoes from Buddhism of the planes of existence and the idea of karma.) Burning off impurities is not fun, and many of these astral spirits seek refuge in humans or torment humans for one reason or another.

The power to exorcise spirits derives ultimately from the High God, "Su-God," and also from a Shinto god he created, called Miroku, identified with the bodhisattva figure Maitreya, here called the "Buddha of the Future." Mahikari sees itself as a supplement to other religions. It recognizes that all religions worship lower deities and prophets created by Su-God; some of them have lost their healing powers, however, which Mahikari offers to restore.

The Mahikari ideology also places the individual's suffering on a grand world-historical plane. In its version of history, mankind once was united on the lost continent of Mu, where people existed in five colors. The yellow people were dominant, and within the yellow group, the Japanese. Mu had all the technological advancements of today: telephones, airplanes, and so forth. It was ruined when the races began to inter-marry. The present world then developed, but is about to be destroyed.

This story combines an apocalyptic vision of coming disaster with a way out. Because of human wickedness, Su-God has recently put strict gods in power, and signs of this change are to be seen in recent earthquakes, droughts, and so forth. Humankind is to be subjected to even greater torments, and only those possessing the amulets of Mahikari will be saved, to become the "seed people" of the next era.

These kinds of disaster-plus-solution texts appear throughout human history and are often called "millenarian movements". Each of these movements appropriates a set of already widely accepted ideas and traditions—for example, the role of a Buddha or Christ in ensuring salvation—and harnesses them to a small-scale organization, to which are attracted people looking for spiritual guidance or discipline or health. These movements take the promise of salvation seriously, and set out to get it here and now.

Amulets and Ancestors

Consider in greater detail how healing works for Mahikari adherents. People come to the sect to be healed; they learn why they suffer; and the ideas they learn are an important part of the healing process. They learn that their souls are polluted by spirits and by material pollution and that Mahikari offers them both a temporary, personal solution through healing and a way to prepare for future destruction through continued membership in the sect. People are satisfied that they understand why things have happened to them, that it is not their own fault, and that they can do something about them.

The healers diagnose the patient's ills by detecting the auras around their bodies. Bodies give off electromagnetic waves, they are told, and the shape of these waves can be detected by an "aura meter." Auras come in different shapes and colors. Healers can also detect spirits around the body. But the main activity of the healer is to channel energy into the body that will heal and also will ferret out spirits bothering the patient.

The healer wears an amulet, a small locket worn on a chain, with a piece of paper inside that has a symbol written on it. This locket is "plugged in" through the central Mahikari organization to God—indeed, the objective properties of the amulet are explained in ways that draw on electric and electronic imagery. If the amulet gets wet it may disconnect, healers are told, and apology money must be paid to Mahikari for it to be reconnected. Monthly dues must be paid, which are offered to Su-God "to keep the line connected for the next month."

The healer, wearing the amulet, raises his or her hands over the patient's body, concentrating rays from God on the body. The healer begins with the patient's "primary soul" and then looks for parts of the body that seem to need attention, perhaps massaging the body to detect such parts. The healing power of okiyome also works for inanimate objects, such as automobiles or movie projectors. (Of those people belonging to Mahikari who were surveyed, 42 percent had repaired their television sets with okiyome; 29 percent had used it to fix their wristwatches.)

In the case of people, spirits usually are responsible for their ailments. The healer must find out the identity of the spirit and then convince it to leave the patient. The patient must enter a state of trance. The healer chants over him or her, and the patient usually begins to move and cry out in ways indicative of the spirit's identity. The patient's hand movements may be characteristic of a particular animal (serpentine movements indicate a snake, and so on). Or the patient may write out words or names on a tablet.

But the healer usually talks to the spirit as well, asking it if it is human, when it died, and, most importantly, why it is possessing the person. The healer scolds the spirit: "Go back to the other world and leave her in peace."

The most common explanation of specific ailments involves relationships with ancestors. Events may have caused an ancestor's spirit to possess you, for one of two reasons. First, you may have neglected the altar of the ancestors in your house. One man's ancestor came back to possess him because the altar was on a filing cabinet and the spirit was disturbed by the noise. In the Mahikari sect people study proper altar care to avoid these problems. Nothing must be above it (so it must occupy the top story of the house), its flowers must be arranged properly, and it must have proper lacquered tablets and be supplied with food every day. Recall that in rural society the altar was the site of the protective household god, and so the anxiety of ordinary people about neglected altars makes sense.

Second, events that happened to ancestors, or to yourself in an earlier life, may have caused your misfortune and caused you to be possessed by an ancestral spirit.

Healers draw on the logic of karma from Buddhism to explain how this works. One woman had been the wife of a warrior (samurai) in a previous incarnation, and when she married he grew jealous and came to bother her. Samurai often appear as the ancestors responsible for possession because they tended to commit all sorts of bad deeds and would be expected to bring misfortune.

But sometimes another kind of spirit is involved: that of a fox or snake, for example. Here, too, there is an explanation of what event caused the spirit to possess the person. One man with cancer of the face was found to be possessed by the spirit of a snake. When he was a boy he had cut off the head of a snake, and the spirit had chosen appropriate revenge.

Trance Psychology

Central to the patient's experience of being healed is the state of trance into which he or she enters. Trance, like any other altered state of consciousness, begins when one dissociates, or withdraws from ordinary states of consciousness (Davis 1980, 132–144). We have all experienced dissociation during daydreaming, when different, sometimes odd thoughts and images wander into one's consciousness. But in the kind of structured trance settings found in Mahikari or elsewhere the patient has been trained to expect certain specific symbols, images, or actions to emerge. Mahikari patients study books of spirit images beforehand; some also rehearse the hand movements of different spirits. They then *project* their fears, anger, sadness, or specific problems onto the symbols that have been made available to them. They respond to questions posed to them about ancestors or animals, and can introduce into their answers their own life problems. Finally comes the moment of release, or catharsis, when the person collapses onto the floor and experiences a strong feeling of relief. (Aristotle used "catharsis" to refer to the moment in a drama when pent-up emotions in the audience are released.)

The psychology of the trance-healing session is not specifically Japanese; Felicitas Goodman (1988) documents trance and possession worldwide. Its particular form in Japan draws on older culturally specific practices, however. One is the duet form of the healing: the process always involves an exorciser and a subject, who then exchange roles (rather than, for example, a single healer and many patients). This duet form is found in much older spirit possession–healing cults in Japan and is familiar to patients. It is especially effective in the way it taps the Japanese emotion of "dependence" on another, *amae.* This emotional relation has its prototype in the dependence of a child on his or her mother, and underlies relations to teachers, employers, and, in the past, the emperor. When the emperor was demoted to the role of ordinary human and state symbol after World War II, psychiatrists (Doi 1986) noted that some people became depressed by the loss of a pole for their dependence emotions.

The healing session helps to draw out longings for someone to depend on, in this specific, highly charged sense, and also longings to be depended on. The alternation of roles allows the person who is missing these roles in everyday life to better assume them. For example, one housewife had become so concerned about pollution in food that she could not bring herself to cook for her family. She then became immobilized out of guilt for not doing so, for no longer being depended on. These feelings emerged during trance, and repeated sessions gave her a way to speak these feelings as well as a new setting for dependence–role playing.

Mahikari combines universal psychosocial processes (such as trance) with culturally specific features (such as the focus on ancestors). Simply by participating in a group, regardless of its content, some people gain a stronger sense of the value of their lives. Members also have a legitimate reason to meddle in other people's lives. But, remembering Malinowski, we might pay special attention to the way the process adds confidence and certainty to the making of difficult decisions.

Take the case of Winston Davis's teacher, Yoshida Sensei, and his wife (Davis 1980, 52–63). Yoshida's father had died in the hospital, even though he had asked his son to take him home to die. Several years later, their daughter died in the same hospital. Later, Yoshida's mother died of a stomach ailment, and Yoshida himself developed ulcers. They joined Mahikari and began to be possessed by a number of ancestors and relatives, and through the exorcism procedure learned the causes of their various misfortunes.

Yoshida's father appeared in the form of a badger. He complained of dying in the hospital and said he had caused the daughter's death as revenge, and added his regret that Yoshida had sold off their land. (Yoshida remembered that he had had trouble selling the land and now knew that his father was behind these troubles.) Yoshida taught his father that he must be a spirit and not trouble them in the earthly world: "Apologize to God and return to the astral world to continue your austerities," he demanded. His father's spirit wept at this. They then agreed that Yoshida could sell some of the land, since it was difficult to farm and surrounded by buildings, as long as he bought some other land as a hedge against inflation. After that the father appeared as a human spirit; he had progressed up the spiritual ladder.

The process addressed the several sources of guilt faced by Yoshida and his wife, explained the series of illnesses, and finally exorcised the guilt by leading Yoshida through a series of emotionally charged sessions. Finally, it legitimated his further action, allowing him to sell off land with a clear conscience.

Who Joins the New Religions?

Women make up 60 percent of the participants in Mahikari; many of these women are unmarried and in the traumatic period after high school during which society views them as in transition to their next state, marriage. Employers still see most women as temporary employees, biding time until marriage. But some women either wish to pursue careers or have not found suitable husbands, and many psychosomatic illnesses occur then.

Healing can explain why marriage is difficult, perhaps because of possession by a jealous husband from a past life, and can also provide an outlet for repressed emotions and desires. Consider several cases discussed by Winston Davis (1980, 161–200). Tanio lived in fear of men. Her own father was often drunk and violent, and she was raised by her mother. In trance the spirit possessing her declared herself to be that of a woman whose husband she stole in an earlier life. Nakata never married because, trance revealed, she was possessed by spirits of aborted children. Eiko was happily married but her family resisted her joining Mahikari. Her own ancestors torment her whenever she worships her husband's ancestors. (Here emerged the classic problem of changing ancestral allegiances.)

These women and men found power in an environment of their own general powerlessness. Inside the sect people experience possession and curing. But outside, as well, they experience miracles. Only 12 of 688 members interviewed said they did not experience such miracles. They found social status within the group. And they found an ideology that explained much of what was happening around them, gave them a way to muddle through it, and promised future salvation.

Whatever we might think about these groups, they are a response to urban ills. Some of them are clearly destructive (and some think even Mahikari to be so). In March 1995, canisters containing the nerve gas sarin exploded in a Tokyo subway, killing 10 and injuring more than 5,000, and the attack was linked to the sect Aum Shinrikyo. Aum Shinrikyo's leader, Shoko Asahara, preaches much the same apocalyptic vision as does Mahikari's Okada Kotama. Aum hands out battery-powered headgear to followers so that they may communicate directly with their leader. (The headgear also attracts recruits from the sciences.) Its teachings combine Buddhism and Hinduism—especially the god of destruction, Shiva. Aum followers had to renounce ties with the outside world and donate all their goods to the cult (Sayle 1996).

The history of state Shinto and its ties to militarism have made the Japanese state very wary of interfering in these sects, even when evidence of criminal actions emerges. In 1989 Asahara was named responsible for killing a lawyer helping to return children kidnapped by the sect. And yet Aum was recognized as a religious body the same year and no steps were taken against its leader. One legacy of state Shinto is thus an extraordinarily lenient attitude toward the new sects.

Magic and Religion

Those practices that we might call "magic" have differing relationships to religion. Some, such as baseball practices, are not based on any belief system whatsoever. Others, such as Trobriand spells, do imply beliefs in spirits but little else. Still other practices, such as healing in Japan, Brazil, and Malaya or among the Cuna of Panama, draw on extensive bodies of knowledge about how spirits work. In all cases some of the older insights by Frazer and Malinowski about the logic and functions of magic can still help us understand why people are attracted to certain practices. Malinowski's notion that all people use science plus magic, with the latter added on to the former, continues to make sense. The forms of magic differ greatly: memorized spells, possession and exorcism, narratives about creation or battles, or about God or the effectiveness of medicine. But each such practice gives the person a sense of control, or understanding, or certainty greater than what was enjoyed before the event. Each practice also seems to reduce anxiety (although once it is relied on, its absence may create anxiety).

These features of "magical" practices all concern their effects. To understand their contents and why Japanese, Brazilians, and Cuna do things differently, we have explored the linkages between each practice and the dominant forms and motifs of the culture in which it is found. Recall the paths taken by healers. Cuna healers seek to reduce a woman's pain by telling a story of battles; Malay healers, a story about cosmic harmony; U.S. healers, a story about breathing techniques and medicines. Japanese healers draw on ideas about the ever-watchful ancestors, the culture form of the duet, and Buddhist religious traditions to construct a convincing combination of texts and practices.

Institutions built on notions of magic can take on functions of healing, religion, and even community. Their practices can provide confidence insofar as they fit general cultural expectations, and this confidence and assurance can cause physical changes in a patient. For better or worse, they can furnish the basis for close-knit relationships in a disorganized world. Far from being merely a set of mistaken ideas, magic continues to be a powerful force in the real world.

7 Science and Religion

*A*s two distinct ways of looking at the world, religion and science could be thought of as one encompassing the other (by explaining the other, or by its innate superiority), or as distinct, albeit perhaps overlapping, ways of knowing. The issue is not new—Galileo's defiance, Newton's astrology, Einstein's rational God—and indeed it does not seem to be easily resolved. In the United States the arguments are perhaps hottest in education—Darwin versus Creation, or maybe Intelligent Design—but here and there appear efforts to let one calmly inform the other. The $1.5 Templeton Prize for contributions to dialogues between religion and science is only the most visible of these efforts.

What can anthropology contribute to reasoned debate? It can broaden the terms of the debate, into a more general examination of how people can creatively draw on two or more distinct ways of knowing. Humans always have relied on the evidence of their own two eyes plus something else—think of the Trobrianders use of practical knowledge plus magic. Together with other social and human science, anthropology also can study natural science as a social enterprise, one involving social networks of scientists and international networks of control (Hayden 2003).

Anthropology also can look at why religious claims can be so powerful, as this volume does to a small degree. We have already considered the powerful evidence that magic and healing through religion seem to work, in the sense that they appeal to people. What can science say about these practices? Can science say anything about the nature of religious belief itself? And, conversely, how can people who believe in religious narratives of creation effectively teach a form of science that emphasizes the natural, evolutionary origins of all life?

Does Prayer Heal?

*T*he medical effects of religious practices have come in for a great deal of scientific study in the past decade. The claims and studies bear on two separate questions: What are the health effects when a patient prays, attends church, thanks or blames God, and so forth? And what are the effects, if any, of "intercessory prayer," meaning prayer by someone else for the patient. Although these two practices often are mixed together in articles, they imply two quite distinct mechanisms. If the first set of practices leads to significantly better health, the results can be attributed to a range of psychophysiological mechanisms—for example, the influence of confidence and optimism on the immune system, in essence the same as a "placebo effect." If intercessory prayer leads to greater health, the results are attributed to God.

A number of scientific studies of Christians in the United States support the claim that praying, believing in God, and attending church make people healthier and longer-lived than people who do not practice a religion. Studies have been done on large samples, often balanced between white and black Americans. Some studies focus on patients and their post-operative outcomes, others on blood pressure levels, and still others on mortality rates in the general population. Current research reports from mainstream medical journals are listed on the Duke University Center for the Study of Religion/Spirituality and Health (*www.dukespiritualityandhealth.org/recentreports.html*). In one National Institutes of Health–funded study (Helm et al. 2000), over 3,000 North Carolina adults were surveyed in 1986 and then monitored over the next six years (1986–1992). The researchers controlled for social support and health behaviors, and found that lack of private religious activity continued to predict a 47 percent greater risk of dying.

Religiosity does not necessarily promote health, however; more important seems to be the relatively positive or negative way U.S. Christians approach a relationship to God. One group of researchers (Pargament et al. 2001) studied what they called "negative religious coping" among black and white patients, a concept that they attributed to patients who wondered whether God had abandoned them, felt punished by God for their lack of devotion, or decided the Devil had made them ill. People who believed these statements experienced 19 percent to 28 percent greater mortality during the two-year period following hospital discharge. Positive religious coping, however, has consistently been shown to promote mental and physical health (for example, Koenig et al. 1992). Frequency of church attendance is a powerful predictor of health in many of these studies, for example, of a strong immune system, indicated by low levels of plasma interleukin-6, an immune system messenger that appears in higher levels among people with chronic illness (Koenig et al. 1997).

Although some of these studies attempt to control for the amount of social support the study subjects enjoyed, it also seems that the social side of church attendance contributes to the positive effects of religion on health. The role of organized religion in offering solace during illness may be particularly important in the contemporary United States, given the mobility of its residents and the tendency to rely on institutions for support for elderly relatives. Prayer also "gives patients something to do so that they don't feel as helpless," notes Harold G. Koenig (2002), one of the Duke investigators. Prayer also may lead to greater relaxation that reduces muscle tension (ibid.).

Even within the medical community, debate has arisen about the mechanisms or pathways that link prayer to health. Writing to comment on Koenig's analysis quoted here, a physician and theologian stated that it was the "spirit of God" that provided the healing because of the patient's prayer (Flynn and Fulton 2002). In so doing, they implicitly link prayer by patients to prayer by others on behalf of patients, or "intercessory prayer," prayer to God to intercede on someone else's behalf.

A small number of medical researchers have designed studies to test the idea that if a team of "intercessors" prays for patients, patients will do better than will patients not receiving prayer from the team. These studies have been controlled, in that patients were assigned in random or near-random fashion either to a prayer-receiving group or to a non-prayer-receiving group, as well as "double-blind," meaning that neither the patients nor the medical personnel knew which patients were in which group.

In one such study, conducted in a coronary care unit in Kansas City, about 1,000 patients were assigned to the two groups (Harris et al. 1999). Fifteen prayer teams of five people each were asked to pray for patients identified by name. Intercessors all agreed to the statement that God "is responsive to prayers for healing made on behalf of the sick," that is, that God intercedes. The intercessors prayed for 28 days for each patient (a time chosen to cover nearly all patients' hospital stays). The researchers then faced the problem of how to measure outcomes. Because the prayers were for a general speedy and complete recovery, they needed a measure of overall goodness of outcome. They devised a scoring system, on which complications added points: the higher the score, the worse the outcome. They then calculated the association between prayer and outcome, using t tests and accepting $P<.05$ as significant for most tests. Both decisions follow accepted procedures, but were the source of much critique afterwards, as we shall see.

The investigators found an 11 percent reduction in the outcome score for patients who had received prayer, with $P=.04$, thus meeting their conditions for significance. The length of stay was not different between the two groups; the study thus agreed with earlier similar studies. The investigators were able to gain exemption from hospital Internal Review Board (IRB) rules for informed consent on the grounds that simply knowing of the study might create anxiety about not being treated with prayer, and because no clear harm could result from no prayer. They note that because half the patients stated a religious preference, there likely was "background prayer noise" caused by relatives praying for control-group patients, so that the study measured the effects of "supplementary intercessory prayer."

How could such prayer work? The study's authors refrain from suggesting mechanisms: it could be God, or it could be unknown physical forces caused by prayer. They defend themselves against the (correctly) anticipated charges of studying relationships without proposing causal mechanisms by citing the pathbreaking clinical trials conducted by James Lind in 1753 aboard the HMS Salisbury, which determined that eating lemons or limes cured sailors of scurvy. He did not know why this was so, they state, but his observations were sound. Cautiously, they conclude: "It was intercessory prayer, not the existence of God, that was tested here."

Well, as one might imagine, a storm of protest appeared in this and other journals. Some questioned details of the study; others stated that $P=.04$ is more acceptable if a causal mechanism is known or proposed than otherwise (a point made widely in the social sciences as well); most argued that science and faith were two different kinds of knowledge and should be kept that way. A few entered into the theological implications of such a study: if God indeed favors people for whom strangers choose to pray, over others, then is he a capricious rather than an all-loving God? (You can continue to follow the thread of these debates on: *http://archinte.ama-assn.org.*)

The cautious entry of medical science into these waters threatens some because it could legitimate studies that show other kinds of practices to have medical effects despite the absence of known causal mechanisms: homeopathic medicine, which features potions containing minute traces of supposedly effective elements, is the most obvious candidate. Other physicians find the mixing of science and religion ipso facto distasteful. Still others find it enormously welcome that they can speak with patients about the patients' religious beliefs and practices—indeed, most of the medical centers or institutes devoted to religion and healing focus on clinical care and not scientific research.

Mapping the Brain

Another approach from medical science to studying religious experience has been by way of brain mapping rather than experiments. Much of this research has focused on determining how the brain state correlates to states of calm achieved through meditation. People who become adept at meditation report common themes, among them a sense of great calmness, a diminishing of the boundaries between the self and other, and a sense of union with the universe or with God.

Andrew Newberg and his colleagues (Newberg, D'Aquili, and Rause 2001) have used single photon emission computed tomography (SPECT) to measure the blood flow patterns in the brains of Tibetan monks during meditation and Fransiscan nuns while in prayer. The subjects were instructed to give a simple hand signal at the peak of their meditative state. At this signal, a radioactive marker was released into the bloodstream. As the marker passed through the brain, images of the peak moment's effects on the brain were captured.

Most often, the measurements showed marked changes in brain activity during meditation or prayer, and these changes were related to the subjective changes reported by the subjects. In particular, the meditation affected the posterior section of the parietal lobe in the cerebral cortex, an area that receives input from several senses and produces the experience of a three-dimensional self oriented in space. Normally this area exhibits extremely high degrees of activity. However, at the peak moments it experienced very low activity levels, as indicated by reduced blood flow. These were precisely the moments that the monks and nuns said were characterized by the sense of a diminished self or a union with God.

Narratives and Pain Relief

*M*ore generally, stories and activities that a patient believes have a beneficial effect may have that effect, either through the calming effects of the storytelling, or the belief that the story or practice has a direct relationship to healing, or merely because of the presence of a medical helper.

Giving Birth in Panama and Malaysia

Consider two examples of birthing magic, one from Panama and one from Malaysia. In both, midwives and shamans help the mother in moving the baby down the birth canal and out into the world. But they do so by drawing on very different sets of images and values. Cuna society, in Panama, holds high the culture of heroes and battles (Lévi-Strauss 1963b). There, a shaman, who can be possessed by spirits, sings to help child-birth. He sings a story of how Muu, the spirit that forms the fetus, has exceeded her usual domain and captured the woman's soul, thereby preventing her from moving the baby down the birth canal. The shaman must carve small figurines, the spirits of which he then leads up the birth canal to overcome wild beasts and defeat Muu and her allies. In his song the shaman describes in painstaking detail the events leading up to his own arrival at the woman's house—the woman experiencing pain, the midwife coming to call him, his own arrival—and then the journey of the friendly spirits. The journey is in the same concrete detail as the mundane events and, in Claude Lévi-Strauss's analysis, the woman is thus likely made to feel the entry of the spirits as real. She now can iden-tify her pain with specific, well-described animals and spirits lodged in her vagina. The detail makes the journey psychologically real to the woman in pain, giving her a lan-guage for her pain and difficulties, organizing her perceptions and feelings.

Now contrast the chants recited by a healer in a Malay village studied by Carol Laderman (1983). As with the Cuna, the ritual specialist only intervenes when the mid-wife can no longer cope with the difficult birth. Malinowski's idea that most people work on a commonsense basis until they reach the limits of their capacities and knowl-edge, and only then reach for magic to extend their grasp, thus once again seems to work well. The specialist, called a "bomoh," recites a story about God's creation of the world and of the first couple, and then about the creation of the individual human. These sto-ries follow generally available Muslim lines. They provide a story for the woman that takes place out of ordinary time, placing the woman's suffering also out of ordinary time and giving it a sense of order, naturalness, and harmony. Just as Cuna culture highlights battle, Malay culture stresses the importance of harmony and control.

Even if the woman does not hear every detail of the story, women do know the story's general outline beforehand, says Laderman, and are soothed by its familiar refer-ences to the creation story, listing of prophets and mythological figures, and litany of the sequence of days leading to birth.

The story responds to a general cultural emphasis on harmony with the universe. But what happens in the individual? Drawing on work in U.S. hospitals as well as Malaysia, Laderman argues that the psychological response to hearing the story creates a biological response, producing endorphins that reduce pain and also reduce anxiety. Endorphins are chemicals found in several areas of the brain, which appear to be responsible for "placebo effect" pain reduction. Not only do these effects benefit the mother, but because anxiety can prevent proper cervical dilation, the reduction of anx-iety may directly lead to more productive contractions, and a quicker, easier birth.

Of course, the ways in which imagery, narratives, beliefs, and emotions affect bodily states, from levels of pain tolerance to changes in the immune system, is a topic under considerable current research. On the one hand, fear can lead to death, as Walter Cannon (1942) observed; more recent research suggests that the "fight or flight" adrenaline response induced by fear, though useful in the short term, is debilitating over longer periods, weakening the heart and the immune system. On the other hand, dissociation (the mechanism involved in trance and hypnosis) and positive imagery reduce pain levels. Just how "magic"—and the many other curing techniques now used in the United States and therefore not so labeled—works on the nervous and immune systems is far from being understood, but it is now widely accepted that such mechanisms do exist.

The "placebo effect" is surely part of the explanation for a number of approaches to curing. Sometimes it is even recognized by practitioners, as in the following case. Americans dramatically increased their interest in voodoo in the 2000s. In New Orleans, the grave of a nineteenth-century "voodoo queen," Marie Laveau, has become one of the most visited graves in the United States (Kinzer 2003). Laveau was a free woman of mixed Native American, African, and European descent, and she has come to stand for a mixed heritage of religion, power, and geographical roots similar to that of Brazilian Candomble. As in the Brazilian case, many adherents profess themselves Catholics, and one practitioner stated that Catholic priests come to him for help. Why this recent rise in popularity? Some ascribe it to post–9/11 searchings for meaning; others to the constantly shifting search for healing and power. One voodoo priest working in New Orleans for over 20 years said that he performed ceremonies to help people but did not know how they worked. "Have you heard of the placebo effect?" he said (Kinzer 2003).

Does Evolution Explain Religion?

*I*n recent years, some evolutionary anthropologists and psychologists have argued that certain tendencies in how we react to the world are the result of adaptations, or perhaps the accidental by-products of other adaptations. Among those adaptations relevant to explaining religious beliefs are the tendencies to impute agency to beings and to impute cause-and-effect relations to events observed in the world. When we are saved from a flood, we look for cause, and we look for an agentive cause, meaning action by an active being of some sort, rather than just impersonal forces. We also become rather good at modeling what other people are thinking, rather than merely assuming that they think what we do. These human tendencies may have originated as adaptive responses to the conditions of early life—assuming that a quick movement in the grass was made by a predator may make us more able to escape being eaten, and who cares if we are wrong most of the time? It is easy to see how one could argue that these responses then gave rise to ideas not themselves adaptive—about unseen agency responsible for death and accidents, for example.

Yet others hold that this line of reasoning could explain virtually any sort of ideas about agents and beings, and that we have to explain not just why we have religious ideas, but why we have *these* ideas and not another possible set. For example, Pascal Boyer (2001) suggests that answers will come from knowledge about the ways our minds work. Over the long haul of human experience, he continues, humans would have proposed lots of ideas about spirits, unseen lands, and mystical causation. Human minds would have found some of these ideas attractive, useful, and relevant to everyday social life, and others much less so. They would have retained the former and discarded the latter. In other words, religions are the ways they are because of selection processes, similar in logic (though not in the precise mechanisms) to those of natural selection in the biological realm.

The selectionist argument begins by noting that spirits resemble humans, except for a small number of differences. For example, consider the following possible ideas about spirits proposed by Boyer (2001, 64–67):

(1) There is only one God! He is omnipotent. But He only exists on Wednesdays.
(2) The spirits will punish you if you do what they want.
(3) Some people get old and one day they stop breathing and die and that's that.
(4) Dead men do not talk (nor walk).
(5) There is only one God! He knows everything we do.
(6) We pray to this statue because it listens to our prayers and helps us get what we want.

Boyer points out that everyone reading this list has an intuition that the first two propositions are bad candidates for religious ideas even though they are about spirits and God; the next two are also bad candidates because they are banal; and the remaining two are good candidates. Why do we have these intuitions? What precisely is it about them that makes the first two pairs not work and the third pair work as candidates for religious principles? It cannot be that religious ideas are strange or that they "transcend experience," because the first two statements also do that, and in any case the people who do pray to statues would say that (6) is very much part of their experience.

Boyer argues that religious representations always preserve certain of our expectations about how the world works, and they violate certain, quite specific other ones. In particular, they preserve expectations about the kind of object the religious object is. The statue that listens is a statue in all respects (it was made by someone, could be destroyed, does not multiply on its own), except that it also can listen to people praying and then relay that information somewhere (or directly grant requests). Gods and spirits are like human beings except that they have special cognitive powers (such as knowing everything that happens) or other powers (such as superhuman strength or speed).

These ideas correspond to the way we think about the world generally. We know the world as consisting of certain kinds of things: persons; artifacts ("things that are made"); animals; trees, and so on. We know many features of each kind. Animals are born and they die; they reproduce; they eat. Artifacts do none of those things; they are made. Each of these kinds has a number of subkinds (artifacts made of wood, or of paper, etc.; animals that are mammals; those that are fish, and so on). These kinds serve as templates for making sense of the world as we learn more about it. When we learn of a new object in the world, a new subkind—say, a human with extraordinary strength, or a two-headed cow—we are able to infer (to assume, or postulate) a lot about that new object, based on our "template knowledge." We infer from the fact that the two-headed object is a kind of cow that it will have the usual properties of animals, and indeed of cows: that it will reproduce, live and die, eat, and so forth.

Religious ideas add new objects to our list of what there is, and we understand them by associating them with a particular template. If a spirit or god is a kind of person, but with some unusual characteristics, then saying that it can travel with great speed still allows us to infer a great many other things about that spirit: that it remembers things, that it exists in a continual manner, that it perceives things, and so forth. But to say that it only exists on Wednesdays frustrates our normal processes of inference. Could it then remember, or even exist in any sense we can understand? Experimental evidence confirms the claim that ideas like a "Wednesday-only god" are relatively difficult for subjects to recall, whereas all-powerful or all-knowing gods are not.

The reasons why proposition (2) fails as a religious idea are a bit different; they have to do with the processes by which ideas are adopted and transmitted across generations. We could certainly imagine especially sadistic spirits telling us to do things and then punishing us for doing them, but why would we adopt and transmit such an idea? What humans in fact do, claim Boyer and others, is to work from our moral intuitions, which recent work in developmental psychology show to be quite basic. "Basic" here means that children and adults think of some actions as being right or wrong in themselves. Boyer argues that we have developed these intuitions as predispositions toward cooperation. For example, we feel outraged when people break in line, even if it is not our line, because they have violated certain rules of social cooperation.

Boyer (2001, 237–240) contends that we then impute moral opinions similar to these intuitions to gods and spirits. We interact with them, and treat their intuitions as similar to ours. We also resent spirits in ways similar to the ways we resent humans. For example, witches may be seen as models of how one should not behave, as beings who act on jealousy, who take but never give, and so on.

This idea, that it is our social lives as well as our minds' mechanisms that shape our religious representations, also helps explain other ways we refer to spirits and gods in practice. We may say that God is omnipotent or that he knows everything, but in practice we represent such beings as using their powers in ways that are most relevant to us. People do not think of God as knowing the contents of all the refrigerators in the world at all times, although that is implied by "all-knowing" (Boyer 2000, 207). Rather, people think of God as knowing our thoughts, or rather those among our thoughts that are relevant to social interaction such as lies, desires, and intents. In other words, God (and gods and spirits generally) know the same sorts of things that we ourselves take into account when we act in society, when we judge the actions of others, and when we judge our own conduct.

This account of religion, then, is based on certain hypotheses about what we are most likely to acquire as children, and pass on to others when we are adults. The major mechanism proposed in this account is what we can call selective retention, that is, selecting some of the ideas floating around in a society for transmission to the next generation. The account is analogous to that proposed by Charles Darwin in order to explain the diversity of species and, like Darwin's, it depends on there being a source of variation. In accounts of biological evolution the variation comes from mutations, changes in the genetic code from one generation to the next. In accounts of cultural evolution the variation could come from a number of sources, including error in transmitting ideas (think of the "telephone game"), adaptive pressures, and sheer human inventiveness.

Can Creationists Teach Evolution?

Of course it is just this sort of argument, explaining religion in Darwinian terms, that is most likely to pique believers in religion who are opposed to Darwin's accounts of anything. The battle between creationism and science is an old one, which I will not rehearse here. Rather, I wish to ask if it is possible for creationists to teach evolutionary biology?

Wheaton College in Illinois has become a visible experiment concerning this question, particularly since PBS aired a documentary on the school as part of its series on evolution. Wheaton is an evangelical college, which maintains a certain degree of conformity to its beliefs. In 2004, a philosophy professor was dismissed when he converted to Catholicism. And yet Wheaton maintains high academic standards in all fields, including the natural sciences, sending many students on to earn doctoral degrees from mainstream universities.

At Wheaton, biology is taught by nationally recognized professors, who emphasize evolutionary processes among their areas of teaching and research. On her Web site, Professor Shawn McCafferty says that her "primary field of interest in science falls under the broad heading of Evolutionary Biology" and that her work runs "from bacteria to humans." Professor Betsey Dyer describes her studies of cell evolution and genomics.

Although I do not know how these two professors teach their subject, at least some teachers at Wheaton combine the teaching of evolution with evangelical beliefs by using a certain version of intelligent design (ID). A PowerPoint presentation for a Wheaton biology class (www.wheaton.edu/Biology/faculty/ppp/powerpoints/Scsem06ID.ppt) emphasizes that ID is "*not* primarily an apologetic tool . . . *not* young earth creationism . . . *not* against micro-evolution," but that it offers an explanation that is more convincing than the random events put forward by "neo-Darwinian theory." The presentation advocates punctuated changes in evolution, with the Cambrian Explosion as an example, and points, as all ID arguments do, to "irreducible complexities" in biological processes.

The presentation clearly and emphatically distinguishes *this* ID approach from others that would clearly fall outside the bounds of scientific knowledge. Some creationists are also Biblical literalists, for whom a day is a day, and for them the earth is only thousands of years old (young earth creationism). Others argue that any claims that change is governed by evolutionary processes contradict God's word (against microevolution). But this ID approach accepts both microevolution and an old earth. It focuses on the two positive claims put forward by ID that are least immediately vulnerable to scientific disconfirmation: that change occurred in quick flashes of time, and that the complexity of some life organisms defies arguments from chance. The latter appeals to common sense—how could the eye have arisen out of random events?—while the former cites such mysteries as the Cambrian Explosion of new life forms (which was partially responsible for scientific "punctuated evolution" theories).

Other narrative strategies explained to me by teachers included the argument that the creation of the first humans by God consisted mainly of granting a human soul to a biological creature. This creature itself may have been the product of evolutionary processes, but these were not processes of *human* evolution. Humanity was created by God; evolution produced changes in physical form.

Now, the "Wheaton position" arouses the ire of those who would remain literalists. The most vehement attacks by ardent creationists are reserved for those who say that there can be compromises, whereby one not only teaches evolution but also acknowledges that God created humans. Wheaton College became the most visible target in these attacks when in 2001 the Public Broadcasting System aired a documentary on the school as part of its series on evolution. One literalist who became deeply involved in the attack was Ken Ham of the organization *Answers in Genesis*. Ham was interviewed on the PBS program and objected to Wheaton's approach. Ham, and Answers in Genesis (or AiG as they portray themselves), indeed pay a great deal of attention to the literal truth of Genesis, and of the Bible in general, and oppose treating it as "poetry" or "literature," as when Wheaton professors take "one day" in the Genesis account of creation to mean a longer period of time.

AiG also turns against Wheaton College for the ways in which its faculty and students portrayed Biblical knowledge on the program (www.answersingenesis.org/ pbs_nova/0928ep7.asp). One contributor to the site puts the question succinctly, in an answer to Wheaton students who defend their instructors as good evangelicals: "Is the Bible Wheaton's final authority in matters of *history* or is that history divorced from things like salvation, morality, faith, etc?" Herein lies the objection to "compromise": once a teacher allows evidence that contradicts Biblical teachings to have equal standing to the Biblical evidence, he or she is compelled to treat the Biblical passages in a nonliteral way, for example regarding the age of the earth. This step ultimately destroys the authority of the Bible. And it is unnecessary: yes, teach evolution, says AiG, but: "fact is, particles-to-people evolution is irrelevant to real experimental biology." In the Amazon.com site for the PBS film, students reacted to the issue of compromise. Some found that solution satisfying, whereas others stated that you could not be a Christian and yet believe in evolution.

There is a point to the critique. Wheaton's *Statement of Faith* states that "the scriptures of the Old and New Testaments are verbally inspired by Jesus Christ and inerrant in the original writing, so that they are fully trustworthy and of supreme and final authority in all they say." It also says that "we believe that God directly created Adam and Eve, the historical parents of the entire human race; and that they were created in His own image, distinct from all other living creatures, and in a state of original righteousness." Wheaton requires its faculty members to sign onto its *Statement of Faith*.

Answers in Genesis now has its own way of presenting its views to a broad public, in the form of the Creation Museum, which opened in Kentucky on May 28, 2007. A series of rooms in the museum show how the world darkens when it abandons a literal interpretation of the Bible. Two teenagers, apparently indoctrinated with evolutionary teaching, are shown at home. The girl is talking to Planned Parenthood and the boy is looking at pornography on a computer. In its story on the museum, *The Times* (Baldwin 2007) quotes Ken Ham on the importance of showing humans and dinosaurs together in the dioramas. The coexistence of dinosaurs and humans issue is dear to creationists' heart because fossil evidence showing that dinosaurs walked the Earth and disappeared long before their chronology says that God made the world contradicts their version of the Bible. "The Bible talks about dragons. We believe dragon legends had a basis in truth."

How to Teach Evolution Islamically

Some Muslims pose the same questions as do conservative Christians. The most successful of all textbooks for teaching science from an Islamic perspective were authored by "Harun Yahya," the pen name of Adnan Oktar, a name chosen no doubt because the two names are the Arabic for two figures shared by Islam and Christianity, Aaron and John.... Across his many books, Yahya returns again and again to the falsity of Darwinian theories of evolution, and to the truth of those theories and findings, such as the Big Bang and the Cambrian Explosion, that show that the universe and new life forms were created rather than evolving. Yahya mobilizes the same arguments for Intelligent Design as do Christians—the low probability of life emerging by chance, the complexity of DNA—and he also draws on contemporary, renowned scientists to buttress his own, creationist position.

In order to argue against human evolution, Yahya claims that the supposedly pre-human hominids in fact were mere variations of humanity. He cites the work of my own colleague Erik Trinkaus, one of the world's foremost authorities on Neanderthals. According to Yahya (2000, 193), Trinkaus shows that Neanderthals were not inferior to humans in their physical or mental abilities. It thus makes little sense to think of them as in an evolutionary series with humans; better to think of them as a "particular human race that assimilated with other races in time." The absence of transitional fossils between species buttresses the same point: life is created and changes, but does not evolve from simple to complex.

But, as in U.S. Christian colleges, Muslim colleges turn out students well versed in evolutionary biology. How do Muslim teachers of a creationist viewpoint teach evolution? I have been visiting classes in an Islamic private school near Paris, and in 2006 I sat in a class on biology and geology to answer this question. The class, the French equivalent of eleventh grade, was taught by a woman in her 40s wearing a beige head scarf and a white lab coat. The six boys and five girls did group projects and answered questions posed during the lecture. When I visited the class, the pupils were studying the organization of the internal organs of the body, moving from the results of a dissection of a mouse they had performed the previous week to the human body, taking note of the similarities and differences across groups of animals (most of which was review or should have been), and then studying the processes by which an individual forms from the event of fertilization. As they examined similarities across animal species they spoke about limbs and tails. Their teacher explained that "the tail disappeared on humans in the course of evolution." When they discussed the unity of all living things, she explained what that meant and then paused.

"Now let me open a small parenthesis. The curriculum is designed to convince you of the theory of evolution but it is just a theory, it is not absolute truth, I cannot say that in 20 years a scientist will not say, no, that is not any longer true—that is how science progresses. For example with the cell, we used to say that it was like a room, and then we became able to see the parts, and then there were biochemical studies. Science is knowledge that is constructed bit by bit; it does not fall from the sky. So, now we teach about the unity of all living things, but perhaps in 20 years we will speak in a different way."

The lesson continued and a few moments later she was explaining that "animals have limbs—some do not have them anymore because in the course of evolution they lost them. Take the snake: it lost its limbs as it developed to a new way of moving through its environment."

I talked with her after class. She came from Tunisia, and received a doctorate in cellular biology in France, and because of her head scarf she could not teach in the public sector. I asked her if pupils ever objected that she taught evolution. "I am sure that some of them do not believe it at all. At the beginning of the year I tell the parents: 'Here is what I am going to teach them because it is in the national program and if you want to brainwash them afterwards or deform the teaching it is up to you!' I do believe in all the stages that humans went through, homo erectus and so forth, that we evolved, and also in the unity of creation, which was by God, but I do not think we have a common ancestor with other species; I do not know what happened in-between." She said she teaches the national curriculum "as if there were always an inspector here in class."

The pupils learn the official scientific position about evolution, and their teacher embraces much of that curriculum—the mechanisms of change through adaptation to changing environments, the evolution of hominid species—but she is careful to present the thesis of the unity of all living things as a provisional claim. Pupils must learn it to succeed—and she must teach it for the school to be accredited and subsidized—but it is not God's truth.

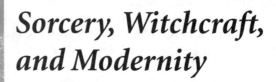

8 Sorcery, Witchcraft, and Modernity

*H*ere is an anthropological stock in trade: all over the world, people think that unseen powers, usually manipulated by humans, cause illness, death, or just plain randomness in everyday life. Anthropologists have used the words "sorcery" and "witchcraft" to refer to these ideas and practices. And here is an anthropological dilemma: many people do not consider these unseen powers as always harmful; indeed, often the same person draws on the same powers to heal or harm. Sometimes terms for "sorcery" also refer to a range of healing practices. Consider the many people in Europe and North America who follow "witchcraft" in order to find spiritual energy or ways of healing (discussed in Chapter 6) and recall the figure in Disney's "The Sorcerer's Apprentice"—hardly an evil character.

Part of our problem with these terms lies in European and North American associations of "witchcraft" with harm, evil, and Satan, thanks to efforts made in the name of Christianity to demonize heretics and control congregations. Do we retain terms that are so ridden with these powerful negative meanings? How do we translate the many ways of talking about the unseen found across the world into a single language of anthropology? Things are still more difficult, because colonialism introduced European terms for "sorcery" into occupied lands. Thus in Cameroon, western Africa, many people use the French word *la sorcellerie*, which corresponds to both English "sorcery" and "witchcraft," to refer to their own ideas about the unseen, ideas that are morally ambiguous.

What do we then do in writing about these things? Most anthropologists writing today use the terms *sorcery* and *witchcraft* (or cognates in other languages), acknowledge the problems that this use poses, and then describe as best they can how things work in the places where they have worked. In fact, this is what we do regarding much of social life: terms such as *kinship, politics,* and, of course, *religion* are not so straightforward either!

La Sorcellerie in Cameroon

*A*ccordingly, the best way to understand the logics of sorcery and witchcraft is to jump into an account of one society, and then describe how things differ elsewhere and how they change over time. We will begin with the Maka people, who live in the southeastern, French-speaking, forested part of Cameroon. The Maka survived German efforts to extract rubber from the region, and equally coercive French efforts to force people to plant coffee and cocoa. After World War II, rising producer prices led some Maka to plant more of these crops, and some of them became wealthy and powerful.

Throughout this period Maka have spoken of an unseen power called *djambe,* a force that lives in the belly of some humans in the form of a small animal, like a mouse or a crab. A myth tells of the introduction of the djambe to human society. A hunter found a djambe in the forest. It asked him to give it a little meat and he did so. That day he killed many animals. Every day he did the same, feeding the djambe and enjoying success in hunting. But then his wife followed him into the forest and spoke to the djambe. It entered into her body, promising to make her rich, but then demanded more and more meat. She killed their animals to feed it, and ended by feeding it her children.

As the ethnographer Peter Geschiere (Geschiere 1997) explains, the myth establishes links between greed and killing, particularly of close kinsmen, and it blames women for causing the djambe to become destructive. Maka say that certain people, called *njindjamb,* "bring out their djambe," which means that they leave their bodies and join others of like mind at nighttime rendezvous. There, ordinary social rules are reversed: men have sex with other men, and women with women, and they finish by eating the hearts of kinsmen. These kin are certain to die if they do not obtain the aid of a healer (*nkong*).

The djambe concept lies at the heart of two problems for the Maka. The first concerns one's kin. The djambe represents the "dark side of kinship." Although if you are to trust anyone it will be your kinsmen, some people, those who "bring out their djambe," eat their kinsmen's hearts. Stories about djambe bring to the surface the possibility that kin may betray one another, a possibility that one sees in everyday life, when kin feel jealousy toward one another and enter into quarrels.

The djambe also brings out the ambivalence of power. One can only have access to power through the use of djambe. No one who exercises authority in the village could do so without having protected himself by drawing on his djambe. Healers, who can counteract harm done by djambe, also gain their powers by way of their own powerful djambe. In the past, healers had to sacrifice kinsmen in order to fully obtain their powers. Indeed, if a boy or girl shows signs of having an active djambe—for example, if all one's younger siblings die—then a teacher might try to teach her or him to channel that power into the practice of healing, so that she or he becomes an *nkong,* a healer.

The ways of talking about djambe illustrate general human problems: do we trust or mistrust our close relatives? Can someone who obtains power be presumed to use it only for good, or is its use for evil inevitable? In each society in the world people articulate and develop these problems in particular ways; often they call on ideas of sorcery or witchcraft to provide language for these anxieties.

Geschiere tells the story of Tsjume to illustrate the "vicious circle of djambe" in Maka society. Tsjume, an elderly man, fell ill and his third wife died. People attributed these misfortunes to djambe, and rumors pointed at Nanga, Tsjume's first wife. She, too, became ill, and most people said she was the victim of her own djambe use (although others said she suffered from fear of djambe attack). But then she died, after being taken to her natal village, and now Tsjume was accused of having caused the deaths of his wives. Nanga's and Tsjume's family quarreled violently over the matter of where Nanga would be buried. A few weeks later Tsjume's second wife died. Tsjume now began to accuse openly a woman who lived in his compound and who enjoyed a spotless reputation. Geschiere heard her reply: "People who know so well what the witches do are the first to leave their bodies in the night."

Tsjume eventually recovered his strength and the matter ended. People assumed that "the witches had settled the whole affair among themselves." The series of accusations showed the social shaping of fear and suspicion in Maka society. People assumed that if a death occurred in the household, that others in the household must be responsible. But how could you decide who is responsible? In the case of Tsjume, people could follow the logic of Maka djambe ideas to decide. They could infer from the fact that Nanga's illness followed closely on that of her co-wife that sorcery was responsible: she was either responsible for the misfortunes or next on the list of victims. Most people thought she was causing the illness until she died, at which point the second possible position, that she had been a victim, became the majority view. Tsjume's final accusations, of a woman who otherwise was above suspicion, elicited a reply that tapped into a key Maka idea, namely, that those who best understand the doings of djambe are those who bring out their own djambe, that is, who attend nighttime revelries and use their powers for ill.

The slipperiness of accusations rests on the postulate that everyone in the society might well have a djambe. What is at issue is not what is inside you but how you use it: do you develop it, and bring it out for use against others? Do you draw on it to become a great healer, or a powerful government official? To exercise power or achieve greatness depends on having "a full belly," meaning that you have an active djambe. Or do you just go about your business and trouble others as little as possible?

Sorcery ideas imply that particular individuals are responsible for misfortune, or that others experience rapid success through use of their inner force. In other words, it explains success and misfortune by pointing to characteristics and actions of individuals. And the specific characteristics of djambe—the uncertainties and ambiguities created in its "vicious circle"—fit with Maka local politics. Maka village affairs are set out and, sometimes, resolved in village meetings, at which the greater persuasiveness of some people over others determine the day. People attribute these powers to djambe, but djambe's inherent ambiguity means that such authority is fleeting. One elder, Mpal, could cut off others in debate. It was said that he did this by tightening their throats so that they could not speak. But one day he was challenged on grounds that his overly active djambe had caused the deaths of several boys. On that occasion another man was able to counter Mpal's powerful djambe by the power of his own indignation.

The moral ambiguity of djambe reminds us of the difficulties of using the English words sorcery and witchcraft, or the French *la sorcellerie,* a word that encompasses both English terms, because of the sense of evil, or at least maliciousness, that these words convey. The difficulty is further compounded by the fact that Maka use *la sorcellerie* to refer to djambe, and *sorcier* to indicate someone who makes use of his or her djambe, for whatever purposes. A man giving testimony in a court case involving sorcery accusations might give his occupation as "*sorcier,*" a self-description that indicates that he has the knowledge and experience to testify, not that he admits committing malicious acts against others. Geschiere notes the problems and in the end uses *la sorcellerie* to refer to these ideas and practices on grounds that the terms fit reasonably well, and in any case they have entered into Maka use.

Azande Oracles

*A*nthropological studies of sorcery and witchcraft nearly always refer back to the pioneering work carried out in the 1930s by E. E. Evans-Pritchard with the Azande in central Africa. Evans-Pritchard underscored the logic of experience, explanation, and proof that underlies these ideas. In this respect he followed his teacher Malinowski, who argued that people everywhere are rational in their everyday behavior. However, Evans-Pritchard examined much more thoroughly than had Malinowski how it is that the institutions of everyday life reinforce a specific set of beliefs. In his 1937 book, *Witchcraft, Oracles and Magic among the Azande,* he paid particular attention to the social logic of oracles, or how Azande would interpret the results of divination through the lens of their knowledge of their society.

The Azande case continues to be cited by philosophers with respect to the "problem of rationality," and we will focus here on the logic of Azande practices as Evans-Pritchard studied them. Azande say that some among them have inherited a substance that lives in their small intestine, called *mangu.* Mangu can give forth emanations that cause misfortune, and this can happen, at least sometimes, without the knowledge of the person in whose body it exists, as a direct consequence of feeling envy or hatred. In this respect Azande ideas differ from Maka ones, although in both societies people focus on the use of these powerful substances rather than the mere possession of them.

Although Azande will point to natural or social causes for unfortunate events, they cite mangu to explain why it was this person who was the victim. Using an arresting idiom, they say that mangu provided the "second spear" of explanation, thrown after the first to clinch the matter. A man hanged himself after a quarrel, but people quarrel every day without killing themselves, so the force of mangu is called on to explain why in this case the man committed suicide. People are killed when a granary collapses on them, and it is clear that termites had weakened the structure, but why it had to be these people who died is referred to the causal logic of mangu.

Sometimes Azande simply say "it must be mangu" and leave it at that. When they decide to accuse someone of causing misfortune, they choose the likely targets: people likely to have hated or envied the victim. How is an accusation evaluated? Usually an oracle of some kind is consulted by an expert. Oracles form a hierarchy from the most common (and least expensive to use) to the most tightly controlled (and most costly), but the form of consultation is the same. You have the expert put a question to the oracle. The question might be: "Did so-and-so cause my son's illness?" but it might also be on a non-witchcraft matter such as: "If I build a house in this clearing will I fall ill?" Among widely available oracles are the stones that when rubbed together either stick or glide in response to questions and the termites that eat parts of a stick pushed into their mound. On the top of the oracle hierarchy is the chicken oracle controlled by princes. When this oracle is consulted, a handler, who works for the prince, administers a strychnine-type poison to the chicken. He then poses a question, directing the chicken to die (or live) if the answer is "yes." The chicken then dies or lives. Sometimes the answer is verified by putting the question the other way around (using a second chicken). Thus, the first time the handler asks the chicken to live if the answer is "yes"; the second time to live if the answer is "no."

How does this oracle, the most important and beyond which there is no appeal, work? Presumably, if the oracles gave random answers to questions they would come to be perceived as unreliable. There must then be some degree of positive correspondence between outcomes and what those involved already know or suspect. Part of the answer lies in what is asked of the oracles.

Some questions will concern matters about which most people already have some knowledge and about which there is already a great deal of suspicion, such that either answer, yes or no, will fit what people think they already know. For instance, a couple was accused of a specific act of adultery, and the oracle came out against them. They had protested their innocence (and may have indeed been innocent this time) but were known to have been carrying on an affair for some time. Upon being confronted with the oracle's decision, the man blurted out: "It must have been another time!" Still claiming his innocence of this act of adultery, he surmised that the oracle had detected a previous adulterous act on his part. In his eyes (assuming his outburst reflected his thoughts), then, the oracle was mistaken but not disconfirmed. Other questions cannot easily be disconfirmed. A person might ask an oracle: "If I build my house in such and such a place, will I die?" If the answer is yes, he will not build there and there is no test; if the answer is no and he does build there, chances are low he will die soon. Similar is the question "If I marry so-and-so, will she die within a year?" If they do not marry the oracle is untested; if they do marry, the chances that she will die soon are again low, and were she to die an additional explanation could be sought in, you guessed it, witchcraft!

Even if we assume that the handlers do not influence the result by varying the amount of poison administered to the fowl, then, the oracle will appear not random but in accord with common knowledge. And of course some bias may enter in, although Evans-Pritchard claimed he could detect none.

What are the consequences of being found guilty? They can be quite severe; once, Evans-Pritchard was told, a man could be put to death for certain offenses. Today a person or couple might be put to work for the prince or fined. But even more commonly, the offender will merely be ordered to make things right. How he or she does so sheds important light on what this business of oracles and mangu is all about. For when one is formally accused of witchcraft—one is presented with the wing of a fowl that died— the correct response is to blow out water and say: "If I possess witchcraft in my belly I am unaware of it; may it cool. It is thus that I blow out water."

Today, younger people are counseled by their elders that even if they are sure they are not guilty, they should just blow on the wing to show that they bear no ill will. The matter is not about guilt but about setting things right, smoothing over the hurt. Of course sometimes the oracle is right on the money, or only slightly off, as in the case of the adulterous couple, and then a spontaneous confession may result.

In analyzing the Azande system we are better off considering witchcraft first and foremost as a set of social practices rather than a pseudoscientific system of knowledge claims (as philosophers often do). Individual Azande may or may not be completely convinced of the truth of each statement uttered about witchcraft and oracles, but the overall effect of the way questions are put, the range of responses, and the focus on restitution rather than guilt, is to make the set of practices believable.

This way of looking at it helps to solve the "rationality problem": the set of statements about and practices of Azande witchcraft is a discourse about social problems, one that gives the members of the society a relatively socially harmless way of talking about conflicts and dissatisfactions, bringing them to light, and also resolving those problems. The moment when water is blown by the accused is a moment of catharsis. Tensions between the parties may be released and somewhat relieved. The overall system of power receives an ideological reinforcement, as the prince's oracle has revealed the truth.

Sorcery and Modernity

*I*deas about sorcery are neither limited to a particular society nor static. Let us return to Cameroon, where the societies that lie in the same forested region as the Maka share a set of ideas about sorcery. One of the major languages of the region, Ewondo, has provided a lingua franca term, *evu,* to designate concepts that correspond to the Maka *djambe.* These societies also share a basic political structure; they are what anthropologists call "segmentary," meaning that they consist of small kinship-based groups, related more or less closely to one another, and much of their political activity is based on these kin ties.

The relevance of local political form for understanding sorcery becomes apparent if we contrast these societies with those lying to the west, in the grasslands portion of Cameroon. These societies were and are organized in a more hierarchical fashion, with chiefs and notables. People living in these societies also believe in an inner force that can be used in a range of ways, but their chiefs have the power and responsibility to ensure that the force remains under control and that it works in the interest of the good. The chiefs can declare when someone is using sorcery in a harmful way, and in the past they could execute them (Goheen 1996). Their power allows them to cut through the "vicious circle" of sorcery force. Of course, they declared their own powers to be beneficial.

In many African societies, sorcery ideas have provided ways to understand contemporary politics and economics. In Cameroon (as elsewhere), the authoritarian character of colonial rule government has continued into the postcolonial period. Intrigues and feuds among national politicians have led to sudden twists and turns, climbs to success and falls from grace. One way to explain these events is through the logic of sorcery. As Geschiere observes, much as Americans continue to search for complete explanations of the assassination of John F. Kennedy, so do Cameroon people try to explain these otherwise opaque fortunes and misfortunes.

Sorcery ideas also may be invoked to explain how some people accumulate riches, and why some of the rich then suffer for it—all the modern houses have gravesites in front of them, noted one man. The phrase coined by Jean-François Bayart (1989) to describe African politics, the "politics of the belly," points to the idea that power comes from "eating" wealth, whether that wealth comes from the outside, in the form of aid or export revenues, or from villagers. It also refers to the means of accumulating those riches, namely, through sorcery, the djambe that lives in the belly. Because sorcery power engenders jealousy and, often, misfortune, sorcery ideas have often caused people to refrain from accumulating visible wealth—even planting coca trees could trigger sorcery consequences.

People also create new sorcery ideas to explain new forms of great wealth, and the existence of wealthy people who appear to live contentedly with their riches. One new idea has been that of the sorcerer who turns people into zombies to work for him. This practice is called *ekong* in the port of Duala, one of the centers of new commercial wealth in Cameroon and also a center for these new ideas. Someone seeking this way to wealth may dream and in his dreams visit a prosperous estate. The owner will offer it to him on condition that he offer the life of his mother or another close relative. The victim—the poor mother, for example—will dream that she is led away with her hands tied. It is then time for her to consult a healer to counter the sorcery (de Rosny 1992). These self-described victims usually are people who live in cities and who are experiencing problems with their families. Healers understand these social sources of the ills and the fears, and their work is a type of family therapy, bringing to light family tensions. But, as the circular logic of sorcery implies, these same healers might themselves be responsible for ekong practices. People turn to ever-new possible sources of powerful assistance, whether new healers, chiefs (in the western region), or the state.

As we saw above, chiefs in the western regions can neutralize harm, and this power also allows them to "launder" new wealth that is suspected of having been earned through ekong. Presenting wealth to a chief allows a newly rich person to be accepted by others, as they presume that the chief will work to ensure that the power behind the wealth works only for the good.

Since the 1970s, the Cameroon state increasingly has intervened in sorcery, as have other African states. State prosecution of sorcerers began in the eastern part of the country, where sorcery is reputed to be the most common and where the absence of chiefs has provided the state with the possibility of a new role. These prosecutions were at the behest of local notables—farmers, village officials, party leaders—who thought they had been the victims of sorcery. In most cases neither a confession nor material proof is offered. Judges, assisted by a prosecutor, hear the cases, and most of the time they find the accused guilty. Judges do not make use of healers to see whether the accused does indeed have active sorcery inside him or her, but rely on testimony of accusers and of healers. In other words, the courts cut through the local practices of accusation, counter-accusation, and divination. Healers function, not to aid the accused or the sick, but to advise judges on the guilt or innocence of a suspected sorcerer.

Throughout Africa, ideas about sorcery incorporate ideas about social tensions and power, and they have changed along with broader social transformations. Even in precolonial times, accusations of witchcraft were made against women much more often than against men. Some cases of rapid social change exacerbated the attacks on women. In Nigeria, for example, the development of the cocoa economy in the 1940s and 1950s led to the rapid proliferation of women traders, many of whom left the traditional patrilocal compound to pursue their activities elsewhere. These women passed on trading capital to their daughters, bypassing traditional inheritance lines that ran from fathers to sons. Local witchcraft ideas already targeted women; the rapid social and economic change in this period led to an increase in witchcraft accusations and to the 1950–1951 Atinga cult of witch finding that accused thousands of women in Nigeria as witches, forcing them to confess, pay a cleansing fee, and eat a substance that would kill them if they ever practiced witchcraft again. In Andrew Apter's analysis (1993) of the movement, newly powerful male traders financed the cult in part to persecute the women traders with whom they competed.

Accusations of witchcraft continue to be a part of modern urban life in many parts of Africa as a way of talking about evil, particularly the evil brought by strangers (Auslander 1993; Bastian 1993). Tabloids and other newspapers carry witchcraft stories across regions of West and Central Africa. Witches in Zambia and South Africa are accused of causing barrenness and AIDS, sickness and economic failure. Witch finders, in southern Africa often associated with the Zionist churches, are recruited by young men to cleanse their villages by identifying the elderly women and men who are preventing the younger people from advancing economically. Witches are not killed but cleansed by having potions rubbed into cuts on their bodies. And yet, an exception to this general pattern, young militants in South Africa have used the "necklace"—the burning tire used to kill suspected informants during the struggle against apartheid—as a weapon against accused witches, leading one chief—significantly, a woman—to create a new town as a sanctuary for the accused.

Sorcery and Reciprocity in New Guinea

In 1998, when the ethnographer Bruce Knauft last visited them, about 600 Gebusi were living in the forests of southwestern New Guinea. The Gebusi once lived in a world of sorcery, but one that was strikingly different from that inhabited by the Maka. Gebusi were known for their absence of warfare and their overall sociability. And yet, until the mid–1980s they had one of the highest rates of homicide in the world; about one-third of the deaths occurring in the period 1940–1982 were from killing, and the overwhelming majority of these deaths were in retribution for a suspected death or illness from sorcery (Knauft 1985). These killings were all within the group, but, contrary to what one might expect to find, they did not engage in particularly great amounts of internal conflict or backbiting. Clearly, a different cultural logic from that we have studied for Africa was at work here.

Knauft explains how Gebusi social life is shaped by the idea of "direct reciprocity": I give you something and you give me its equivalent in return. Anthropologists find that in many societies two modes of reciprocity underlie many social norms and values, regarding agriculture, material exchange, marriage, relationships with spirits, and general sociability. In direct reciprocity operating in Gebusi society, the movement of goods, a service, or a person in one direction is supposed to be countered by a movement of a similar good, service, or person in the other direction. In marriage, it means that if my village receives a woman (or a man) from another group, we must make sure that a woman (or man) from our group marries one of them. In the case of "generalized reciprocity," giving something to another group will eventually be reciprocated, but perhaps from a different group, in a chain-like fashion. My group might take a spouse from one group, and give a spouse to another group. If direct reciprocity implies closure, generalized reciprocity implies an opening toward the outside.

For the Gebusi, both marriage and sorcery involved direct reciprocity. Marriage was supposed to involve women moving between groups in balanced fashion, and if a marriage in one direction was not followed by one in the other, tensions resulted—and sometimes these tensions led to sorcery accusations. Sorcery itself was structured along the lines of direct reciprocity, for if a woman was the victim of sorcery, then a female sorcerer had to be discovered and killed, and that killing put an end to the matter. Discovery was accomplished through divination and the use of mediums. Mediums also allowed the living to communicate with the spirits of sorcery's victims, who lived in the forest as beautiful birds and animals, the spirit familiars and protectors of the living.

The severe consequences of being suspected of sorcery meant that no one seems to have practiced it, and Gebusi refrained from claiming positions of leadership for fear that their actions would be seen as typical of sorcerers. By the late 1990s, sorcery accusations had nearly disappeared. Most Gebusi had joined one of several local churches and now faced the highly powerful spirit, God. All the people who had acted as mediums to ascertain the identity of sorcerers had died or given up their ties with spirits. If someone did level a sorcery accusation, he or she could be hauled into court and charged with slander. Many people continue to believe in sorcery, but in some places, at least, the practice has ceased.

Why is this so? The contrast with the African cases discussed earlier provides some clues. Maka and other people saw in the accumulation of riches and emergence of inequalities a threat, and sorcery has provided a way of talking about, and sometimes acting against, that threat. The Gebusi with whom Knauft has lived have welcomed the introduction of "modernity" in the form of consumer goods, schools, churches, and protection against warfare. They see abandoning sorcery as a way toward that modernity. Many of them did a "direct exchange" between the older spirits and the new God, and see sorcery practices and churchgoing as incompatible. Their new lives bring them into constant contact with people from other ethnic groups at the large station area; these contacts radically alter social life, which now includes a large, depersonalized domain of social interactions at school, office, church, or sports events. The modernity experienced here is attractive, individualizing, but also passivizing—Gebusi now receive lessons, speeches, sermons, all of which instruct them to supplicate and hope for the best.

This outcome was contingent on the particular experience of the Gebusi and differed across New Guinea societies. Knauft suggests that such locally important elements as the relatively friendly character of the local police and the tolerant attitude of church officials made it seem attractive to Gebusi to ally themselves with these local officials. In the case of the police, this reliance contributed to the decline of sorcery accusations, because accused sorcerers now were sent off for jail terms or released for lack of evidence rather than killed. The legitimacy of these state institutions, itself due to this set of contingent factors, then led to sorcery's decline.

Sorcery and Sacrifice in Sri Lanka

In the healing practices associated with Buddhism in Sri Lanka, human agency is assumed to lie behind most illnesses and other misfortunes of everyday life. People spread illness and misfortune through malicious talk, through poisons and effigies; ill will toward others may cause harm even when the perpetrator is unaware of what he or she is doing—an idea we have just seen with the Azande. Expressions for sorcery refer to the sorcerer "binding" the victim to the sorcery to create the kind of intimacy otherwise associated with kinship or sexuality. Sorcery may result from feuding among the spirits of deceased kin that continues down through the ages.

In one case reported by Kapferer (1997, 41–42), a hospital worker who had become seriously ill underwent a series of exorcisms in order to discover the cause of the illness. In trance, the victim described a land dispute that had begun when two sisters of his great-grandfather had not been given the land they deserved at the time of their marriage. It was the spirits of these sisters and their descendants who were behind the man's troubles. His illness was "the monstrous forming of the accumulated anger growing within a body of kin through the generations" (Kapferer 1997, 42).

As in Africa and New Guinea, then, Sinhalese sorcery strikes often among kin and expresses suppressed angers and resentments. A range of anti-sorcery rituals and specialists are available to counter the work of such spirits and persons and to restore health. The force of sorcery is represented and embodied in a demon and deity that exists within and in tension with Buddhist ideas and practices. The term *Huniyam* or *Suniyam,* connoting emptiness, refers to the sorcery force and to the demon/creator. The ambivalence of Suniyam runs throughout anti-sorcery rituals, and recalls a similar tension between sorcery and healing in Cameroon society.

The master anti-sorcery rite is called the Suniyama. An expensive ritual, it requires the sorcery victim or his or her sponsor to build an elaborate structure said to be the palace of the first human King, Mahasammata, and his Queen, Manikpala. The palace represents earthly desires and sources of envy, which have brought on the victim's misfortunes. As the ritual unfolds, the victim moves from outside the place into its bedchamber, also said to be the center of the world and a space of the Buddha, a place of enlightenment. The victim, whether male or female, plays the role of the Queen, who, at the beginning of history, was the first human to be struck down by sorcery. As the victim moves toward the center of the palace, he or she leaves behind all thoughts of desire. A series of sacrifices are performed, and at the ritual's end the palace is destroyed (thereby destroying the reasons for sorcery). Thus the Buddha's power is invoked to regenerate the victim, but paradoxically by means of sacrifice and destruction.

The ritual was created by a sorcerer, Oddisa, to save Queen Manikpala from illness caused by sorcery. Performing it not only cures a victim, but also enacts Buddhist ideas and, in effect, the history of Sri Lanka. The ritual therefore is very attractive to new elites. The ritual's dual function of curing and enacting also helps explain the emergence of a deity, Suniyam, worshipped in urban temples and shrines in Sri Lanka (Kapferer 2003).

These shrines are located in boundary areas of cities, and in areas plagued by violent crime. They are visited by people suffering from a wide variety of ailments, or by those who seek help in business or schooling, or to hurt competitors, to stop the police from making an arrest, or to exact revenge. Kapferer (2003, 122–123) stresses the association of the god Suniyam with violence: during the insurrections of 1989–1990, when thousands of young people were killed or jailed, the shrines were crowded with parents seeking either revenge or the return of their children.

Witchcraft as Satan versus God

*I*n early modern Europe and North America, misfortune was thought of in a dualistic framework, where God and his followers confront Satan and those in his grasp. Witch hunts in various parts of Europe resembled those in Africa today, except that the source of the witchcraft was not the individual but her or his ties with Satan.

In the United States, witchcraft is surely most closely associated with the celebrated 1692 trials held in Salem, Massachusetts. I would argue that witchcraft ideas in New England once functioned much as they do in Azande society, to encourage confession and purge the society of its fears and tensions. But rapid social changes of the late seventeenth century created new fissures in village society that were given strong moral and emotional colorations by Puritan preachers and church members. Much as in contemporary Africa, older tensions were exacerbated and witch hunts grew in importance.

New England Puritans

The Puritans of seventeenth-century New England held strong religious ideas about the church as a community and about the immanence of evil in the world. A church in this society was not a building or even an association to which one could freely belong. In its narrow and most compelling sense it was a community of people who felt themselves elected by God, as "saints," who had joined in a covenant that bound each to the other. Church members were responsible for one another, such that the sins of one person would lead to misfortune for others (Miller 1956, 141–152). As John Winthrop put it in his sermon on "Christian charity" delivered to the Pilgrims onboard the Arabella en route to the New World in 1630: "We must be knit together as one man and must delight in each other, make other's condition our own, rejoice together, mourn together, labor and suffer together, always having before our eyes our commission and community in the work" (quoted in Demos 1982, 299).

This sense of common destiny was reinforced by the constant copresence of church members in a village. You encountered your fellow parishioner in his store, where he sold you bread, or near your fields, where you might get along or be embroiled in a dispute over boundaries or water. Common destiny and a shared life worked tolerably well as long as everyone prospered tolerably equally. But sharp differences in economic and social standing had begun to emerge, along with ideas of individualism. These new and dangerous ideas were, ironically, exacerbated by the opportunity afforded in the New World: the abundance of land and the fragility of new institutions.

Puritans also held that a strong line divided good from evil in the world. Evil was incarnate in the witch. As the prominent preacher Cotton Mather put it: "There is in witchcraft a most explicit renouncing of all that is holy and just and good." The witch showed "the furthest effort of our original sin" (quoted in Demos 1982, 304). Witches' meetings were imagined as inversions of all that was holy, involving trampling on the cross and defiling the Host. (And, indeed, contemporary Satanic cults do practice some of these rituals of inversion.) In this respect, witchcraft served to sharpen and perhaps to strengthen the moral boundaries between the community and Satan's forces.

In this context, in which all actions were to be scrutinized for their good or evil, ordinary people understandably could experience a great deal of anxiety about whether their actions and feelings came from God or Satan. Puritans believed in predestination, that God has damned or saved us before we were born, but not revealed to us His decision. Puritans saw the world as full of signs or marks of God's will, so that one might recognize in himself the signs of Election, or of damnation (and indeed becoming a member of the church required that one declare oneself saved). But Satan could be behind such feelings, trying to induce damned individuals to enter the church. Even the most highly placed church member could not easily escape gnawing doubts as to the reliability of his or her own certainty. One story has it that a woman in a Boston congregation, tormented by her uncertainty, threw her child into a well to seek relief of certain damnation. (Hers was, however, an incorrect interpretation of the strictly unknowable nature of Election!)

Evil and Accusations

In this context of gnawing doubts, the presence of Evil, and the ideal of a morally as well as socially close-knit community, fears of evil within—the witch—were endemic. Throughout the early modern period in Europe, accusations of witchcraft were an expected part of life. England had somewhere between 300 and 1,000 executions for witchcraft between 1542 and 1736. Accusations fit the general pattern already noted. Most of the accused were women; indeed, in one detailed record for the period 1560–1680 in Essex County, only 8 percent of the persons tried were men. The typical English witch was an older woman, perhaps widowed, from the poorer segment of the community. Often she was a beggar. She was usually accused of bewitching someone not only in her own village but in her part of the village. Witches were neighbors. The historian Keith Thomas argues that accusers were beginning to chafe at the demands of charity, as the ethics of the time gradually became more individualistic. And yet moral responsibility for charity still was preached by the church and probably felt as legitimate by the better-off citizens. Harsh words, even curses, by those whose appeals for financial assistance were denied would have spawned some guilt in the hearts of these newly individual-minded villagers, and to assuage this guilt, argues Thomas, they projected it onto the "witch" (Demos 1982, 298–300).

Witchcraft accusations were brought from England to New England—indeed, in particular from Essex County, England, to Essex County, Massachusetts. In seventeenth-century North America there are recorded 93 witchcraft cases, of which 16 led to hangings, the Salem outbreak excepted. If we count the Salem trials as well, the total rises to 234 cases and 36 executions—an "accusation rate" of seven accusations per 100,000 people in North America, compared to less than one accusation per 100,000 in England, and about 5.5 for the most "active" county in England, Essex. Clearly, then, events in Salem pushed the rate of accusations far beyond their usual frequency (Demos 1982, 11–12).

Accusations functioned in similar fashion to what we observed for the Azande. The activity of a witch could explain why an unexpected event happened, even when the physics of the matter were perfectly clear. For example, a man on maneuvers with his militia accidentally discharged his gun, which ricocheted off a tree and struck another man, killing him. The first man was charged with manslaughter, but people continued to ask why the rather odd accident had happened. In the event, a woman was accused of witchcraft. She had owed money to the deceased and had been his landlord: she was thus close to him and yet in a socially ambivalent relationship to him. But to blame a single individual was insufficient to account for the presence of witchcraft in the community, where everyone was in some way responsible for everyone else. And so, on a subsequent Sunday the preacher widened the field of blame to include the entire community, whose general moral decrepitude, he charged, had permitted Satan to enter among them and do his evil work (Demos 1982, 3–9).

In such a case the matter would rest there, and so it had been in Salem before 1692. Events in that year represent an abnormal, outrageous set of actions. Yet the people involved were ordinary village folk, much like all the other folk peopling the eastern seaboard then and afterward.

The Salem Outbreak of 1692

First, the events. In February 1692, several girls in Salem village began acting very strangely: alternately prancing about and hiding under chairs, making strange, "foolish" speeches that no one could understand, and taking to their beds, moaning and complaining about pains. The authorities of the village interpreted this behavior as witchcraft. One of the first girls to act strangely was the daughter of the village minister, Samuel Parris. As she lay on her bed, Parris and others began to question her, thinking that she might be the victim of witchcraft. The questions put to her and to several other girls were in the form of: "Was it so-and-so?" Much as with the Zande oracle, certain names were put forward and others were not. The girls were urged to name someone, and they did name several women, including Tituba. Three women were then questioned by two members of the provincial legislature, who lived in nearby Salem Town. Tituba confessed to having committed witchcraft; the other two denied the charges.

The accusations snowballed, and the public hangings began in June of that year. Between June 2 and September 22, 19 men and women were hanged, including a minister, the Reverend George Burroughs. The hangings were finally stopped by the intervention of Boston-area ministers who were troubled by the willy-nilly hanging, though not by the principle of hanging witches. On October 12 Governor Phips forbade any more imprisonments for witchcraft, and all prisoners were set free during the following year.

The events raise some troubling questions. First, why were the experiences of the children interpreted as the torment of witches? Were Puritans generally likely to make such interpretations? The nature of the experiences was not all unpleasant, after all. The girls' strange speech suggests the speaking in tongues of the Pentecost spoken of in the Bible and known to the ministers. Indeed, in the very same year of 1692 a Boston servant girl exhibited similar syndromes: spasms, outbreaks of strange speech, and, upon meeting some of the accused Salem women, violent behavior toward them. But in this case, Cotton Mather drew on her behavior to form a group that met with her, chanted psalms, and had similar experiences, which began to be seen as a kind of religious ecstasy.

Later, in the early eighteenth century, the same sort of outbreak in Northampton, in western Massachusetts, was interpreted by the minister of that town, Jonathan Edwards, as a sign of the "pouring out of the spirit of God." This movement led to what came to be called the "Great Awakening," a period during which a wider range of religious experiences and behaviors were accepted (Miller 1956, 153–166).

Second, why were the charges believed? The accusers were young girls, and there was only their own testimony to support their charges. Were the distinguished jurors who found the accused guilty themselves imbeciles? How can we understand their findings?

Finally, why, in this instance but not before or after, did the outbreak expand as it did? Several hundred people were accused, 150 imprisoned, and 19 executed. Earlier outbreaks in New England since 1647 had resulted in a total of 15 executions. Those executed were local people, marginal, following the general pattern: accuse your neighbor if he or she is powerless and likely to be suspected by others on grounds of unpleasantness.

The events in Salem might have been just another minor outbreak. By April, only six people had come under public suspicion of witchcraft. But then the number of accusations picked up and were aimed at people of high status outside the immediate community. The accused included the wealthiest ship owner in Salem Town and two of its seven selectmen, two sons of a former governor, themselves prominent public figures, and even Lady Phips, wife of the governor! And unlike all previous outbreaks, most of the accused were people outside of Salem Village, in the nearby village of Andover (Boyer and Nissenbaum 1974, 22–30).

Salem and Disruption of the Moral Community

The historians Paul Boyer and Stephen Nissenbaum have given us an account of the anomaly of Salem based on the peculiar social tensions of the time. In 1636, Salem Village (today the town of Danvers) was founded but was under the control of Salem Town. The town, not the village, levied and collected taxes and set the prices to be charged for farm produce at the village gate. The village was not legally independent at the time of the witchcraft outbreak (Boyer and Nissenbaum 1974, 37–109).

The town had become a major export center, with a rich merchant class. (Many in China thought the greatest naval power of the day was the "country of Salem" because so many ships bore the name.) By keeping the prices of produce down, the town had prospered for 30 years, and because the town's population had been growing, the farmers had been able to prosper as well. But the population of the village outside the town was growing, too, and the average land holdings per household diminished dramatically at the end of the century, from 250 acres in 1660 to 124 acres in 1690. With less acreage and more farmers, a disparity developed between the amount of food needed by the town and the amount being produced. By the early 1690s, the average income of many of the farmers had declined, and tensions developed between the town and the village.

Not all families fared equally well or poorly in Salem Village. Two families who played leading roles on the witchcraft stage were the Putnams and the Porters (Boyer and Nissenbaum 1974, 110–152). Both had arrived in the 1640s from neighboring parts of England, and both soon became prosperous farming families in the village. But by the 1690s the two large groups of descendants of the original immigrants lived on opposite sides of the village.

The Porters had settled in the eastern half of the village, where they operated two sawmills, sold lumber to town merchants, and eventually married into town families. They and others in the eastern half of the village were able to benefit from townspeople's demand for goods and services. Their land was better for farming as well, and they were also close to the road that ran along the eastern edge. Near them were other small entrepreneurs, traders, and shop owners, all of whom increasingly saw themselves as sharing interests and outlooks with residents of the town. By and large they wished to preserve the close relationship of town and village and feared the future domination of an independent village by the local church. Among other fears was that the church might impose restrictions on the movement of produce outside of the village. The Porters were accused of witchcraft, which they denied. The accusers did not dare to confront the powerful Porters directly, and so they tended to target people who were associated with them.

By contrast, the fortunes of the Putnams were tied up exclusively with the village. Their original grant was of lands in the western portion of the village, where expansion could only be further westward. They were landlocked, with no nearby roads, and with poor, hilly land. They tried to diversify in the 1670s, setting up an iron-smelting plant, but the effort failed. They were fated to stay on the farm, but the farm was getting smaller, as by the third generation the remaining plots were each barely enough to maintain their standard of living.

It was this third generation of desperate Putnams that furnished the leaders in witchcraft accusations. Foremost among them was Thomas Putnam, Jr., his wife Ann, and their 12-year-old daughter Ann. They had been deprived of an estate that had been awarded to Thomas's half-brother (who, to make matters worse, had married a Porter). Several of their children had died. Their frustration and rage was vented at persons who could be attacked in the village and then expanded outward to include outsiders, upwardly mobile, who were insufficiently deferential. The Putnams were involved in the prosecution of 46 accused witches. The daughter, Ann Putnam, was the principal afflicted girl and accuser (Boyer and Nissenbaum 1974, 30–36, 133–152).

For the Puritans, self-interest was the enemy within the body of the community. "Our community are members of the same body," said John Winthrop in 1630 to the first Pilgrim contingent. From this perspective, the town, with its taverns and rich merchants, was to be seen as bringing moral danger to the Church and its community. The minister in Salem village, Samuel Parris, had never been accepted by all villagers, and the Porters were among those whom he saw as his enemies. He felt besieged and insecure, and he channeled his frustrations and anger into his sermons on Judas and on the sense of filth and corruption in the community. And he led the charge against the witches.

Within the village, a remarkable geographic pattern emerged that confirmed the importance of social and economic divisions in the witchcraft trials. Of the 25 accused witches who lived in or near Salem Village, only three lived in the western half of the village and four in the center; all the others lived in the eastern half, most of them along its boundary with Salem Town. (By contrast, of the 32 adult villagers who testified against the accused, 30 lived in the western half of the village.) This distribution of accused witches underscores the degree to which the town was seen as a danger to the community by the accusers. Among the accused was John Proctor, a tavernkeeper who was envied by the Putnams for his success and who was also condemned as too worldly, and John Willard, an outsider who married into the village and then began to buy up coveted farmland in great quantities (Boyer and Nissenbaum 1974, 181–189).

The Porters themselves were of too high a status in the community to be accused by people who would encounter them frequently. But those on the fringes of their circle were accused; for example, a man who had recently married one of their sisters. Other victims were marginal to the community in other ways. Several victims were poor women who were judged as being disrespectful to their benefactors. Cotton Mather had warned that those "who through discontent at their poverty, or at their misery, shall be always murmuring . . . witchcraft is the upshot of it" (Boyer and Nissenbaum 1974, 208).

Historian Beth Norton has added a new dimension to the accusations by pointing out that some of the accusers had fled from villages and towns attacked by Wabanaki Indians in the late 1680s and early 1690s. For example, Abigail Hobbs's confession (on April 19, 1692) marked a critical juncture in the building of Salem tensions. Abigail lived in another village, and her confession signaled the enlargement of the circle of accused beyond Salem. She stated that she had encountered Satan as a "black man," an expression often used for Indians, in Casco Bay and Falmouth, settlements farther north that had been targets of attacks by Wabanakis. Norton argues that Abigail's confession linked witchcraft and Indian attacks in the minds of Essex County residents, and that this linking led to the explosion of accusations that followed (2003, 78–81, 112–132).

Evidence and Confessions

That these people could be witches was not doubted. Everyone accepted that witches did exist. Satan's struggle for the souls of people was evident in the world, and misfortune always had a moral tinge to it. As the historian Perry Miller has written, Puritanism had no room for failure. When failure came, it was due to the work of Satan in the world, and among his favorite vehicles were witches.

What was the evidence for witchcraft? According to the canons of evidence of the day, several kinds were admissible (Boyer and Nissenbaum 1974; Demos 1982). One was empirical evidence, which included behavioral traits: these could be positive, such as great physical strength, or negative, such as the inability to recite the Lord's Prayer all the way through. These signs were largely upheld through the proceedings. The category also included odd physical markings, such as the supposed third "witch's teat," a third breast on women. Such bodily evidence was considered to be God's message to humans, but it was generally rejected in the Salem case as being unreliable.

Of long-standing evidentiary value was the category called "Anger followed by Mischief," that is, when after a quarrel or even a sharp look someone was stricken with a malady. This evidence eventually was rejected because of the difficulty of ascertaining the empirical links between the "anger" and the "mischief."

Finally and most dramatically, there was Spectral Evidence—in this case, when the afflicted girls saw figures of the accused coming to them and harming them. This evidence could, of course, be produced at a moment's notice. Mary Warren, one of the girls, tried to recant her own accusations against previous witches when the other girls accused her master, John Proctor. The others responded to her defection by immediately seeing specters around *her*. At this threat, she retracted her recantation and returned to their side. But when "respectable" townspeople began to be accused, some of the ministers remembered that Satan was capable of creating specters and images to mislead the God-fearing, and at that point spectral evidence began to be doubted publicly. Increase Mather, the leader of Boston's clergy, condemned the use of both Spectral Evidence and Anger followed by Mischief. Mather said that even when one saw a specter, it could be Satan causing mischief and trying to impune the righteousness of a good person.

Of course, many people confessed before the case could come to trial. Those who did confess, here as elsewhere, were not hanged but released. From the perspective of a modern trial court this course of action seems very odd. Why release confessed criminals and hang those who insisted on their innocence? But from the perspective of comparative witchcraft studies it is what we would expect. As in the Azande case, the confession purged the community of tensions and, in this instance, of the deep guilt it felt for straying from the righteous path. As with the blowing out of water among the Azande, the confession gives a language for conflicts, the language of Satan and witchcraft. (Possibly, although this is not documented, some may also have thought, as do Azande, that it was possible to cause evil through witchcraft without intending to do so, just by being angry with someone.)

Here is another way the Salem events went wrong. The first three women to be accused had confessed but after that confessions virtually ceased. Why? Boyer and Nissenbaum argue that a cultural change was just then occurring in New England, one that gave just enough moral sanction to individual pride and "face" that many people were no longer willing to confess for the sake of community. Now they wished to act on their individual consciences. But the logic of accusation and confession had not quite caught up with their new sense of obligation and responsibility. From this point of view the events in Salem are a terrible result of uneven moral and cultural transition, away from one world view, that of the Puritan, toward another, that of the outward-oriented Great Awakening (Boyer and Nissenbaum 1974, 209–216; Miller 1957, 153–166).

In order to understand the events at Salem in the 1690s, we must take seriously a number of competing perspectives. The unusual outbreak in 1691–1692 at Salem Village happened where it did largely because of the unusually high level of tensions that divided the village and set it against Salem Town. The events happened when they did because several rising trajectories of anxiety came together at this moment and place: the social and religion tensions within the village were rising at the same time that fears of Indian attacks from the west and at the same time as a crisis in Massachusetts governance. The accusations had the content they did because of the long history of ideas about witches and Satan; they died down as sharply as they did because of local doubts and debates among influential churchmen about those ideas.

As Mary Beth Norton (2003) argues, these events involved all of Essex County, Massachusetts, and not just Salem Village and Town. Indeed, one of the distinctive features of the 1691–1692 events was precisely the extent to which Salem villagers accused people living in Andover and Salem Town, with whom they had had little or no contact. We might, however, draw parallels between the way in which rising levels of economic tension and anxiety in Salem created a geographically expansive pattern of witchcraft accusation, and the ways in which accusations in some African societies have reached beyond the usual range of kin and neighbors to include the rich and the powerful. In both contemporary Africa and late seventeenth-century New England, new patterns of trade, gain, and political power created new lines of worry, hostility, and resentment.

Note that at the same time that we can see parallel, powerful, psychological changes in two very different times and places, we also explain each set of changes in terms of local ideas and forces. The anthropological insistence on locally based accounts of change precludes easy recourse to vague psychological notions, such as "modernization," or political economic ones, such as "globalization," as if such concepts explained a local series of events. At the same time, the anthropological insistence on comparisons and regional analyses can lead to better understandings of the mechanisms and processes underlying social change. Earlier, we saw an example of such an analysis in the case of Bruce Knauft's studies of sorcery in South Coast New Guinea societies. Knauft first showed the particular set of events that made sorcery accusations plummet in the society he studied. He then pointed to very different trajectories in other New Guinea societies; these contrasts allowed him to point to the "differences that made a difference" for this region of New Guinea.

For Salem, Norton argues (262–265) that the trajectories of accusations and confessions depended on the specific social character of each village. Salem Village, long racked by internal dissension, produced many who denied the accusations against them, and thus led to the reliance on spectral confessions. In nearby Andover, the site of many accusations, people were accustomed to proceeding by consensus. In that town, many people, especially women and children, acceded to the demands of their male elders that they confess. For example, Mary Tyler later told Increase Mather of the series of pronouncements made to her by her brother-in-law, magistrates, and the Reverend John Emerson that she was a witch; Emerson seems to have tried to beat the devil out of her. She succumbed to these accusations and confessed. Most telling was her brother-in-law's assertion that "God would not suffer so many good men to be in such an error about it" (i.e., her guilt), in other words, not to confess would be intolerable since so many prominent people had stated that she was a witch.

9 Worship, Hierarchy, Conflict: Focus on Hinduism

*I*n previous chapters we have approached a particular aspect of religion and drawn from various traditions to highlight certain cross-religious practices, and to encourage comparativist thinking. But this approach carves up one set of practices and ideas, experienced by actors as coherent, into components. Here we invert the priority to explore the ritual, intellectual, and sociopolitical dimensions of the Hindu tradition in India. I try to give a multidimensional portrait of one religious tradition by moving from worship rituals and ideas about deities to social hierarchies and political conflicts. In later chapters we will refer back to some of the material covered here to rebuild a comparative look at religious dimensions of nationalism, laws, and violence.

Sacrifice, Offerings, and Deities

*I*n India, sacrifice, offerings, and devotions are directed toward gods, of which there are many. About 80 percent of India's 800 million people consider themselves Hindus, and most of them, daily and in countless ways (including sacrificial ways), carry out rituals of offerings and homage to the gods (Fuller 1992, 29–56).

Some gods are entirely specific to a village or district. Others may have locally specific forms, but are also manifestations of pan-Indian gods. Particularly important are Vishnu and Shiva. These two gods stand in complementary relationship to each other, Vishnu as the preserver and Shiva the destroyer, Vishnu the king and Shiva the ascetic (the renouncer of worldly pleasures), Vishnu at the center of the world and Shiva outside of it. (Brahma, not to be confused with the Brahmin caste grouping, is less prominent in worship, but is in fact the creator.) Because creation is cyclical—creation following destruction in the cycles of cosmic history—both are necessary elements in the world.

Vishnu is usually worshipped through one of his ten incarnations, in particular as Rama or Krishna. The ancient epic of the Ramayana tells of Rama's life as the king of the northern realm of Ayodhya (later the site of intense conflict; see below). The epic represents his life as the model for a righteous king's conduct. The Ramayana is known throughout India (and much of Southeast Asia) in various versions, some emphasizing Rama's divinity. It is read or viewed today in the forms of sacred texts, popular stories, comic books, and shadow puppet plays, and during 1987–1988 it appeared as a hugely popular television series—a series which also raised popular enthusiasm for Hindu nationalist politics.

Krishna is portrayed as a warrior or as a mischievous child. His battles are recounted in another well-known epic, the Mahabharata. But he also transcends mere human warfare. In a section of the epic called the Bhagavad Gita, he counsels his cousin Arjuna to remain above the world even as he is forced to continue his battles. Krishna is also worshipped as a youth and remembered for his romance with the cowherdess Radha.

Shiva has many manifestations. He may be represented by a phallic linga statue, or as a human-looking image. Shiva has sons, Skanda and Ganesha, the latter represented with an elephant head. Both Vishnu and Shiva may have different wives in different temples, although Vishnu is most often represented with the goddess of fortune, Lakshmi.

Vishnu and Shiva each has followers, Vaishnavas and Shaivas, who worship them either by these names or in their local manifestations, often alongside other, lesser deities. Each temple in India is in principle unique, and each is dedicated to a particular, local form of a deity. For Shiva and Vishnu, this localization of worship means that they are addressed by a distinctive name. In the south Indian temple to Minakshi, for example, Shiva is present as Sundareshwara, Minakshi's consort. At a temple in Benares, Shiva's holiest site on the Ganges river in north India, he is addressed as Vishwanatha (Fuller 1992, 37–38).

Priest purifies the image of Shiva with water, Shiva temple at Yanaimangalam, Tamil Nadu state, India. (COURTESY OF DIANE MINES.)

As with the Virgin Mary, one person and yet also distinct in her many manifestations in the thousands of Marian shrines (see Chapter 10), these Shivas are many and one. Indeed, some Hindus say the same of Vishnu and Shiva, that they are one, Vishnu–Shiva. Many temples have legends explaining how it was that Shiva or Vishnu came to occupy a spot at that particular temple—after a battle, or a great deed, or to become the consort of a local deity. The one-and-yet-many conception thus is basic to Hindu religion, but at the same time a feature that at least some Hindus find requires an explanation, usually in the form of a legend.

The same unity-and-multiplicity is found with respect to the Goddess, Devi, who exists in multiple forms. As Durga, she fights off demons; as Kali or Shakti, she is power itself and is supreme over the gods, often shown trampling on Shiva. She manifests herself as not only a consort of one of the great gods, but also in local forms, where she not only brings powers of heat, and sometimes disease, but also fertility—all being forms of her power, shakti. In south India each local settlement has its own tutelary goddess, known by one name throughout that region. Thus, in much of Tamil Nadu (Fuller 1992, 43) the goddess is Mariyamman: Mariyamman of this place versus Mariyamman of that place—different goddesses and yet also localized forms of the single Goddess.

But Hindus also have local, lesser deities, and because Vishnu and Shiva, concerned with the cosmos, are unlikely to respond to requests for assistance in everyday matters, worshipers turn to local, lesser deities, such as the god-queen Minakshi mentioned earlier, or still lesser deities worshiped by particular castes. These deities may be ghosts who were enshrined as a means of controlling their powers, or they may be humans, who can be especially relied on to respond to human problems. A village might have dozens of these deities, worshiped by different persons or groups, or approached for particular problems.

Thus some Hindus identify little goddesses, matas, that occupy various places in the environment—in a thorn bush, under a three-brick "altar," in a house. They are associated with the Goddess, and their festival is on her day of Navaratri, but they are distinct from her. As with the kami of Japan (Chapter 3), these deities are many and mostly unnamed. They may enter certain men and women and possess them, and through this possession heal a child or answer a vexing question posed by a fellow-villager.

At the other end of the deity scale, modern religious and political movements have taken specific gods as symbols for their idea of an all-Hindu India. A prominent Bengali nationalist, Bankim Chandra Chatterjee, created a form of the goddess as "Mother India," Bharat Mata (Fuller 1992, 42). In her temple at Benares she is represented not as a personage but as a map of India—a literalistic fusion of the goddess with the nation and the state!

Do Hindus Sacrifice?

The Hindu ideology best known to the outside world is that of renouncing violence and avoiding eating meat. And yet animal sacrifice continues to be an important part of religious practice, especially, but not exclusively, in eastern and parts of southern India. Goats, pigs, fowls, and, ideally, a male buffalo are slaughtered and offered to deities— smaller animals to lesser deities and the buffalo to goddesses, and in particular to the

Woman cooking ponkal, *a dish cooked from "raw rice" and suitable for Brahmans, to be offered to the "backyard god" pictured to the left, at Yanaimangalam.* (COURTESY OF DIANE MINES.)

Goddess in the form of Durga, who slew the buffalo-demon and whose victory is celebrated on Durga Puja or Navaratri (Fuller 1992, 83–105; Hiltebeitel 1985).

As in most religions where it is practiced, Hindu animal sacrifice is both a substitute for the giver and a gift to the god, a way of both honoring the god and transacting with him or her. Animals are often sacrificed to "hot" deities who bring violence, and particularly epidemic diseases such as smallpox. The offering appeases them and honors them, asks for the disease to be removed, and for the deity to protect the sacrificer. The meat offering is a substitute for the sacrificer; it is offered, consumed by the goddess, and then taken back to be eaten as prasada ("blessed food," "grace") by those present, who thereby take in the grace of the deity. The deity is both responsible for disease and the source of grace, and the twinned acts of sacrifice and consumption bring together these two functions.

Although in the term used to denote it, sacrifice (bali) is contrasted to worship with vegetable foods (puja), in ritual practice it often complements vegetable worship. Animal sacrifice may conclude a sequence of worship events, or vegetables and meat may be separately offered to two complementary deities.

How can sacrificial practices continue to coexist with the principles of nonviolence? It is not as if sacrifice is a marginal practice that has somehow escaped the attention of

Brahmans. Indeed, in eastern India a Brahman priest often purifies the sacrificial animal before its slaughter (which is carried out by someone else), and the offering may take place at a major temple. One Brahman in west India told the anthropologist David Pocock (1973, 72–73), when asked about the animal sacrifices he conducted on the occasions of building house foundations, that "of course it's violence (hinsa). So what? You can't have a foundation ceremony without a blood sacrifice, it's essential and that's that." Although he was never present at the actual killing of the animal, the Brahman considered these and other sacrifices to simply be a necessary way of responding to the demands of certain deities.

Buffalo sacrifice was outlawed at independence in 1947, and from time to time the police try to break up sacrificial rituals. Stories circulate (Fuller 1992, 104) as to how officers who made these attempts were rendered blind by local goddesses until they allowed the ritual to proceed.

The Vedic Roots of Indian Sacrifice

Sacrifice once served as the mainstay of Indian religion, of what is often called the Vedic religion that preceded Buddhism and modern Hinduism. Indian religious ideology shows a change from practicing animal sacrifice to renouncing meat consumption (a change that parallels—in quite different form, of course–changes in Jewish ritual practice).

Hindus have available a large number of older sacred works, including the early texts (the Rig Veda and the Upanishads) composed over the millennium 1400–400 B.C.E and known collectively as Veda, "knowledge"; the two later epics already mentioned, the Ramayana and Mahabharata (conventionally but controversially dated between 500 B.C.E and 400 C.E.); and subsequent treatises on law, state craft, and devotions. Evidence for early sacrifice comes from the four Sanskrit texts called the Vedas. The Vedas consist chiefly of hymns for use in sacrificial ritual; the oldest, the Rig Veda, describes how the world and its institutions were created by sacrificing Purusha ("Man"). The four exemplary, male victims—horse, bull, ram, and he-goat—served as substitutes for human sacrifice, and were killed and cooked.

Agni, the god of fire, is said in these texts to be present at all sacrifices. Fire, today as well as in antiquity, is required for sacrificing even grain and milk products—recall the clarified butter placed onto the fire in household worship, and the camphor flame used at temples. In the Vedas, Agni is described as receiving the sacrifice with his tongue of flame, and carrying it up to the other deities with his smoke. The very first hymn in the Rig Veda (1.1.1) is to Agni:

> "I pray to Agni, the household priest who is the god of the
>   sacrifice,
> the one who chants and invokes and brings most treasure."

By the sixth and fifth centuries B.C.E the older Rig Vedic religion of sacrifice was submerged by new religious ideologies. One important break with this tradition comes with the teachings of Gautama Buddha (563–483) that one must renounce violence.

Buddhist teachings became the religion of state under Asoka (r. 268–239), who constructed a new imperial state in India. Buddhism supplanted the sacrificial religion of the Vedas. But post-Rig-Vedic texts within the Hindu tradition also appeared after 500 B.C.E (in particular, the Upanishads) that deemphasized sacrifice and instead stressed the individual's obligation to adhere to a moral code, the dharma, that forms part of a universal moral and physical order. In this code every action has its consequences according to the laws of karma, such that one's deeds in this life or in a previous life shape one's current condition. Ideally, one would be able to renounce this life and pursue the goal of liberation (moksha) from the eternal cycle of suffering and rebirth (samsara).

In the first centuries of the common era (C.E.), a new "Brahmanic religious synthesis" developed, with renunciation of violence and sacrifice at its core. Sacrifice continued as a central element in Hindu life, but now as a submerged line of practice under a quite different ideology. Animal sacrifice now was conducted alongside vegetable offerings.

Today, particularly in south India, one may find two deities, side by side, in a temple. One, the dominant one after whom the temple is usually known, only receives vegetarian offerings. The other deity requires, and receives, animal sacrifice. The vegetarian deity's image may be screened from the sacrifice as a sort of insulation. The great gods do not divide into two complementary deities in this fashion; worship of them is more thoroughly shaped by the Brahmanic synthesis, in which the great god, vegetarian worship, and vegetarian Brahmans are absolutely superior to all else.

Offerings and Grace

Let us focus on the more common vegetable offerings to deities, or puja. These offerings may take the form of an informal family rite or that of a village temple festival. You may perform puja to ask a favor from a deity (usually a minor deity; greater ones tend to be above that sort of thing), or when you recite sacred Sanskrit texts about the exploits of a goddess, or when you join a group in singing devotional Hindi songs to Krishna.

A relatively simple puja might be focused on the ancestors of a joint family, of parents, sons, their wives, and children (Fuller 1992, 57–82). Here is an example: in a village in Madhya Pradesh, central India, the father regularly worships his agnatic (through males) ancestors in the home. Just before noon he bathes himself, offering some of the water to his ancestors; his wife and sons' wives meanwhile prepare an elaborate meal. He takes a plate of the food, a dish of clarified butter (ghee), and a brass pot with water from the bath, and, in the kitchen, kneels before a piece of flaming cow dung. He sprinkles water around the dung and places some of the butter on the fire. Again he sprinkles water, and this time places some of the food on the fire. After a third sprinkle he bows before the flame, his hands pressed together, touching his forehead. He then joins his family for their meal. Because some of the food has been offered to the ancestor, all the meal now contains the "grace," prasada, of the ancestors. Homes also contain altars with images of family deities and teachers; women as well as men worship there daily or occasionally.

Worshiper receives from temple priest as prasada *a garland that had been offered to Shiva, Shiva temple at Yanaimangalam.* (COURTESY OF DIANE MINES.)

Here is a second example: in the southern Indian state of Tamil Nadu, where in a village temple a priest is ready to honor Minakshi, the goddess-queen of an ancient kingdom, and her consort Lord Shiva, in one of his many local manifestations. Each of the deities is represented by a two-foot-high movable image, set up in the temple complex and draped with white cloth. Musicians play, and their loud drumming signals the close of each ritual stage. A chanter recites sacred formulas (mantras). The priest purifies the images by rubbing them with a series of liquids, including sesame-seed oil, milk, and water that has been infused with divine power through the chanting of mantras. The gods' images are adorned with clothes, jewelry, and flowers, and their foreheads are marked with three stripes of white ash, the mark of Shiva. Food is held out to the deities while water is sprinkled around the offering. The priest waves oil lamps and a candelabra with seven camphor flames in front of the images. People attending the ritual then crowd in to place their hands over the flames and touch their fingers to their eyes, and to accept white ash from the priests to place on their foreheads.

This temple ritual may be reduced or elaborated. The images may be purified with water before the ritual, and at its conclusion butter may be poured onto a flame as a final offering. More foods may be offered, and distributed to all worshipers. Or the ritual may be reduced to a presentation of one camphor flame to the deity, with a plantain on the side as an offering. The reduced ritual is still valid (it counts as puja); the elaborations are not superfluous (they add to what is accomplished).

Forms of offering vary within India and abroad. Major Hindu communities are found in Africa, Europe, and the Americas, and Hindus make up a large proportion of

Girl with food that she has offered and received as prasada, *part of an annual offering she makes to fulfill a vow, temple to Murukan, son of Shiva, Pattamadai, Tamil Nadu state, India.* (COURTESY OF DIANE MINES.)

the populations of some Caribbean islands, Fiji, and Bali. Men and women may worship at home or in a temple, where the deity may be an incarnation of a great god, usually Vishnu or Shiva, or a local deity. Festivals all revolve around making offerings to the gods. Festivals vary across India, but include the springtime Holi, celebrated in north India to mark the burning of the demonness Holika and the start of the agricultural season, and a sequence of festivals in September–October, in particular the festival of lights, Diwali, a time for welcoming, and escorting, departed ancestors. (The celebration of Diwali at my own university is one of the season's highlights, with students of all religious affiliations lining up overnight to get tickets.)

All forms of offering, simple or elaborate, involve purifying, communicating, and making offerings. Some objects are by their origin pure, such as cow products, from butter to dung to the ash of the dung, and thus can be used in rituals. You can purify something by pouring water over it, thus the importance of bathing, particularly in the Ganges, and sprinkling water at an altar.

People and deities communicate through multiple channels: chants, music, words, and gestures. Before the gods one always shows respect through the gesture called namaste or pranam, holding the hands together and touching the forehead. It, too, may be succinct or elaborated: a supplicant may merely hold up the hands to the forehead, or may bow down, even touch the feet of the deity. You also indicate respect to other people by drawing on this same repertoire of gestures, and according to how they rank in the social hierarchy relative to you. Through this gesture you honor "that bit of god which is in every person."

We also see the deities—and they see us. We exchange darshan, "vision," just as we exchange gestures and words. A priest can attribute this power of seeing to the statue of a deity by painting eyes onto its face. This act brings up a critical point about images in India: the image is not the same as the deity, but the deity comes to be in the image, and also, at any one moment, exists in many different images throughout India. Worshipers enhance the exchange of vision by placing a light, especially a camphor flame, by the altar.

These exchanges of vision already imply the commingling of human and divine essences, but this exchange focuses on food. Whatever we do to dress a deity, sing to it, or chant over it, we must feed it. The food may be anything that people eat, but it is always offered to the deity, taken back, and distributed to those present—family, neighbors, or temple-goers. It may simply be set before the god, or it may be set on fire—"the flame is the tongue of the gods." The consumed food becomes the embodiment of the deity's power or "grace," the literal meaning of prasada, the food offering. Anything that has been placed in contact with the deity and then returned to humans—ash, water, food, flowers—is prasada, and conveys that divine power to the human partakers.

We can see that puja is most importantly *transaction:* something is given and something is received, and by this event the worshiper takes on something of the divine being.

Reform and Devotional Movements

Opposition to sacrifice was one element in broader movements for religious reform and national self-determination. Some of these movements were influenced by Western rationalist ideas about religion, but the movements also incorporated Brahmans' ideas about proper Hinduism. Brahmans had relegated sacrifice and meat-eating to non-Brahmans, but new movements for reform urged all Hindus to renounce meat-eating (Fuller 1992, 155–203).

Reform movements began in the early nineteenth century with Ram Mohan's Brahmo Samaj in Bengal, which claimed to have discovered a "rational" and monotheistic Hinduism in the Vedas and Upanishads. Indeed, Hindu reform movements share with many Islamic and Christian ones an emphasis on returning to the sacred texts, not as a way of escaping the present but, quite the contrary, in order to rationalize religious practice and purge it of undesirable traditions and superstitions. In the Hindu case, the practices to be discarded included most spectacularly the self-immolation of widows (sati) and the exclusion of untouchables. The still more influential Arya Samaj movement, which spread across north India after 1877, was less radical in its reform agenda, but it, too, called for an end to animal sacrifice as a barbaric incongruity in a religion dedicated to nonviolence. Arya Samaj was dedicated to universalizing the Hindu message and making it accessible to members of all caste groupings—and, indeed, to uniting Christians and Muslims under the banner of Vedic principles.

A different kind of reform comes from the proliferation of Agamic schools, designed to lead priests to memorize the important texts to be used for ritual, those thought to have been produced by Shiva for Shivaite temples (Fuller 2003). These schools produce priests who may be no more expert or adept at performing the physical acts of worship and offering, but who now know what to say during their physical acts. These schools promote the idea that one must learn the content of religions before learning to practice it—an element of reformism that we will find elsewhere as well (see Chapter 11).

Some reform movements have emphasized devotion, and these movements appeal particularly to middle-class Indians. Urban, middle-class associations bring people together to sing songs of bhakti ("devotion") to gods. Most popular are songs about the exemplary devotion of the cowherdess Radha for the god Krishna. The songs sung in their praise are erotic and religious. These associations provide new ways for urban dwellers to create social forms of religiosity, and in some cases also to maintain religious purity in an urban world of social intermingling—hence their appeal to some middle-class Brahmans.

These devotionalists joined nationalists and other reformers to oppose animal sacrifice. In Gujarat, west India, where Vaishnava (Vishnu-centered) devotionalist movements campaigned against sacrifice, many villagers have simply abandoned the goddesses who demand animal sacrifice. The convergent pressure of these movements has been to flatten out worship: all deities should be treated the same, as vegetarians. Mahatma Gandhi contributed to this pressure, raising his own Vaishya caste's vegetarian dietary code into a universal moral imperative that "Hindus shall not eat meat" (Fuller 1992, 103).

Within the collection of practices, teachings, and ideas called "Hinduism," a tension has persisted between a notion of religion as effective action, where an offering produces a result, and religion as obedience or devotion to transcendent deities. This tension has itself produced some of the diversity of practices observable in Hindu settings, whether in South Asia or elsewhere, and it invokes broader differences about what religious practice really is: obedience to a deity, or actions taken to obtain material or spiritual benefit?

Bathing at Benares

*T*he Hindu pilgrim's goal is to multiply his temple experience through journey, to "exchange vision" (darshan) with deities many times in many places. Each site is called a "crossing place, ford" (tirtha) to somewhere beyond; a pilgrimage is a tirtha-yatra, a journey to a ford (Fuller 1992, 204–223).

The prototypical goal is Benares (Kashi, Varanasi) in north central India (Eck 1982). This "City of Light" lies alongside the Ganges, a river said to have descended from heaven to earth. Over seventy landings line its banks, some containing temples to Shiva, who makes Benares his earthly home. Benares has always been an earthly crossing, the place where the old trade route across northern India crossed the river Ganges. As with other places of pilgrimage, it is also a spiritual cross, one where earth and heaven meet. Here the dead may be assisted in crossing over the Ganges to the condition of moksha, liberation from rebirth, the ultimate goal of the Hindu. Here, too, the gods may descend from heaven to earth. Shiva lives not only in the city's many temples, but also in its ground and buildings: "The very stones of Kashi are Shiva," goes the popular saying.

The gods descend and pilgrims cross at many other fords throughout India. Of the thousands of places where Shiva, or the hero Rama, or the goddess Durga have emerged to split rocks or crushed enemies, a few cities are particularly favored. Some are associated with Rama, and in particular his capital at Ayodhya. Others, including several associated with Krishna, are on mountains; still others mark the four corners of India.

Benares is the most widely acclaimed of all, however. To many Hindus it is the center of the universe (as is Jerusalem to some Christians, Mecca to some Muslims, Beijing to some Chinese), and located directly under the heavens. Benares also encapsulates worship in India: temples in other parts of India, from the Himalayas to the southern tip of the subcontinent, have replicas in Benares. One may visit these replica temples and exchange vision with their deities without leaving the city. The city has absorbed their power. And in one new temple the devotion is of "Mother India," Bharat Mata, represented in the form of a relief map inside the temple where the image would usually be. The map shows the major pilgrimage places, which pilgrims can view and thus "exchange vision" with all at once! But this logic of replication also goes in the reverse direction, for Benares is replicated elsewhere in hundreds of temples called "Shiva Kashi" found throughout India (Fuller 1992, 208–209). The deities are here, in this city, because gods and God, the spiritual force behind all the gods, is everywhere. One pilgrim, longing for the black stone dedicated to Shiva found near his own village, remarked: "I miss God."

Benares also attracts pilgrims to bathe in its particularly sacred waters and to cremate their dead. The pilgrim's first duty is to bathe in the river on one of its many landings. Pilgrims bathe in the Ganges to partake of its purifying powers, brown and replete with ashes and bacteria though it is. Indeed, usually they take the popular "Five Fords" trip along the riverfront, where they bathe at each of five landings (ghat). At each stop, the pilgrim recites a statement of intention, that he or she is undertaking this pilgrimage, and if the pilgrimage is made to fulfill a vow or with a goal in mind (which is not necessary), a statement to this effect is added, such as "I am making this pilgrimage in hope of bearing a son." Each stop has stories of kings and gods associated with it, and nearby are temples, or phallic linga statues devoted to Shiva, or even a mosque (Eck 1982, 211–251).

The last bath is taken at the landing of Manikarnika, at the center of the three-mile long waterfront. This bath is the most important. The site has a cremation ground and a large sacred well nearby. Shiva is in the temple, but Vishnu built the well as the world's very first tirtha. And a manifestation of the Goddess or Devi guards the well.

Manikarna is called the "burning landing" because when seen from the river one sees the plumes of flames from the crematorium located among the temples. Those who die in Benares are cremated next to the Ganges and their ashes are scattered over the waters. Some who die elsewhere have their ashes brought, or even mailed, to Benares. When one's ashes lie on the Ganges, one's spirit crosses over from earth to liberation. But even failing this, pilgrims will say prayers for the dead to ensure that the ancestors will dwell in heaven. So important are these rites that when long-lost ashes from the cremation of Mohandas K. Ghandi's body were discovered nearly a half a century after the event, they were carried to the Ganges to be poured into the waters (*New York Times* January 31, 1997).

Newly arrived corpses are placed by the river's edge before being dipped into its waters for their final bath and then hoisted onto the funeral pyre. The eldest son circumambulates the pyre, lights it, and when the burning is finished, walks away without looking back. Members of an untouchable caste in charge of the cremation ground throw the ashes into the river, where they are gradually carried downstream.

The religious importance of seeing sacred places and images helps us understand why a rapid bus tour of a large number of sites makes religious sense. Pilgrimage is the major reason why Hindus travel, and they do so by the millions every year, traveling on foot, by bus, or by train. They value the journey itself: joining others in travel, making merit by giving alms, seeing many deities, getting away from normal routines, and experiencing another realm—both another part of the country and a glimpse into the beyond. Hardship may itself be felt as a proof that merit has been earned through the journey, even if it is not explicitly sought out.

Or, pilgrims may choose a bus tour that, without the hardship of journeying on foot, offers a greater number of chances for darshan with deities. The anthropologist Ann Grodzins Gold (1988, 262–298) traveled by bus with a group of pilgrims from northwestern India to the eastern coast of Orissa. The pilgrims were from different castes and came from town and village settings. The villagers included Brahmans (the order or varna associated with the priesthood), Rajputs (traditionally a warrior caste and of the second-ranking Kshatriyas order), and people from farming, gardening, and other miscellaneous castes. The pilgrimage did not erase these distinctions; indeed, the castes stayed apart; "the fact that we were sharing a pilgrimage did not act as a leveler of rank" (Gold 1988, 269).

On the road, pilgrims sang songs about the deities Ganesha and Rama, and about the Sun King, from whom a woman in the song takes darshan each morning. They stopped at one site after another. Upon reaching a tirtha-yatra they would bathe in the waters, view the images in the temples, make gifts to priests and beggars, and occasionally perform a short offering ritual. They traversed the country where Lord Krishna had spent his childhood and observed darshan tableaux of his babyhood. They made a whirlwind tour of Benares's many temples, which left a colorful blur in their minds. The deepest and most favorable impression was made by the sea. "These Hindus had seen countless icons in their lives," remarks Gold (1988, 284) after one pilgrim, emerging from the famed temple at Puri, said with a shrug that "Well, God is God." But, she continues, they had seen "only one sea."

What did the pilgrimage mean to them? None of Gold's fellow pilgrims thought that bathing in sacred waters would cleanse them of bad deeds. Rather, and in a more diffuse way, the entire experience of getting out of everyday routines, taking many powerful darshans of gods, enduring the hardships of the road, and giving alms to beggars would be good for the soul. Hitting the road and seeing the gods lightens the pilgrim of goods and attachments and concerns, bringing her or him nearer to "the deity within himself." Approaching one's inner divinity prepares oneself for the moment, perhaps in some future life, when one will finally attain release, moksha. "Sweeping the road ahead," suggested one widow.

While some pilgrims thought that pilgrimages causally improve one's chances of eventually achieving moksha, others were more skeptical. One pilgrim told Gold (1988, 288) that traveling and bathing could not effect what God determines, although He would reward giving alms: "From what does moksha come? From his own hand, God's, that's from whom. It does not come from wandering. Whatever you give, in whatever place give it. From this comes moksha. What kind of dharma is dirtying the water? But dharma is giving-and-taking."

In scholarly debates as well, Hindus are of two minds about what pilgrimages get you. On the one hand, some commentators on the classic texts assure the pilgrim that: "Even if a man be a sinner or a rogue or irreligious he becomes free from all sin if he goes to Benares." But others equally clearly say the opposite, that it is the inner self that must be purified through meditation. After all, observes one scholar, "Fish are born and die in the water (of tirthas); and *they* do not go to heaven."

Muslim–Hindu Violence

During the 1980s and 1990s there took place violent conflicts and riots pitting Hindus against Muslims. The flash point for some of these was located in the northern Indian city of Ayodhya, Rama's birthplace (van der Veer 1994). Ayodhya is a holy tirtha over the holy river Sarayu and a place for the pilgrim to "cross over" from the mundane world to make contact with Rama. Many Hindus claim that Rama was born on a site in the city where the Moghul (Muslim dynasty) ruler Babar built a mosque in the sixteenth century. Moghul rulers allowed Hindus to worship on this site, even inside the mosque compound, and the subsequent Muslim dynasty endowed Hindu temples in the city.

In the twentieth century, relations between Muslims and Hindus deteriorated as in much of South Asia. Hindus launched attacks on the Babar mosque during the celebration of the Day of Sacrifice in 1912, and again in 1934. The situation heated up further after the 1947 Partition and the flight of many Muslims to Pakistan. In 1949, a statue of Rama appeared in the mosque. Hindus and Muslims naturally interpreted this event in very different ways. For the Hindus, Rama had appeared in their midst, giving them a sign to liberate his birthplace from the Muslims. For the Muslims, their mosque had been defiled. Riots ensued, and the army was called in. The government closed the mosque, and it remained closed to both Muslims and Hindus until 1984, when national politics came to a head in the city.

By the mid-1980s there had emerged a strong Hindu nationalist party, the Bharatiya Janata Party (BJP), which garnered support from Hindu nationalist movements and in particular from the Vishva Hindu Parishad (VHP). The VHP was an attempt to create a united Hindu organization. Given India's diversity in religious practice and beliefs, creating a unified Hinduism would be a daunting task. What Hindus plausibly shared, however, was a belief in certain sacred objects and symbols. One was the sacred river the Ganges, and in 1983 the VHP organized a drive to symbolize Hindu unity based on shared water. Large trucks were sent throughout the country, each carrying enormous bronze pots with water from the Ganges. This water was given to villagers en route, and the pots were replenished with water from local sacred sources, symbolizing Hindu unity—and giving the VHP a way to firm up its local support network.

Hindu unity meant opposition to Muslims, and the VHP called for mosques to be removed from several sacred spots, including in Ayodhya. By 1989 the VHP had begun to mobilize support for building a new temple in Ayodhya. In November, just before Indian general elections, Hindus were urged to send or bring bricks for the temple, and bricks poured in—from Hindus in Europe and the United States as well as from throughout India. The VHP was eventually stopped from building the temple by the ruling Congress government, but the flames thus fanned led to massacres of Muslims, and numerous Hindu deaths as well, in northern and eastern India.

One year later, violence erupted again, this time brought on by the political party, the BJP. The BJP joined forces with the VHP in part to oppose the government's plan to reserve a greater number of jobs and positions for lower-caste people. (In its mass support and vote-getting, the BJP appeals most to urban, upper-caste people.) Despite police bans, some volunteers bent on rebuilding "Rama's temple" made it to Ayodhya, where many were killed. In December 1990, to further dramatize BJP support for the Hindu nationalist cause, the party leader L. K. Advani began a "chariot-led procession" to Ayodhya. Perhaps because the Ramayana epic had been serialized on television a few years earlier, Advani decked his party out as Rama's army. His chariot, drawn by an air-conditioned Toyota, was carved and gilded to recall Rama's chariot. He carried the bow of Rama, brandishing it to ward off his enemies. Supporters, marching alongside, were decked out in warrior garb and handed bows as well.

The procession began from a place in Gujarat, west India, widely associated with the tenth-century destruction by a Muslim ruler of Hindu temples. This choice of starting point played up anti-Muslim sentiments. The procession moved across India before being halted in the eastern state of Bihar, where Advani was arrested—an arrest which then led to the collapse of the fragile coalition government. Mass strikes and riots followed; all trains and buses that passed anywhere near Ayodhya were canceled, but nonetheless many people were killed. Then in 1992, supporters of the BJP/VHP rushed to Ayodhya and demolished the temple. The riots that ensued led to over one thousand deaths, mostly of Muslims (van der Veer 1994).

Though religious sentiments were front and center during the campaigns and riots, we would err in thinking of these conflicts as the emergence of "primordial" or traditional sentiments in opposition to the nation-state. The conflicts and riots developed out of a modern idea of a Hindu nation-state, itself with roots in colonial constructions of religious communities and postcolonial electioneering. In the nineteenth century, the British created the idea of a "Hindu majority"—and a Muslim minority—through the census. They interpreted these categories as native Hindus versus foreign Muslims. This view has had an effect on later Indian notions, promoting the idea that one's primary loyalty is as a Hindu to the "Hindu community" or as a Muslim to the "Muslim community," rather than to local communities or leaders. And it was on these notions that Advani and other Hindu nationalist leaders drew to mobilize support for Rama and anger against Muslims. Although Hindu–Muslim tensions predate colonialism and independence, the kind of violent religious nationalism exhibited in this case (and in many other places) is to a great extent a modern creation.

And for most Hindus, as for most people, anywhere, these nationalist claims have little to do with the practical bases and emotional pulls of religious practice. "Ram is supposed to dwell in our hearts, not in a temple," said one north Indian villager (quoted in Fuller 1992, 261). "We don't need to learn about our dharma from politicians seeking votes."

10 Imagery and Faith: Focus on Worldwide Catholicism

With Augustine, the Catholic Church set out to do two things that one might think near-impossible: to spread throughout the world and to do so all the while maintaining a strict hierarchy centered on the Pope. What follows is a very specific window into this truly transnational religion: through its use of imagery in promoting faith.

Relics and Images in Catholicism

Catholic imagery has been based on different types of meaning and multiple associations in the minds of worshipers. When we think of Catholicism we usually think of elaborate representations of saints, Jesus, and Mary. But Catholic images also draw on other kinds of symbolic meanings to become powerful, multivocalic foci for worship and social life.

A famous example is the Shroud of Turin, a cloth held in Turin, Italy, since 1578 that has on its surface an image of a bearded face, said by some to be the image of Christ. The shroud is venerated by many Catholics, not just because it is a likeness of Jesus but because they think that it was produced by direct and miraculous physical contact with his face, in a fashion similar to the process that produces a photograph. This claim of direct contact generates in many pious people a sense of direct communication between the viewer and Jesus. The arguments about the Shroud's authenticity turn exclusively on this issue of contact, not on its resemblance to Jesus. In fact, the iconic qualities of the image on the Shroud, its resemblance to conventional ideas of what Jesus looked like, are precisely what skeptics point to when they claim that it is only a painting. The relative weight of iconic and indexical meanings is thus of great importance for the Shroud's religious status.

Christianity is, after all, founded on ideas of contact and physical presence, in particular the idea of incarnation, the embodiment of godliness in tangible form as Jesus Christ. The central ritual of the Church is based on the worshiper's direct contact with Christ through eating and drinking of his body. Holy Communion enacts the miracle of the Eucharist, in which ordinary bread and wine are consecrated by a priest and, at that exact moment, turned into the body and blood of Jesus. This countlessly repeated miracle parallels the sacrifice Jesus made of himself for the sake of humanity.

The idea that Christ is in the bread and wine was popularly assumed for centuries. It was finally codified in 1215, when the Fourth Lateran Council ruled that consecration does indeed convert the ordinary substances into Christ, or, in the technical language of the Church, that "transubstantiation" takes place. The Council also ruled that Christ was whole in every particle of bread and wine "under two species." This second idea, called "concomitance," responded to the concern, evidently widespread at the time, that when one dropped crumbs of the bread on the floor one was dropping bits of Christ, that chewing the bread was chewing his bones, and so forth.

The History of Relics and the Host

Relics preserve the history of religious miracles through their own history of physical contact with sacred persons or events. They make up an important part of the history of Catholic religious objects—which is also the history of Catholic politics. Religious objects have mediated between the community and the church hierarchy, between local and universal perspectives, between religion and the state, and between cultures.

The central Church ritual, communion or the Eucharist, is based on a miracle of incarnation. In the early Church the ritual of communion was expansive and collective. The priest said "Peace be with you"; the lay worshipers responded in kind and exchanged the "kiss of peace" with each other (men with men, women with women). Worshipers then brought forward their sacrifices of bread and wine to be consecrated by the priest. Communion was thus the Church partaking of Christ and worshipers communing with each other. Christianity drew on its Jewish roots but also broadened them. Communion widened the bounds of the Jewish seder to include the entire community beyond the realm of one's family and friends. Communion thus modeled socially the universal ideal and ambition of the Church (Bynum 1987, 48–69; Feeley-Harnik 1981, 107–168).

Communion recreates for a brief moment what is in effect a direct physical link to Christ. But Christian churches also relied on other kinds of sacred indexes to maintain a sense of connection among churches and among worshipers. As the Church expanded in Europe and North Africa it created a network of churches under the control of Rome. Churches were built on shrines or as shrines, sometimes near or around cemeteries located just outside city walls, where the buried remains of saints sanctified the ground of the new church. There was a practical consideration at work as well—the belief current at the time was that on the day of Resurrection, the first bodies to be taken up to heaven would be those buried near the body of a saint (Ariès 1974).

A Christian shrine or church usually contained sacred objects, an image or relic that gave the shrine its religious status. A relic was a remnant of a saint—a bone, bit of hair, or an entire corpse—or an object that had been made sacred by contact with a saint (or Jesus). It was movable, and so separate from the place itself. Except in Ireland, where the pre-Christian Celtic veneration of places continued unabated, it was the relic, not the place, that was considered sacred.

Saints' bodies, sometimes partially or wholly mummified, have been favorite relics for churches. In the early churches they were often exhibited to worshipers and pilgrims. Today as well, the faithful consider saints' bodies to be capable of working miracles. Some bodies exude healing fluids, such as a marble sarcophagus in the French Pyrenees that accumulates clear water. Throughout the year the water is collected by individuals and used for healing, and the remainder is pumped out each July 30 at a special ceremony. Soil may be taken from the burial place of a saint and used to heal, particularly in Ireland and the Americas. A small church near Santa Fe contains such a miraculous source of earth. Bones are also used as church relics, today usually contained in elaborately sculpted boxes or reliquaries.

The logic of sacrality through contact reaches beyond body parts and sacred soil. Paintings and statues may acquire sacred status from having once been in contact with a sacred person or object. For example, some paintings of the Virgin Mary draw their religious force from their historical ties to what is called the True Icon (*Vera Icon*) of Mary: a painting said to have been made by Saint Luke and considered to be holy because he, a holy person, painted it, and not because of a property of the representation itself. Paintings that are understood as copies of the True Icon are found in Italy, Spain, and most famously in Poland. Our Lady of Czestochowa, the national icon of Poland, is a painting of a dark Madonna, and it is housed in a fourteenth-century church in the southwestern part of the country. It is the object of the major pilgrimage for Polish Catholics. It is said to derive from the Saint Luke painting. Other paintings or statues are touched to the painting in Czestochowa, and from that contact derive a special (indexical, we would say) power. Copies of the True Icon become as effective as the original in working miracles. (At least by the sixth century c.e. we find stories of paintings carried into battle to ensure victory.)

Images versus Relics

By the late fourth century, a lively traffic in saints' remains had developed across Europe. Remains were sent as gifts, sometimes stolen from crypts in Italy. This traffic was encouraged by the idea that remains could be divided up, and the saint became present in each fragment (analogous to the idea that Christ was totally present in every fragment of consecrated bread). As Theodoret of Cyrus proclaimed: "in the divided body the grace survives undivided and the fragments, however small, have the same efficacy as the whole body (Bynum 1987, 48–53).

During the eighth century a rapid rise in missionary activity led the Church to develop rules for creating new churches. In 787, the Second Council of Nicaea declared that a new church had to possess a saint's relic in order to be consecrated. The new rule further increased the demand for relics. People began to scour the Roman catacombs for bone fragments that could be attributed to early Christian martyrs, and a virtual flood of these bone fragments poured forth from Rome out into northern Europe. The hunger for relics turned major discoveries of bones into momentous cultural events. In the early ninth century Saint James' bones were discovered in northern Spain, and the site of this discovery, known thereafter as Santiago de Compostela, became the third most important Christian pilgrimage site after Rome and Jerusalem (Nolan and Nolan 1989, 160–171).

The propagation of relics not only expanded the bounds of the Church but also provided a firm spiritual foundation for the empire created by Charlemagne. From the ninth century onward, the oath administered to witnesses was taken on saints' relics, and read: "May God and the saints whose relics these are judge me that I speak the truth" (Rothkrug 1980).

During the early years of Christian expansion, there were no official procedures for evaluating relics, or indeed for canonizing saints. A local church could declare someone to have been a saint and then build a church around him or her. The remains would be disinterred and placed on an altar within the church. If the body was found to be intact, or in the language of the times, "uncorrupt," this condition was attributed to its holy qualities, which had continued to reside in the body after death. (Note that in this tradition intact bodies were signs of purity; by contrast in the Greek Orthodox practices, discussed in Chapter 4, total disintegration of the flesh is a sign that the soul was received into heaven.)

Many of the relics were, in fact, fakes: countless pieces of wood from Christ's cross circulated throughout Europe, as did chalky stones from the Milk Grotto in Bethlehem said to be colored by milk Mary used to nurse Christ. The market pressures also encouraged theft: one Roman deacon named Deusdona contracted to steal the remains of Saint Peter and to supply them, broken down into small parts, to the Franks. As their authenticity increasingly was doubted, their value declined. (Compare with Gresham's Law in economics: "bad money drives out good.")

The Church responded in two ways. First, it began to exert authority over the status of holy man or saint. It carried out its first canonization of a saint in 993 and gradually gained control over that process. Second, the Church tried to substitute images for relics. Early Christian art (like Islamic art) had been largely decorative. Many people felt that the crafting of human figures would be tantamount to worshiping graven images, a fear inherited from Judaism. In the words of Saint Epiphanius in the fourth century C.E.: "When images are put up, the customs of the pagans do the rest." But popular use of imagery, pictures of saints, developed in the late fourth century and became widespread by the sixth. The Church came to encourage this trend in the interest of promoting universalism. Saints, after all, were many, and their stories often emphasized local miracles and military victories rather than the universal message of Christ that was central to the Church. Basing the legitimacy of a local church on relics underscored the local bases for worship rather than the Church's universalism. To the extent that the Church was able to refocus worshipers' attention toward paintings or statues or other images, it would be able to emphasize the universal figures of Mary and Christ, whose bodies were not available to be relics (Nolan and Nolan 1989, 160–171).

To meet popular objections that only relics were sacred—and the practical point that only relics would share in the resurrection—Church authorities encouraged the crafting of reliquaries: elaborately carved boxes, often with jewels and gold, or statues in the image of a saint that contained minute pieces of the saint's bone. These objects were both relics and images. Images such as paintings or ordinary statues were also said to have had direct contact with a sacred person, or, as in the case of the True Icon mentioned above, to have been painted by a saint, or to have been once physically touched to a painting that was painted by a saint, and so forth, along a historical chain of direct, sacred contact. These efforts drew on popular ideas about contact and sacrality but also promoted universal images.

A More Hierarchical Ritual

The Church's efforts to emphasize its universal message over local sacrality gained momentum in the eleventh, twelfth, and thirteenth centuries, a period of growth in the political power of the Church. What we often call the "age of faith," or, in reference to the great energies devoted to church crafting throughout Western Europe, the "age of cathedrals," also saw a shift in the relationship of people to the institution of the Catholic Church. Rome began to exercise more control over local churches, and in each church priests recast their role vis-à-vis lay persons in a more hierarchical or vertical way.

The eleventh century saw the growth of powerful monasteries, which resisted secular control, the struggle for priority in spiritual affairs over the kings, and the Crusades, which began in 1096. The church became "monumental" in several senses. Doctrine was systematically formulated, most notably by Thomas of Aquinas (1225–1274); the great cathedrals of northern Europe were built; and Rome was able to exert ever-greater control over the behavior of individual churches. It was the great age of pilgrimages to such sites as Santiago de Compostela in northern Spain, to England's Canterbury Cathedral, the site of Thomas à Beckett's assassination in 1170 (and the destination of the pilgrims in Chaucer's *Canterbury Tales*), and the first great Holy Year pilgrimage to Rome in 1300. Many religious orders that promoted pilgrimages—Dominicans, Franciscans, Carmelites—were founded during this period.

All these developments added to the general sense of a Christiandom united by movements of people, the mobilization of popular energies, and a central, controlling power lodged in Rome. In worship itself, these changes led to a great focus on the priest's role, as the representative of Rome, over and against that of the people. Communion and other aspects of liturgy became more centralized, more in the hands of priests and monks. Saint Thomas himself wrote that priests engage in the communion of Eucharist on behalf of others. Saints once had come from the popular ranks, even after canonization became a Church monopoly. Now male saints began to be drawn entirely from the ranks of priests (Bynum 1987, 53–69).

The ritual transformation that most evidently represented this change was the shift from *receiving* communion to *seeing* the Host. By the twelfth century churches had begun to offer communion less frequently and instead to concentrate the attention of worshipers on Christ's presence in the bread and wine at the moment they were consecrated by the priest. Christ could be seen on the altar and adored there. Physical contact was downplayed in favor of, again, the image of Christ, albeit an image of the Host that had become Christ.

As priests emphasized the "adoration of the Host" other changes were made as well. Elaborate containers for the Host, reliquaries, were made and placed so all could see. Holes were made in some church walls so that even horses could commune by viewing the Host. The Host began to be raised up for general view; this practice of "elevating the Host" first occurred in Paris in 1200. Fifteen years later Pope Innocent II declared as dogma the miracle of transubstantiation, the change of bread and wine into Christ's body and blood. In 1264 a new feast day, the feast of Corpus Christi, the "body of Christ," began to be celebrated. By the fourteenth century a new kind of vessel called a "monstrance" ("displayer") was created to display the consecrated Host. As the historian John Bossy (1983) writes, the "socially integrative powers of the Host" were transferred from the mass to the feast of Corpus Christi.

From the twelfth century onward, receiving the Host became something priests did. Already by the eleventh century only priests could take Christ in their hands; others had to receive a wafer directly in their mouths from the priest. The priest once had carried out the consecration of the Host in full view and standing facing the worshipers—after all, in the early church it had been their bread and wine that had been brought to be consecrated. But now the priest celebrated with his back to the people. He took communion for their sake with his back turned. Special "rood screens" were constructed to seal him off from view. In these churches communion became a mystery, a miracle that touched only the priest, who was sometimes venerated precisely because of his privileged contact with Christ. In the words of Saint Francis of Assisi (1181–1226): "He touches Christ with his own hands."

The "two species" of the Eucharist now were treated differently. When communion was offered to worshipers, the consecrated cup was sometimes withheld and ordinary wine substituted. The reason given was that the church feared that a careless parishioner could spill Christ's blood. The wafer now became the focus of this longed-for ritual act. It became a strongly held symbol of the unity of the church and of fears of its being desecrated. Anti-Semitism was often voiced as an accusation that someone had defiled the wafers. Stories circulated of Hosts turning to flesh and bleeding in protest against misuse (for example, by sorcerers) or in an effort to warn churchgoers against an approaching danger (Bossy 1983; Bynum 1987, 53–69).

The Host increasingly became a symbol of the church, rather than a source of redemption for the individual person. Some people protested this church control; these protests included demands to receive the Host "in both species," that is, as consecrated wine and bread. A hunger for the chalice and communion intensified, and ordinary people, particularly women, experienced religious devotions and ecstasies as sensing and eating God.

The central objects that located or founded a church also shifted from relics of saints (with the host as one of many relics) to the general adoration of Christ and the Virgin Mary. In 1150 the pope rejected his former title, "Vicar of Saint Peter" for the new one, "Vicar of Christ," shifting his grounds for authority from the presence of Saint Peter's body in Rome (a relic), to his direct receipt of authority from Christ.

The Church also began to desacralize relics and to replace them with images of saints. It developed the idea of the saints and Mary in the "communion of saints," or "the unity under and in Christ of the faithful on the earth, the souls in purgatory, and the blessed in heaven." Dead souls were enrolled in the new brotherhoods and orders as part of this universal community. This idea of the communion of saints allowed one soul to pray for another. Helping other souls through prayer became a major activity both in church masses and at pilgrimage sites.

Christ Incarnate

The Eucharist, as it became the focus of church activity, is best seen as Christ's incarnation—it gave the worshiper direct contact with Christ. Recall that it was only in 1215 that the Church proclaimed as dogma the eucharistic miracle of transubstantiation. The elevation and adoration of the Host began about then, and Corpus Christi followed in 1264.

These steps addressed what we can think of as the problem of Christ's relics (Nolan and Nolan 1989). After all, according to the church, Christ ascended to heaven 40 days after the Resurrection, leaving no body behind to generate relics. In popular opinion he did leave some relics behind: his blood and the earth that was touched by it; pieces of the cross and nails from the cross; garments worn during the Passion; the Shroud of Turin. The church gradually accepted the idea that his milk teeth, foreskin, and spilled blood could, in theory, have remained on the earth even though he ascended to heaven. Popular pressure was for more relics of Christ, perhaps because of the more difficult access to Christ through communion.

The steps taken by the church in the thirteenth century to promote the worship of Christ may have been responses to this pressure. The doctrine of transubstantiation not only provided an officially sanctioned opportunity for direct contact with Christ incarnate, but it also allowed numerous further miracles, at least in the popular imagination.

Sometimes the Host was said to really become flesh and blood. In at least one shrine, in Lanciano, Italy, are small pellets of blood and a strip of flesh said to have been formed from consecrated bread and water during the celebration of Mass by a doubting monk in the eighth century. Bavaria has a shrine where sacramental wine, spilled on an altar cloth in 1330, formed an image of Christ. Christ could now become real, the object of worship (and sometimes even contact) within a more hierarchical church (Clark 1967, 410–434; Nolan and Nolan 1989, 216–290).

Mary and Marys in European Societies

The church has also promoted the adoration of Mary as Mother of God. This "cult of Mary," which undoubtedly draws on older images and ideas of a virgin mother goddess, first appeared in Turkey in 431 and expanded across the West. At some point a popular idea developed that Mary herself was conceived in her mother, Saint Ann, free from the original sin that everyone else receives by virtue of Eve and Adam's transgression in the Garden of Eden. This idea of "immaculate conception"— conception in the womb free of original sin—spread on a popular level but was not immediately accepted by the church. In the sixteenth century, the Council of Trent declared Mary free of original sin, but only in 1854 did Pope Pius IX declare as dogma that Mary indeed had experienced an immaculate conception.

Marian worship on a widespread, dominant scale dates from about the eleventh century and is due in part to the activities of the Cistercian order, all of whose churches were dedicated to Mary. The popular idea that she was bodily assumed into heaven was officially proclaimed as Roman Catholic dogma in 1950. As with Christ, this doctrine meant that very few relics could be claimed to be available: her sash and veil, a few strands of hair, pieces of milky rock white from her breast milk—slim pickings indeed. More popular were images of Mary, usually as the Pietà, holding the body of the dead Christ.

This image of Mary drew, intentionally or not, on much older notions of a virgin mother goddess who bears a child who later dies in her arms. Inanna, the Queen of Heaven in Sumerian mythology, gives up her son Dumuz to torture and death. The Egyptian Isis nurses and mourns for her son Osiris. (And as we shall see, such pre-Christian images are found in the Americas as well.) Pietà images are especially popular in German culture (70 percent of these images are found there), probably because of the long-standing tradition of imperially founded nunneries. Around 1300, Dominican nunneries began to promote the image of a suffering Mary, a representation of their own direct, personal, at times erotic relation to Christ. The pietà image generally becomes popular during times of sadness and war, because it provides an especially apt image for suffering. For example, many new pietà statues were carved after the trauma of the Thirty Years' War in the seventeenth century, and again after the First World War in our own century (Nolan and Nolan 1989, 191–209).

The numerical analysis of to whom a shrine is dedicated shows how sharp has been the change from saints, usually based on relics, to Mary, always based on a shrine image. In the period before 700 C.E., 92 percent of the shrines formed were dedicated to a saint. That percentage dropped to 20 percent in the "high medieval" period of 1100–1400, and has remained about the same since. The percentage of shrines dedicated to Mary was only 6 percent in the early period, but 73 percent in the high medieval period, and level ever since. Shrines dedicated to Christ have remained at below 10 percent throughout the common era (Nolan and Nolan 1989, 155).

Marian Apparitions and Modern Life

Over the past 150 years, Mary has taken on a new identity in the popular imagination, less as Mother of God and more as an individual who intervenes on behalf of individuals in modern, industrialized societies. She begins to appear in the sky to troubled individuals and to offer solace and instructions. Hundreds of such apparitions have occurred in the past two centuries, but seven were approved by local bishops and gained international attention; these occurred in France, Belgium, and Portugal. These visions include the apparitions of Mary at Lourdes, France, in 1858, and in Fatima, Portugal, in 1917. Both were eventually accepted by the Church; most others were not (Zimdars-Schwartz 1991).

In 1917, in Fatima, three children reported a series of appearances of Mary. One of the three, Lucia dos Santos, later discussed in her memoirs her religious upbringing as well as the events surrounding the apparitions. Lucia took her First Communion at age six rather than at the usual age 10. She tells of how the priest told her to kneel before the image of the Virgin and to ask Mary to take care of her heart; when she did so, she saw the statue of the Virgin smile at her, and she heard the Virgin say she would do this for her.

Pietà of Mary and Jesus venerated at Theirenbach in Alsace, France, c. 1350.
(MARY LEE NOLAN AND SIDNEY NOLAN, *CHRISTIAN PILGRIMAGE IN MODERN WESTERN EUROPE*, p. 200.)

Lucia was 10 when, together with her friends, she saw the Virgin appear on six separate occasions. Mary spoke to the children, saying that they had come from heaven, and that she would take them to heaven. All three children reported hearing the same words. Others came to the place where the apparitions occurred. Some of these other watchers reported seeing a small cloud appear over the tree where the children saw the Virgin and the tree's branches bend.

At the time, the children reported hearing three secrets from the Virgin. In 1941 Lucia revealed two of them. The first concerned the nature of hell. The second was a prediction of war unless the world became devoted to her Immaculate Heart. Mary further specified that her followers would need to secure the consecration of Russia to her Immaculate Heart and to convert that country's people. If such steps were not taken, she warned, the world would be annihilated. Lucia wrote the third secret down, and in 1957 her note was sent to Rome. In 1977 Pope John Paul I visited her (Zimdars-Schwartz 1991, 190–219).

Other reported sightings of Mary followed in the late 1940s, and manifested the worries held by many European Catholics about the general loss of faith and the coming clash with communism (Christian 1984). Marian apparitions provided a kind of collective catharsis, a general focusing and release of these tensions, and have continued unabated through the 1990s.

One of the more recent apparitions has been occurring frequently on a hill just outside Medjugorje, Bosnia, since June 24, 1981. Six children saw Mary on the first day; since then more than 20 million pilgrims have come for a view. The children moved the place for their visions into the church, until the bishop ordered them out. Since then some people have reported nightly appearances of Mary (Bax 1991; Zimdars-Schwartz 1991, 220–244).

Pilgrims to the site often return with stories of personal conversions and healing. One Irish woman described her visit as at first just a "holiday." But then she saw the concrete cross that had been built on the site, and saw the sun behind it turn blood red, with a small piece of the sun missing after it had moved behind the cross. On her return home she attended a funeral mass and when the priest held up the Host she saw it as "the image of the sun at Medjugorje and I really believed in the presence of Christ—the sun had been the Host with the piece missing like when the priest breaks off a piece—and I was overcome and cried."

Medjugorje spreads. An Italian family bought a white plaster statue of Mary during a visit to the site, and in February 1995 reported that tears of blood had begun running down the statue's face. Crowds began to flock around the family's home near Rome, and the local bishop had the statue removed. CAT scans of the statue showed no hidden mechanisms; laboratory tests showed the blood to be human; DNA matches with the family's blood were proposed. In the end, the bishop became a believer in the miracle (Warner 1996; Bohlen 1995).

In the United States, an American returned home to New Jersey after a visit to Medjugorje in 1988 and reported that he had been healed of a back injury and hearing loss. Mary appeared to him in his backyard six months later, stating that she had work for him to do. In August 1992 he publicly announced when the second visit would happen, and 8,000 people came to witness the event. About the same number showed up in Cold Spring, Kentucky, when a local pastor predicted an apparition (Steinfels 1992).

The Church has been ambivalent about the apparitions. On the one hand, the apparitions encourage popular faith, and their message is in keeping with the interest of the Church. On the other hand, the apparitions occur outside Church control; they challenge the hierarchy of the Church by providing an alternative source of religious enthusiasm to worship in churches. The Church has given official recognition to the apparitions at Lourdes and Fatima, but not to Medjugorje. There, the local Franciscan fathers, who for centuries functioned as the parish priests, have encouraged people to enjoy the special grace provided by the visions. But the Bishop of Mostar, whose district includes the apparition site, has forbidden worshipers to make the pilgrimage and has called the apparitions "theatrical practices." His ruling has been part of an effort, backed by Rome, to wrest control of the parishes away from the friars, and Mary, here as elsewhere, has become a key token in that struggle (Bax 1991).

Religious sentiments in Catholic Europe have always included some resentment of the power and privileges of the clergy. For those visitors to the sites of apparitions who share these anticlerical feelings, the Church's rejection of visions makes the visions even more attractive. The apparitions usually are reported from marginal regions during times of trouble—Bosnia and southern Italy in the 1990s, economically depressed parts of the United States in the 1980s, post–war Western Europe.

Spanish Shrines

As the Church increasingly came to promote Mary as an object of worship, people have made her into a local protector as well as the symbol of Church worship. In agrarian parts of northern Spain, each valley of herders and farmers contains a number of small villages. Each village parish has its own active patron, whose image is in the village shrine and who protects the village as a whole. The shrine may be an isolated chapel at the boundary of several villages or the parish church at the village center.

In the Nansa river valley studied by the ethnographer William Christian (1989) are 14 such village parishes. Of these 14, one has Christ as its patron, three have the souls in purgatory (*Las Animas*), and 10 have a particular aspect or realization of the Virgin Mary. Thus, in one village the patron is Our Lady of the Queen's Ford; in another, Our Lady of the Light; in a third, Our Lady of the Bridge; and so forth. Each shrine, each saint, protects a particular territory, a "territory of grace," acting as patron to its inhabitants.

Some of the shrines to Mary are located at boundaries of villages or herding districts. In one district, three statues of Mary are found right at the meeting point of three villages' lands, each facing back toward "her own" village. In local stories, the Virgin is said to choose the spot where the shrine is to be built. In one case a shrine was placed at one spot, but during the next night two oxen came and moved the shrine up the hill to the place where she had desired it to be placed. The Virgin keeps the sheep at home, say local herders, and calls down divine power to protect them. William Christian calls the shrines "energy transformation stations."

One of these patron saints is Our Lady of the Queen's Ford, the patron of the village of Tudanca. The shrine is located in a chapel about five kilometers behind Tudanca. The saint's name comes from a nearby ford, but the patron is also identified as Our Lady of the Snows, an aspect of Mary recognized by Rome and given a feast day, August 5. Over the centuries, celebrations of the feast day have waxed and waned, depending both on the level of nearby economic activity and on the attitude of the parish priest toward the shrine. Currently the shrine is visited only by some Tudanca residents; in other decades, however, it has received attention from people of other villages as well. The shrines patronize and protect their own villages, but they may be appealed to by anyone, especially people from neighboring villages.

In the first week of May each year the image is carried down from the isolated chapel to the parish church in town, where it remains for three months and is the center of church devotions. The period when the image is in the church is also the period of plowing and sowing the fields, and its presence may once have been intended to protect the crops. On the feast of Saint James, July 25, the image is carried in a procession of all the villagers, organized in the following order: children first, then lay men, priests with the image, and women. The villagers thus see themselves as a whole composed of parts. "The villagers for once in the year," writes Christian (1989, 70), "see the village as a social unit, abstracted from the buildings and the location that makes it a geographical unit."

It is the women who continue up the mountain to the shrine and replace the image in its resting place. A woman keeps the key to the shrine, and when, on the patron's feast day of August 5, a mass is held at the mountain chapel, even the priest has to wait for her to unlock it. In other villages, too, special roles in the devotion to the patron are handed down from mother to daughter. Women are the chief worshipers at the shrines.

These patrons are firmly planted in the rural landscape. Each exists and acts on her own. Some of the names are unique, appearing nowhere else in Spain. Others do appear elsewhere, but then are given additional local tags to emphasize their individuality. A shrine to Our Lady of Carmel, for example (a common name for the Virgin Mary), will become Our Lady of Carmel of Cosio, or of another village. These shrines have existed for a long time; some may predate Christianity (when clearly they were known and worshiped by other names).

From the standpoint of these "localized devotions"—worship activities focused on a local manifestation of Mary or a saint—Mary appears as many distinct patrons woven together into a general community of sainthood. The Mary of the Snows is an agent distinct from the Mary of the Bridge, despite the fact that all are manifestations of the one Virgin Mary, Mother of God.

Many in One

Recall a similar feature of worship in India. In south India each local settlement has its own tutelary goddess, known by one name throughout that region. So throughout the state of Tamil Nadu, for instance, once finds Mariyamman of this place versus Mariyamman of that place, as different goddesses and yet also localized forms of the single Goddess (Fuller 1992, 43). This many-in-one is quite similar to that found in northern Spain and elsewhere in the Catholic world. Mary exists in both a highly local and a universal form at the same time in the consciousness of some Catholics, as does Mariyamman (the similarity in names is a coincidence) for Hindus.

The parallel stops at the level below Mary, however, for whereas Hindus have local, lesser deities as well as the major gods, most Catholics have only the major textually sanctioned figures to turn to—Mary, Jesus, saints. In Catholicism the distance between God and local, reachable spiritual beings is mediated by proliferating the number of forms of Mary, and remaining entirely within a restricted pantheon.

There is an irony in the fact that the adoration of Mary was encouraged by the church as a way of unifying and centralizing devotion, but that Mary became the vehicle for differentiated devotions and representations. Of course, even in the universal language promoted by the church one has different names or "advocations" (different forms of a deity) of Mary, a variety that in part stems from the very images the church used: Mary of the Immaculate Conception, Mary the Pietà, Mary of the Assumption, and so forth. Mary is shown in different contexts, and these images become signs of different attitudes or emotions. But it also may be that relying on replicable images as the basis for Catholicism (or any other widespread religion) itself gives rise to this dual character, the "one Mary or many Marys" problem. Once the image takes on any local roots it begins to be thought of as the image of a local individual. The very replicability of the image poses a problem: is it one or many? If one, what are all these other objects? If many, are they different actors?

A Japanese Comparison

Just as Catholics have created "many Marys" to provide nearby, accessible images, so have Japanese men and women turned to deities called "bodhisattvas," or "Buddhas-to-be." These deities, who put off their transition to Buddha status in order to help humans, are nearer to hand when one needs help than are the distant Buddha figures.

Especially important among them is the goddess Kannon, who ensures fertility and safety in childbirth. In India, Kannon was the many-armed god Avalokitesvara, and became (via a gender change) the important Chinese goddess Kuan-Yin, and then the Japanese Kannon. The bodhisattva Kannon is capable of rescuing people from earthquakes, fires, shipwrecks, witchcraft, execution, snakes, and thunderbolts, and of giving a woman the child she wishes, son or daughter. She is sometimes depicted as associated with the waterfall because of her power; her many arms are likened to the many different streams of a fall. She also has lesser spirits called *jizo* who act as guardians of travelers and children. Travelers often set out small statues of jizos on their routes, and especially when they are embarking on a pilgrimage. But one may also set out a jizo as a concrete way to take a request to Kannon. These requests are most commonly either for forgiveness for having had an abortion or for safe delivery of a child.

Kannon is both a single goddess and many personal guardians. She can be depicted as a single protector, or as highly individuated. For example, a shrine to Kannon at Kyoto is supposed to contain "60,000" statues of Kannon, one for every face there is in the world; this way of representing her is supposed to guard all the world's people.

A debate has arisen in Japan over the practice of buying jizo statues from a temple to atone for an abortion. Setting out the statue is thought by some to help guide the fetus across the river that separates the world of life from the world of death. These statues, called "water child jizos" (Mizuko jizo), are sold by Buddhist temples for several hundred dollars each. More than 2,000 temples now offer these statues, and temple leaflets warn that failure to appease the spirit of a dead fetus could lead to cancer, heart disease, back pain, rebellion of children against parents, and so forth—a list long enough that anyone who fails to buy the statue will surely find herself victim of the fetus's spirit. Is this service a way the temple serves people's needs or, as one magazine called it, a "business of terror"? Some women continue to visit the statues for years or even decades after the abortion, dressing them up against the cold or pouring water over them to quench their thirst (WuDunn 1996).

Jizo statuses set out to atone for an abortion or to ask for safe delivery of a child, at the shrine to Kannon near Kamakura, Japan. (COURTESY OF JOHN RENARD.)

Generalized Devotions

Priests entering the Nansa valley have had to work with the shrines already in place, but sometimes they have tried to discourage devotions at the shrine. In most cases, devotions go dormant, reappearing a decade or more later. The priests bring with them devotional emphases of the papacy, and often of a religious order. They try to refocus the devotions of villagers on universal images of Mary and Christ, rather than on her specific manifestations, what one priest called approaching "to the main doors, not the side doors" of the church.

These "generalized devotions," in William Christian's (1989) phrase, are based on the circulation and promotion of images that are highly interchangeable. In homes and in parish churches one finds paintings, lithographs, pamphlets, calendars, and rosaries. These images could be substituted easily one for the other, or replaced with a new batch, without any loss of religious significance. The images are usually of Mary as the Madonna, and sometimes of the cross, and they are used in family devotions. They often come from Rome or from the religious orders currently in papal favor, and their propagation and use is intended to underscore the universality of the Church. For example, the Dominican brotherhoods have promoted the devotion to the Holy Rosary at home using personal rosary beads. The brotherhoods teach people that saying prayers with the beads will allow one to share in all the prayers said by all members of the brotherhood throughout the world. Other orders, including Capuchins and

Passionists, have provided images of saints or Mary that correspond to their particular religious emphases.

Mary has played her part in efforts to reuniversalize worship, both through her interchangeable pictures in homes, and through her role in regional and national shrines. Many villages in the Nansa valley have been visited on trips to the regional shrine to Mary, which was approved by the Vatican in 1954, on the 100th anniversary of the papal proclamation of the Immaculate Conception.

Jesus, Mary, and the Nation–State

Of particular importance in changing local worship practices has been the devotion to the Sacred Heart of Jesus, begun in 1673 when a nun in Paris had visions of Jesus Christ in which he urged her to devote herself to his heart as a symbol of his love for humankind. But it was not entered as general feast of the church until 1856, when it quickly became an image to which popes and rulers tried to rally the faithful. In 1899 Pope Leo XIII consecrated the world to the Sacred Heart of Jesus, and King Alfonso of Spain did the same for Spain in 1919, with the backing of a conservative government. Images of the Sacred Heart entered the Nansa valley about that time as well (Christian 1989, 84–85).

Because of its association with the political right, in the 1930s statues commemorating the Sacred Heart became symbols of the Nationalist forces, the right wing fighting under Franco to topple the government. The national monument to the Sacred Heart was frequently "executed" by the Loyalists, and pictures of the ruined monument were circulated by Franco's side to rally Catholic support.

Elsewhere too, the Sacred Heart of Jesus became a symbol of conservative governments. In late–nineteenth-century France the relation of a largely Catholic people to a secular state (and largely secular capital city) was a continuing source of tension. In 1871 many Parisians rose up against the Thiers government, in part because of the state's capitulation to Prussian forces. The government, which had fled to Versailles, brutally suppressed the uprising, known as the *Commune,* and regained control of the city. Shortly thereafter, in an attempt to underscore the central place of the church in French life, the government constructed the magnificent church on the hills of Montmartre called Sacre Coeur—Sacred Heart. Though much loved by tourists (and many Parisians), the association between the building and the suppression lives on in the minds of many on the left. (I happened to be living in Paris in 1971, the year of the Commune's centennial, and I witnessed Sacre Coeur being pelted with tomatoes and stones.)

At the same time, images of Mary surface as symbols of national resistance. In communist Poland, the national shrine of Polish Catholicism dedicated to Our Lady of Czestochowa has for centuries been associated with national resistance against foreign conquerors. The Polish Primate under communist rule, Cardinal Wysynski, mobilized the nation around the shrine image, beginning with the rededication of the nation to this "Queen of Poland" in 1956, and following with hugely successful annual pilgrimages of the shrine to every single town in Poland.

The state's use of religious imagery underscores the changes in how the Church represents itself. In the ninth century, a person was sworn in on relics as the clear chain of direct contact to local sources of sacrality. By the late nineteenth century the state was staking its claim to loyalty on images of and devotions to Mary or, in particular, to Christ. Christ seems more immune to the differentiation process that has made Mary many. Indeed, the role of Mary in Catholicism as a firm local identity goes far beyond Spain, as we shall see.

11 *Sacred Speech and Divine Power*

*I*t is hard to think of a religion in which set ways of speaking—spells, prayers, recitations—do not play central roles. Humans are talking animals, and we use our powers of speech to understand and shape events in both the visible and invisible worlds. Most rituals we have examined so far have had certain speech forms at their center: invocations of ancestral spirits (in Africa, Sumatra, or New Guinea), stories and spells that heal (in Japan, Panama, or the United States), and pronouncements that channel the meaning of images (in the Catholic mass or Dogon masked dances).

Some religious traditions place particular emphasis on the centrality of the spoken word to religious practice. For the Navajos of the American Southwest, the world was brought into being by the Gods when they spoke and sung it into existence. Speech and song bring this creative power into the present world, for good or evil. So, too, for the Dogon, who understand the world as having been spoken into being. In both Hindu and Buddhist traditions, the word that is spoken and heard has primacy over that which is written and read—in the latter case a direct chain of transmission is broken. It is not only in the European traditions of Moses, Plato, and Jesus that writing has been understood as secondary to speech (mistakenly so, argues the philosopher Jacques Derrida), but in other religions, of greater and smaller scale, as well. Written scripture may play an important role in these traditions—"scripture," after all, means "writing"—but it does so as the written record of what was originally an act of speech.

Certain religious movements portray their own distinctiveness by contrasting their emphasis on the spoken word to the reliance of competing faiths on images. In seventh-century Arabia, Muhammad and his followers contrasted the word of God, which they followed, to the images of polytheists, which they condemned. Moses responding to Aaron's setting up of the golden calf, or Joseph Smith and Brigham Young leading the Mormons across the United States, both condemned the worship of "graven images" and urged their followers to focus on the word of God. Luther chastised the Christians of his time for following the Church rather than scripture, and the "letter of the Bible" has been the watchword for Protestant movements of reform ever since. Each of these leaders has accused other faiths of forgetting or ignoring God's words.

But speech, like images, can be meaningful in more than one way. When we speak we refer to concepts, and through them to things in the world. We also call up associations in the minds of our hearers, associations linked to their memories of hearing such words before, or to the style, rhythm, or voice tone of the speaker. Thus, the way in which a sermon is delivered or a hymn sung can be as meaningful to worshipers as the manifest content of the sermon or hymn. We also understand some speech as directly accomplishing something, as having force as well as meaning: a marriage vow seals a pact; a spell compels a spirit to act. Within a religious tradition people often discuss and debate how best to understand their own speech. Is a sermon better if it is carefully crafted beforehand (as clearly a human product), or is it better if it is spontaneous (allowing the Holy Ghost to offer direct inspiration)? Can a prayer, or a mass, or the recitation of a verse work directly on the universe, or is it only a request to a deity or god?

We consider the relationship between ways of speaking and divine powers in three religious traditions: Islam, in which God's speech sets out a proper path for humans to follow; Navajo religion, in which humans draw on the creative powers of the first beings when they sing prayers of blessing or healing; and several Protestant religions, in which God reveals his word through scripture and spontaneous, inspired speaking. Finally, we return to Islam to trace the steps of the pilgrimage to Mecca, which follow the example of the Prophet Muhammad, handed down through chains of transmitted speech.

The Qur'ân as Recitation of God's Speech

For Muslims, speech is sacred and powerful mainly as the source of commandments from God and as the vehicle for carrying out, through prayer and worship, those commandments. Muslims' sacred book is the Qur'ân, a word that comes from the Arabic root meaning "to recite." The Qur'ân is the collection of verses spoken to Muhammad by the angel Gabriel, who conveyed them from God. The revelation of these verses took place between 610 and 632 in Mecca and Medina, in Arabia. The Qur'ân preexisted these revelations as God's speech—indeed, most Muslims regard it as eternal (Graham 1987, 79–115).

The revelations were handed down orally long before they were first written down, and even today Muslims consider it important to memorize and recite these words of God. In its written form, the Qur'ân is arranged as 114 chapters, each divided into verses, and arranged, not in the order in which they were spoken to Muhammad, but, by convention, from the longest to the shortest.

Unlike the Hebrew Bible or Christian Gospels, the Qur'ân is not a collection of long narratives. It contains brief parables and stories but mainly consists of directives and exhortations to Muhammad and his people. Muslims learn the fuller stories of the prophets and of Muhammad's life from other narratives, not from the Qur'ân itself. Much of the Qur'ân is about how Muslims ought to live: values, social norms, and what we generally call "law." These guidelines for living are called sharî`a, "the way." (Law in the narrower sense of enforceable jurisprudence is designated by the term *fiqh*.)

The following passage, from the third chapter of the Qur'ân, exemplifies the way in which several kinds of messages are typically combined. It reads:

Say: 'God has spoken the truth; therefore follow
the creed of Abraham, a man of pure faith and no idolater.'

The first House established for the people
was that at Mecca, a place holy, and a guidance to all beings.
Therein are clear signs—the station of Abraham,
and whosoever enters it is in security.
It is the duty of all men towards God to come
to the House a pilgrim, if he is able to make his way there.
As for the unbeliever, God is All-sufficient nor needs any being.
(Qur'ân 3:90–92)

A lot is contained in this passage. Muslim children and adults will memorize it in Arabic, learn its meaning in their own language (if they are not Arabic speakers, as most Muslims are not), and then be taught the ways to understand it by a religious teacher. Most Muslim children begin to learn the Qur'ân at a young age, and as they grow up they will likely attend Qur'ân interpretation sessions in the local prayer house or mosque.

The passage is addressed to Muhammad, as are all Qur'ânic verses. It shows him precisely how to admonish and guide the people of Arabia, some of whom had become his followers. God directs him to say a certain passage to the people, a passage that identifies Muhammad's mission as pulling people back to the true path of worship of God from which they have strayed. How that path is identified is important: it is the "creed of Abraham," the same creed delivered to Jews and later to Christians. These people had their own "messengers," similar to Muhammad: the Jews had Moses, to whom was revealed the Bible, and David, to whom was given the Psalms; Christians had Jesus, to whom was revealed the Gospels (in this, the Islamic view of Christ's mission). Jews and Christians are "people of the book," and have been accorded special treatment in Muslim-held territories. Muslims believe that Jews and Christians eventually strayed from pure monotheism (the doctrine of the Trinity is a particular target) but that people of all three faiths worship the same God. *Islam* means "submission [to God]" and is intended as a return to an old faith, not the creation of a new one.

The passage then refers to a historical event, the construction by Abraham of the Ka'ba, the large, cubic, black-draped structure in Mecca around which Muslim pilgrims process during the annual religious pilgrimage. The duty to make the pilgrimage, for those with the means to do so, is based on this passage in the Qur'ân, short though it may be, and the fact that Muhammad made such a pilgrimage in 632, the year of his death.

The final sentence in the passage implies a warning to the unbelievers, those who do not yet accept God, and reminds them that God does not need them, but, it is implied, they do need to heed his call.

The Qur'ân is treated not just as a book to be read, memorized, and studied, but also to be celebrated through song and calligraphy. Contests of Qur'ân melodic recitation are held at regular intervals throughout the Muslim world, in which the beauty of the voice control and melodic interpretation, as well as the fit of melody to content, are the basis for judging winners. (Indonesia and Malaysia, two non-Arabic speaking countries, routinely win prizes at the international finals.) Much Islamic art is based on the artistic interpretation of the form of the written Qur'ân, and intricate writings of the names "Allah" and "Muhammad" are found on almost every conceivable surface in

Islamic calligraphy in the Congregational Mosque in Isfahan, Iran. The inlaid tile design shows both cursive and geometric styles; the inscriptions include Qur'ânic passages and, in this Shi'i setting, invocations of both Muhammad and 'Ali.
(COURTESY OF JOHN RENARD.)

Muslim societies. Many Muslims also believe the spoken and written words have the power to ward off evil or heal people of illness.

The Qur'ân is God's major gift to humans, analogous to the presence of Jesus among humans in Christian understanding. It is an exact replica of the words spoken to Muhammad; therefore, the forms of the spoken and written words themselves take on sacred value. It is also evidence of direct historical contact between God and

Muhammad. This direct contact is crucial to Islam's religious foundation, and explains two areas of study within Islam: one that proves that Muhammad was illiterate and could not possibly have created the Qur'ân, and a second that shows the Qur'ân to be inimitable in grammar and rhetoric. These lines of investigation, taken together, prove that the Qur'ân is from God. (Contrast the lack of importance to most Christians of the original sound and shape of the Greek words in the Gospels.)

But Muslims debate among themselves about what the implications of the Qur'ân's divine source are for everyday life. Many Gayo Muslims, for example, consider prayers (*do'a*) that include Qur'ânic verses to be directly effective in healing, or giving one invulnerability, or harming one's enemy. One of my friends, for instance, used a passage from chapter 61 of the Qur'ân as the beginning of an invulnerability spell:

And He will give you another blessing which you love:
help from God and present victory.
Give good tidings, O Muhammad
to believers.

To which he would append a plea ending in the lines:

Let my blanket be from God,
my cloak from God,
my shawl from God.

My friend thought that when he uttered the prayer, God gave him a cloak and shawl, as the material realization of God's promise to give "help from God and a present victory." In his own memory, these divine gifts had served him well during battles fought in the 1950s, making bullets and knives skip off his clothes as he fought. But in the 1980s others pointed out to him that the Qur'ânic passage had been revealed to Muhammad as a message of peace, to stop fighting. One scholar objected to my friend that reciting the Qur'ân could not automatically confer any power on the reciter; that all power came from God and that He knew all that happened in the world anyway and would do as He pleased, regardless of what mumbo-jumbo ordinary men and women chose to recite. All that we can do, he said, is to live good lives and worship God, and then perhaps He will choose to reward us.

The Creative Power of Navajo Speech and Song

*T*he view that speech directly confers power, limited within Islam to one, often criticized view about the Qur'ân and God, flowers fully within Navajo religion. Like Muslims, Navajo place speech at the center of religion, but as the source of creative power rather than as the source of divine commands.

In Navajo tradition, the individual human being has the power to change the world through language (Witherspoon 1977). A person can do so because the world itself was created through language, when First Man sang the song known as Blessingway. Among the first creatures, the Holy People, were Long Life Boy (thought) and Happiness Girl (speech), to whom First Man said: "You two will be found among everything." Indeed, their names are found in nearly every Navajo prayer and song as signs of the powers to create. They also are the parents of Changing (or Earth) Woman, the being who is associated with the earth's fertility.

The sung prayers known as Blessingway tell the story of creation. They also reenact creation each time they are told (Wyman 1970). They may be performed as a separate ritual—for example to bless a house—or be incorporated into other rituals in which, by invoking the events of creation, they endow the ritual with that same creative power. Navajo sand painting also draws its powers from the story of creation. After the Holy People built the first house, they decorated the floor with bits of shale, rock, and mineral dyes. They drew all the forms of life that they eventually were to create, depicting them in the forms of holy people. They then recited a long prayer to these holy people, and in that act created a causal pathway between sand paintings and the sacred powers of creation.

Blessingway and many other prayer cycles identify and associate everyday people and conditions with the Holy People and the events of creation. Blessingway contains many lines that link powers given to the Holy People to powers desired by the speaker, such as:

May the power that enables you to inhale also enable me to inhale.

Let the dark flint which arises to protect you always arise to protect me.

Often these sections of the prayer provide long catalogues of body parts and powers, underscoring the identification of the Holy Person's body with that of the prayer reciter. These identifications are intended to transfer the properties of the Holy People to that of the person who is the object of the ceremony. For example, Navajo singers will help ensure a good birth for an expectant mother by performing a Blessingway ceremony that identifies the Holy People of the Earth, themselves associated with fertility and life, with the mother and child (Gill 1981). The singer will collect earth from a cornfield and water from a flowing stream, both nurturing life, and apply them to the woman. The prayers recited include the Earth's Prayer, which underscores these identifications through passages such as the following:

Earth's feet have become my feet by means of these I shall live on.

Earth's legs have become my legs by means of these I shall live on.

Earth's body has become my body by means of this I shall live on.

Earth's mind has become my mind by means of this I shall live on.

Earth's voice has become my voice by means of this I shall live on.

. . .

It is the very inner form of Earth that continues to move with me, that has risen with me, that is standing with me, that indeed remains stationary with me.

Now it is the inner form of long life, now of happiness that continues to move with me, that has risen with me, that is standing with me, that indeed remains stationary with me, surprising, surprising. (Wyman 1970, 136)

The pair of terms *long life* and *happiness* are the principles personified in the Holy People Long Life Boy and Happiness Girl (Wyman 1970, 19–46). They are linked to all the components of the earth. The effect of these pairings is to transfer to the mother and expected child these two essential qualities, long life and happiness.

Prayers such as these are used for healing when Holy People are thought to have been responsible for the illness. If a person has trespassed on a holy site, the Holy People may place a spell on that person; the Holyway ceremony is designed to induce them to remove the spell. The singer addresses a particular holy person by name and makes an offering of tobacco smoke to him. In the Holyway stories associated with the ceremonies, the holy person is sent tobacco, smokes, and then agrees to help cure the patient. The holy person addresses the patient as "grandson," placing himself in a relationship in which he can be compelled to aid the ill person, his "grandson." The prayer draws on the knowledge contained in these stories by demanding, not requesting, that the holy person cure the patient:

This very day you must remake my feet for me,

This very day you must remake my legs for me.

The prayer ends by asserting that the cure has occurred:

With my body cooled off, I am walking about,
with my body light in weight, I am walking about,

. . .

As one who is long life and happiness I am walking about

Pleasant again it has become,

Pleasant again it has become! (Gill 1981, 128–129)

In this, its concluding section, the prayer performs the act of bringing the patient to health. The verb is in the progressive mode—"I am walking about"—indicating that the patient will continue to enjoy health. Most importantly, the prayer identifies the patient with Long Life Boy and Happiness Girl: he or she has become "one who is long life and happiness."

Speech and Grace in Protestant Churches

So far we have considered ideas about how speech relates to power; now we introduce a third concept, that of the grace of God. Ways of speaking found in many Protestant churches introduce the idea that speech by everyday people can, when accompanied by God's grace, be divinely inspired.

In the sixteenth century, several Christian scholars, notably Martin Luther (1483–1546) in Germany and John Calvin (1509–1564) in Geneva, protested against certain Church teachings. The worship movements that Luther, Calvin, and others established thus came to be known generally as "Protestant" because of this series of protests. Although differing strongly among themselves, these movements shared the dual conviction that, first, people could be saved only through faith and by the grace of God and, second, that scripture, not human institutions, was the ultimate source of religious authority. As the billboard outside the Lutheran Church near my home in St. Louis proclaims today: "Only by Grace; Only by Faith; Only by Scripture."

Protestants make the claim that faith and grace connect individuals to God in opposition to the Catholic claim that the Church, through its sacraments, creates that connection. For the Catholic, the miracle of the Eucharist means that Christ is produced in the bread and water of the Mass. For most Protestants (and, from at least the ninth century onward, for some Catholics), the objects of a mass are signs of, not the substance of, Christ. Moreover, for them the ritual of the Eucharist does not automatically confer merit or salvation or grace on the individual worshiper. Nor do chants said on behalf of the dead aid the dead in their struggle through purgatory to heaven. The individual has free and direct access to God, and God may bestow grace on anyone. The gift of the Word of God thus may reach anyone at any time and place and in unpredictable ways. Faith is all that is required (Clark 1967, 99–115).

In the wide array of movements and churches that followed Luther's break with Rome—Methodists, Baptists, Lutherans, and so on—this emphasis on universal access to God's grace and revelation of grace through speech and hearing led people to develop many and varied ways of worship. Quakers and some Baptists have stressed the universal nature of the minister's role, that anyone may be visited by the Holy Ghost and moved to preach. Charismatic and Pentecostal churches (and certain movements within Lutheranism) have encouraged worshipers to let the Holy Ghost visit them and lead them to speak in tongues, as did the apostles after the death of Jesus. But other movements denied the universal access of people to grace and salvation. John Calvin argued that God has predetermined who is to receive his grace and be saved, and who is to be condemned to hell. This doctrine of *predestination*, held by the Puritans in early North America as well as Calvin's followers in Europe, implied that one's good works had no bearing on one's fate after death.

The Letter and the Spirit of Scripture

The ultimate authority on all religious matters for Protestants is scripture, and not the teachings of a church or pope.

But what is "scripture"? One interpretation of the Protestant slogan "only scripture" (sola scriptura) is that the written text is paramount. Luther was indeed an outstanding biblical scholar, learned in Greek, Latin, and Hebrew, and did argue for the importance of the scholarly interpretation of the text as written. Early Protestant preaching never strayed far from the text of the Bible. What came to be called "Fundamentalist" movements, but might more correctly be called "literalist" emphases on the literal meaning of the text, follow from this focus on the written word.

For some Fundamentalist churchgoers in the United States today, literal truth resides in the 1611 King James Version of the Bible. Some of these Christians call modern translations "perversions." KJV is the Bible "as it is written" (Ammerman 1987, 53). Rather than considering the Bible as a whole, and worrying about contradictions between various parts, Fundamentalists (along with many other Christians) tend to refer to a verse or a phrase, on which they then elaborate, both in sermons and in discussing everyday life. People turn to individual verses that they have memorized, and they also use the language of some of those verses in everyday conversations, speak of their sicknesses as "suffering in beds of affliction" or having "a thorn in the flesh" (Ammerman 1987, 87).

This literalism can lead some Fundamentalists to a point at which they are nearly using the Bible for divination, as in the case of a man who decided to order a tent from Sears and Roebuck Company because he found listed among the permitted foods in 14 Deuteronomy the "roebuck" (Ammerman 1987, 54).

This interpretation of scripture can, of course, be used to underwrite claims of special authority grounded in learning. But these claims are often countered within the tradition of Luther and Calvin by appeal to a second understanding of scripture. Luther, Calvin, and other reformers looked beyond the text to the divine message it conveyed (Graham 1987, 141–154). They placed no special value on the original languages of the Hebrew Bible or the Greek Gospels, and indeed Protestant reformers have encouraged translation as the best way to spread God's word. In this respect they differ from Muslims, for whom there can be only one Qur'ân, the Arabic-language speech of God. (Indeed, most Muslims consider it impossible to "translate" the Qur'ân; English and other versions are usually called "interpretations" or "renderings.")

For the Protestant reformers, then, speech and writing was best thought of as a window to God's word, transparent to its referent. It is the Word, not the particular letters, that is holy. The Bible as preached, translated, interpreted, and witnessed in one's life is the key to the proper understanding of God, not the scholastic analysis of the Hebrew or Greek constructions. The Word of God is thus the meaning of scripture. It can take different forms, including the presence of Christ himself in the world, as the Word made flesh.

God can thus communicate his word in very different ways. Luther underscored the importance of inner communication with God, communication that did not depend on learning. He wrote that "no one can understand God or God's word rightly unless he receives it directly [literally, "without mediation"] from the Holy Spirit." And Calvin wrote that "all of scripture is to be read as if God were speaking," and that the spirit of scripture was more important than the letter of scripture. In their view, God can communicate with ordinary people through many media: the revelations recorded in scripture, the embodiment of the divine in Christ, and the visiting upon any of us of the Holy Ghost (Graham 1987, 143, 147).

Because these inner modes of communication—hearing with help from the Holy Spirit—must accompany the reading of the Bible, Luther linked speech and hearing to the central value of faith:

If you ask a Christian what work renders him worthy of the name Christian, he will not be able to give any answer at all except the hearing of the word of God, that is, faith. Therefore the ears alone are the organs of the Christian person, who is justified and judged a Christian not by the works of any member, but through faith. (quoted in Graham 1987, 141)

The writings of Luther and others thus could be taken to give to individuals the right to hear God's word, no matter what statements were made by the authorities of a church. This radical giving of spiritual rights to individuals surfaces time and again in subsequent history.

Election and Signs

Most Protestant Christians would agree that God bestows his grace where he sees fit. But how and when does he see fit? Can our actions bring on grace?

The struggles over this issue within Christianity trace back to the very roots of the religion. On the one hand, Christianity drew from Judaism. It began, after all, as a sect within Judaism, where obedience to the Law determined the fate of individuals and of the universe. The idea that good works redeemed one's soul were developed by the Church into elaborate doctrines of penance, masses, and salvation. Many Protestant traditions also incorporated such a notion, Methodism among them.

But Christianity became, not a sect within Judaism, but a new religion, and did so in large part by adopting ideas from Hellenism, the world view that pervaded the Mediterranean world (Jaeger 1961). Hellenism included the idea of divine grace that is visited upon humans rather than achieved by them. This concept accorded well with the idea of an all-powerful God, and indeed with the unpredictability of the God of the Hebrew Bible. After all, if God does not need humans then he will dispense grace in ways that fit his plans, not our works.

The idea that God's grace is entirely independent of human actions finds its most eloquent exposition in Paul's letter to the Romans, in a section where Paul is distinguishing between the older idea of the Jewish "chosen people" from the Christian idea that God chooses, or elects, some people (and not others) both from among the Jews and from among the Gentiles.

. . . [W]hen Rebecca had conceived children by one man, our forefather Isaac, though they were not yet born and had done nothing either good or bad, in order that God's purpose of election might continue, not because of works but because of his call, she was told, "the elder will serve the younger." As it is written, "Jacob I loved, but Esau I hated."

What shall we say then? Is there injustice on God's part? By no means! For he says to Moses, "I will have mercy on whom I have mercy, and I will have compassion on whom I have compassion." So it depends not upon man's will or exertion, but upon God's mercy. For the scripture says to Pharaoh, "I have raised you up for the very purpose of showing my power in you, so that my name may be proclaimed in all the earth." So then he has mercy upon whomever he wills, and he hardens the heart of whomever he wills.

You will say to me then, "Why does he still find fault? For who can resist his will?" But who are you, a man, to answer back to God? Will what is molded say to its molder, "Why have you made me thus?" Has the potter no right over the clay, to make out of the same lump one vessel for beauty and another for menial use? (Romans 9, 10–21)

Just as the potter may select some pots for greatness, and others for quick destruction, without the pots having the right to answer back, how can we, God's creations, question the will of God, our Creator?

The doctrine of election formed a central part of the teachings of Saint Augustine in the fifth century (Burns 1994). Because original sin cost humans their free will, he wrote, all our fortune, good or ill, is due to God's grace. In the sixteenth century, John Calvin developed this argument into the idea of predestination, which became founding doctrine for the Presbyterian Church. As inscribed in the Westminster Confession of 1647, which the English Parliament accepted the following year, the doctrine was stated in the form that "some men and angels are predestined unto everlasting life, and others foreordained to everlasting death" (Weber 1958, 98–101).

This doctrine left its adherents with a radical uncertainty about their future. Calvin taught that no one can know whether he is saved (although Calvin apparently thought he was), because the damned can have all the mental states possessed by the saved except for the final state of trust in God. So although a strong feeling of faith in God is necessary for salvation, it is insufficient as a source of reassurance about salvation.

This uncertainty has one opening, in the "doctrine of signs," that even if we cannot know with certainty about our salvation, we can see signs of it. These signs could be in one's ability to succeed in the world. Some Protestant theologians argued that one had a duty to assume that one was saved and act accordingly. Individual psychology led believers in the doctrine toward intense worldly activity in the hopes that leading a rational, systematic life for the greater glory of God on earth would itself be a sign that one has been called to serve God—has been elected. Some added an additional tenet that helped close the logical circle: that only the elect had faith strong enough to keep them hewing to this path. Thus, success and profit are themselves signs of election.

Although this line of thinking brought even Calvin's heirs back to a position in which good works counted for something on the religious plane, it was not a return to Catholic doctrine. The Calvinist still has no possibility of absolution; if he is damned then there is still nothing he can do about it. Furthermore, in the idea that a life spent for God was a sign of election, it was the whole life that mattered, and not the individual work, as in the Catholic calculus of sin and absolution.

Max Weber (1958) drew on these religious responses to develop his theory that what he called the "Protestant ethic" provided a psychological push for the development of modern capitalism in Europe. He noted that the pioneers of modern capitalism in Europe were mainly Protestant rather than Catholic, despite the fact that Protestant theologians were far more restrictive regarding what we might call the modern business necessities of interest and competitive pricing than were their Catholic counterparts. Luther, for example, wrote that "the greatest misfortune of the German nation is easily the traffic in interest. . . . The devil invented it, and the pope, by giving his sanction to it, has done untold evil throughout the world."

Weber's idea was that Protestantism spurred on the development of capitalism, not directly through its doctrine but through the psychological consequences of that doctrine. Men tormented by the unknowability of election were spurred on to succeed in the world, to build edifices of successful businesses as monuments to their worldly success. Weber called this cast of mind "worldly asceticism": denying pleasure to oneself but doing so in a life very much devoted to this world. The capitalist experienced loneliness, since no one could save him and God was distant; had a hatred of material, sensuous life, since it had no positive religious role and tempted people to idolatry; and threw himself into a social life that was solely work for the glory of God.

Weber advanced his thesis by studying the sermons and diaries of Calvinist theologians in the seventeenth and eighteenth centuries. Richard Baxter, for example, served in Cromwell's government as well as in the Puritan Church. He preached hard, methodical work as a religious labor (and opposed sports). The divine quality of this work will be "known by its fruits," he wrote. As a consequence, these men preferred specialization and the division of labor for the greater returns to labor they brought, and thus the greater indication of their own personal election.

The doctrine of election—or "particular election" as it came to be called—was by no means universally accepted by Protestants. An especially widely effective treatise written by Jacobus Arminius in 1608 and called *Declaration of Sentiments* argued that God wishes all people to be saved and gives them the means to do so. Living the good life, stated Arminius, can bring one to God's grace. This position (often called "Arminianism") implied that humans are "perfectible." This argument was taken up in the eighteenth century by John Wesley. The movement he founded was named Methodism for the methodical life he urged Christians to lead. Methodists and other movements accentuated the emotional work required to bring about certainty of salvation and to lead the person into the state of grace.

Baptists gained their distinctive position within the array of Protestant churches through their argument that only those who had gained their faith should be baptized into the church. They thus rejected infant baptism. But Baptists themselves split over the issue of election, with some teaching that Jesus died for everyone; others, that he died only for the elect. Those who held the first view were called "General Baptists" and included the group that left England for Holland in 1607, some of whom then journeyed to Plymouth, Massachusetts, in 1620. Those holding the second view, called "Particular Baptists," founded churches in England and also sent groups to America. Today, some Presbyterian and Reformed churches in Europe and the United States advocate the doctrine, but may place more or less emphasis on it.

Singing and Certainty among U.S. Primitive Baptists

One group of churches that has attempted to remain faithful to Calvin are the self-styled "Primitive Baptists" of the southeastern United States. These churches are scattered throughout the Appalachian mountains, but I draw here on a study conducted in the early 1980s by James Peacock and Ruel Tyson (1989) in the Blue Ridge mountains straddling North Carolina and Virginia. In this sparsely populated region, both elders and other worshipers travel from church to church to worship, often staying Saturday nights with friends. Services include hymn singing, one or more sermons preached by elders, and large meals spread out on communal tables. The churches belong to the Mountain District Association.

The Primitive Baptists adhere to the Westminster Confession, and they actively wrestle with the difficulties the doctrine presents. They attempt to uphold election and reject the idea that we can earn our salvation or have certain knowledge of it. As one preacher put it, "every time you feel inspired, it didn't necessarily come from the Lord." But they also hold to the idea of signs of salvation that one can sense in the world. These signs include the experience of community attained through fellowship and church services, "a sweet meeting," such as one preacher recollected in a sermon in the early 1980s. "Oh, my friends, sometimes we've sung songs here that've lifted us up," he reminds them. And the beauty of their singing is a sign, a foretaste of heaven: "Beyond the little foretastes of experience now, ah, in heaven's pure world today there are angels that sing" (Peacock and Tyson 1989, 112).

"Hymns are small sermons," notes one church elder. Peacock and Tyson describe how, concerned with not overstepping the boundary between faith in their salvation and (mistaken) assurance about it, they choose their songs carefully: "Amazing Grace" and "Guide Me O Thy Great Jehovah" affirm God's absolute sovereignty and "In Sharon's Lovely Rose" expresses hope of reaching heaven, but "Blessed Assurance, Jesus Is Mine" is unacceptable because it presumptuously claims assurance of salvation. In their style, too, they express resignation and modest hope, but avoid the joy that could dangerously approach certainty. Upbeat tempos and complex harmonies are avoided; unison singing in a dignified cadence is preferred. Peacock and Tyson recall the tears running down the cheeks of the congregation while singing; their participation in the service is no less emotional than that of their more animated Pentecostal brethren, but it bespeaks a resigned, stoic attitude in the face of God's great and unknowable will (Peacock and Tyson 1989, 114–118).

Sermons pose two related dilemmas for the preacher. Does one prepare an elaborate sermon and risk the sin of pride, or wait for the Spirit to emerge inside one, and risk incoherence? Does one urge people to perform their duties as Christians and risk strengthening the erroneous idea that doing their duties will win them salvation, or refrain from any exhortations and miss the opportunity to guide them along a righteous path?

Preachers do not, in fact, preach from outlines or notes. To do so would be to insult the "Spirit that bloweth where it listeth." Sermons come from the heart. "If I can't feel that power, I ain't preaching the Gospel. I may stand up there and quote scripture and so on, but it ain't the Gospel," remarked one preacher. For, as Luther and Calvin proclaimed, the Bible is the inspired word that emerges in and through humans, not the dead letter of the written book. It was the word of God that produced the Bible and inspires people today as well. Or does not: an elder may rise to preach and after quoting scripture, sit down when he finds he has nothing to say (Peacock and Tyson 1989, 118–126).

In their sermons preachers strive to avoid implying that religious experience is evidence of salvation or that good works can lead one to salvation. Elder Bradley used a sermon he preached in a North Carolina church to trace his own path. His experience preaching and "saving souls" had led him to think that preaching could bring a person to salvation. He realized his error after revisiting the passage in the Letter to the Romans on election. His sermon reminds us how what appears to be an obvious reason for preaching is indeed in error from the perspective of the doctrine of election, and also how the apparent gloominess of this perspective can be in fact the basis for joy:

Finally came to the conclusion that this which I'd been taught, that salvation was dependent upon men hearing the gospel, repenting of his sins and believing on Jesus, that God was using this the preacher to reach the dead sinner, that this was totally contrary to that which was taught in the word of God, but that this salvation depended upon God's own sovereign pleasure and that he made choice of a people in a covenant before time began. And, oh what a joyful sound it was, and how beautiful it was for me then to see things in that order! To see that God planned this salvation, and if God planned something you can rest assured it's not going to come to naught. That which God has planned will be executed. God declared this salvation before men ever had being in himself. (Peacock and Tyson 1989, 122)

The "sweet meeting" that comforts the soul depends on community: preaching, singing, and eating together makes up what these Baptists call "the visible church." But here enters a difficulty: if your group consists of both the damned and the elect, how can you construct a solid community? Two ideas of community have emerged in the Mountain District, roughly corresponding to the contrast between North Carolina and Virginia churches, and these two ideas have consequences for practices of speaking, singing, and gathering in fellowship.

Two Models of Church Authority

For reasons of topography and modes of livelihood, the churches in North Carolina are dispersed in fields and hills, whereas those in Virginia are located in villages (Peacock and Tyson 1989, 87–117). The North Carolina churches are less well attended than the latter group, and worshipers are more likely to live individualistic lives, usually as independent farmers. Charisma, direct divine inspiration, governs the lives of the elders, and it appears in their sermons, which often recount personal experiences. Songs of stoic resignation, sermons about doctrine, moods of individualism, and antibureaucracy sentiments characterize the North Carolina churches.

In contrast to this individualistic structure and attitude, the Virginia churches have created some degree of bureaucracy, and their elders emphasize organization over charisma. The lives of those attending services are more likely to involve work in government civil service or small businesses (although here, too, many farm). Sermons are more likely to dwell on duty. Singing has changed in some Virginia churches, evolving in the direction of mainline Protestant church singing, with major keys predominating and harmonies explored.

Peacock and Tyson recount how the two groups of churches have come into conflict over their differing ideas of authority and community. The North Carolina churches have favored allowing individual churches and members to go their own ways, as the Spirit moves them. Charisma, the gift of grace from God, dominates. Those in Virginia have stressed the importance of following rules and obeying duly constituted authority.

The contrast surfaced in a dispute during the 1980s about the right of a church to exclude some of its members. Churches do exclude members, and members cannot join other churches. Because members and elders rotate where they worship they can effectively keep out the excluded. In this case, one church excluded a majority of its worshipers on grounds that they had associated with a sinner. They had shown themselves not to be of the elect and so had to be thrown out of the church—much as did the

Puritan churches of seventeenth-century New England that we read about earlier. The church is responsible for community as a whole, and must exclude sinners.

But the excluded members then formed their own church and asked to be recognized by the Mountain District. The rule-following Virginia churches supported the exclusions and refused to recognize the new church, because doing so would contradict the righteous authority of the church that had thrown them out. The North Carolina churches supported the right of the members to form a new church. They felt called to do so, and who can say they are mistaken in their calling? (Peacock and Tyson 1989, 71–85).

At issue was not just who makes the rules, but who has access to the Word of God. If the Word of God is given to anyone and everyone, at any time and place and in unpredictable ways, then the worship and preaching of anyone should be recognized and attended to. If an individual is called by God, his or her subsequent actions should be respected. But if the right to provide an authoritative interpretation of scripture is held by those persons capable of correctly reading it, then all others should obey that authority. Here the North Carolina churches stood in favor of the availability of God's word to anyone; the Virginia churches, of the importance of a duly constituted hierarchy based on knowledge and the consent of the community acting as a whole.

This tension about authority and community plagues all Christian movements that attempt to structure themselves around the ultimately unknowable grace of God. The Virginia churches have changed as had the Quakers in 1700, toward hierarchy and a "routinized" authority. The North Carolina churches have resisted this pull.

Charismatic and Pentecostal Churches

Other Christian churches in the same part of the United States have maintained an independent stance but have taken different positions on the question of whether we can perceive and experience signs of our own election or salvation.

Many Fundamentalists, such as those in the Northeast U.S. church studied by Nancy Ammerman (1987) doubt that everyone who claims to be saved is so, and they look for signs of salvation, most importantly some outward, noticeable change in the person's life. They should have given up smoking and drinking. They also should show confidence in the Lord; constant worries are signs they have not yet been saved.

Throughout much of the South, Holiness churches are scattered in hills and towns much as are the Primitive Baptists. Preachers and ordinary people often travel long distances to worship. The focus of worship is on the relationship between the individual and God, as in all the movements we have considered so far. But here the role of rather dramatic signs is paramount, for snake-handling is often part of the service. Surviving a snakebite, or a drink of poison, or an electric shock is a sign of God's grace. The women and men who have been bitten sit together in services as the "true believers," or the "true saints." These signs, having survived, are signs, or "charismata" that are given by the Holy Ghost. They are proofs of Jesus' power to save them; cups of strychnine are called "salvation cocktails" (Covington 1995; La Barre 1964).

One church name says it all: "The Church of Jesus Christ with Signs Following." The phrase is in reference to 16 Mark, a key chapter for worshipers at Holiness churches and for many other churchgoers throughout the South—just as the Primitive Baptists and other believers in particular election take their cue from 9 Romans. In 16 Mark, Jesus appears to his apostles and upbraids them for not believing those who said they saw him risen. He then commands them to go into the world and preach the Gospel, and says:

He who believes and is baptized will be saved;
but he who does not believe will be condemned.
And these signs will accompany those who believe:
in my name they will cast out demons;
they will speak in new tongues;
they will pick up serpents, and if they drink any deadly thing,
*   it will not hurt them;*
they will lay their hands on the sick,
*   and they will recover.*

Mark continues to relate that these apostles did indeed go forth and do the work of the Lord, and the Lord confirmed the message "by the signs that attended it" or, in the King James Version, "with signs following." Here ends Mark, and from here derives the name of the Holiness church mentioned above.

The relation of speaking in tongues to salvation is further evidenced in 2 Acts, the second key text for Pentecostal and Charismatic churches. It relates, speaking of the apostles:

When the day of Pentecost had come,
*   they were all together in one place.*
And suddenly a sound came from heaven like the rush of a mighty wind,
*   and it filled all the house where they were sitting.*
And there appeared to them tongues as of fire,
*   distributed and resting on each one of them.*
And they were all filled with the Holy Spirit and began to speak in other tongues,
*   as the Spirit gave them utterance.*

Because these events took place on the Pentecost (the Greek name for the Jewish Feast of Weeks), religious movements that seek to experience what the apostles did are called Pentecostal, or Charismatic because of the adherents' desire to receive the charismata, the gifts of grace visited upon them by the Holy Spirit. Participants in these movements believe that their own speaking in tongues and ecstatic experiences are signs that they are saved—they have renounced the doubt that plagues those who adhere to particular election, and embrace the idea that anyone may be saved—and yet these signs of salvation are still required.

Perhaps it is the strong need to overcome strong doubt that explains the great lengths to which some worshipers go to prove their salvation to themselves and their fellow worshipers. Some handle snakes; others swallow poison. Snakes may have been chosen precisely for the shock the handling delivers to outsiders. "Spread the Word! We're coming down from the mountains!" announced one preacher. The Holiness churches in which snakes are handled date only from about 1900. As with the Primitive Baptists, the churches value their independence. They are usually scattered throughout rural areas and are visited by a series of preachers. They first practiced snake handling in 1909, in Tennessee. Apparently it was not until 1918 that someone died from snakebite, and he was denounced as a backslider, someone who had lost his faith, when he died (La Barre 1964).

Snakes are typically brought out in their cages partway through the service, after a sermon and singing have taken place. Sometimes music continues, usually on a guitar, and worshipers begin to dance and enter trance states, at which time someone may pick up a snake and handle it before dropping it back into the cage or passing it on to someone else. The handling may take place in a more subdued setting, the snake passed from one person to another. Women and men handle the snakes. Perhaps 20 or more people are known to have died from snakebites in Holiness meetings; some state governments have responded by forbidding the use of poisonous snakes.

The Church of Jesus Christ with Signs Following in Alabama received national attention in 1992, when the church's preacher, Glenn Summerford, was accused of attempting to murder his wife by forcing her to put her hand in a case filled with poisonous rattlesnakes. She claimed he was trying to kill her because he could not divorce her and retain his position in the church. He claimed he did it to prove her innocence and that the snake bit her because she was backsliding. He was convicted and sent to jail, and his church, lacking any institutions for succession, disbanded. Other preachers soon began to hold outdoor snake-handling services, however (Covington 1995, 1–63).

But snake handling is just the most spectacular (at least to date) of a wide range of practices intended to bear witness to the divine presence within oneself. It is itself the most visible sign of the powerful need to bear witness in a striking and public way to God's grace, to the presence of the Holy Spirit in oneself.

Much more widespread than snake handling are practices of speaking in tongues. Even the relatively staid Lutheran churches of suburban St. Paul, Minnesota (near where I grew up), have begun to encourage members to speak in tongues. Some report a sense of release and of grace as the incomprehensible words flow out of them. They do not speak of the experience as like a trance, but as an experience over which they have some control.

Charismatic movements are growing within Roman Catholicism as well, and in 1981 John Paul II met with Charismatic church leaders and gave his approval to their movement. Worldwide anywhere from 50 to 75 million Catholics can be considered to be Charismatic. And Pentecostal churches are growing rapidly throughout the world, particularly in South America and Southeast Asia. In Brazil, where Umbanda and Macumba had become popular as supplements or alternatives to Catholicism, many are finding that Charismatic churches that focus worship on God but offer the opportunity to speak in tongues combine the best of both worlds.

All these movements are seen by participants as bringing the divine into themselves through the mediation of the Holy Ghost. The religious experience provides a material sign that God has accepted the worshiper and that he or she can hope or know of salvation. This particular emphasis on the individual's avenue to grace through personal experience—often spoken experience—is a key characteristic of Protestantism.

The individual's relation to God through the inspirited Word is markedly different from the idea that contact with God is through the miracle of the Eucharist, itself mediated by the priest. Protestantism relocated God's miracles, his charismata, signs of grace, from communion and the icons of Mary and Jesus, to the individual's ways of speaking. Doing so made possible new forms of community and authority based on those ways of speaking, of which the churches discussed here are but a few instances.

In these religious traditions—Islam, Navajo, Protestant—speech is linked to power through the individual. The speaker who speaks truly and clearly is able to do so because of a relationship with the divine. This relationship is complex and debated, but across religious traditions an idea emerges that sacred speech, in its utterance, places the speaker in contact with the divine. Reciting the Qur'ân is repeating God's own words and can confer power on the speaker. Chanting Blessingway reenacts the events of creation that accompanied the first chanting by the First People. For some Protestants, a true worship service requires speaking in a holy way—in tongues, or when called by the Holy Spirit to preach, or when reading from the Bible in a state of inspiration. This inspirited speaking is in some respects the equivalent of the worshiper's contact with an image—the drawing in of power through an "exchange of vision" with a Hindu statue is probably the closest equivalent. Catholic, Hindu, Japanese, and other traditions also rely on prayer for worship, of course. But the traditions studied in this chapter have taken the spoken element of worship and made it into the privileged element. When this is done—and it is done in different ways in each tradition—the subjective state of the individual also becomes a matter of increased concern. If an object is the center of worship, its objective qualities—its separation from the worshiper—give the process of worship an air if not a doctrine of objectivity: the worship succeeds if certain steps are taken. The Catholic mass is objectively efficacious even if the priest or the worshipers have their minds elsewhere. But once the words uttered by the worshiper become the whole of worship, those daydreamings endanger the very idea of worship. "Thought is the inner form of speech," say the Navajo; "no actions are effective without the correct intention" echo Muslims. Speech is close to thought, or ought to be, and words uttered must be accompanied by the proper state of mind if they are to reach their destination. Subjectivity now takes center stage.

The Pilgrimage to Mecca

*E*ach year during the pilgrimage month of the Islamic lunar calendar, more than a million Muslims from throughout the world gather in the holy places in and around Mecca. These men and women have traveled to Mecca to carry out their religious obligation to make the pilgrimage. All the pilgrims must carry out a series of very specific actions, moving and worshiping together, before completing their task and returning home. The principal goal of the pilgrimage is to obey God's commands, as they were made clear to humans through his messenger, Muhammad. The steps of the pilgrimage were set out by Muhammad and transmitted through chains of speaking and hearing.

Following the Footsteps of Muhammad

We have already seen that Muslims consider the Qur'ân to be God's major gift to humans, and in this respect the Qur'ân's role is similar to that of the Torah for Jews and that of Christ for Christians. But Muslims also consider as divinely inspired the actions of the Prophet Muhammad—not because he was divine himself, but because he spoke and acted as God's messenger. The collection of reports about his statements and actions are called the "hadith." These reports supplement the Qur'ân as the second basic source for guidance and law in the Muslim community. Much of Islamic ritual as well as everyday life is based on what Muhammad did as contained in these reports, and it is in this way that Muslims developed the pilgrimage, or hajj.

The pilgrimage is meaningful for Muslims in the first place as a repetition and commemoration of the Prophet's actions, "following in his footsteps," as many returned pilgrims said to me. But it was also dictated by God in his revelations to Muhammad. Several years after Muhammad and his followers had fled from Mecca to Medina to escape persecution, came the first revelation concerning the pilgrimage, quoted in the last chapter of the Qur'ân:

The first House established for the people
was that at Mecca, a place holy, and a guidance to all beings.
Therein are clear signs—the station of Abraham,
and whosoever enters it is in security.
It is the duty of all men towards God to come
to the House a pilgrim, if he is able to make his way there.
(Qur'ân 3:90–92)

The house mentioned in this passage is the large cubic structure called the "Ka'ba," which is draped in gold-bordered black silk cloth. The Ka'ba is the centerpoint of the religious world for Muslims. It is toward the Ka'ba that Muslims worship five times daily, and it is around the Ka'ba that they walk when they make the pilgrimage.

In Islamic tradition the Ka'ba dates back to the prophet Abraham, who journeyed to Mecca with his son, Ishmael, and Hagar, Ishmael's mother. (In the Islamic version of the sacrificial trial of Abraham, it was Ishmael, not Isaac, whom he was ordered to sacrifice.) Abraham built the Ka'ba on God's command. The angel Gabriel then brought down a black stone to place in its corner. The stone, it is said, was white, but turned black on contact with the sinful world.

By the seventh century C.E. Mecca had become a trading center in the Arabian peninsula, and it was here where Muhammad was born, grew up, and received his first revelations. His triumphant return to Mecca from Medina marked the victory of Islam over the polytheistic Meccan elites, and his first pilgrimage, in 632, the year of his death, became the model for all pilgrimages since (Peters 1994).

Making the pilgrimage is one of the five ritual obligations, or *rukns* (pillars), of Islam. The pilgrimage has always attracted Muslims from throughout the world, but the development of steamship travel in the nineteenth century and air travel in the twentieth has led to a boom in pilgrimage activity. By the mid–twentieth century about 30,000 people made the journey each year; today about two million pilgrims, from the 60 or more countries with sizable Muslim communities, arrive in Mecca each year. Pilgrims come from near and far: the largest delegations are from Nigeria, Pakistan, Turkey, and Yemen, and then Iran, Indonesia, and Iraq. Some pilgrims stay on to study and teach; most return home bringing new ideas and trade goods. Islam was founded by a trader amid vast networks of desert caravans; the contemporary pilgrimage enlarges those networks of trade and communication to the scale of the entire world.

Precisely because these holy cities occupy such a central place in the Muslim popular imagination, they have sometimes been the targets of political movements. During the 1979 pilgrimage, an armed group seized control of Mecca's Grand Mosque and broadcast denunciations of the Saudi government over a citywide loudspeaker system. Iranian anti-American demonstrations at Medina in 1982 led to arrests and revived debates about whether religion and politics could legitimately be separated in Islam. Since then the Saudi government has prohibited delegations from making the pilgrimage when they feared political disturbances (or health risks, as in the 1996 ban on Nigerians during an epidemic in Nigeria).

Although the details of the hajj are taken one by one from accounts of that first pilgrimage, the steps can be sorted into the three stages of rites of transition that were discussed in Chapter 4. Indeed, Victor Turner (1974, 182) argues that in larger-scale societies pilgrimages perform some of the same social functions that are filled by initiation rituals in smaller-scale societies, in providing the place for a religious experience outside the bounds of everyday social life. The pilgrim separates himself or herself from ordinary social life, enters a liminal stage in which distinctive everyday identities are exchanged for the shared identity of the pilgrim, and then returns to the social world. Each transition point is marked by clear religious duties.

Rites of Separation

Although a Muslim may visit the holy places in Mecca and Medina at any time during the year, the pilgrimage itself may be performed only on the eighth, ninth, and tenth days of the last month of the Islamic lunar calendar—the pilgrimage month, Dhu'l-Hijja. (Because the lunar year is 11 days shorter than the solar year, the pilgrimage season cycles back through the solar year.) Unlike pilgrimages made by Christians, Jews, or Hindus to their holy cities, the hajj is a series of ritual actions performed together, simultaneously, by all the Muslim pilgrims for that year (Ruthven 1984, 23–48).

Weeks or even months before these key days, pilgrims have been gathering and departing from villages, towns, and cities all over the world. In Indonesia, as in many other countries with large Muslim populations, each group receives an official send-off from a local government official. As recently as two generations ago, departing pilgrims from the Gayo highlands received a different kind of send-off. They were fed at a ritual during which prayers for the dead were recited on their behalf because most who made the journey were older, and many would not survive the two- or three-month sea voyage. The ritual was held before they left because otherwise they would not receive one.

Travel, whether by land, sea, or air, is for much of the way a secular affair. Only when approaching the port or airfield of Jiddah must pilgrims take steps to enter the state of consecration, or *ihram*. Each pilgrim announces his or her intention to undertake the pilgrimage, renounces shaving, cutting the hair, and sexual intercourse, and changes clothes. The new pilgrim's clothing consists of identical, simple, white seamless garments. Men leave their heads uncovered, and women must not have cloth touching their faces. Some pilgrims even ride roofless buses once they approach Mecca. Each of these measures maintains an unbroken physical link between the pilgrim's head and God, and signals his or her surrender to God.

Moving in the Liminal State

Wearing identical clothing, renouncing normal relationships to their bodies, and concentrating their lives on worshiping God defines the pilgrim's position during the days of pilgrimage. In the liminal state, between their previous lives of various occupations, nationalities, wealth, and status, and their future lives as returned pilgrims, these men and women live and move as equals, sharing some rudimentary Arabic, simple accommodations (for most pilgrims, anyway), and the same daily objectives.

The clothes mark the fact that all pilgrims are religiously equal. As Muhammad's grandson Husayn stated, "The pilgrim offers himself to God as a beggar." Pilgrims mingle with one another even while onboard ship or plane as pilgrims, leaving ordinary social status aside.

Once in Arabia they gather in groups by country and are led through the pilgrimage steps by a group leader, usually someone from their country. For many pilgrims this is their first international experience, rubbing shoulders with others whose language they cannot understand. Arabic prayers and a few short greetings are usually the only form of verbal communication across these groups. Even the American Black Muslim leader Malcolm X (1973, 339) was shocked by this universalism, as he wrote in a public letter to his mosque in Harlem. "For the past week, I have been utterly speechless and spellbound by the graciousness I see displayed all around me by people *of all colors.*"

Pilgrims arrive steadily at Mecca. As they do, they make seven lefthand circles (*tawaf*) around the Ka'ba. Indeed, the root meaning of *hajj* is "to describe a circle." Huge masses of pilgrims move slowly around the silk-draped structure. Each tries to touch or kiss the black stone set into its eastern corner. The Iranian scholar Ali Shariati (1977, 31) described the experience of the tawaf as that of "a small stream merging with a big river. . . . Suddenly, you find yourself floating and carried on by this flood. You have become part of this universal system. Circumambulating . . . Allah, you will soon forget yourself."

The Ka'ba already served as a holy site before Islam, but its guardian was the deity Hubal, whose statue was kept inside the structure. Many other deities were worshiped as well, and the circumambulation was part of worship. Muhammad retained this practice and the veneration of the black stone when he undertook the first pilgrimage, and his followers, though surprised that he did so given the stone's association with paganism,

Major rituals and places of the hajj. (COURTESY OF RICHARD T. ANTOUN, *MUSLIM PREACHER IN THE MODERN WORLD,* p. 173.)

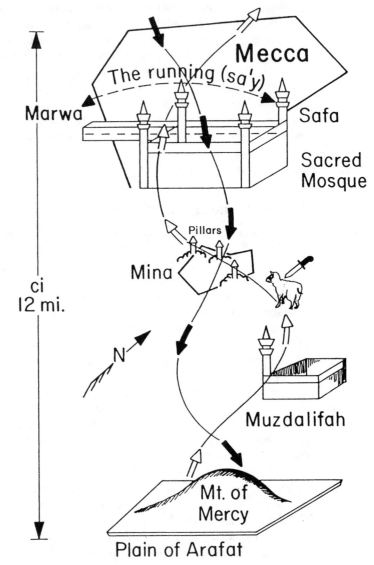

followed suit. The rigorous logic of following the Prophet's actions won out, here as elsewhere.

After the tawaf the pilgrim does the *sa'y,* "running," which does indeed consist of simply running (or, for the older, walking) back and forth, seven times, along a street in Mecca. The running commemorates the time when Hagar was abandoned under a tree at Mecca by Abraham. When her food and water ran out she began to run wildly between two high points, pleading with God for help. When Ishmael raised his hand, there was a well, which became known as the well of Zamzam. The well marked the spot where Mecca was then built. Pilgrims collect water from the Zamzam well and bring it home with them; often diluted with rainwater, it will be used to heal or bless others. The running covers about two miles, and some pilgrims must be pushed in wheelchairs.

The circumambulation, also called the *'umra*, is sometimes performed separately out of season as the "little hajj." Travel agencies throughout the Muslim world offer umra packages—a Muslim may travel to Saudia Arabia at any time of year, circumambulate the Ka'ba, visit the holy sites, and return home.

The Hajj Proper

Pilgrims then begin the events that constitute the pilgrimage proper, the events that are performed only on the prescribed days. They must travel to the plain of 'Arafat by sunrise on the ninth day of the month. It is at 'Arafat, a barren plain about two miles from Mecca, where Adam and Eve were reunited after their expulsion from heaven. Here, too, Muhammad delivered his final sermon in 632, in which he set out most of the details of the hajj. A vast tent city is erected on this plain on the days before to the ninth, and there the pilgrims are assigned quarters.

At 'Arafat the pilgrims spend the ninth day in prayer and meditation, gathering around the Mount of Mercy at the edge of the plain. After performing the midafternoon worship, the millions gathered together stand, awaiting sunset, shouting cries of "God is great." This standing (*wuquf*) is the central event of the hajj proper. The special status enjoyed by this rather unspectacular (relative to the tawaf that precedes it and the sacrifices to follow) event comes from its role in replicating Muhammad's final sermon, and from the shared sense pilgrims derive from it of showing humility before God.

Pilgrims then disperse and return toward Mecca, stopping to spend the night in the city of Muzdalifa, where they are to rid themselves of all resentments toward others. There, too, they collect pebbles, which they use the next day to throw at three pillars near Mina, on the return road to Mecca. This *rajm,* or stoning, of the statues is understood to be a stoning of devils. No mention is made of it in the Qur'ân; as with the veneration of the black stone in the Ka'ba, it is performed solely because Muhammad did it on his pilgrimage. As interpreted by most participants, it commemorates Abraham's resoluteness to obey God, for it was on this spot that he prepared to carry out God's command to him to sacrifice his son. The devil appeared to Abraham, and tried to instill doubt in his heart about the sacrifice. Abraham stoned the devil until he fled. After the crowding and rushing of the previous two days the stoning also undoubtedly releases tensions. Some commentators have harnessed the energies visible during the stoning to religious mission; Ali Shariati urged pilgrims to think of the pebbles as bullets used to kill one's enemies.

Pilgrims then carry out a sacrifice in memory of Abraham's submission to God's will. Usually they buy a goat on the spot and arrange to have its throat cut. The meat is distributed to the poor, much of it immediately frozen on the spot by Saudi authorities. The day after this event is called the *yaum an-nahr,* or day of sacrifice, and, as we noted in Chapter 10, it is celebrated throughout the Muslim world by similar sacrifices. The pilgrimage is thus both a duty for all Muslims and the occasion for a worldwide ritual observance.

Reintegration to Normal Life

The pilgrimage proper is complete at this point, and the pilgrims gradually make the return to normal social status. They begin by cutting some of their hair. Women snip off just a bit, but men often have their heads shaved. Now all prohibitions are lifted except for that on sexual intercourse. Pilgrims return to Mecca, perform another circumambulation of the Ka'ba, collect Zamzam well water for the return trip, and now can again engage in sexual intercourse. They are urged to spend several days in "eating, drinking, and sensual pleasure." This urging emphasizes that the pilgrims are now leaving the state of consecration and returning to normal society—the rite of passage has ended.

Those pilgrims who return home immediately find themselves enjoying a new status, that of hajji (male) or hajjiyah (female), someone who has made the pilgrimage and returned to society. Many now wear white for everyday activities or when they attend the mosque to signal this new status. Their status may lead to other achievements: they are probably looked on with greater favor by their local bank; they may be chosen for office. They certainly have much to tell about from their journey. But they also enjoy a sense of religious accomplishment, having fulfilled the most difficult of God's commands.

How Is It Meaningful?

Ordinary Muslims undertake the pilgrimage for a variety of reasons—they are obeying a divine command; they are fulfilling a duty expected of them socially; they may be advancing their own social status. But is this all we can say? In what ways is the pilgrimage with its many component actions meaningful?

The pilgrimage presents a challenge to our usual ideas of the meaning of a religious act. It is not performed with a separate goal in mind, such as atonement or cleansing. The religious historical event that is commemorated in each segment of the ritual is sometimes but not always clear. The only overall, uniting idea of the pilgrimage is that it is made up of actions that were performed by Muhammad on his first (and only) pilgrimage.

Scholars do suggest parallels with earlier rites, either those performed on the same spot as a contemporary ritual and taken over by Muhammad, or parallel rituals within the Semitic ritual tradition that were adopted by Muhammad as properly monotheistic. For example, the wuquf, or "standing," was part of earlier Hebrew practice. Muhammad made the entire plain of 'Arafat a place of standing before God. The 'umra was originally a sacrifice of firstborn livestock and was held in the early spring, much as with Passover, in the month of Rajab (at that time the lunar calendar was made concordant with the solar, so that Rajab always occurred in the spring). The sacrifice was carried out at the Ka'ba. As late as the twelfth century C.E., local Muslims were still carrying out this older sacrificial 'umra in the month of Rajab.

In fact, although the 'umra is thought of as a little hajj, 'umra and hajj were once distinct events. The essence of the 'umra is the tawaf, the circumambulation of the Ka'ba, while the essence of the hajj is the standing before God at 'Arafat. In origins, the one is sacrificial, the other is an act of submission to God. Muhammad then tied them together in one long series of events.

This kind of explanation may provide a historical account for why certain events became part of the overall pilgrimage. They do not account for the meaning of the rite for those people who take part in it. Muslim commentators have offered several broad lines of interpretation.

One interpretation links the performance of the hajj to the overall meaning of Islam as *surrender*. According to the important twelfth-century theologian Al-Ghazali, devotion to God demands self-abnegation, surrender to his will. Therefore, God has

Man returned from the pilgrimage proudly displays his new clothing, Isak, Sumatra.
(COURTESY OF J. BOWEN.)

imposed on the Muslim actions that in themselves have no emotional or intellectual appeal, such as the running back and forth between two points, or sa'y.

A second interpretation identifies symbolic or iconic meanings for each individual place or object that the pilgrim encounters. The Ka'ba is the House of the Lord. You will meet God in a seamless shroud, so you meet him today wearing such garments. The tawaf resembles the movement of angels that encircle the Throne of God, which itself is situated directly above the Ka'ba in heaven. Ali Shariati (1977) sees the "running" as standing for purposeful activity on the earth.

A third line of interpretation seems to me to be closest to the ways in which pilgrims themselves interpret their experience. This approach locates meaning not in the events but in their historicity, as commemorations of past events. The running commemorates the moment when Hagar was looking for water for Ishmael and Gabriel created the Zamzam well. The stoning marks the moment when Abraham stoned the devil. The sacrifice commemorates Abraham's willingness to sacrifice his son. At the very least, every event commemorates Muhammad's pilgrimage—and this insight returns us to a key element of Islam, that practices and texts constantly refer back to the life of the Prophet for their authenticity.

And what is the specific goal of the pilgrimage? Despite the fact that worship is always conducted facing the Ka'ba in Mecca, and that "Mecca" has become a shorthand for a central place or goal, in fact the central event in the pilgrimage, the standing at 'Arafat, takes place outside Mecca itself, as does the sacrifice, both in places that are virtually uninhabited during the remainder of the year. Within the hajj framework, for instance, the pilgrim is never still, but is hurried around the Ka'ba, down the road to 'Arafat, back to Mina and then to Mecca, around the Ka'ba again, and then home. What the pilgrimage is really about is commemoration of Muhammad's actions, not the visit to the holy places (which, one should again note, can take place at any time of the year).

Pilgrims expand this sense of historicity from particular commemorations to a more diffuse sense of being in the place where their religion was born, being "at the source." "Everywhere," writes the Pakistani religious leader al-Maudûdî of the typical pilgrim, "he sees the relics of those who lived God, and sacrificed their lives for His sake. Every grain of sand witnesses the glory and grandeur of Islam, and every piece of stone declares: 'This is the land where Islam took birth, and whence God's word rose high'" (quoted in Cragg 1980, 60). As the leader of U.S. Muslims Waris Deen Muhammad said in conversations in St. Louis in 1996, "on the pilgrimage you come near to God; you are visiting Him."

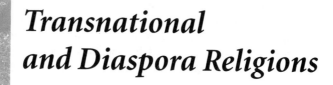

12 *Transnational and Diaspora Religions*

S ome religions are made up of the practices and ideas found in one society and deeply rooted in the life of that society. Such is the case with those societies in highland New Guinea, eastern Indonesia, and the Southwestern United States that we studied in earlier chapters. Even within broad, world-wide religious traditions, local versions of the religion may be quite specific to one society—Catholic beliefs and practices are very different in urban Chicago and rural Spain, for example. But increasingly, the possibilities of long-distance movement and communication have made it possible for people to maintain strong transnational religious connections and to consult sources of knowledge that are no longer strongly tied to one place—the internet only being the most obvious example of this dislocation of knowledge production. Although many have stressed the degree to which individuals thereby become empowered as religious agents, these global networks and sources also may make it easier for religious leaders to exert supervision and control over the far-flung faithful.

Transnational and Diaspora Religions

W e often use the terms "diaspora" and "transnational" to refer to these long-distance connections. Usually, diaspora refers to people who see themselves as temporarily or permanently separated from a religious center or, at least, an historical point of origin. The nature of their displacements vary: to speak of a "South Asian diaspora," for example, is to refer to a broad variety of peoples, religions, and origins in the Indian subcontinent. Most of those who traveled to Europe or the Americas did so to seek better lives, and many brought high levels of economic and social capital with them. Others, recruited as laborers for British plantations in Malaya or Fiji, occupied lower rungs of new local socioeconomic ladders. Jewish and African diasporas reflect histories of forced expulsion and enslavement, and slave traders tried to wipe out the memories of African origins that form part of a diaspora culture—but with only partial success, as we shall see below.

In recent years many scholars of religion have used "transnational" to refer to networks that sustain continued movement and communication across national boundaries. Although initial migrations from a central point may have created the transnational situation, the view of religion and society associated with transnational religious movements and networks may have nothing to do with origins and returns. It makes little sense to speak of "diasporic Christianity" or "diasporic Islam" because these religious referents do not designate a people but an allegiance to a set of religious norms or authorities. Nor do I find it useful to speak of North African immigrants to Europe as in a "diasporic" situation, as their own view of things is for the most part turned toward integration into European society and, at the same time, conformity to global religious norms (see Chapter 13), and not, in the 2000s, to a point of origin and eventual return. I prefer to reserve "diaspora" for an orientation characteristic of a movement or group of people that highlights a history of emigration and keeps in mind and memory a promise of return.

The Jewish Diaspora: History and Ritual

*T*he locus classicus of the concept of diaspora is of course the dispersion of the Jews.

Sacrifice and the Temple

Let us go back to the process of centralizing worship on the Temple that preceded exile. Jewish ritual had been organized around sacrifice, first mentioned when God takes Abel's offering and refuses Cain's in Genesis, an event that introduces homicide and guilt to the world. David and his son Solomon united the tribes of Israel into a kingdom during the tenth century B.C.E and built a Temple in Jerusalem, where sacrifice regularly took place. At least by the seventh century B.C.E, when Josiah forbade sacrifices "in the high places," meaning the scattered local altars, sacrifice had become exclusively centered on the Temple.

But Israelites were also considering other ways of reshaping political and religious society, and at this time we also read emerging criticisms of the notion that God is best worshiped through sacrifice. The prophet known as first Isaiah, writing sometime before the exile, quotes God as wearily castigating his sacrificing flock (1:11):

What to me is the multitude of your sacrifices?
  says the Lord;
I have had enough of burnt offerings of rams
  and the fat of fed beasts;
I do not delight in the blood of bulls,
  or of lambs, or of he-goats.

God then orders his people to stop approaching with hands "full of blood," but instead to focus on their own purity (1:16):

Wash yourselves; make yourselves clean;
  remove the evil of your doings
   from before my eyes;
cease to do evil.

Sacrifice was made impossible in 586 B.C.E, when the Babylonians destroyed the Temple and sent the Jews in exile to Babylon ("by the waters of Babylon . . ."). Some dreamed of a restored Temple, where sacrifice would once again be carried out—Ezekiel (45–46) speaks in great detail of how the Temple will be rebuilt and burnt offerings made. But after the end of exile, when Cyrus of Persia permitted the Jews to return to Jerusalem in 538 B.C.E, religious practice became primarily about maintaining the laws of ritual purity. Ezra, the chief creator of a post-exile life, was himself a priest and a scribe, not a hereditary king. Furthermore, many Jews continued to live outside of Judea, in the diaspora areas of Syria, Egypt, and Babylonia. If they did not have the Temple close at hand, they did have the Law of Moses as contained in the first five books of the Bible, the Pentateuch. It was in the period after return from exile that this Law was compiled in roughly the form we know it today.

Over the final centuries before the Common Era, Judea passed from Persian to Greek rule, and the Jewish community itself became more and more internally differentiated. Even as the upper classes moved into the political and cultural world of the Greeks, others emphasized, by contrast, the importance of hewing to the Law. These groups included various pious groups of hasidim, the Maccabees (leaders of a successful revolt against the Greek rulers in 167 B.C.E), and the later Pharisees, students of the Bible and strict followers of the laws of ritual purity. Debates ensued over "what is a Jew." Is a Jew anyone who claims to be a Jew, or only those people who maintain ritual purity? The Pharisees held to the latter position, and their answer prevailed: a Jew was someone who observed the Law as it had been handed down from Moses to the authorities of the day.

Religion had shifted from the group's sacrifice of animals, to each individual's avoidance of certain tabooed animals. From destroying life in atonement for sin, religious life was refocused on living according to the Law. This change was further intensified when Roman rulers destroyed the second Jerusalem Temple in 70 C.E. and then expelled the Jews from the city in 135. Gone was the possibility of worship through sacrifice. Scholars, rabbis, became the leaders of the community, and sought to rebuild religious life around the idea that by obeying the Law in their homes, Jews could experience the divine without a Temple. A general, shared religious life could be created through the medium of the Law, and observing the proscriptions contained in the law would also keep the Jews separate and distinct. Taboos and boundaries became central elements in everyday life.

Passover and History

Jewish ritual life today contains many references to those historical events of dispersal and survival that transformed the ways of worship. The history of Pesach, or Passover, with its central meal, the seder, illustrates how Jewish ritual life was moved from public sacrifice to domestic celebration and observance of taboos (Bokser 1984). Pesach began as two spring festivals. Shepherds would sacrifice a lamb or kid from their flock on the full moon during the month when the animals were born. The lamb (the pesach) would be roasted whole and eaten completely during the night. At about the same time, farmers would celebrate their early spring harvest by offering unleavened bread, to symbolize the separation of the old grain (in the form of fermented dough used to leaven bread) from the new, harvested grain. (Two other agricultural festivals, Shavuot, "weeks," and Sukkot, "harvesting booths," celebrated the later harvests.)

At some point in early Jewish history these celebrations of harvest and birth were merged into one ritual and were given a new meaning, the celebration of the Jews' deliverance from Egypt. The unleavened breads, in the form of matzohs, now became signs of the haste of flight: not enough time was available to leaven the bread before leaving Egypt. And in celebration of this event the book of Exodus (12:19) orders Jews that for this day "No leaven shall be in your houses"—leaven defined for these purposes as contact between grain and water for more than 18 minutes. Sacrifice was still carried out, first at altars throughout Judea, and then, after Josiah in 621 B.C.E forbade all sacrifices in "high places," at a single gathering at the Temple in Jerusalem. Each family brought a lamb to be sacrificed in commemoration of the lamb sacrificed in Egypt. They killed the lambs around the Temple, and gave some of the blood to the priests to be thrown at the base of the altar, then roasted them and ate them with unleavened bread.

After 70 C.E. Temple sacrifice could no longer be made, and the rabbis replaced the earlier focus on sacrifice and harvest with an exclusive focus on the covenant with God and its document, the Torah. Passover was now solely a commemoration of the flight from Egypt, and it was held at home (not at the synagogue, perhaps to avoid implying that the synagogue had replaced the Temple). The matzoh replaced the sacrifice as the main element of the meal, although a piece of meat on a bone remains as a reminder of the now-lost practice of sacrifice of the pesach itself.

Ritual Life Today

Jewish lives today combine feast-day commemorations of past events with everyday observance of religious laws, but the different ways Jews combine legal and ritual life have given rise to several distinct religious categories. About half of the 18 million people considering themselves Jewish live in North America; most of the remainder live in Israel, Europe, and Russia; Jews in each of these places generally regard themselves as either Orthodox, Conservative, or Reform. Orthodox Jews (a category including Hasidic movements) stress observance of legal rules; they hold that the Torah and the commandments are God's word as revealed at Sinai and continue to be binding on all Jews. Conservative (or Historic) Jews also recognize the validity of the Torah, but emphasize the historical continuity of the Jewish people and the capacity of the people to change law and practice. Reform Jews (along with the smaller Reconstructionist movement) focus on the spiritual essence of Judaism rather than the idea of a ethnically based nation and have been more willing to abandon older rituals and laws.

What divides these groups is mainly attitudes toward religious law; what unites them is mainly the observance of major holy days. For Jews as for Muslims, people living in different countries and cultures participate, in the same day and in much the same way, in rituals of commemoration. For Muslims, these calendrical rituals are mainly about sacrifice and pilgrimage; for Jews, they are mainly about deliverance and atonement. Muslim rituals are patterned after the acts carried out by Muhammad; therefore, what Muslims emphasize is the importance of precisely following the commands given in the scripture. Jewish rituals have changed radically over time in their forms and in their meanings, and Jews emphasize the historical events that the rituals commemorate. Jews consider the Passover celebrations and other holidays as primarily about remembering an event that defined their subsequent travails and identity, and about hoping for the future Messiah.

At Passover celebrations today families read the Exodus tale from a liturgy called the Haggadah. Although brought out in numerous editions with new material, all Haggadah texts recite the story of the persecution of the Jews in Egypt and their deliverance by God. A cup of wine is left for Elijah, whose arrival is supposed to herald the Messiah. And many also celebrate the survival of the Jewish people and the birth of the modern state of Israel as additional holidays.

On other holidays, too, different stories make the same general point, that through their covenant with God the Jews, despite their persecution, were delivered from evil. Purim, a time of games and merrymaking, nonetheless commemorates the hanging of Haman and the slaughter of the other enemies of the Jews of Persia through the intervention of Esther. Hannukah, a celebration of freedom, observes the victory of the Maccabees. Sukkot, once, like Passover, a harvest feast, became a period to recall the long journey out of servitude (Schauss 1938).

Jewish festivals have changed over the years to reflect shifting concerns. The fasts and the agricultural festivals of Sukkot and Shavuot have receded in importance, and new holidays, such as those commemorating the Holocaust and Israel's Independence, have come into being. And yet ritual preserves a common element, of linking the current generation to key events in the past, some of them disastrous events for the Jewish community that nonetheless point toward that community's Covenant with God.

But this history may be interpreted in widely varying ways, and these variations return us to the central issue of boundaries and identity. The Passover Haggadah reminds Jews that "in every generation they rise to annihilate us," and the story of Esther can be read at Purim as chiefly saying one must slaughter one's enemies before they do you. In 1996, between Purim and Passover there occurred terrible suicide bombings in Tel Aviv and Jerusalem, and some Israelis drew on those possible readings of history to argue that continued war was inevitable, peace impossible. And yet others argued that Purim was chiefly about resisting oppression; Passover, about faith in deliverance, and that reacting to the bombings with oppression and lack of faith was in effect giving in to terrorism.

Central to these debates is both history and the Covenant, which is embodied in the Torah, the first five books of the Bible (Genesis, Exodus, Levicitus, Numbers, and Deuteronomy) given to Moses as the Law. At a boy's major rite of passage, when he becomes a "son of the commandments" or bar mitzvah, he shows his ability to read from Torah. Recently, as we saw in Chapter 3, some Jews have added a ritual for girls, the bat mitzvah. For many Jews prayer in Hebrew and reading of Torah remain daily rituals. In daily prescribed prayers the worshiper praises God and petitions Him for the restoration of the Temple. Orthodox and Conservative Jews pray in Hebrew; Reform Jews often use their vernacular language. On the head and left arm, the worshiper may wear the tefillin boxes containing Biblical quotations to remind the wearer of his religious duties. Although many events take place in the synagogue, home is the center of ritual life. The threshold of many Jewish homes is marked by a small box on the door post, the mezuzah, which contains a biblical passage proclaiming God's unity. "Here O Israel, the Lord is our God, the Lord is One." (Deuteronomy 6:4)

Jews have always felt that correctly applying Torah to daily life required further writings. Out of a consensus within the Jewish community on the correct understanding of scripture in the second century C.E. came the Mishna, a collection of rules and spiritual teachings. Scholars then wrote further commentaries on the Mishna, and these commentaries, called gemara, were joined to the Mishna to form the Talmud—in fact, two Talmuds, coming from scholars in Babylonia and Palestine.

Let us take an example of how scholars explicated the Law. The Torah gives as the fourth commandment:

six days shall you labor and do all manner of work;
but the seventh day is for the Lord, your God;
you shall not do on it any manner of work (Exodus 20, 9–10)

But the Torah does not tell its readers how to apply this commandment. Questions arise, and arose to Jews trying to observe the Law, and rabbis attempted to arrive at answers. What is "work," and does it depend on where you are? Scholars specified that carrying heavy objects on the sabbath was permitted in private—that was not work—but not in public places. When in the day does the Sabbath begin and end? Days begin in the evening, and scholars gradually pushed back the exact moment of its beginning. When may one break these rules? Health reasons were listed.

Some scholars have pointed out the resemblance between the multipl cross-references and layers of commentary in these texts and the hyperlinks across computer sites available on the World Wide Web. Recognizing the similarity, in 1996 the historian Eliezer Segal produced sample texts and commentaries in hypertext format. In a different vein, and recalling the role of temple worship, New York City's Temple Emanu-El broadcast its 1996 Rosh ha-Shanah service over the Internet, with the headline "Can't Get to the Temple? Get to the Computer" (*New York Times* September 16, 1996).

Movable Boundaries

Strict observance of religious laws may require ways to modify the ways those laws are carried out. For example, on the Sabbath one may not carry anything except within one's private domain. "Carrying" has been defined to include carrying an infant, or pushing a wheelchair. But what if an invalid needs to attend services, or an infant needs to be carried to the synagogue? One can, decided the rabbis, create a cooperative private domain, called an eruv, which might include the houses of a Jewish community and its synagogue. The eruv must be enclosed in some way, for example with posts and wires, as are, often unbeknownst to most residents, parts of some U.S. cities (including an area around the Congress and White House).

Often unobtrusive, eruvs have surfaced in at least one public debate in London over whether public, non-Anglican, religious objects were appropriate—and in particular religious objects that defined boundaries (Trillin 1994). Orthodox Jewish residents of a northern London neighborhood proposed to construct an eruv around their six-and-a-half-square-mile area, using 20-foot posts connected by fishing line, and mainly along existing roadways or rail lines. In the ensuing debate opponents of the eruv, including some in the older generation of Jews, argued that England's cohesion depended on religious differences remaining private affairs (in a context where the Anglican Church remains the Church of State, headed by the Queen). A younger generation of Jews, and in particular several Orthodox groups, argued that their religious freedom depended on building the eruv (see further discussion in Chapter 15).

The Lubavitchers of Brooklyn

Devoting their lives to the Law, some Jewish "pietist" movements place special emphasis on correctly observing the many commandments (mitzvot) from God—said by some to be 613 in all, positive and negative. Centuries of persecution, especially in eastern and central Europe, have intensified the desire to maintain internal cultural order through following the commandments. The pietists called Hasidim, who grew in the late eighteenth century under the tutelage of holy men in the Ukraine and eastern Europe, hold that obeying these rules brings the entire cosmos closer to light and goodness.

The most important Hasidic group today is probably the Lubavitchers, whose headquarters since 1940 has been in Brooklyn. The Lubavitchers venerate their leader or Rebbe, the holy man (zaddik) who mediates between God and the world. The Rebbe is specially blessed by God and that blessedness is passed on genealogically. All seven generations of Rebbes have been descendants of the movement's founder, Schneur Zalman (b. 1745), each a son, or son-in-law (and usually also cousin because of close intermarriage) of his predecessor.

Recent Rebbes have had strong influence in Israel. Lubavitchers, along with some other Orthodox groups, argue that non-Orthodox rabbis (Reform and Conservative) have no standing, and the marriages and conversion they perform are worthless. They also hold that only Orthodox Jews, those who maintain the laws of purity and agree that the Torah remains fully active as Law, have the right to return to Israel under the Law of Return, and in 1988 they nearly succeeded in making their view into the official Israeli position. In the 1980s and 1990s the Orthodox religious parties, which often held the balance of power in the Israeli Parliament, the Knesset, would from time to time call the Rebbe in Brooklyn to check the propriety of the positions on religious matters.

Many Lubavitchers were certain that the seventh Rebbe, the Paris-educated Menachem Mendel Schneerson (1902–1994) was the Messiah, at whose coming the Temple would be rebuilt. Some flew to Israel at his death to await what they called "the ultimate retribution" for centuries of persecution. In September 1996, two years after the death of Rebbe Schneerson, the new Israeli Prime Minister, Benjamin Netanyahu, made a special trip to Queens, New York, to say prayers at the Rebbe's grave (on a trip where he did not meet with the leaders of American Jewish organizations).

In her book *Holy Days,* Lis Harris (1985) describes everyday life for one Brooklyn household that belongs to the Lubavitchers. Harris underscores the meaningfulness that the women of the household find in living a life of restrictions and rules. The enforced rest on the Sabbath, when no cooking, not even turning on a light, may be done, gives them leisure and freedom from working for others—an important theme in the context of historical persecution of Jews. "No one is master of any Jew on the Sabbath" states one woman, Sheina, who had married into the community. Such rules "force me to think about the sanctity of the ordinary facts of my existence" (Harris 1985, 125).

Sheina had grown up in an Orthodox home, but a personal tragedy and chance meetings with Lubavitchers had led her to join the community. She had agreed to a marriage arranged by a rabbi, and had come to joyfully embrace the many rituals and commandments of the Hasidic life. Of the purifying bath in the communal bathing-place, the mikvah, not used by most Jews, she said that a community is supposed to build a bath even before a synagogue, so important is maintaining purity. For Sheina, rules that prohibit sexual intercourse between husband and wife for two weeks each month (during and after menstruation), and a ritual bath at the end of the period, make sex more passionate, "like a new bride every month" (Harris 1985, 140).

A similar passion for obeying the Law pervades Sheina's weeks of work before Passover to rid her house of the least bit of leavened food—grain that has come into contact with water for more than eighteen minutes. Exodus (12, 19) commands that "no leaven shall be found in your houses," and Hasidic housewives labor hard to comply. Sheina cleans her house from top to bottom, replaces the stove top with a special Passover cook top, and brings out an entire set of Passover cook ware that is sure to be free of leaven. Her matzohs come from a nearby bakery, where bakers race from kneading the dough to scoring it to baking the matzoh—all in nine minutes, well within the limit! Sheina and her husband also sell all leavened goods—packaged foods and whiskey (made from grain), for example—to a non-Jew, and then buy it back after Passover. The goods remain in their house, locked away, but the transaction means that the Law has been obeyed, because the goods are not theirs.

Sheina's Passover meal, like most such meals, featured the foods symbolic of exile and suffering: the meat, of that eaten before leaving Egypt, the egg dipped in salt water and the bitter herbs, of sadness and suffering. But the meal followed hours of discussion about the truth of exile as the Jews' present condition. All those present agreed that the state of exile was permanent until the Messiah should come, and that all attempts at assimilation to the larger world were futile.

Transnational Religion: Africa and Brazil across the Atlantic

*I*t is a mistake to think of the world evolving from an order of nation-states to an order of transnationalism and globalization. Certainly, the seventeenth-century creation of the Westphalian system in Europe, by which religions were stated to be the province of the prince in his or her domain, began a process that led to the assumption of increasing powers by states and contributed to the rise of thinking about nations. But long before and long after the seventeenth-century European treaty were the expansive and expanding realms of Christendom and Islam, the spread of Theravada Buddhism, and the spread of civilizations in the southern part of the Americas. Even if we think of the term "transnationalism" as properly postdating the importance of "nation," the phenomena so named—networks and movements of people and knowledge across vast distances—has been part of human social and religious experience far longer than has the confining of legitimate belief and worship to a princely, or parliamentary, realm.

The history of religious innovation across the Atlantic is an important case of these often neglected trans-state socioreligious networks. Afro-Brazilian religions developed in the context of the slave trade and enforced Catholicism. Yoruba religious ideas and practices, in particular, shaped the development of Candombé religion in Brazil, with its center at Salvador de Bahia, but so was Yoruba religion shaped by people returning from Brazil (Matory 2005). The case of the Black Atlantic shows us that even as African images and ideas became the basis for New World religious creation, there also emerged a trans-Atlantic network of men and women who shaped developments on both continents.

The slave trade brought large numbers of African people to the southern and central portions of the Americas as well as to the colonies in North America. Slavery lasted longer in the southern regions, until 1888 in Brazil. Many of the Africans were taken from what is today Nigeria and Bénin. In particular, Yoruba people were brought to Brazil and Cuba, and Fon people were brought to Haiti. Slave traders and slave owners tried to wipe out cultural traditions and mixed slaves from different regions, as an effort to prevent Africans from organizing rebellions (Walker 1990).

Because slave-owners prohibited the practice of African religions, some Africans translated ideas and deities of West African religions into the images and language of Catholicism. Slavers thought that they were imposing Catholicism; Africans understood that they were preserving older traditions. In Brazil these traditions today are called Umbanda and Macumba in Rio de Janeiro and Candomblé in the northeast region of Bahia. They combine, in different proportions, African qualities, especially in Bahia, and Brazilian innovations, especially in Rio, with Catholic imagery and ideas from a Euro-Brazilian movement called Spiritism.

In Rio a woman presides over services in a small storefront center called the Spiritist Tent of Granny Maria Antonia of the Congo, one of many places to which people come to worship and seek help from the spirits (Guillermoprieto 1990). In this center as in many others there is a particular "patron" spirit, Granny Maria Antonia. She is understood to be a woman who was born in Africa and was brought as a slave to Brazil, where she died. She is of a recognizable type of Afro-Brazilian spirit, the "Old Black Woman." Also exhibited at the center are statues of Christian figures: the Virgin Mary, Jesus, St. George (of dragon-slaying fame), and others. Each resembles corresponding statues in, say, European Catholic churches. But each also corresponds to an Umbanda deity called an Orisha, and can be traced back to its original in Yoruba society, West Africa. Today people freely offer the Orisha as well as the Catholic name for each image; a century ago any but the Catholic identity would have been strongly denied to outsiders.

In this schema of cross-religious translation, God is Olorun, the creator of the world. The image of Jesus is also identified as Oshala, the creator of human life. Saint George, depicted slaying a dragon, corresponds to Oshossi, the hunter god, and St. Lazarus, protector of lepers, to Omolu, a deity governing disease. Mary is identified with Yemanja, the mother of some of the other Orishas. Furthermore, and here note the parallel with our Spanish valley, other Orishas who are mothers are also identified as manifestations of Mary. These maternal deities are associated with the water and sea as well.

The lifting of the veil surrounding this momentous project of religious translation was not followed by the crafting of new, original statues. In Yoruba and Umbanda thought the Orishas have no concrete form; they are forces and principles rather than personages. Thus the process of rendering African deities in Catholic form added a new visual and individuating dimension to worship, and the Catholic images remain as foci for Umbanda worship. The identification extends to ritual occasions as well. People observe the Catholic feast days that apply to their "translated" deities, but do so in a way that corresponds to the Afro-Brazilian meaning of the deity. For example, Yemanja (Mary) is identified with the sea, so people flock to the sea on the Catholic feast-days for Mary and once there they offer gifts to Yemanja, wading out into the water and letting the sea carry them away.

Umbanda and Candomblé in fact bring together three religious traditions. Alongside of Catholic and Yoruba religions is the doctrine of Spiritism or Kardecism, popular among the elite in Europe and Brazil in the late nineteenth century and today adhered to by millions in Brazil, either as part of Umbanda and Candomblé or on its own. Spiritism provides a means of healing people from physical and mental afflictions. The doctrine attributes a wide range of events in the material world to the desires and actions of spirits. Sometimes spirits possess people, and when they do they can cause the person to suffer illness. Specialists can communicate directly with these spirits, ask what their wishes are, and restore the person to health.

Umbanda in Rio

Umbanda was in fact born as a revolt against the elitism of Spiritism in Rio (Brown 1986). By the 1920s, Spiritism had become a highly intellectualized and European-oriented set of practices. Lighter-skinned Brazilians (Brazilian color coding of individuals contains many categories, from very dark to very light, rather than a simple black/white dichotomy) controlled the séances. They were speaking with the likes of Voltaire and Plato. If an Indian spirit appeared, possessing one of their own, they would refuse to allow him to speak.

In the 1920 a middle-class Rio man, Zelio de Moraes, suffered an illness that left him partially paralyzed. His father, a real estate agent, was a Spiritist and took him to his group for healing. There he was visited by the spirit of a Jesuit priest, who revealed that the illness was spiritual, and that he had a mission, which was to found a truly Brazilian religion that would be dedicated to the worship and propitiation of Brazilian spirits. These spirits included *caboclos*, spirits of Brazilian Indians, and *pretos velhos*, spirits of Africans enslaved in Brazil.

Zelio received additional messages from other spirits. The "Indian of the Seven Crossroads" told him the new religion would be called Umbanda. Zelio then did as he was told, and founded the first Umbanda center, today called the "Mother House." This center, the Spirits' Center of Our Lady of Piety, attracted a largely white and middle-class clientele. But the spirits that spoke through the participants were those of Indians and Africans, giving them the voice denied to them by the Spiritists. The movement grew rapidly, attracting a diverse range of participants.

The social and political roles of these movements have changed dramatically in this century. At first tolerated, it was repressed as heretical in the 1930s, 1940s, and 1950s by the Catholic Church, with support from the Brazilian state. State repressions began to loosen in the 1960s, and since 1970 people have enjoyed relative freedom to worship openly. The initial reason for this tolerance was political, as politicians seeking office sought support from the large communities of Umbanda-Candomblé followers. But the change also has been motivated by social and cultural changes (Walker 1990). In the past thirty years many Brazilians have sought their "roots," and some, including many of lighter skin color, have found them in the links back to Africa. Many of these people, mostly of the middle class, have found these links through the experience of possession by an African spirit. In doing so, they have moved away from the Catholicism, which once was virtually required of those seeking high social status. Being known as follower of Umbanda or Candomblé is no handicap to political office, and participation in the movements can be combined with a range of political and social doctrines. The Brazilian secretary of public works in the 1980s, for example, calls himself a "Marxist-Spiritist," believing in both reincarnation and Marxist-Leninism.

These movements also have become part of a broader popular culture in Brazil. On New Year's Day, the major newspapers in Rio run the Umbanda seers' forecasts for the next year. In Bahia state, the home of Candomblé, pop-singing groups have risen to the top of the charts with songs based in Candomblé; new wave filmmakers have drawn on the Orishas for their subjects, as in the popular film called "The Amulet of Ogun." The Orisha named Esu, who controls roads and pathways, was adopted as the patron deity of all communications facilities, and a statue to him stands in front of the post office in Salvador, Bahia's capital (Murphy 1994). The urban poor are drawn to these movements. Two million of Rio's six and one-half million people live in squatter settlements called *favelas*. For them, "survival calls for imaginative solutions, and Umbanda is nothing if not the triumph of imaginative thought," writes the reporter Alma Guillermoprieto (1990).

Let us return to the Granny Maria Antonia center mentioned earlier. The center is a two-story house located in a lower middle-class neighborhood in central Rio. A black woman named Stella Soares runs the center. Stella, a former nurse, insists that all who attend don white uniforms; this measure makes everyone more nearly equal, she says. Certain specific spirits visit the center and possess those who attend its services. They are the spirits of individual Indian and African people rather than Orishas. They include the Indian of the Seven Crossroads, the Indian of the Coral Cobra, and the "Indian who tears up tree stumps with his bare hands." They speak; they embody the local identity of black and Indian Brazilians, and through the experience of being possessed the worshipers can experience several identities, several sides of themselves. Her clientele includes dozens of mainly white, middle-class initiates, who go into trance, but also many very poor black clients. "Once they have changed into their white clothes," she says, "you cannot tell the difference."

Are these religions part of Catholicism? Catholic priests call on people to abandon Umbanda, claiming that it has nothing to do with Catholicism, and some practitioners (probably an increasing number) consider themselves to be followers of Umbanda and not, or no longer, Catholics. But many other Umbanda followers claim status as Catholics. They point to a number of close relationships between Umbanda practices and Catholicism. The images in worship are all Catholic. Some Candomblé priests require initiates to be baptized Catholics before they can join in the rituals. The story of how the first center was founded also underscores the connection with Catholicism—it was, after all, the spirit of a Jesuit priest who commanded Zelio to open up his center. Catholic feast days are observed, and many Umbanda practices reinforce the link to the Catholic Church. For example, on August 16, the feast day for Saint Lazarus, Umbanda priestesses drive by churches where the mass is held and sprinkle popcorn on all so that they will receive benefits from Omolu, the deity associated with the saint.

As we saw in Chapter 10, Catholic images, and especially the image of the Virgin Mary, have served to mediate translations of religion across vast social and cultural divides, first within Europe, and then out across seas with the expansion of the Church. But the very capacity of the image to carry multiple meanings—what we have called the multivocality of the image—has allowed subordinate groups to contest the dominant meanings. Spanish villagers insist on their own Mary's capacity to protect and nurture; Mexicans, of the Virgin of Guadalupe's role as a national symbol; Brazilians, of Yemanja/Mary's powers over the sea; Christians throughout the world, on Mary's willingness to appear to them and to deliver messages of hope and struggle. Each set of claims to Mary is asserted over and against official counterclaims that underscore the unity of Mary and Christ and the single authoritative voice of Rome.

In this example, transnational Catholicism appears not as a single set of ideas and practices, but a set of contested images, and, in the case of Afro-Brazilian religions, part of a contested legacy of religious survival and creativity.

The Black Atlantic

But in the nineteenth and twentieth centuries, Brazilian-born men and women traveled to West Africa and helped shape the development of religious practices in Nigeria (Matory 2005, 46–72). Following uprisings in Brazil during the mid-nineteenth century, thousands of people were able to return to West Africa, and most of them gravitated to the now bustling seaport of Lagos. The British encouraged the immigration of these and other people, including slaves freed by British vessels, and these "return migrants" began to build up a sense of Yoruba identity. The cultural nationalism that developed in Yorubaland included a sense of the superiority of Yoruba religions, and this sense was then carried to Brazil in the late nineteenth century. Thus, what some had thought to be "survivals" of West African ideas in Brazil in fact were brought to Brazil as part of a continual traffic across the Atlantic by African-Brazilian men and women.

The Brazilians developed a notion of religious purity that was absent from the Yoruba side of the Atlantic. Matory (2005) chronicles how by the 1930s traders working the route between Lagos and Bahia were nourishing a Brazilian appreciation for "pure

African" goods (good for trade) and religion (good for prestige, and thus for trade). Thus Afro-Brazilians began to "purify" Candomblé of what they saw as accretions from Catholic or other influences. In particular, the head of a Bahia Candomblé temple, Mãe Aninha, was able to successfully claim that her knowledge of African practices made her version of Candomblé more pure and authentic. She was able to jump to the top of the Bahia hierarchy through these claims. (A second wave of "purification" of religion came in the 1980s with new Nigerian religious experts visiting Bahia.)

Thus Candomblé incorporates into its central practices a concern with purification and cleansing that is not central to Yoruba practices. Contemporary Yoruba practices emphasize maintaining health through restoring the balance of elements within the body. Candomblé healing, by contrast, emphasizes expelling polluting elements from the body (Matory 2005, 128–133). The deity Esu may have been adopted as the patron saint of communications, given his position at crossroads and thresholds, as mentioned above, and he is the guardian of the centers, but because of his liminal position he also is responsible for introducing disorder, and can be bribed into bringing disease and misfortune. Cleansing an afflicted person of these misfortunes requires using products thought of as "pure African" such as kola nuts. Thus the trans-Atlantic production of notions of African purity has reshaped the practice of healing.

The same logic has been at the heart of ideas of Brazilian identity as linked to Africa. Celebration of the African roots of Candomblé was a way for Brazilian cultural leaders to oppose the dominance of the United States. And beginning in the 1980s, increased, and often state-financed, trips by Brazilian Candomblé priests to Nigeria and reciprocal visits by Nigerian priests have led to a movement to recognize the independence of Candomblé from Catholicism and its place in a trans-Atlantic network and history of religions. As Matory (2005, 152–181) so well shows, these trans-Atlantic affiliations by no means diminish attachments to nations and to territories. Brazilian nationalism increasingly is based on these trans-Atlantic memories and connections. Conversely, the houses (or "nations") of Candomblé are rooted in specific parcels of land in Brazil.

Indeed, Matory's (2005, 177) affirmation that "diaspora is therefore better described as a *pluralization* of territorial identities than as an abandonment of them" serves well in examining other transnational projects as well. In the next chapter I focus on Muslims in Europe, where far from developing a deterritorialized or new sort of transnational citizenship, one sees men and women developing citizenship projects in two or more countries.

Mary in Mesoamerica

*B*ut first let us move northward in the Americas to Mesoamerica, where Mary's resonances with local stories and traditions made her a particularly powerful symbol.

The Virgin of Guadalupe

In Mesoamerica, today's Mexico and Guatemala, the Mary of Guadalupe has served as a symbol of nation and people, sometimes in opposition to foreign rule. During and after the Spanish conquest of the region, from the mid-sixteenth through the late seventeenth century, the native Mayan people of eastern Mesoamerica organized rebellions. These rebellions soon incorporated the symbols of Catholicism, reworked in Indian terms. The insurgent movements often included figures anointed as Christ or king. In some cases, villagers were visited by the Virgin Mary, who then instructed them to start a new church organization. She would leave proof of her visit in the form of an image that she created either on cloth or as a statue (Lafaye 1976; Wolf 1958).

The two most influential cases involved the Virgin revealing her image to a peasant (in both cases, as it happened, named Juan Diego) during the sixteenth century. The first apparition, in which Mary left her figure on a cloak, took place in 1531 in Tepeyac near Mexico City and became known as the Virgin of Guadalupe; the second, known as the Virgin of Ocotlan, occurred about 10 years later in Tlaxcala state, when Mary imprinted herself on an ocote tree.

The Virgin of Guadalupe was to become the master symbol of Mexico. The Mexican War of Independence was fought under her banner, and her shrine at Tepeyac became the major Mexican shrine. In the official story of the events, the Virgin addressed a Christianized Indian named Juan Diego in 1531, 10 years after the Spanish conquest of the area. The Virgin commanded him to go to the archbishop of Mexico and tell him that she wished a church built in her honor on Tepeyac Hill. Juan Diego tried twice to win the archbishop's approval, but was unsuccessful. Mary then performed a miracle. She told Juan Diego to gather roses in a dry spot where roses never grew, and then to present them to the archbishop. He did so, but when, standing before the archbishop, he unfolded his cloak, there appeared from inside, not roses, but the image of the Virgin miraculously imprinted on the cloak. The bishop immediately acknowledged the miracle, so the story goes, and ordered a shrine built on the spot where she had appeared.

This particular spot was not, however, a random choice. It had once been the site of a temple to the goddess of fertility Tonantzin. Tonantzin, Our Lady Mother, is associated with the moon, as is Guadalupe's image. Indeed, for at least the next 50 years worshipers called her Tonantzin as well as Guadalupe, and this still is the case in parts of Mexico. Stories about Tonantzin continue to be told in Mexico: in one, she intervened when God wanted to punish his children, by challenging him to try to produce milk so she could nourish her children.

These associations or "syncretism" are not unique to the New World, of course. William Christian speculates about preexisting deities where there now are shrines in Spain. In Ireland, in particular, statues of the Virgin often are erected in spots formerly considered sacred because of an unusually shaped rock formation or a sacred grove. And in the Church of Saint Germain in Paris, a black image of the Egyptian goddess Isis was displayed as the Madonna until 1514.

Guadalupe and Mexican Resistance to Spain

In later centuries, rebellions against Spanish control frequently formed around cults of the Virgin Mary. In 1721 in Cancuc (Chiapas), the Virgin appeared to a young girl and asked her to place a cross in her hamlet, build a chapel around it, and offer incense. A local Mayan leader then claimed to have ascended to heaven where he spoke with the

Virgin Mary, Jesus Christ, and St. Peter, and was told that the people were to appoint their own officials and no longer had need of the Spanish. This man, Sebastian Gomez, then appointed bishops and priests, all using the symbols of the Catholic Church.

Devotions in the local church had already become "localized" in the sense in which we used the word earlier: worship focused on locally specific images of the Virgin that were understood as protecting the village. Services consisted of giving offerings and prayers to these advocations of Mary and to other localized saints, rather than addressing prayers to God. Gomez and his followers now renamed Cancuc "Jerusalem" and referred to the Spaniards as "the Jews who persecuted the Virgin Mary." Although the movement was suppressed, it illustrates the ways in which local opposition to Spanish rule was elaborated in what were once the conqueror's own images, the sacred images of Catholicism itself.

By choosing Mary and the saints as key images, those local movements that did not reach the stage of open rebellion managed to insulate themselves (and popular religious practice generally) against charges of heresy. The Spanish Inquisition investigated these religious movements and looked for evidence of idolatry, in particular prayers said to images that asked them to directly heal illnesses. The Indians whom the inquisitors interrogated denied that they acted in this way, claiming that they merely appealed to the patron saints and to the Virgin Mary for help. Because the Spanish Church accepted as legitimate both the cult of the patron saint and the possibility of visitations by the Virgin, the inquisitors were unable to find solid ground to prosecute Indian religious leaders (Lafaye 1976).

Why was it the Virgin Mary (and not Christ) who became Mexico's national symbol? The answer is in part due to the way the Church itself portrays Mary and Christ, and perhaps in part due to local family dynamics. The Virgin is associated with struggle and life in Mexico, while Christ is associated with defeat and death. On the religious plane, these distinct associations stem from the crucifixion of Christ, on the one hand, and the nurturing role of the Virgin, on the other. The anthropologist Eric Wolf (1956) argues that on the family plane, the associations grow out of the distinct sentiments the child forms toward his or her mother and father, in both Indian and Mexican families. The child experiences a paradise of closeness to his or her mother, and sides with the mother in her struggle against domination by the father. Mary thus brings out a wealth of early pleasant memories; Christ, the object of struggle. Sentiments formed in the family are expressed in the culture through the symbols of the Virgin and Christ.

On the plane of politics, the Virgin Mary, in the specific advocation of the Virgin of Guadalupe, is associated with the struggle against Spanish military and religious colonization. Many Mexicans interpreted Guadalupe as the goddess Tonantzin who has returned to liberate Mexico. This interpretation follows an indigenous logic of cyclical history, in which gods depart only to return later. Mexico appears as a new paradise, to which came the Virgin to herald independence. In one seventeenth-century text, the Virgin of Guadalupe is linked to the woman portrayed in the Revelation of John, "arrayed with the sun, and the moon under her feet, and upon her head a crown of twelve stars," and who is to realize the prophecies of Deuteronomy. Not coincidentally, the image of the Virgin of Guadalupe in the shrine today is adorned with a sun and moon and the twelve stars.

The Virgin of Guadalupe thus links family (mother), politics (liberation), and religion (salvation). Against the background of these linkages we can understand how it was that in 1810 the patriot Father Miguel Hidalgo y Castilla began the revolution for Independence with the cry: "Long Live the Virgin of Guadalupe and down with bad government."

The political and religious associations have continued in full force into this century. In the early twentieth century, the church, trying to render more uniform the devotions of the faithful, attempted to replace the Virgin of Guadalupe with the Sacred Heart of Jesus from Rome. This attempt was perceived in Mexico as an effort to supplant a Mexican figure with a European one, and it was strongly, and successfully, resisted. And in 1996, the Bishop of Guadalupe, speaking to a reporter in Italy, declared that he considered the peasant Juan Diego to have been a mythical figure (*St. Louis Post-Dispatch*, September 7, 1996). The remark led to his immediate removal from office!

South Asians Overseas

*T*he case of trans-Atlantic religion tells us that when we study diasporas or transnational networks we should expect to find continuities, local innovations, and a back-and-forth across geographical divides. Yes there are broad similarities and persistent elements in religious practices that can be traced to the Nigeria-Bénin region, but there also are profound differences in basic conceptions of being and healing. These differences can be traced in part to the complex history of interactions across the Atlantic and in part to the distinct local projects of developing identities and statuses in which religious practitioners have been engaged.

As we move to the example of South Asian diasporas we should expect to find a corresponding multidimensional story of movement, adaptations, and interactions, rendered all the more complex by tensions across religious divides within South Asia. Population movements outward from South Asia have occurred at different periods and for a wide variety of reasons. Between 1830 and 1920, millions of men and women from British India became indentured workers, mainly on plantations, in other sites of British settlement, from Trinidad to Mauritius, and South Africa to Malaya. Over time they developed cultures and practices as part of local development of ethnic divisions of labor: in South Africa and Malaya, for example, as the "third group" between dominant categories of whites and blacks, or Malays and Chinese, respectively. As majorities in other places, they endeavored to create a Hindu-based local identity, as in the case of Mauritius examined below.

Many others migrated later and in more favorable economic circumstance, particularly those Muslims moving to North America from the 1960s on, and, somewhat lower on the economic ladders, Muslims and Hindus moving to Britain after the Second World War (see Chapter 13).

Mauritius and Hindi Language Ideology

In his study of ideologies of language and origins in Mauritius, Patrick Eisenlohr (2007) traces processes of purification parallel to those discerned by Matory for Brazil.

Mauritius, located just east of Madagascar, has a majority Hindu population brought from India to work on plantations. Muslim South Asians are the next largest population category. The Mauritian Creole language is spoken by nearly everyone, and the major local language of Indian origin, Bhojpuri, has changed considerably from the version spoken in India. Precisely because of these situations of linguistic mixing and change, some Hindu nationalists promote a "pure" Hindi language as a badge of their ancestral ties to South Asia. More broadly, Hindu Mauritians promote an identification with an ancestral Hindu culture, whose spiritual values underpin their own citizenship qualities and practices on Mauritius. Put another way, Hindu Mauritians' sense of who they are in Mauritius does not involve ideas of assimilation or integration to a preexisting culture—Mauritius has no indigenous population—but the cultivation of putatively pure linkages backward in time and overseas in space to India.

But viewed from India these linkages are the contemporary efforts of Hindu nationalist organizations to solidify Hindu-ness (*Hindutva*) at home by way of connections to the diaspora. The threatened position of Hindus or threatened disappearance of Hindu religion and culture abroad serves as one more rallying cry for Hindu unity at home (van der Veer 1994, 114–118). Therefore, the Arya Samaj, the VHP, and the once-banned RSS (Rashtriya Svayamsevak Sangh) work through Hindu organizations in Mauritius, such as the state-subsidized Hindu House and Hindu Council, which in turn exert pressure on the Hindu-dominated government and civil service. The Mauritius Hindu organizations and the local offices of the transnational Hindu organizations, such as the VHP, enjoy overlapping officials and coordination of activities.

Hindu nationalists symbolize Hindu unity across the oceans in the very same ways they do so at home, by symbolically articulating the unity of all Hindus via symbols of religious purity. For example, in 1972 the Mauritius minister of commerce and industry consecrated the island's own most important place of pilgrimage as "Ganges Lake" by flying in water from the Ganges river to dump into the lake. The India VHP sent a well-known Hindu teacher to experience darshan with the most important temples across Mauritius (Eisenlohr 2007, 35–44). VHP rhetoric was particularly effective in drawing parallels between the Indian Hindu experience of Muslim invaders and the Mauritius Hindu experience of colonialism. And they also may play on the parallel contemporary grievances: of Hindu Mauritians against what they claim to be Franco-Mauritian Creole privileges, and of Hindu Indians against Muslims, derided as preventing national unity.

But these activists present their actions as nationalist, in that preserving and enhancing Hindu unity also strengthens what they see as the identity of Mauritius, one in which Hindu traditions play a central role and a Sanskritized version of Hindi guarantees access to the sacred text of the religion. Hindi is increasingly taught in schools, and modern standard Hindi versions of sacred texts are distributed and read throughout the island. It is important to stress that the importance of the Hindi language to Mauritian Hindu self-conceptions is not a survival of past practices. The ancestors of today's Hindu Mauritians spoke vernacular Bhojpuri, and today's version of that speech is heavily inflected with local borrowings. Hindu Mauritius activists have enrolled "classical" Hindi in a campaign to construct pure ties to ancestral traditions—not unlike the ways in which Brazilian Candomblé preachers mobilized ideas of a pure

African tradition in their efforts to raise the status of their temples within the Bahian hierarchy.

Husayn in Trinidad

Let us now return to South Asia, but this time to trace the ways in which a religious ritual has been transformed in meaning as it journeyed overseas.

Each year, Shi'i Muslims throughout the world commemorate the death of the man they call the Imam Husayn, the grandson of the Prophet Muhammad, at the Battle of Karbala in 680 C.E. There, in present-day Iraq, Husayn's small army was besieged and then slaughtered by the larger forces of the Caliph, Yazid. The battle signaled the end of efforts by the party (shi'i) of 'Ali, the son-in-law of the Prophet Muhammad and Husayn's father, to lead the Muslim community. It meant that those who continued to follow the descendants of 'Ali would remain a permanent minority party in the Muslim world. Its memory has given to Shi'is their central, unifying topos.

Throughout the year, but especially during the feast of Ashura, on the tenth of the month of Muharram, women and men commemorate the defeat, mourn the suffering of Husayn and his family, and direct their wishes and vows to them. These rituals of commemoration and request are not merely instrumental events, but occasions of great emotional power. Shi'is hold 'Ali and his descendants to have carried with them the sacrality of Muhammad as well as to have been the legitimate heirs to rule the Muslim community.

Many Shi'i communities stage processions or *ta'zîyas*, in which they enact the suffering and death of Husayn. The plays are staged as processions, at which spectators participate by weeping at Husayn's fate. They also signal the capacity of Husayn to mediate on their behalf with God, and thus they remind the participant of the universal possibility of salvation.

These processions have been transformed as Shi'is traveled from the homeland in Iraq or Iran to other lands. In India, the term "ta'ziya" came to refer to huge models of tombs, and in particular of Husayn's tomb in Karbala, that were carried on wooden or bamboo frames in procession, and then submerged in sacred waters at the journey's end—an action that you now will recognize as adding a typically Indian touch to this Shi'i Muslim ritual. Shi'is continued the devotional dimensions of the commemoration through private readings of elegies, while the more public processions became the occasions for a wider range of emotions. Some Sunnis and even Hindus participate in the public processions: Sunnis, too, venerate Husayn, and some Hindus consider Husayn to have been a deity. Some treat the ta'ziyas as sources of healing power, procuring garlands from the structures to hang around their infants' necks. Hindu drummers often provide rhythmic accompaniment to what, for many, becomes a parade, a festival. Sunnis and Shi'is sometimes did come into conflict on these occasions, as the two communities held different explicit views on the event—Shi'is find the caliphs that came before and after 'Ali to have been illegitimate, Sunnis think the opposite and that the Shi'i practices verged on idolatry. But these conflicts erupted only when other conditions pushed toward open conflict.

When South Asians moved in large numbers as laborers to Trinidad (and else-where in the West Indies), they brought the "Hosay" (*Husayn*) ritual with them. Even more than in India, non-Muslims joined in the public processions, which marked a shared, South Asian identity. Non-Muslims participated in part because some already would have done so in India, and in part because they took the ritual as a means of protesting against their conditions of indentured servitude. Plantation estates com-peted with each other to build the most impressive ta'ziyas. The aspect of mourning and breast-beating that was central to the processions when they were predominantly Shi'i now passed out of use.

As the event became more "carnivalized," other Trinidadians not of Indian descent joined in, making it a national celebration. Afro-Trinidadians join in building the mod-els and the drums, and many join in the procession itself. The imam's blessing is wit-nessed by many non-Muslims present and working alongside both Sunni and Shi'i Muslims (Korom 2003). And yet the Husayn commemoration does after all have its roots in Shi'ism, and this value remains present, to be mobilized at particular moments, as when the Bilal Muslim Mission of the Americas began to teach the Islamic meanings of the event, and to ignore those meanings that do not have global Islamic roots. The esoteric elements, such as the moon imagery that has remained attached to the procession since its arrival from India, remain out of public discussion. These efforts could in time lead to a drive to purify the Husayn commemoration of its "Hosay" elements; for the moment, they have led to active debates among Trinidadians as to whether the event is mainly Islamic, or Hindu, or Indian.

In the story of the Black Atlantic and that of Hindus overseas, themes of purifica-tion recur. It may be generally true that diasporas' ideas of identity seek a purity, free of contextual complications, that is less a concern in homelands.

13 Focus on Muslims in Europe

*I*n this chapter we focus on the ways in which Muslims have adapted to new countries of residence in Europe and at the same time have continued to participate in transnational religious networks. We will see how their histories of migration have shaped how they and other Europeans have come to see themselves and each other.

As with Catholicism and Buddhism, Islam always was transnational in its conception, in the sense of having a global reach. Sunnis and Shi'is alike envisioned the Islamic state as transcending preexisting boundaries that were ethnic (or "national" in today's sense) so as to include all Muslims. In that sense many Muslims saw the ideal political arrangement as one in which all Muslims would be in one state, with one ruler. Even today, some Muslims envision a future time when a single Muslim state or caliphate will unify all Muslims.

Muslims established a presence in Europe early in Islamic history. They expanded into Europe from two directions: from northern Africa into Spain (and for a brief period into southern France), and, later on, into the Balkan Peninsula. The former left a rich Islamic heritage, which many in Spain claim today; the latter created Muslim majority societies in today's Albania, Bosnia (and, of course, in Turkey).

In the remainder of Europe the presence of Muslims is due to the colonization of Muslim-majority lands in Asia and Africa. France, Britain, the Netherlands, and Italy all had colonies with Muslim populations. France invaded Algeria in 1830 and by the century's end had made it part of French territory. By the turn of the twentieth century, France was recruiting male laborers from northern and western parts of Africa, as well as from elsewhere in Europe, to work in its factories, and these patterns of "circular labor migration" continued to develop during the first half of the century. The Dutch ruled today's Indonesia and Suriname, and the British today's India, Pakistan, and Bangladesh, and some Muslims from those Asian regions moved to the Netherlands and Britain. Italy's ventures in northern and eastern Africa led to some migration later from those areas to Italy.

Migration and Transnational Ties

*L*arge-scale movement of Muslims to Europe only began after the Second World War, however, when the demand for unskilled labor to rebuild Europe far outstripped the European supply. Muslims from Kashmir and what is today Bangladesh came to Britain, benefiting from policies that allowed free movement within the Commonwealth. The unrest and uncertainty produced by the Algerian War (1954–1962) led many French Algerians to settle in the metropolis with their families. By the late 1960s, Moroccans and Turks were moving into the Netherlands and the Scandinavian counties. Worldwide recession in 1973–1974 led European countries to limit labor migration, however. Since that time most Muslims arriving in Europe have come to join a close family member already enjoying legal residence, to claim asylum on grounds of conflict or persecution, or as an illegal entrant. In those areas of Europe that had experienced relatively little earlier labor immigration, including the Scandinavian countries and Italy, asylum seekers make up a relatively large proportion of the Muslim population. Elsewhere the older patterns of labor migration continue to shape today's immigration patterns.

In the 1980s, the Europe-born children of the major wave of Muslim immigration came of age and began to demand public recognition of their religion. They wanted to have mosques, halal food, and to be allowed to dress in a recognizably Islamic fashion. They did so at the very moment when the rise of what came to be called "political Islam" elsewhere in the world—Khomeini in Iran, new political movements in North Africa and the Middle East—stoked fears about Islam in Europe. Debates about the character of European Islam thus began at about the same time as the rise of a strong anti-immigrant trend in many countries, and the rise of anti-Islamic sentiment.

The distinct trajectories of Muslim migration have produced widely differing profiles of Muslims in each European country. France and Britain stand out in this regard because most of their Muslim residents (or their parents) came from former colonies, giving them some knowledge of the host country's language and customs and thus facilitating integration. Although the Netherlands colonized the world's largest Muslim population in Indonesia, most Dutch Muslims today are from Morocco and Turkey, without prior knowledge of Dutch. Turkish Muslims arriving in Germany may have known some German language because of the long history of labor migration from Turkey to Germany, but Moroccans, say, traveling to the Netherlands or to Norway, or Senegalese arriving in Italy, are unlikely to arrive with more than a smattering of words in their new country of residence, and their hosts are, in turn, unlikely to know much about Morocco or Senegal.

Adding to these differences were variations in migration patterns across Europe. In some countries immigrants have tended to live and socialize mainly with others from the same country of origin, and such ethnic concentration has made integration and understanding across religious lines more difficult. Today we see the sharpest conflicts on religious grounds precisely in those counties where Muslims live apart from others.

South Asians in Localized Britain

We can see these processes and mechanisms more clearly if we focus on several cases. Let us first look at Britain. British Muslims tend to come from a small number of places. About one-half of the Muslims in Britain are from Pakistan; Bangladesh and India provide the next largest numbers. Many of these Muslims come from just two districts in South Asia, Mirpur in Pakistan and Sylhet in Bangladesh. About 60 percent of UK-resident Pakistanis are from Mirpur, and in some cities with large Pakistani populations this percentage is higher (Lewis 2002, 216). New migrants sought out those they new from home districts, and once further immigration was restricted in 1962, new residents came under the rubric of family reunification, which favored residents of districts already overrepresented in Britain.

Pakistanis have been the most active and visible in British Muslim affairs and organizations, adding to the effect of this concentration on non-Muslim British perceptions of Islam in Britain. Muslims are also overwhelmingly perceived as non-English looking; of the relatively small number of converts, most are black British or Caribbean.

Furthermore, Muslims tend to live in a small number of places in Britain. Nearly half live in the London area; others have settled in Bradford, Birmingham, and a few other large industrial cities. These concentrations magnify those of origin to the extent that people from the same origins settled together: half of all Bangladeshis live in East London, and the Mirpur migrants have concentrated in Bradford and a few other places.

Subsequent developments in Britain added to the strength of transnational ties to specific places of origin. As Muslim populations grew in each city, mosques tended more and more to attend to people from one origin district and often who followed one particular South Asian school of Islamic thought. Many parents have sought spouses for their children from their own districts of origin; these intercontinental marriages continue to be organized in new generations.

Philip Lewis's (2002) study of Bradford provides an excellent picture of this organization. Early Muslim migration was by single men, who made few demands in the religious sphere and settled together regardless of origins. It was when families began to settle in the city in the late 1960s that fission began, following lines of community of origin (Lewis 2002, 56). Groups from different countries or districts within countries tended to settle together. Mosques were major agents of fission, because they were headed by religious officials, imams, who held allegiance to a specific South Asian movement, such as the Deobandi school or the Barelvis.

Bradford Muslims tended to form local associations specific to an ethnic or regional identity, such as the Azad Kashmir Muslim Association, the Gujar Khan burial society, or the Pukhtoon Cultural Society, all of which provided communication and mutual aid. Public funds were available to organizations that identified themselves as representing ethnic or racial minorities. Reinforcing these ties to South Asian localities was the practice of organizing support for Bradford political candidates around what had been local caste groups, *biradari,* in Pakistan. Pakistani political parties also shaped allegiances for Bradford elections, as when Islami Jamhoori Ittihad, the Pakistan coalition opposed to the Pakistan People's Party, brought together the same component groups within Bradford (Lewis 2002, 74).

The role played by mosques has grown in Bradford. Once Muslim families began to immigrate to Britain in the 1960s, more and more mosques appeared and became centers for spiritual development and religious teaching. They also began to make demands to local authorities on religious grounds, in contrast to the demands based on racial or ethnic discrimination claims made by the state-subsidized associations. In Birmingham it was in the mid-1980s that the rise of mosque influence coincided with a greater receptivity on the part of city authorities to considering the interests of Muslims to produce new guidelines for school policies toward Muslims on dress, provision of halal meat, and so forth.

But even as Pakistanis have claimed an Islamic public identity, that identity continues to have a strong Punjabi cultural content (Werbner 2003). Urdu remains both an important link to Pakistan as well as a vehicle for religious instruction. In that sense, it maintains an ethnic or regional consciousness in a way that knowledge of classical Arabic does not. Arabic can be understood as a vehicle for Islamic knowledge that transcends place; Urdu inevitably retains its Asian association. The enclave existence of some Pakistanis also facilitates and is reproduced by the transcontinental marriage, which Lewis (2002, 217) states accounts for over half the marriages in cities with high Muslim concentrations such as Bradford.

The concentration effects of the migration process also lend a particular texture to discussions within Islamic communities about religion and culture. For example, Katy Gardner's (2002) study of burial practices by Bangladeshis living in East London considers their decision to bury a deceased relative in Britain or to send the corpse back to Bangladesh for burial. The Muslim undertaker she consulted estimated that 60–70 percent of Bengali corpses are sent to Bangladesh (and specifically to Sylhet district) for burial. And yet sending corpses requires embalming, a practice these Muslims consider to be forbidden. It also violates the hadîth known to them, commanding Muslims to bury soon after death. The major reasons given to Gardner for sending back the corpses despite these rules are that the deceased's close relatives need to visit the grave regularly in order to pray for the soul, a necessary practice to ensure that it reaches heaven. Because there are no Islamic burial grounds near the Tower Hamlets area where they live in London, these visits would be difficult to carry out in Britain. Sylhet people also view their homeland as particularly holy because their spiritual leader (*pir*) Shah Jalal was buried there.

North Africans in Centralized France

In Britain, then, how Muslims migrated has reinforced their transnational ties to their origin places. In France, by contrast, the political culture of secularity (*laïcité*) and explicit government policy produce a marked split between official and unofficial practices of category politics. Officially, individuals are treated as citizens, and are not assigned to ethnic or religious categories, a refusal that makes the work of demonstrating ethnic or racial discrimination particularly difficult. However, in everyday life both public actors and ordinary people are engaged in a process of assigning others to such categories, most notably that of *maghrébin* (North African), based on various features of appearance, a process of everyday ethnicization that can produce comic results when, as in my own experience, some, but not other, children of a "native family" are suspected of being North African because of their slightly dark hair or features.

The demographic character of Muslim immigration to France differs in a number of ways from that in Britain. About 60–70 percent of Muslim immigrants to France have come from three countries of North Africa. Algerians and Moroccans have contributed the largest numbers, followed by Tunisians. Turks and West Africans form the next largest groups. The dominance of North African Muslims in the public sphere is even greater than these numbers might suggest, for a number of reasons. The North African countries had historically close colonial ties to France, and Algeria was part of France until 1962. North African immigration in the 1960s and 1970s was massive and concentrated in industrial cities. If "black British" immigrants set the tone in Britain, it was North African Muslims who did so in France, thereby making Islam identified with one region.

Men who came to France in order to work in the 1960s and 1970s were usually housed in large public housing units (HLM) where they were mixed together. Thus, immigration did not begin with origin-specific neighborhoods, as in some British cities. In any one neighborhood in the poorer suburbs of Paris or Lyon, or in the center of Marseille, one finds Moroccans, Malians, and poorer French families living together. People from one country surely seek out one another, but this is less the case for their children, who are more likely to identify with other Muslims, or other "Maghreb people" (a category that is itself the product of immigration), or people of similar socioeconomic situation. Certain ties can reinforce country allegiances, as when an association or a mosque is predominantly associated with one country, or a Sufi order preserves ties to a particular saint. But even those mosques, religious schools, or associations sponsored by Muslims from a particular country rarely are exclusivist, because they usually do not seek to reproduce a particular theological or ritual tendency. For many in the generation of Muslims born in France, it is the experience of being discriminated against as "Maghrebin" or "Arab" that creates their sense of "ethnicity" (Cesari 1998).

The common Arabic language has facilitated some degree of cooperation across the three North African communities, as has a relatively shared degree of religious jurisprudential reasoning (following the Mâliki *madhhab* or legal school) and religious practices. This cooperation exists both at the national level, for example, in the activities of the largest national organization, the Union of French Islamic Organizations (*Union des Organisations Islamiques de France, UOIF*), and usually at the local level in the forms of shared worship in mosques. In cities or neighborhoods where cross-ethnic cooperation is high, the shared Arabic language facilitates common participation by North Africans (but not others) in congregational prayers. Indeed, the growing distinction, and sometimes tension, is between the older generation's preference for sermons in Arabic and younger Muslims' preference for French.

By contrast, Turks have not had the same historical ties to France, and they more often settled together in neighborhoods in eastern France and around major cities. Many of the Senegalese and Mali immigrants have distinct forms of religious practice and social organization, in particular the Sufi orders focused on a specific teacher in West Africa (Soares 2003). Other Muslims, from the West Indies or the Indian Ocean islands, for example, have organized into ethnically specific associations and formed a grab-bag national organization to represent their interests as "non-Maghrebins."

Within the North African category, although Algerians are numerically dominant (one-half of North Africans, one-third of all Muslim immigrants), and they control the important Paris mosque, Tunisians and Moroccans play important leadership roles in a number of national organizations, and Tunisians, in particular, despite being a "minority's minority," only one-fifth as many as the Algerians, have taken on major roles as leaders of religious schools, particularly around Paris. Moroccans, for their part, make up 40 percent of all imams (sermon-givers at Friday prayers) in France.

Thus, in France no one country group is predominant across categories, the way that Pakistanis dominate in Britain, and the Arabic language serves as a (potentially) uniting element across the most politically active groups. Furthermore, whereas differences in religious affiliations (and lineage ties) in South Asia were replicated in British cities, the same is not true for France. Pakistan is severely divided into religious movements, each defined vis-à-vis the other, and each associated with a set of transnational organizations (the Tablighi Jama'a, Deoband-affiliated schools, the Barelvis, and so on). The demographic concentration of emigrants from one Pakistani region facilitated the replication of these oppositions in Britain. This competition of religious associations is less intense in North Africa, or at least it is not as concentrated in a small area, and the emigrants come from a wider range of districts in Algeria, Morocco, and Tunisia. The Tablighis are present, but they do not have a set of opposed Pakistani organizations next to them in, say, Paris. The divisions that one does see tend to be by country of origin rather than by any religious orientation: thus, Algerians versus Moroccans vying for control of a mosque, or each, along with Comorians and others, having their own mosque and associations.

The associations that attract the most enthusiasm from young people in France are based in neighborhoods and usually with a nonreligious central activity: sports, employment, music, and so on. It is here that the strongest identifications form, and these are not necessarily inflected by ethnicity in a specific sense or by religious affiliation, but by a perception that they are perceived by others as North Africans or as Arabs.

This specific context for the deployment of ethnic, religious, and other processes of self-identification have meant that younger French Muslims tend to reflect on distinctions between Islam qua religion, and the tradition or culture of their parents and the "country of origin." (This emphasis contrasts with the British case, where many younger Muslims continue to identify themselves in terms of an integrally linked package of specific ethnicity and Islam.) As one young French Muslim woman told a sociologist, "I became a practicing Muslim thanks to France, because it provides structures so that we might learn Arabic and our religion. I am glad to have come to know my religion, true Islam, because, "back there," it is too traditional and troublesome (Venel 1999, 71).

Further Variations

In other countries we find other, specific sets of transnational ties between those Muslims with a foreign origin or ancestry and their countries of origin. Spanish Muslims, for example, come overwhelmingly from neighboring Morocco and maintain close ties with their home country; Spain even owns two cities located in northern Morocco. Patterns of Muslim migration to the Netherlands resemble those in Britain to the extent that immigrants remained separated into country groupings, except that they came from a wider array of countries. Each large Dutch city is likely to have several mosques, each allied to a different transnational community, and each with a preference for its own language. Utrecht, for example, has two Turkish mosques, two Moroccan ones, and one for Surinamese Muslims. Languages for sermons are correspondingly different: Turkish, Arabic, Urdu for South Asian-origin Surinamese, Dutch for Indonesians and Javanese-speaking Surinamese (Landman 2002). Like Britain, the Netherlands encouraged each immigrant community to develop its own institutions, in the Dutch case reflecting an older, and now largely abandoned, way of organizing society around the major religious and political "pillars."

Although Germany has a broad policy of recognizing and supporting (through taxation) religious organizations as public entities, divisions among Muslims are sharp and are reproduced in mosques. Schiffauer (1997) traces the history of mosques in the southern city of Augsburg, and shows that the current proliferation of mosques is the result of a series of fissions, which were the direct product of competing loyalties to Turkish political organizations: the official Turkish Islamic office of the Diyanet, the fascist Grey Wolves, the major Turkish Islamic party (called the AKP by the 2000s), and the Islamic association Milli Görüs. Until recently all these groups considered Germany to be a country of *hijra,* of temporary immigration, and they were more interested in promoting political and religious positions important in Turkey than in constructing a Muslim society in Germany itself. As one indication of this contrast in social focus, Schiffauer (1997, 162) reports that in the 1990s he could find not one sermon among all those available on cassettes in the bookstores that discussed problems of Muslims in Germany—in contrast to France, where this is the topic of nearly all of the many cassettes for sale!

Transnational Islam in Three Senses

*A*t this point let us return to the conceptual issues raised in the last chapter around "transnational religion" and see how they apply to the situation of Muslims in Europe. We can distinguish between three uses to which the phrase "transnational Islam" is put. One has to do with population movements across countries; a second involves the workings of transnational religious institutions; the third points to the global field of Islamic reference and debate: movement, institutions, normative reference.

Muslims may move across national borders for social or economic reasons, and in this first respect can be said to participate in transnational movement in precisely the same way as do Haitians who move to North America, or middle-class Europeans who live and work in more than one country. There is nothing necessarily "Islamic" about these attachments and travels just because they involve Muslims, although they *may* define or create trajectories along which religious ideas are carried and changed. Many of the North or West Africans, Turks, or South Asians who migrated to European countries in search of work have remained profoundly attached to their countries of origin. Many of them make frequent trips to these countries; those who retained their original citizenship may return to vote; some have chosen to have their bodies "repatriated" for burial.

Of course, different populations develop distinct trajectories: in France and Italy, for example, West Africans travel more frequently to origin countries than do North Africans, for reasons having in part to do with the greater participation by the former in transnational Sufi movements. In this respect, Senegalese in Italy or France (and Turkish workers in Germany) resemble the now classic cases of transnational movement between Caribbean countries and the eastern United States.

Certain transnational institutions *are* tied to religious practice, however, and these transnational religious institutions have been a second focus of study for those interested in "transnational Islam." Some Muslims belong to religious organizations that either promote cross-national movement as part of their religious practice, or encompass and promote cross-national communication within their religious hierarchy. One of the most prominent in Europe (and North America) is the Tablighi Jama'at (Metcalf 2001). The movement has its origins and center in northern India, and sends missions out to urge Muslims residing elsewhere in the world to return to the correct practice of Islam. Diverse Sufi orders also maintain ties and communication between new places of residence and their centers, as they have been doing since the tenth century. Their devotions focus on a living or dead saint, and they carry that devotional orientation with them as they travel. Sufis in Manchester or Paris have local leaders, but they also maintain their ties of devotion to saintly leaders in Pakistan, Senegal, or elsewhere (Soares 2003; Werbner 2003).

These Sufi groups maintain particularly strong ties to a homeland and maintain these ties across generations. In that respect, these transnational religious movements develop a diasporic character in the form of representations and imaginations of a homeland. For example, the Mouride order, founded in the 1880s by Sheykh Amadou Bamba, is centered in Senegal, where its followers consider the mosque to be the Mecca of West Africa. The order maintains close ties among followers living in Europe and North America through local associations and through periodic visits by the current head of the order (the founder's son). Trade and spirituality pass along these networks, although they are open to others from West Africa as well.

An Iranian order, the Shahmaghsoudi, illustrates another geographical possibility: centering an order in the diaspora. Founded in California, the order includes over 75 lodges throughout the world and was created to provide alternative forms of Islam to those promoted by the Iranian Revolution. At the same time, it taps into the centuries-old Oveyssi Sufi tradition. Whereas Senegalese Mourides take their affiliation with them as they move out into other parts of the world, Iranians already in exile came to the Shahmaghsoudi order as a way to recapture something of their Iranian spiritual heritage (Werbner 2003).

A third possibility is illustrated by a lodge north of Paris simply called the "Sufi and Cultural Association," who acknowledge as their teacher a Sufi master living in Tunisia and part of the al-Alawiyya order. The active participants are French men of origins in diverse Muslim-majority countries who grew up together and converted to the Sufi path as an alternative to drugs and delinquency.

Alongside these and other religious-based organizations are ethnic ones, such as the various associations of Turks in Germany, of Kashmiris in Britain, or of Senegalese in Italy. In these countries, ethnic-based associations can bring together people of differing religious affiliations and at the same time provide a more open route to interaction with members of the host country.

In studies about Islam and transnationalism in Europe, it is these transnational, diasporic religious movements that have received the most attention. The reasons for this research concentration are probably multiple. These movements provide a sociologically clear entity to study, with members, leaders, and group activities. They involve movement and communication across borders, and so are clearly "transnational" in a way that links their study both to migration literature and to current writing about globalization. Finally, the Sufi ties of some of these organizations may make them intrinsically more attractive to some anthropologists and sociologists, intellectually so because they have their own rituals and genealogies, and perhaps ethically so to the extent that many social scientists prefer Sufism to the more pared-down versions of Islam associated with modernist and (non-Sufi) reformist movements.

This emphasis within sociological and anthropological studies has led to the relative neglect of a third form of transnational Islam, namely, the development of debates and discussions among Muslims about the nature and role of Islam in Europe and North America. These debates and discussions have led to the creation of networks, conferences, and increasingly formalized institutions for systematic reflection among scholars. These activities and institutions focus on the dilemmas faced by Muslims attempting to develop forms of Islamic life compatible with the range of Western norms, values, and laws—in other words, how to become wholly "here" and yet preserve a tradition of orientation toward Islamic institutions located "over there."

This third sense of "transnational Islam" as a public space of reference and debate draws, of course, on Islam's history of movement, communication, and institutional innovation. Islam has an intrinsic universality (which it shares with Christian religion) and also more specific universalistic dimensions. The message of the Qur'ân was to turn away from localized deities and worship the transcendent God. The capitals of Islamic polities shifted from one city to another (Baghdad, Damascus, Cairo, Istanbul), meaning the caliphate was and is not limited to one particular region or center—and indeed in some contemporary imaginings, such as those associated with Hizb ut-Tahrir, they can be entirely deterritorialized. Mecca remains the religious focal point of Islam, but the Islamic era began with the flight or migration (*hijra*) from Mecca to Medina.

Other features of Islamic religious practice promote the sense of a worldwide community, the *umma*, among ordinary Muslims. The role of Arabic as the primary language of scholarship and the development of a global jurisprudence (albeit with several schools or traditions) made possible international communication among scholars. The standardization of the Qur'ân, the requirement to pray in Arabic, and the popular enjoyment of reciting and writing verses of the Qur'ân promote among ordinary Muslims the sense of participation in a universal message. The annual pilgrimage brings together a sampling of Muslims, and the Saudi government's quota system ensures that pilgrims will meet a geographically wide range of fellow pilgrims. Daily, theoretically five times daily, Muslims turn their bodies in the direction of Mecca in order to carry out the obligatory rituals of worship (*salât*). Even those Muslims who refer to their allegiance to a spiritual leader or to the Shiite legacy of 'Ali more than to their membership in the worldwide umma would deny that Islam is or should be defined or bounded by local or national borders. This sense of Islam's transnational character is diffuse but powerful, and it derives its power from the ways in which rituals reproduce, and histories remind Muslims of, the shared duties and practices of Muslims across political boundaries. In its impulse to refuse particularistic loyalties to ethnic groups or to a nation-state, this consciousness first and foremost creates an imagination of an Islamic community transcending specific boundaries and borders.

This consciousness in turn supports the legitimacy and indeed the imperative to search anywhere in the world for the highest authority on Islamic matters. This imperative creates specific networks of authority, learning, and communication that are more historically and sociologically specific than the general sense of global *umma*-hood. Some sources of religious authority—Meccan jurists, Cairene muftis—owe their status to their institutional associations and affiliations; they have been at least recognized, if not always acknowledged, by Muslims throughout the world and over the centuries. Other sources of authority, such as the star of al-Jazîra television, Yûsuf Qardâwî, have followed more specific paths to positions of authority, but nonetheless find audiences in many countries.

The scope of influence of these authorities varies greatly, but in each case, and this is the critical point, it reaches far beyond the borders of the home country. The communications between these sites and Muslims living elsewhere in the world take many forms: newspaper columns, internet sites, cable television, or books. Moreover, links to authority sites often demand a competence in Arabic and a familiarity with the genre conventions of the advice column or the fatwa. These sites are not the only ones available to Muslims, of course, and those in, say, northern India, Iran, or Java require additional or distinct linguistic competencies and take different institutional forms. But to claim the highest level of scholarly expertise and authority, one must be able to read texts written in classical Arabic and perhaps be able to recite these texts as well.

This orientation is more specific and can be more particularistic than that toward the *umma,* in that different populations of Muslims pay attention to different sources of authority (and scholars do so more than ordinary people) but it, too, draws on a general feature of Islam, namely, the idea that it is to the most learned, wherever they may reside, that the Muslim ought to listen. It has to do much more with the worldwide communication of ideas than with the movement of populations and does not depend on it. Muslims may communicate and debate across political boundaries without necessarily migrating or forming transnational religious movement.

Can European Societies be Muslim?

*L*ife in Europe raises long-standing questions about whether Muslims' obligations to God change when they move to lands not ruled by Muslims. In the early centuries of Islam, scholars developed a distinction between two realms, the *dâr al-islâm* or abode of Islam, versus the *dâr al-harb* or abode of war (Abou El Fadl 1994). The former included the countries ruled under Islamic principles; the latter referred to all other places, where, presumably, Muslims would not be free to worship. Today, many Muslims find discomfort in this way of viewing the world. How is one to define "Muslim societies," the dâr al-Islam? Does one look to the correctness of the government, the piety of the people, or simply the fact that most people living in the country profess Islam as their religion? Is a majority-Muslim country whose government represses its people, and prevents the free expression of religious ideas to be considered part of dâr al-islâm? Conversely, why should countries not governed by Islamic laws but where Muslims are free to worship be considered as belonging to an "abode of war?" As many Muslims in Europe began to think about religion in terms of the essentials of worship and spirituality, this category seemed increasingly out of date.

Some Muslims have proposed alternatives. Referring to the protection given to religious minorities by international law, some scholars have proposed *dâr al-'ahd*, "abode of treaty," while others have proposed *dâr al-da'wa*, "abode of predication," or *dâr ash-shahâda*, "abode of witness," emphasizing the possibilities open to Muslims in these lands. For many Muslims in Europe, the key issues are not labels—Muslim world versus non-Muslims lands—but of the social and cultural conditions for Muslims to live fully satisfying lives as Muslims. Two categories of Muslims would not accept this proposition. Some consider religion a private matter not in need of new institutions, and hence see no particular challenge to living in Europe. Others consider it provisional to live anywhere but an Islamic state, a category that includes neither European nor most Muslim-majority countries.

The practical significance of this question emerged most recently regarding bank interest. One of the more pressing questions for Muslims who are planning to reside permanently in Europe is whether they may take out loans at interest to purchase homes. The Islamic prohibition against lending or borrowing at interest would seem to prevent them from so doing, but in the late 1990s some Muslims living in Europe put the question to the European Council for Fatwa and Research, a collection of jurists of various nationalities who now reside in Europe. The council is led by the highly influential Egyptian jurist, Sheikh Yûsuf al-Qardâwî, who lives in Qatar. In 1999, the council responded to the question in the form of a *fatwâ*, a non-binding legal opinion issued by a qualified person or group. The jurists stressed that the prohibition on usury does mean that Muslims everywhere should take steps to avoid borrowing from banks that charge interest, and should devise alternative ways of financing homes, such as paying more than the stated price but in installments. However, if Muslims in Europe could not practice such alternatives, then they could take out a mortgage for a first house (Conseil Européen 2002).

In their argument the jurists cited two considerations. First, the doctrine of extreme necessity (*darûrat*) allows Muslims to do what otherwise is forbidden under compulsion or necessity. Why is it a necessity to own a house? Renting keeps the Muslim in a state of uncertainty and financial insecurity, stated the council. Owning a house allows Muslims to settle in close proximity to a mosque, and to modify their house to accommodate religious needs. Moreover, Muslims living in Europe had reported to the council that mortgage payments were equal to or lower than rents.

Second, the jurists argued that while living in non-Muslim countries, Muslims may make contracts that violate Islamic law. Past jurists belonging to two of the traditional schools of Sunni legal interpretation, the Hanafî and the Hanbalî, had made this argument, they said. Muslims cannot change the institutions that dominate life in their host countries, and thus they are not responsible for the existence of an interest-based financial system. If they were forbidden to benefit from banking institutions, then Islam would have weakened them, a result that would contradict the principle that Islam should benefit Muslims.

The ruling did not change the traditional prohibition of lending at interest, but exempted Muslims living in Europe from the prohibition because of a combination of empirical circumstances: the importance of owning a house, the high level of rents, and the absence of viable alternatives. These circumstances allow the jurists to apply the principles that necessity allows for exemption, and that Muslims may use otherwise invalid financial instruments when they live in "non-Islamic countries."

As noted earlier, in the late 1980s many Muslims in Europe shifted from seeing themselves, and being seen by others, mainly as immigrants, to taking on identities mainly as Muslims. Some, at least, Muslims and non-Muslims began to see religious commitments and practices as distinct from ethnic particularities and immigration histories. This shift has had a number of repercussions that have played themselves out over time and at different rhythms in different countries, but I think that we can best understand these changes as the creation of a number of new possibilities in self-identifications and in treatment by others. These new possibilities do not resolve to one single trend, such as "individualization," but engender new tensions.

For Muslims, the shift has made possible several different ways of thinking about what it means to be a Muslim in Europe. For some, being a Muslim becomes a matter of faith and private religious practice, along the lines of older forms of European Protestantism. For others, it becomes a tradition to which they can refer, but to which they do not feel bound or obligated. Such, for example, is the position taken by self-styled "secular Muslims" in France. The opposite is equally possible; many Muslims have to come to see Islam as a set of norms and constraints that are detached from any one time or place and opposed to the traditions of various home countries. Muslims may see Islam in this last way and become highly involved in European public life, or, to the contrary, they can withdraw from public life on grounds that one can best live as a Muslim if one remains detached. These possibilities are all well represented among European Muslims today.

The "secular Muslim" approach is most present in France because the secularist media find this approach closest to proper French attitudes. Writers such as Malik Chebel promote in their books and through frequent television appearances an "enlightened Islam" that would consist of philosophy and spirituality, but eschew the legal and institutional aspects, which, he writes, do not fit well in Europe. "Self Islam" was the French title of a recent popular book that brings together the notions of religion as mainly and properly individual and internal. Several sociopolitical movements use the phrase "secular Muslims" (*Musulmans laiques*) and call for keeping Islam out of the public sphere, and eradicating beliefs and practices deemed inimical to the republic. In this approach, individuality, privacy, laïcité, and European values are bundled.

What could be called the "public Islam" approach argues that this bundle must be untied, and that the public presentation of Islam does not conflict with European values. The Swiss intellectual Tariq Ramadan (2002), for example, argues that at the level of values one can find a convergence between Islamic norms and those of Europe, and that to do this one need not abandon the ideal of a visible, public Islamic presence. (Ramadan also argues for a geopolitical strategy of encouraging this convergence within each distinct cultural or religious tradition.) The "young Muslim" movements once associated with Ramadan seek to change political life as coalitions of Muslims, rather than as coalitions of secular citizens. If the "secular Muslim" approach grows out of French secularism, the "public Islam" accords best with countries supporting a multicultural recognition of ethnic differences such as Britain.

Opposed to both these stances are separatists, either those who simply keep to themselves, such as the Tablighi Jama'at, or those that promote the eventual recreation of an Islamic state, such as the Hizb ut-Tahrir or its more radical offshoots. Muslims who are attracted to one of these movements make the same distinction between "religion" and "tradition" as do those who see themselves as "secularists" or as "publicly Muslim." But whereas a figure such as Tariq Ramadan sees a way to adapt Islamic norms to Europe, on condition that Europe accepts Muslims' public presence, the Hizb ut-Tahrir does not.

For non-Muslims, the shift in frames, from immigrants to Muslims, also can produce diverse effects. By and large, European governments have moved toward recognizing Islam as a legitimate faith, deserving of the same recognition and resources as are accorded to forms of Christianity and Judaism. At the same time, however, highlighting the religion of a certain segment of the population emphasizes an element that separates them from the majority population, religion, and places into the background crosscutting elements that form the basis for allegiances and solidarity, such as occupations, political allegiances, or cultural interests.

As a result of these differences in migration histories, Muslims differ markedly across Europe in their own sense of identification. A 2006 Pew Global Attitudes Survey (2006) asked Muslims in different countries around the world to choose between religion and nationality as their primary identity. While 42 percent of French Muslims said they were French first and Muslim second, only 7 percent of British Muslims and 3 percent of Spanish Muslims put nationality first. (Pew reports that American Christians choose between religious and national identities in almost exactly the same proportion as do French Muslims.) These same differences also show up for the population of each country as a whole. When asked if there is a conflict between being a devout Muslim and living in a modern society, 74 percent of all French people said there was none, about twice as high a figure as that for other Europeans or Americans. Indeed, French people are more positive about modern Islam than are people in Indonesia, Jordan, or Egypt!

The distinctive feature of the French experience within Europe is that there, and there alone, both colonial history and current policies push in the same direction, toward integration. Today's French Muslims, or their parents or grandparents, came from former French territories in North or West Africa, where they learned that they were now part of the grand story of France, albeit in second-class roles. French Muslims today are demanding long-denied equal status and respect, as did African Americans in the United States. Their experience is quite unlike that of, say, Moroccans arriving in Denmark, where no common pasts, languages, or experiences prepare their way, or, for that matter, South Asians in Britain, who never were told that they could become English—and many of whom today demand a distinct mode of governance under sharî'a law.

Nor do French Muslims live in ethnic enclaves. The housing projects around Paris contain people from different parts of Asia, Africa, and Europe, and stand in stark contrast to all-Turkish neighborhoods in Belgium and or all-Pakistani parts of British cities. Young Muslims who emerge from this mixed environment speak only French, demand French-language sermons in their mosques (and increasingly get them), and they flock to French-medium Islamic schools and institutes.

French policies also push toward integration, with a mix of carrots and sticks. Headscarves are out at school, but some enlightened mayors are giving land for mosques. The state gives newly arrived men and women hundreds of free hours of French language lessons, in an effort to make them more competitive for employment. Contrast recent Dutch policies (applied mainly to poorer counties) that require would-be immigrants, even the spouses of Dutch residents, to prove that they already speak good Dutch *before* arrival, but provide no help in learning the language.

Whether Muslims living in Europe come to consider their countries of residence as part of the "Muslim World" may depend less on whether Islamic law ever gains official recognition, or Islamic private schools grow and flourish, than on whether they find themselves recognized as equal citizens. Or perhaps they will rephrase the question, and suggest that there are no more Muslim and non-Muslim worlds or countries, but places where one is more or less respected in one's quality as a Muslim man or woman.

14 Religion, Radicalism, and Violence

*T*his chapter will be devoted to the question of what role religion plays in the genesis and development of violence and war. At first glance, it would seem reasonable to say that religious beliefs often lead to violence and warfare. Hundreds of recent books and articles about contemporary violence blame religion, whether regarding Islam and terrorism, Hindu violence in India, or conflicts between Catholics and Protestants in Northern Ireland. Case closed, it would seem.

Upon a closer look, however, each case for religion's direct role in violence seems fuzzier. Archeology and ethnography of small-scale societies show no consistent role for religion in the genesis of war. An overview of the anthropology of warfare (Ferguson 1990) argues that a range of material factors, such as competition for scarce economic or political resources, best explain the occurrence of large-scale violence, and that structural and psychological factors, such as political scale or resentment, then channel and shape what follows. Recent anthropological analyses of genocide support these claims, though they give greater prominence to political power struggles (Hinton 2002). Religious loyalties and affinities may lead people to join a cause, or reinforce the resolve of fighters, but so may loyalties to social or ethnic groups, or to a nation or cause. There does not seem to be anything intrinsic to religion that predisposes people toward, or away from, violence or war.

More generally, anthropologists long have abandoned generalizations about humans as naturally aggressive (as in the view promoted by Hobbes) or naturally peaceful (as in the contrary view proposed by Rousseau). It is more interesting to reflect on the fact that everywhere, and in all ages, one finds people engaged in conflict and peace, hostility and acceptance. Hindus may protect cattle from harm, but some have killed Muslims for sacrificing their own cows. Some Muslims have bombed in the name of God, but most draw on their religion for its lessons of patience and submission. Indeed, most of the time people do not fight others on grounds of religious difference.

The more interesting question concerns the social and historical conditions surrounding violence, and the roles that religious ideas and orientations may play with respect to the mechanisms that lead people to engage in or refrain from violence or warfare. This way of putting a general question—focusing on conditions and specific mechanisms—usually produces more interesting answers in the social sciences than do broader questions such as, "does religion promote violence?" Other questions have similarly benefited from such whittling-down. For example, the "contact hypothesis" held that familiarity breeds acceptance. It turns out, however, that it is specific social mechanisms that breed acceptance, such as cooperating on a specific task, and that simple contact has no predictable result (Forbes 1997).

As in previous chapters, we will consider a series of case studies to discern the relevant dimensions to our question. The two types of religious phenomena most consistently linked with images of violence today are the small-scale movements often called "cults" and politically active forms of Islam, and we will consider each in turn. Elsewhere in the book we have considered specific acts of violence, for example, those committed on persons undergoing initiation (Chapter 4) and the killing of people accused of witchcraft (Chapter 8).

Cults, Sects, and Violence

*A*mong the many new religious movements appearing in the past decades in Europe, North America, and elsewhere, most conduct their affairs as peaceably as do more established religious groups. Those that commit acts of violence, directed toward themselves or toward others, thereby become widely known. These acts contribute to a popular sense that a "cult" or "sect" is likely to involve brainwashing, terror, and physical violence, despite the fact that these features occur relatively rarely. We consider two recent movements that did involve violent acts and then ask what is true of them that is not true of other, peaceful movements.

Aum Shinrikyo

The Japanese movement Aum Shinrikyo at first resembled many other Japanese New Religions in promoting meditation and ascetic practices under the leadership of a charismatic person, in this case the the blind Asahara Shoko (Reader 2000). Asahara earlier had joined a religion called Agonshu, whose adherents practiced yoga and meditation and sought special psychic powers. Like many others in Japan, Asahara was attracted by the movement's teaching that the world was threatened by environmental or nuclear disaster. He left to form his own group in 1984, which began by setting out goals and ideas that were similar to those of other Japanese religious movements (Davis 1980). Members sought greater psychic powers, perhaps through contacts with ancestors, in order to purify themselves or to solve their everyday problems. Like other such religions, Asahara's saw people as being reborn according to their karma, and most people as falling into undesirable rebirths.

Starting in the mid–1980s, Asahara began to preach a coming conflict between good and evil, but at first he saw his mission as purifying the world to avoid conflict. He urged followers to form *sanghas,* using the word for Buddhist monasteries. His demands were strict: those who would join the sanghas had to break off all ties with their families and friends. Even under these conditions, over 1,000 people did join a sangha, and perhaps

8,000 more joined the movement. As with other Japanese new religions, many of the recruits were educated young professionals. Asahara offered them the chance to engage in research, much of it aimed at giving them superhuman powers; some of it consisting of fabricating amphetamines and hallucinogens along with poisons and explosives. The recruits practiced ascetic regimes and meditation along a path set out by Asahara. Disciples could purchase containers of what was supposed to be the guru's bathwater, or vials of his blood, which would give them his special DNA (and which probably produced effects through the addition of hallucinogenic drugs). They had to rent a helmet that would connect them with the guru's brain waves and enable them to reach his state of meditation (Hall, Schuyler, and Trinh 2000, 76–110).

The stated purposes of these practices changed over time. At first they were supposed to give practitioners personal powers and thereby enable them to save humanity. But as Asahara failed to reach his own goals of massive recruitment, his disillusionment led him to turn toward a more dramatic form of apocalyptic preaching, in which he said that mass destruction was coming and only a few people on earth would be saved. In itself, this doctrine is not so different from that adhered to by many Christians in North America who believe that at the coming moment of Rapture only a few saved souls will be brought up to heaven to avoid the destruction that will follow on earth. But (as readers will be quick to add) doctrine does not determine people's ideas or practices. In this case, Asahara responded violently to his failure, blaming the world for what had happened. He turned inward, demanding complete obedience from his followers, and set an example by having his wife beaten until she complied with his demands to lead an ascetic life. He had others beaten and forced to follow regimes involving near-starvation or other extreme practices, and in 1988 one of his followers died after a regimen involving repeated immersion in baths. Asahara was waiting for legal recognition of his movement as a religion and covered up the death; worse, he ordered the killing of a follower who was about to defect and tell the authorities of the death. The murder changed Asahara's writings and preaching; now he warned of Satan corrupting some in his movement, a logic akin to that of the Salem witchcraft accusations.

The violence escalated, as did opposition from families of those who had cut their ties to the outside world in order to join one of Aum's sanghas and from some disillusioned adherents. Asahara ordered the murder of an opposition group's lawyer and his family. His entry into electoral politics in 1990 failed miserably, adding to his humiliation, and leading to a decision to destroy large numbers of his opponents. He may have ordered as many as fifty people killed. His efforts to develop weapons of mass destruction culminated in the sarin gas attack on the Tokyo subway in 1995, which killed twelve people and injured thousands, leading to the arrest of Asahara and many of his followers.

Order of the Solar Temple

The Order, or OTS in its French version, came to the world's attention in 1994, when police investigating the burning of vacation villas in Switzerland and Québec found that they contained bodies neatly arranged on the floors and killed with bullets to the head. The dead turned out to be successful men and women from Switzerland, France, and Belgium—among them a nuclear engineer, a mayor, and wealthy businesspeople.

A year later more people died in the same manner near Grenoble, France. Letters sent out the day of the 1994 deaths explained that those who died were in fact in "Transit" to another world. It turned out that some had killed themselves, while others had been "assisted" in their journey. Some dissidents had been outright murdered.

The Solar Temple Order developed in the 1970s from the partnership of Joseph Di Mambro, a French former member of Templar and Rosicrucian orders, and the Belgian homeopathic doctor, Luc Jouret. Di Mambro had earlier joined a movement in France that saw itself as the successors to the medieval Knights Templar, and some survivors of the massacre-suicides compared the fate of the Order to that of the knights (Hall, Schuyler, and Trinh 2000; Introvigne and Mayer 2002). The Knights Templar was formed during the Crusades in the twelfth century in order to protect Jerusalem. Their order was chartered directly by the Pope. During the twelfth and thirteenth centuries they succeeded brilliantly both in combat and in amassing and investing wealth from donations. They established parallel lay organizations that functioned as shadow churches with their own rituals. Their secrecy, success, and activities in the financial world aroused envy and suspicion, and once they failed on the battlefield, the Church and the King of France, Philip the Fair, moved together against them. In 1310, Philip had 54 knights burned at the stake for heresy.

The mystique of the knights has propelled them into literature (most recently in *The Da Vinci Code*), and into the popular imagination. The red (or "rosy") cross they wore gave the name to the Rosicrucian order, and Masonic orders claimed descent from both Templars and the Rosicrucians. Hundreds of such "neo-Templar" and Rosicrucian orders have formed over the past two centuries, each combining mysticism, chivalry, secrecy, and promise of delivery from death. The Vatican II reforms that lessened the sense of mystery and tradition associated with the Catholic Mass gave a further boost to the creation of such orders (and to New Age movements generally).

It was out of this cauldron of movements and mysticism that the Solar Order emerged, based on ideas about a "Solar Christ" and the existence of "Ascended Masters" who move in and out of historical existence. Jouret had been ordained as a priest by a dissident Roman Catholic priest, and became the Grand Master of the Solar Order. Drawing on his homeopathic medical background, Jouret lectured throughout the French-speaking world, linking health concerns to the Order's ideas, and selling cassettes, books, and lecture tickets in health food stores and New Age bookstores. Jouret's lectures were by all accounts spellbinding, and he had clubs for people to join—on nutrition, gardening, music, and so forth. His message was that a vital essence in ourselves was troubled when we felt sick, and that the same essence in our environment was troubled, a line of thought leading him to predict ecological apocalypse. His appeal was in his ability to link together a number of New Age themes: astrology, health and environmental consciousness, a mixing of science and faith, and to tie these to the mystical countercultural Catholic traditions, in which francophone Catholics disaffected by the liberal reforms of Vatican II could rediscover history and mystery.

Even as he was predicting that humans would find it difficult to make the crossover from this age to the Age of Aquarius, Jouret came under suspicion in France, where active anti-cult organizations watch out for such movements. He developed a new center in Québec, where the Order's initiation ceremony happened to be videotaped by a member. The tape shows how the internal structure of the Order worked in a ritual. The Order was governed by an inner group, below which were three degrees of initiation, each with three internal ranks. In the videotaped ritual, initiated members wearing white robes with red crosses enter an outer room, line up, and raise swords toward the light emanating from a single candle. A priest blesses a new member, at which point Jouret emerges from behind a door to bless the group. Behind that door was the inner sanctuary where a few initiates would be admitted to witness images, which probably were holographic projections but were experienced by the initiates as visitations by Ascended Masters. They saw apostles of Christ, grand Templar masters, Moses, and other world figures. Di Mambro himself was considered to be the reincarnation of the Pharoah Akhnaton, Osiris, and Moses.

The Order demanded the members donate money and sought a high degree of control over their lives, to the point of rearranging marriages in order to produce "cosmic children" who would create a New Age. Some rebelled at these measures, and dissidence increased when it became known that the spectral appearances of Ascended Masters were the result of technologically sophisticated image projections. By the early 1990s, police and anti-cult groups had begun to investigate the Order. In 1993 Québec police raided an Order building, found weapons, and arrested Jouret and others; they eventually were convicted of weapons charges. The trial added to the group's negative publicity and built up their feeling that the outside world had conspired against them.

The group's leaders responded by declaring that cosmic messages indicated the need to make a "Transit" out of this world and into another (specifically, to the star Sirius). They then took the steps that led to the murder-suicides of 1994 and 1995 in Switzerland, France, and Québec. Would the massacres have taken place had there been no outside intervention against the group? It is hard to say, and it did not take much to push the leaders over the edge, but letters sent by the group pointed to police raids and arrests as the reason for their decision to embark on the Transit at the moment they did so.

French and French-speaking authorities were quick to apply the standard analytical framework used in these countries to denounce "cults" (les sectes): the members were gullible people, marginal to their societies, who had been brainwashed by dangerous leaders. However, most followers of the Order were solid, middle-class citizens. Why, then, did this group march toward destruction, and why did many of its members willingly commit suicide?

As with Aum Shinrikyo, the best account of the group's "success" focuses both on their internal social and psychological dynamics and on the effects of external pressures on the group. Even by the late 1980s, the group's message of apocalypse considered the end of the world to be part of a long-term cycle of birth and death, the idea of 6,000-year cycles found in Hinduism. These events would develop naturally, without any need for the group to take action. In this respect, the Order resembled Aum Shinrokyo at a similar, early stage of development. The group amassed money and arms for survival in face of a coming catastrophe, not in order to kill others, and in that respect resembled the mainly peaceful activities of survivalist groups in western parts of North America. Apocalyptic beliefs thus do not appear themselves to be a sufficient cause of violence.

It was a combination of perceived threats and fears that they were losing their hold on their followers that led the leaders to move to a new stage of killings and suicides. By the early 1990s, Di Mambro and Jouret had begun to express desires to leave this earth. At the same time, police investigations of Order finances and firearms procurement combined with dissent within the movement to create a sense of external threat in the minds of the leaders. Of course, that they responded by killing dissidents requires a further psychological explanation. The members' reasons for maintaining their involvement also are unclear, but most likely had to do with that enjoyment of being in on a secret, being one of the few to know what really is going to happen, that adds strength to secret societies around the world, whether in Masonic temples or New Guinea societies. If we can believe the letters sent out just before the mass suicides and killings, the members of the Solar Order saw themselves as leaving a sullied world for a purer one. Whether they would have followed through with the Transit even without outside opposition is difficult to say, but surely their drive to do so came initially from within themselves, through a conviction nourished by age-old narratives of Christian martyrdom, mysticism, and dispensed salvation, maintained through rituals of access to wisdom, and reinforced by contemporary concerns for psychological and environmental purity.

The series of events that led to the destruction of the Order appear in a number of other cases of small apocalyptic groups, such as Heaven's Gate, whose adherents committed suicide near San Diego in 1997, and the Peoples Temple of Jim Jones, living in its communal settlement in Guyana, South America, where 918 people died in 1978. All three groups believed that they had come from, and would return to, another world. They felt persecuted, and were particularly threatened by defectors and dissidents. Attacks on some of these groups added to this sense of persecution: the fate of the Branch Davidians convinced many cult leaders that they were next in line to be destroyed. In their efforts to restore authority, reclaim charisma, and remove themselves from their persecutors, they took violent action against themselves and others. These actions also were statements to the world. The Order and Heaven's Gate sent out press releases before destroying themselves. Jim Jones said: "We've got to be in the history books."

These and other groups that ended in violence had apocalyptic expectations about the soon-to-arrive end of human history. Their expectations led them to engage in practices intended to deliver them from catastrophe, but that had the indirect effects of promoting strong norms of internal solidarity and loyalty. In the society at large they were confronted by a strong group of cult detractors whose efforts to expose, oppose, and sometime destroy cults reinforced their feelings of persecution.

Persecution does not in itself lead to violence, of course. Scientologists have been subjected to more governmental scrutiny and harassment than was, say, the Order of the Solar Temple and, although Scientologists may have carried out revenge actions against dissidents, there has been nothing approaching the behavior described above. The difference lies in part in the internal ideas: even though Scientology does demand secrecy and conformity from adherents, it does not (as far as we know) organize its activities around the idea of an impending apocalypse.

But then again, the belief in an apocalypse does not necessarily lead to violence either, as is evidenced by the millions of (relatively) peaceful churchgoers in the United States who believe that the end of the world is near, the "dispensational premillenarianists." One could believe that the world will end and draw a wide range of consequences from that belief: that one should better the world to attract a savior, that one should lead an ethically correct life so as to achieve salvation, or that one should convince others to do so as well in order to save the largest number of people. For a movement to move from apocalyptic beliefs to violence demands additional internal elements as well as a perception of external repression. Movements such as those described in this chapter moved from a simple belief that the world would terminate in an apocalypse to a drive to either to flee the world or bring about its end. This turn toward world-ending or world-fleeing action was led by a small number of individuals, whose charisma and paranoia allowed and drove them to carry it off.

Christian Violence

However, Mark Juergensmeyer (2003, 19–36) describes the violent actions taken in the name of Christianity in the United States at the approach to the millennium and argues that some of these actions indeed were based on Protestant theology. For example, the Reverend Michael Bray was convicted of firebombing seven abortion clinics in the 1980s. He justified his actions, and the actions of others, who had killed abortion doctors, on the basis of a view that the federal government was comparable to the Nazi regime.

Bray found a theological grounding for his position in the work of Dietrich Bonhoeffer, the German theologian who was hanged for his role in a plot to kill Hitler, and Reinhold Niebuhr, who wrote on the question of when one might legitimately kill another person, linking this personal question to the old topic of the just war. But Bray added that in the contemporary United States it was necessary for religious groups to decide when someone could be killed, an idea that went far beyond what Bonhoeffer or Neibuhr would have advocated. This view fit with the position taken by some on the Christian Right, to the effect that Christianity must act in God's name regardless of what secular politics decides. Within this "dominion theology" Bray followed the "reconstructionist" position derived from John Calvin but championed in the twentieth century by Princeton theologian Cornelius Van Til. Reconstructionsim urges Christians to follow God's authority in all matters. This and other versions of "post-millennialism" hold that Christ will return only after one thousand years of Christian rule, and that, therefore, it is the duty of all Christians to work to establish a Christian dominion on earth—and not only in the United States.

Explaining Where Violence Occurred: The Hindu–Muslim Case

In Chapter 9, we examined the conflicts between Hindus and Muslims in India in the context of a chapter about Hindu religion. Here we return to these conflicts, but now as part of an effort to account for violence taken in the name of religion. In the earlier account, we came to understand that the violence was justified in religious terms. But here, where we are concerned with explaining violence and religion, we need to understand why violence occurs in some places and not in others. Here we can make a more general point about how not to understand violence and how to approach an adequate account of its eruption.

All too often, when violence breaks out anywhere in the world, we look for causes in other features of those places. When, during the 1990s, Hindus and Muslims attacked each other in some cities of India, we might be tempted to say that, in general, the coexistence of Hindus and Muslims leads to conflict and violence. But in most places, most of the time, in India as elsewhere, religious and ethnic groups live side by side in relative peace. Religious or ethnic differences do not, of themselves, cause conflict (Bowen 1996; Brubaker and Laitin 1998). What we need to do, then, is look for other features of social life that promote conflict.

Ashutosh Varshney (2002) asked precisely this question of Hindu–Muslim violence in India. Varshney begins by noting that 95 percent of the Indian population was not involved in the riots of the 1990s, that riots took place in cities, not villages, and that a handful of cities account for most of the deaths. These cities are scattered throughout India. Rioting and deaths are thus not generally true of India or even of urban India, and not of one region rather than another. To uncover the factors accounting for violence, Varshney ingeniously paired cities of similar size and religious composition, but where one member of the pair did experience violence and the other did not. He then looked for differences that consistently occurred in these pairs, differentiating the high-violence from the low-violence city.

It turns out that the best predictor of non-violence in Indian cities is the degree to which stable, formal civic associations, such as trade unions, professional organizations, or political parties, brought Muslims and Hindus together on a regular basis. How did the presence of such ties lead to peace? In places with such associations, peace committees were formed at the threat of riot, and moved across communities, preventing escalations and contradicting rumors. Without them no one stopped the escalation of violence and often intra-community associations fanned the flames. Now we can understand why rural areas would be much likely to have such conflicts: in villages, everyone already exists in a kind of civic association, with everyday encounters on a face-to-face basis and village organizations dealing with justice, farming, and politics. Varshney's study thus emphasizes the importance of what Robert Putnam (2000) has called "bridging" social capital, meaning the networks and friendships that reach across social divisions, over "bonding" social capital, meaning networks that strengthen solidarities within social groups, and which thus may harden social divisions.

This analysis highlights the proximal social mechanisms that prevent or dampen down conflict between Muslims and Hindus. But one may then ask: why did some cities develop these civic associations and others not? The answer to this question lies in a deeper history, one that refers us back to the activities of the Congress Party and other political organizations in the 1920s. Congress tried to develop such interreligious associations in India's cities, but only succeeded in those places where the major divisions in the city were along lines other than that of Hindus versus Muslims.

Let us see how these pathways developed in two cities: Calicut, a trade-oriented city in the southern state of Kerala, and Aligarh, an industrial city, known for Aligarh Muslim University, located in the northern state of Uttar Pradesh. In the early twentieth century, conflicts among Hindu castes dominated social life in Calicut, making it possible for the Congress party to create political, trade, and cultural associations that brought together Hindus and Muslims. When Hindu–Muslim violence did break out in 1921, the Malabar riots, it did not spread.

In Aligarh, however, tensions between Muslims and Hindus dominated civic life and prevented the formation of civic intercommunal associations. Instead, politics replicated religious affiliations. The middle-class Hindu Arya Samaj movement developed influence within the local Congress Party, whereas the Muslim League, born of Aligarh Muslim University, championed the creation of Pakistan and thus was in opposition to Congress's ideal of pan-Indian union. During the 1990s' violence, politicians and peace committees worked across religious lines in Calicut to prevent local riots, but *within* religious communities in Aligarh to fan the flames.

The historical causal chains thus run from long-standing lines of cleavage within each city, to the political creation (or not) of crosscutting civic associations, to the contemporary activities of those associations, to the presence or absence of major Hindu–Muslim violence. One intriguing by-product of this analysis is that strong political tensions between upper-caste and lower-caste Muslims, as in Kerala, help to dampen down conflict between Muslims and Hindus. Class conflict thus promotes peace!

Varshney's study reminds us that when we seek to understand conflict (or for that matter any social phenomenon) we need to look at cases where it is absent as well as those where it is present, lest we erroneously attribute causality point to a spurious variable, one that co-occurs—"innocently," we might say—with conflicts, but that also co-occurs with peace. And, to stay with our concern in this book, religious difference is one such variable. Because we often see and hear about instances of conflicts between groups of different religious affiliations, we often mistakenly think that religious difference "causes" conflict.

But if we ask of a wide sample of cases what the causes are of intrastate conflicts, we do not find such an association. One such analysis (Fearon and Laitin 2003) found that religious or ethnic diversity does not predict a greater likelihood of conflict. (The best explanations seem to be conditions favoring insurgency, such as rough terrain and a weak state).

Struggle and Authority in Islam

*A*pproaching ideas by viewing them in a social context is nowhere more important than when we consider doctrines of large-scale religions, such as Islam or Catholicism. Each has doctrines that can be drawn on to justify violence and war, such as the Catholic doctrine of the just war (Regan 1996), or the Islamic idea of the jihad, to which we now turn. What role do these doctrines play in conflicts: do they cause them, mobilize people, or play roles at certain specific moments?

Historians note that Islamic ideas of jihad (Arabic jihâd, from the verb jâhada, to struggle or strive) have developed in response to particular sets of social norms and practices. In eighth-century Arabic, war between tribes was expected and ongoing, and most scholars interpret the Qur'ân's statements on jihad in that light (Peters 1996).

Multiple Approaches to Scripture on Jihad

The Qur'ân contains two kinds of verses with respect to war. One set of verses explicitly limits legitimate war to situations where Muslims are first attacked, such as chapter 2 verse 190, which says "and fight in the way of God with those who fight you, but aggress not: God loves not the aggressors." Other verses mention no such conditions, such as chapter 9 verse 29, "Fight those who believe not in God and the Last Day and do not forbid what God and His Messenger have forbidden—such men as practice not the religion of truth, being of those who have been given the Book—until they pay the tribute out of hand and have been humbled." Even this second set, however, links fighting to the expansion of the Muslim political and religious community, the *umma,* and the subjugation and payment of tribute by neighboring peoples. Indeed, maintaining control over armies before and after the beginning of Islam required periodic raiding of neighboring tribes, if not expansion of a community's borders, in order to retain soldiers' loyalty by redistributing wealth (Berkey 2003).

Early jurists confirmed the idea that the umma, led by a caliph, a rightful successor to Muhammad, had the collective obligation to urge other peoples to convert and join the umma, or to submit to Muslim rule and pay tribute. This obligation gave rise to the idea that the world was divided into the *dar al-Islâm,* the world of submission to God, and the *dar al-harb,* the world that was subject to warfare and conquest. These jurists also developed laws of just war, including the rights of enemy combatants and of non-combatants, rules regarding when attack was permitted, and norms concerning how to fairly divide the spoils.

In the modern period, jurists have developed several quite distinct sets of ideas about jihad. Modernist Muslim thinkers writing from the late nineteenth century onward drew on the first kind of Qur'ânic verses mentioned above to argue that the normal state of relations among nations, Muslim or non-Muslim, is the state of peace. War is justified only when necessary to defend oneself. Furthermore, they said, God wants people to come to Islam out of study, reflection, and conviction, and not under force of arms. The Qur'ânic verse, "there is no compulsion in matters of religion" (2:256) is often quoted to buttress this argument. This line of thinking has been continued by such influential Muslim figures as the Egyptian jurist Sheikh Yûsuf Qardâwî, and by Sheikhs of al-Azhar University in Cairo.

A second, opposed line of reasoning was put forth by Islamic groups seeking to fight their own Muslim governments and seeking religious justification for their attacks. Sayyid Qutb (d. 1966), for example, argued that armed aggression against the Egyptian government was justified because Egyptian leaders, although they professed Islam, in fact had left the faith and thus were legitimate targets for attack (Qutb 1978).

As in so many matters, Islamic texts and traditions may be cited to support a wide range of actions. Many contemporary Muslim scholars underscore this quality of Islam (a quality shared by all religions). However, there is a different tendency that one finds in all religions that depend on a scripture, a tendency that one might call the "retreat to literalism," whereby one claims that scripture has a single, unambiguous meaning. Interestingly, this has not been an important position among Muslim jurists, who generally have held that either there is no single correct Islamic position on legal matters, or that there is, but that humans, imperfect as they are, cannot be expected always to arrive at it. Under these two views, differences in interpretation of the Qur'ân and the hadîth either are planned by God, or are forgiven by Him (Abou El Fadl 2001).

It is, rather, Muslim public intellectuals who have invoked their claims as to what Islam "really says" to advance particular stances. One saw this "retreat to literalism" practiced, very understandably, by Muslims in the United States just after the destruction of the World Trade Center towers on September 11, 2001. Some scholars were featured in media coverage as saying that "Islam is a religion of peace" and that it "could never approve of such attacks." Similarly, verses from the Qur'ân promoting peaceful coexistence among peoples and attacking those who kill were cited widely, as if they, and not the statements coming from terrorists, represented true Islam. Rare were the authorities who stated that scripture contains lots of messages, and that one can find verses and interpretations of them that support attacks on unbelievers, as well as the peace-oriented verses more widely quoted.

Of course, the weakness of the "retreat to literalism" was immediately apparent when other Muslims quoted verses that urged Muslims to fight infidels, or that spoke in a highly negative fashion of the Jews. The appropriate response to this practice of citing out of context was to speak of the historical circumstances in which these verses were received, and of the interpretive traditions and alternatives built up around them. But this way was closed to those who had begun the debate by their own literal, and thus ahistorical, way of interpreting scripture.

The problem in searching for a single "Muslim position" on jihad, or even regarding particular actions, is that the major ways in which legal opinions, *fatwa* (pl. *fatâwa*) are produced is in response to a specific question. The choice of question can shape the answer. For example, shortly after the invasion of Afghanistan in the fall of 2001, influential U.S. Muslim scholars posed a question to Sheikh Yûsuf Qardâwî, the Egyptian scholar living in Qatar, whose broadcasts on the television station al-Jazîra are followed by Arabic-speaking Muslims throughout the world. The scholars asked whether Muslims serving in the U.S. armed forces ordered to fight in Afghanistan ought to obey their orders. Qardâwî answered that they should, because they had taken an oath to do so. Subsequently, others put a different question to him: should Muslims bombard women and children in Afghanistan? Qardâwî answered that they should not. Looked at in two different ways, the same actions could be judged as advisable or reprehensible.

Throughout Islamic history, the idea of jihad has provided a justification for unifying against an enemy, and in many cases it has provided the basis for a new political system. In West Africa, for example, the norm of jihad was instrumental in expanding the realm of Islamic rule and constructing stable and prosperous communities. The "chain" of jihad spread through the region over two centuries, from the 1670s in the far western Sahara, to the anticolonial movements of the late nineteenth century.

West African jihad movements responded to a difficult question for Muslims then and now, namely, in the absence of a single Muslim ruler, a caliph, who is it who has the authority to create an Islamic polity, or to declare jihad? In West Africa of the eighteenth century, established Muslim political authority was weak and distant, consisting of an Ottoman Empire effectively confined to the Mediterranean, and an independent Moroccan authority with little reach below the Sahara (Robinson 1985). It was thus new leaders who took it upon themselves to announce the combat against non-Muslim rulers and colonial powers.

Commenting on the contemporary struggles among Muslims over political authority, Gilles Kepel (Kepel 2002) has argued that recent instances of terrorism under the banner of jihad are not signs of the strength of political Islam, by which he means political projects to create Islamic states, but rather signify the decline and defeat of such projects, a thesis first argued by Olivier Roy (Roy 1994). Violence by armed Islamic groups occurs when an earlier movement for political Islam, which was supported by an alliance of a devout bourgeoisie and young Muslim groups, rejects extremist Islamist projects and opts instead for projects of multiparty democracy and focusing on Islamizing civil society. Violence thus is the result of the combination of the preexistence of a cultural repertoire which includes a doctrine of jihad, the development of highly controlled movements with goals of establishing an Islamic state, and rising external resistance to and rejection of those goals by mainstream Muslim populations.

"Radical" Islam

Since 2001, a number of social scientists have studied the pathways that lead ordinary Muslims to join any one of a number of small or large groups that stand apart from mainstream Muslim organizations. Most of these groups have peaceful objectives. The Tablighi Jema'at, for example, aims at reaching Muslims who have become lax in their daily religious duties of prayer and piety, and it recruits them to spread this message to others. Tablighi members often stand out in their societies for their choice of long beards and "Islamic" dress, the men wearing long white robes. Although a few Muslims move from Tablighi membership to more militant, or even violent organizations, others move in a different direction to higher education or electoral politics. In its missionary "call" for Muslims to become better Muslims, it resembles the work of orthodox Jewish Chabad organizations, which make a similar plea to Jews.

Quite different in its objectives is the Hizb ut-Tahrir, which is overtly political and often appears radical in its demands, which include the creation of an Islamic state and, in the meantime, the disengagement of Muslims from civic participation in non-Muslim states. They tend to dress like other well-educated and articulate members of the society where they live, despite their call for a distinct Muslim society. In these respects they resemble the U.S. conservative Protestant groups, led by (recently deceased) Jerry Falwell, Pat Robertson, and others, who call for the restoration of God's dominion on earth as part of the preparation of the return of Christ.

Although we may consider the Tablighi Jema'at and the Hizb ut-Tahrir to be "radical" because they stand out from the more mainstream Sunni Muslim organizations, their doctrines and practices are no more so than are the corresponding Jewish and Protestant organizations mentioned above. Some Muslims in Britain call for governance by scripture, but so do some Protestants in the United States!

Other movements adopt a militant and sometimes violent stand against the governments of their own countries, and call for new regimes that would follow Islam. Muslims have fought or are fighting in Kashmir against Indian control, in Chechnya against Russian rule, in Bosnia against the Serbs, in Algeria against the military-backed regime and, in the case of Hamas, for the liberation of Palestine. One may be for or against these local jihads—the United States aided the jihad against the Soviets, and many in Europe and North America supported the Bosnian struggle—but their character is akin to other internal wars that do not include an Islamic ideology, even if fought mainly by Muslims. For example, the PLO includes Christians and its goals historically were primarily secular; the GAM movement in Aceh, Indonesia, although Muslim, did not have an Islamic dimension to its demands. Other armed movements of course have nothing to do with Islam—most terrorist attacks in Europe in the 2000s have been by separatist groups in Corsica (against France) and Basque country (against Spain), and the bloody combat between Catholics and Protestants in Northern Ireland has only recently come to a close.

Competing Authorities in the Afghan Struggle

The history of struggles in Afghanistan underscore the connections between varying ideas of jihad and struggles over political authority. From the beginning of the resistance to the Soviet-backed regime in the 1970s, to the victory of the Taliban in 1996, Islam has provided a repertoire of ideas of authority, on which various individuals and groups could call in order to rally people behind them. In this respect, the question of jihad has been subsumed in broader questions of political authority (Edwards 2002).

The traditional social forms for armed combat in Afghanistan were tribal. Tribes fought under their own leaders, sometimes perhaps allied with each other, particularly if they spoke the same language. In a place with many different ethnic groups and language families, centralized authority never has been easy to develop. When, in the late 1970s, Afghan tribes began to form armed groups, or *lashkar,* to attack the troops of the Soviet-backed government, the most effective rhetoric for gaining intertribal unity was that of Islam. Various actions taken by the regime could be cited as defiling Islam, and thereby provide a rallying cry for all groups. An intertribal "jihad council" took collective responsibility for actions, preventing tribal rivalries from fractioning the antigovernment coalition.

Eventually, tribal and larger ethnic rivalries stymied efforts to mount a unified military front. But in their efforts to do so, rival claimants to lead the resistance or to govern Afghanistan called on different elements of the Islamic tradition to justify their claims. The three most important kinds of religious claims were saintly lineage, the prestige of a foreign religious education, and the promise of a "return to village religion." None was decisive, but each was legitimate in Islamic terms as a basis for claiming the right to lead the jihad.

Claiming descent from a saint, or better yet, from the Prophet Muhammad, attracts followers in most, if not all, Muslim societies. Continuity through direct contact over the generations is a general feature of Islam. The Prophet's statements are only valid if an unbroken chain of reliable witnesses has transmitted them. Relations of teachers to students create a chain of spiritual learning. Descent from parent to child is a particularly accepted basis for claiming to have inherited a mantle of religious authority. In Afghanistan, the strong tribal norms that bind people together based on patrilineal descent reinforce the appeal of these claims.

One man making such claims was Hazrat Sibghatullah Mujaddidi. Mujaddidi came from a family that claims to have descended from Sheikh Ahmad Sirhindi, a central figure in the development of Indian Sufism in the seventeenth century. The family was invited to Afghanistan in the late eighteenth century by the first Afghan king, and established a political base among Pakhtun tribal groups (the largest ethnic category in Afghanistan). These tribesmen became their disciples in a Sufi order (Edwards 2002, 253). The family enjoyed considerable power in making and breaking subsequent kings. Mujaddidi increased his own authority when in 1953 he earned a degree in Islamic jurisprudence from al-Azhar University in Cairo. This combination of lineage and a prestigious degree gave him considerable legitimacy in the eyes of Pakhtun Afghans. In 1979 he sent letters out to his followers throughout Afghanistan calling for mass uprisings against the government. In Herat, 200,000 people responded to his call, saying, as he himself recalled it, "Oh, this man is the right man. We shall start." The uprising was brutally suppressed by Soviet troops, a failure that considerably lessened his capacity to mobilize people for jihad. In any case, ties of loyalties to Sufi leaders (*pirs*) had weakened considerably in the course of the twentieth century.

The chief beneficiaries of this weakening in the struggle to lead the jihad were the new Islamic political parties. The legitimacy of claimants to lead these parties rested on their early involvement with party organizations and their foreign Islamic credentials. A key source of legitimacy was a professor of Islamic law at Kabul University, Ghulam Muhammad Niazi, who in the late 1960s was the principal sponsor of the Muslim Youth Organization, the origin of later Islamic movements. Two of the most important contestants for Afghan jihad leadership, Ustad Burhanuddin Rabbani and Engineer Gulbuddin Hekmatyar, based their claims in large part on their respective ties to this professor. Rabbani claimed that he had been Niazi's chief assistant at the university. Hekmatyar countered that it was another man from the Niazi tribe, Abdur Rahim Niazi, and not Rabbani, who was Professor Niazi's true heir, and that Abdur Rahman Niazi had worked closely with Hekmatyar in the early days of the Muslim Youth Organization. The Rabbani–Hekmatyar rivalry was ethnic as well as purely political: Rabbani was a Persian-speaking Tajik, whereas Hekmatyar was a Pakhtun. Their respective parties became increasingly polarized along ethnic lines in the late 1970s and 1980s.

Why were their ties to a university professor so important to these two rivals? Professor Niazi was acknowledged as the first Afghan to have studied with members of the Muslim Brotherhood in Cairo, and to have brought their ideas to Afghanistan. It was Ustad (a religious honorific) Rabbani who had translated works by the Brotherhood figure Sayyid Qutb into Persian, but Professor Niazi's status as the first to have learned the new ideas of the Brotherhood underscores the importance of precedence in determining authority in Afghan society. It also shows how the older ties to Sufi teachers and other Afghan scholars had diminished in importance, supplanted by a new kind of genealogical tie, that to prestigious foreign, and presumably better, formulators of Islamic knowledge (Edwards 2002, 239).

The rivalries among Hekmatyar, Rabbani, and other leaders led to the destruction of Kabul, murder and plunder in towns and villages throughout the country, and the rise in the mid–1990s of a new movement, the Taliban, or "students." Their claims to legitimacy in leading a jihad against the tribal rulers and party leaders were, again, based on religious norms, but this time norms having to do with the ideal of an indigenous Islam of the Afghan village. The Taliban argued that this ideal had been corrupted by the work of the parties and by the predominance of Kabul University. The Taliban warriors had grown up in refugee camps along the frontier and in Pakistan, and had attended religious schools, *madrasah,* in Pakistan. They held out the possibility of a restoration of an earlier Afghan Islam and the rejection of all foreign influences, whether Soviet, Western, or Arab. Ironically, it was their subsequent naïve welcoming of Saudi and Egyptian members of al-Qaeda that led to their destruction and the return to power of the regional tribal leaders. But much of their original appeal to Afghans was their refusal to follow either tribal loyalties or city-based party politics.

David Edwards's scholarship shows how we can understand calls for jihad as part of specific struggles for autonomy and power. The traditions and literature around jihad form part of a number of distinct cultural repertoires on which Muslims can call; these repertoires differ across societies, such that the resonances of and alternatives to jihad are quite different in Afghanistan than, say, in Indonesia or North America. Edwards shows that the Afghanistan repertoire includes several sets of values and actions centered on genealogy, honor, and tribal loyalty. In Indonesia the "jihad repertoire" does not reflect those concepts, but instead has associations with long-standing Christian-Muslim tensions over missionary activities and conflicts over power and resources in local contexts. In North America and Europe the concept of jihad has no local purchase, but can only be used to refer to conflicts occurring elsewhere, for example, in Palestine and Chechnya.

Indonesian Jihads

A brief look at recent violence in Indonesia will help to distinguish between the causes of violence and the factors that make it last and grow in strength. Muslims make up the large majority (around 85 percent) of Indonesians, but Christians occupy important positions in society, and in several regions of the country they form the local majority. Although open conflict between Muslim and Christian groups has been relatively rare in Indonesia (attacks on Chinese being determined by a different set of tensions), in the late 1990s bloody conflicts between Muslim and Christian groups did arise in the eastern island area called the Moluccas. What caused this sudden change in Muslim-Christian relations?

Christianization is a centuries-old phenomenon in eastern Indonesia, but much of the conversion in Maluku took place in the nineteenth century under Dutch rule. Some Muslims had lived in the region, especially in the largest city of Ambon, for centuries, but many more began to arrive from the large island of Sulawesi beginning in the early 1990s. These newcomers took over many informal sector jobs, such as market-place sellers and pedicab drivers. They drew on relatively tight social networks to dominate these sectors, as do new immigrant groups throughout the world. Tensions between Muslims and Christians rose after the economic crisis of 1997, when the control of jobs became a matter of survival. In Ambon, patronage networks stretch all the way up to the highest offices, with the governor, high-ranking army officials, and a former mayor of Ambon controlling both employment opportunities and local gangs.

In 1998 a small incident involving a bus conductor and an obstreperous passenger touched off fights between rival gangs (whose numbers had swelled with recent arrivals from Jakarta). Unlike other conflicts that had exploded elsewhere in the country, in particular in Kalimantan and Aceh, here the lines of social cleavage corresponded to nationwide divisions between Muslim and Christian communities. Christian networks throughout Indonesia began to warn of plots to Islamize all of eastern Indonesia. Islamic groups reminded their supporters of long-standing efforts at Christianization, and warned that warriors from the 1940s Christian-controlled Republic of South Maluku were waiting for a chance to launch a separatist movement. Some factions of the armed forces that had continued to support Suharto after his downfall from the presidency gave material aid to Muslims.

Here the tensions leading to violence were material: conflict over jobs between poor Muslims and poor Christians, and conflicts over political power between Muslim and Christian politicians. But each side was able to draw on the repertoires of defense and survival to mobilize their co-religionists. Christians were as able to do this as were Muslims; the fact that Muslims had a convenient word at hand did not in itself give them an edge. Slogans used by protagonists do not furnish adequate analytical frameworks.

Joining the Global Salafi Jihad

Quite different again is the global jihadist movement, what Marc Sageman (2004) calls the "global Salafi jihad," and which targets the "far enemy," meaning non-Muslim nations removed from areas of conflict. These people, who are linked in one way or another to al-Qaeda, differ in important ways from men and women fighting for the liberation of a particular territory, such as Palestine or Kashmir, and from people fighting on religious grounds against their own government, as in Algeria or Central Asia. The global Salafi jihad aims to create an Islamic state, and it sees the West as standing in the way of that aim. Those jihadists who turn to terrorism differ importantly with other movements, such as the Hizb ut-Tahrir, who work toward the creation of a worldwide Islamic state but do not engage in terrorism to do so.

The profile of these mujahîdîn contrasts with certain popular images. They are, relative to others in the countries from where they came, relatively well educated, usually in secular subjects. Other than the Indonesians, who did often attend religious schools, these terrorists came from technical faculties, and approached Islam in a manner similar to the way they approached those secular subjects: as a set of propositions to be learned directly from scripture, and not mediated by traditional disciplines of jurisprudence.

Why did they join the movement (al-Qaeda or an affiliate)? Most did so away from home: Egyptians and Saudis while in exile in Sudan in the early 1990s, Indonesians while in Malaysia, and many from North Africa and elsewhere while in Europe. "Lonely people looking for companionship" (Sageman 2004, 93) met new friends at a mosque, and sometimes these new friends bought them into contact with someone urging a global jihad. They may not have been particularly devout, but they translated their personal alienation into a wholesale condemnation of the West and of the regimes it supported. They may have begun their violent activities in the late-1980s anti-Soviet jihad in Afghanistan, where they were trained by Pakistanis (working from CIA financial aid), but it was more likely that if they had a jihad experience it was much later, sometimes in Afghanistan or in Bosnia.

These jihadists were not recruited and certainly not brainwashed by senior al-Qaeda personnel. Theirs was a pathway that began as social and led gradually to incorporation into a tight friendship group in which radical Islamic ideas became the stuff of their everyday lives. They eventually joined the jihad as a group rather than as individuals (Sageman 2004, 110). In other circumstances, the group's ideas would have been those of left-wing terrorist groups in Europe preaching the virtues of Maoism, or right-wing groups spouting anarchist ideas. Or they would have been nonviolent ideas that also would have given them the sense of order and purpose they craved: perhaps the structure of a political party, or a social movement, or a more mainstream religious group.

Sageman (2004, 111) makes an important methodological point in his study: if you interview people already in a religious movement, they will tend to say that they joined it because of its ideas, because at that point they have bought into the group's ideology. But studies that draw on data about preexisting social networks and activities find that friendship, casual social contacts, and kinship play important roles in recruitment.

But there remains a leap from joining an organization to sacrificing yourself for the cause. What adds this dimension of radical commitment? Clearly religious belief plays a part. The jihadi terrorists met others at mosques, and they spent time listening to sermons, and watching videos about the jihad in various parts of the world. They internalized a script that explained why bad things were happening to good Muslims, and in which the role of the West was paramount. But the exposure to Salafi ideas is far from sufficient to explain why someone becomes a terrorist. As Sagemen (2004, 119) points out, al-Qaeda has recruited virtually no one from places where its headquarters have been located or where it has held training camps, in Afghanistan, Pakistan, and Sudan, and where presumably exposure to their ideas has been greatest. Those people who join al-Qaeda are living temporarily away from home, and they join in part to find a home. Joining a movement accentuates the sense of separateness from everyday life: you dress differently and commit your life to the organization. Here we can recall the Japanese Mahikari movement we examined in Chapter 6. The appeal of the movement depended in part on the script that explained current ills suffered by patients and also set that explanation in the broader context of a mythic Japanese history. People who already experienced tensions and wished to find religious solutions found the movement enticing.

But most people who meet this description do not join any particular movement. Recent work in the sociology of religion (Lofland-Stark 1965; Stark and Finke 2000) adds an additional social dimension to this analysis. People who end up joining a religious movement are likely to have recently moved away from previous social ties, and, after initially encountering the new doctrine, to form positive social bonds with one or more members of the new group. In other words, there may be cognitive reasons why a group's script is attractive, but one also needs the socioemotional dimension—initial detachment from a former group, subsequent reattachment to the new group—to account for joining. This general pattern has held for studies of the Reverend Sun Myung Moon's Unification Church as well as the Egyptian Islamic movements influenced by Sayid Qutb's writings, the Islamic Liberation Organization and the Jamaat al-Muslimin (Sagemen 2004, 126–135).

Recruitment to Terrorism

*E*ven if we understand how people might call on religion to justify killing others, we still do not understand how it is that a small number of people join terrorist groups, or bring themselves to kill other people. What roles do religious beliefs and practices play in recruitment and killing itself?

We might begin by looking at terrorist acts and asking to what extent religions play a role. We might suppose that over the past decade, Islam has been behind most or all terrorism in some respect. But we might do so because of the small number of spectacular events, particularly the attack on the World Trade Towers on September 11, 2001, and because terrorism associated with Islam is a relatively recent phenomenon.

Fortunately, a 2007 study of terrorist attacks in Europe provides some sense of the relative magnitude of different types of terrorism. The EU report (Europol 2007) found 498 attacks during 2006 that it (and the member states) counted as terrorist, or involving violence within the state intended to destabilize the political order. Of those attacks, one involved Islam (in Germany), and 424, thus the vast majority, were separatist, mainly in Corsica, directed against the French government, and in Spanish Basque country. Most of the remainder were from left-wing groups operating in Greece, Germany, Italy, and Spain. Now, about one-half of all arrests made in cases of terrorism were of Muslims, but even more importantly, over half (342 out of 706) of all terrorism arrests made in the EU in 2006 were made in France, with the majority targeting Corsican separatists. Of course, attacks in 2004 in Madrid and in 2005 in London caused a large number of casualties, and those years look different than does 2006, but then again in still earlier years it was Catholic–Protestant conflicts in Northern Ireland that caused a great number of attacks.

How Are People Able to Kill?

Beyond the matter of religion's role in recruitment, do religions make it easier for people to kill when they are moved to do so for other reasons?

The psychiatrist Robert Jay Lifton (Lifton 1986) has discussed the psychological mechanism of "doubling" in killers, a process whereby a person creates a second self, cut off from his or her everyday self (or former self) that in its very thinness and separation from the rest of the world makes it possible to commit violence. Violence may be for many ends, of course. A doctor may create a "medical self" that can commit the violence of slicing open a living body for a life-sustaining medical operation, a soldier may create a "military self" that can shoot an enemy soldier at close range, or a member of a militant religious group may create a heroic version of him or herself as devoted to and even willing to die for a cause.

It is with respect to these processes of "doubling" that the specific actions taken by certain movements become more understandable: that movements that seek to lead their members toward violence will insist that they cut off ties from their everyday or former lives, that they will provide a charismatic figure who will exemplify the heroic doubled self for recruits to emulate. For example, many Palestinians invoke the right to fight an occupier to justify attacks against Israelis in occupied portions of the West Bank and Gaza. In 1991, Hamas carried out its first attacks inside Israel. Shortly thereafter many of its leaders were deported, and in their exile they began to develop the strategy of using young men and women to carry out suicide attacks, a method requiring little training or equipment, but the willingness to die for a cause.

The profile of suicide bombers suggests that they are typically young people who have found no way to advance in life, who have few social ties, and who find acceptance in religion. Those people, usually men who spend large amounts of time in the local mosque, might be noticed by Hamas leaders who then recruit them. They promise that the recruit will be a hero in this life and enjoy the privileges of martyrdom in the next—and that his family will receive both honor and significant material support. Then they isolate him, have him write letters about his impending martyrdom, and prevent him from reestablishing contact with his family (Stern 2003).

Similar steps are taken by leaders of Christian cults. James Ellison, the leader of a Christian Identity movement in rural Arkansas called the Covenant, the Sword, and the Arm of the Lord, sought to convince male recruits that they were new men with a distinctive mission. He had them dress in combat fatigues and told them that they were the white race's last hope against the "Zionist Occupied Government" of the United States (Stern 2003). Followers of the Christian Identity movements believe that they will live into the Endtimes, a period described in Revelations during which the Antichrist will rule the world. They take as their duty to fight the Antichrist; their combat will lead toward the Apocalypse and the return of Jesus Christ. Because many such groups believe themselves to be already in the Endtimes, they seek out the identity of the Antichrist, who is variously described as the "world government" of the United Nations, or of a secret conspiracy developed by the Illuminati, or Zionism.

The specific identity of the enemy is less compelling to members than is the sense of a sacred and world-preserving mission. The rhetoric of the mission and the vision proposed to them fits with the Protestant teachings they have grown up hearing and believing: "End of Times, I've heard of that for years as a child in the Baptist Church. Everyone is left to fend for themselves," said one former member of Ellison's group (Stern 2003, 22). Thus prepared doctrinally for what they hear, and given a new sense of unity and purpose, with little contact with mainstream society, they can be led toward conflict, and even death.

Religion in general has no consistent relationship to violence or war: for every terrorist killing in the name of a deity there are countless other co-religionists leading peaceful lives. Furthermore, if religious ideas can provide a basis for inducing people to follow leaders in battle—and such has been the case from the Crusades to the small-scale violence associated with sects and jihadist groups—so can a range of other ideas, from racial or ethnic purity, to defense of the nation, to pretensions to imperial domination of the world. Religion monopolizes neither peace and charity nor war and violence.

15 Secularisms and Religions in Modern States

We have said a lot about religions so far in this volume, but less to say about all that is not religious, what we often refer to as "the secular": a secular state, or way of life, or set of beliefs. Here people often plunge into confusion. The United States is based on a "wall of separation between church and state," so we might wish to hold it up as an example of a secular state. But presidents of the United States hold prayer breakfasts; they say "God bless America" and the like in official speeches, and it is difficult to imagine a successful candidate for the office who does not say that he or she believes in God—and we expect reporters to pose the question! What then distinguishes the United States from, say, India, Germany, or Egypt on this issue? What is a secular state and what do we mean by secularism?

How to Think About "Secular States"

In fact, despite deep differences in history, political ideology, and religious conviction across contemporary nation-states, most of them overlap considerably on the question of the state's involvement in religious life, or so runs the argument of this final chapter. I focus here on large-scale religions in modern history. Two similarities appear again and again across modern states: political authorities claim, and usually wield, authority over religious leaders; and states apply doctrines of "evenhandedness," that inevitably involve some involvement in religious life. I will explain these two claims here, but they will become clearer as we explore several cases.

First, in nearly all countries the state asserts its own political priority over religious authorities, meaning that state authorities, whether they be judges or elected officials, have the right to determine matters of public policy, not religious leaders. Of course they differ in how they do this. France tries to keep religion out of political discourse entirely, as does Britain (despite the Anglican Church's capacity as the "established church"). The United States makes no such refusal, and legislators often justify votes by saying God so directs them. In India, judges refer to religious texts when faced with cases concerning marriage or divorce, as they do in Israel and Indonesia.

But in all these countries, a civil political body has the ultimate say in policy matters, and legislators will follow deliberative rules and procedures that are not religious in nature. In the United States, a law is enacted and a judicial decision taken as the result of deliberations and voting that are not subject to religious bodies or authorities, and no religious text has direct legal force. India, Israel, and Indonesia, though they apply religious law in their courts, all assert the capacity of their parliaments to stipulate what counts as religious law. Egypt admits only God's Word as a legitimate source of law, at least in theory, but in practice, judges work from the basis of a corpus of legal rulings. All these states could thus be said to be "secular" to the extent that religion is legally subordinated to the state, though not in the sense that law has no religious content.

Secondly, most states (though not all) proclaim neutrality or even-handedness toward religions. This even-handedness usually involves some degree of involvement in defining what counts as a religion. Some states support religious bodies even though they remain resolutely secular in their political philosophy. No one is more explicit about secularity as a constitutional principle than France, but the French state pays the salaries of religious-school teachers and finds ways to aid religious groups to build places of worship. With the United States we might expect that the "free exercise" clause of the Bill of Rights would give religious groups legal advantages over other kinds of groups, but as we shall see below, religious groups win legal cases when they argue for equal treatment and not when they claim special rights qua religion. We will make similar arguments below for some states that apply Islamic law.

Three Meanings of "Secular"

In what follows, I will insist on distinguishing three meanings of the secular: legal structure, social processes, and individual orientations. Or rather, these three phrases designate distinct levels of analysis: the political and legal, the historical and sociological, and the psychological and phenomenological.

Secularism is perhaps most appropriately used to talk about how, in their constitutions and political philosophies, modern states define and regulate the place of religious bodies and religious discourse in political processes. States decide whether and how to recognize a particular body as a religion, set out its rights and duties, and formulate overall policies and philosophies of governance. Some of these philosophies or ideologies may be secularist, in that they proclaim the evacuation of religion from the sphere of public policy. Thus, France proclaims itself to be a secularist or "laic" state, the U.S. Bill of Rights prevents the government from "establishing" a religion, the Indian constitution proclaims the state to be secular, and so forth.

When we look at the long-term social processes that characterize many modern societies, we often talk about the *secularization* of society, by which we mean the effects that the division of labor have had on separations among social institutions. As work became relegated to a separate sphere, the state came to see itself as distinct from religion, and the family became a specialized sphere of socialization, each domain took on its own norms. Norms of family life and work may have been strongly shaped by religious belief, but gradually we came to see each domain as governed by its own rules, properly distinct from each other. This process has been long and is by no means simple. For example, even as marriage and divorce began to be regulated primarily by state bodies, many have continued to see them as mainly religious in nature, whether as a sacrament, as in Catholicism, or as a contract governed by revealed norms, as in Islam. Secularization does not imply a loss of faith and is compatible with a religious perspective on all domains of one's life; it does mean that each of the social institutions in which one participates has its own set of norms.

Finally, we may mean by secularization the *decline of religion* in some sense, if we believe that individuals become less likely to view matters of social life or even ultimate concerns in religious terms. Sometimes we speak of this decline to mean that individuals lose their faith in the existence of religious truths or their beliefs in the existence of religious beings. Sometimes, however, we mean that, whatever the nature of their beliefs, individuals have less to do with organized religions. Some, particularly European scholars, speak of the "privatization" of religion in this second sense.

Although social scientists once assumed that secularization processes entailed the loss of faith, because religion was destined to shrink into a private sphere and eventually to disappear, this idea of an inevitable link between these two levels now clearly is mistaken (Casanova 1994). Secularist political-legal structures and the secularization of society by no means always lead to a decline in participation in organized religion or to a loss of faith. Or, to put it positively, one may have a society where the majority of people retain a high degree of religious commitment and yet the society is highly secularized, and the state exercises little direct action on religions—the United States is an excellent example of this combination.

Secularism and Pluralism in the United States

U.S. history on religion, nation, and state is more complex than the phrase "separation of church and state" might imply. Running through the history of debates and laws in the United States about religion and public life are two contradictory but strong lines of argument. One stresses the constitutionally mandated separation of church and state and the dangers to freedom posed by government entanglement in religious affairs. The second stresses the historically dominant role played in U.S. public life by Christianity—or more narrowly Protestant Christianity, or more broadly a Judeo-Christian tradition.

The first argument stresses rights and laws. The second argument stresses historical tradition and shared values. Each has its claims to an antique lineage: the first, to Christian suspicion of government as inevitably corrupting (a view held by Saint Augustine, for example); the second, to the tradition of civic republicanism, where the state ensures that the community follows a set of moral, including religious, norms (Taylor 1990).

The rights argument for separating religion and state is based on the first 16 words of the Bill of Rights, which reads: "Congress shall make no law respecting an establishment of religion, or prohibiting the free exercise thereof." Many heated debates in our recent history—by the courts, in legislatures, among ordinary citizens—turn on how these 16 words are to be interpreted. Does the first clause, the establishment clause, prohibit all federal or state aid to religious schools, or all public displays in government buildings of religious symbols? Or does it more narrowly prohibit only laws that give special privileges or powers to a particular church? Does the second, the free exercise clause, protect the rights of schools to set aside a moment for silent prayer? Or does this practice run afoul of the first clause? What rights do parents have to further their children's exercise of religion? To what extent may Christian Scientist parents legally withhold medical aid from their children on religious grounds? May religious communities withdraw their children from school before the legal minimum age? Certain of these issues, such as the right to withdraw children from school, involve finding the right balance between the Constitution and the legislative power of the states. Other issues, such as silent prayer in the schools, may be seen as requiring a weighing of the two clauses against each other.

Religion in the Early Centuries

The emphasis on limiting the powers of government over religion was motivated by the colonists' experience of religious persecution (Berman 1990). This persecution occurred not only in Europe, but also in the colonies. The same religious groups that fled persecution abroad soon practiced it in their new homes. Authorities in New York and Massachusetts expelled Lutherans and Quakers along with Catholics and Jews. Even the relatively tolerant colony established by William Penn forbade deists to live in the colony and kept Jews from holding office.

The main purpose of the establishment clause was thus to prevent that kind of intolerance from developing at the federal level. The strongest advocates of the clause, James Madison and Thomas Jefferson, were fresh from their struggle to disestablish the Anglican Church in their home state of Virginia. Few other churches had universal pretensions; most were organized along *congregational* lines, meaning they were governed by the local congregation for the local congregation, and did not aim to become a universal church. Indeed, most residents of the colonies were Puritans, whose religious leaders were far more concerned with reserving church membership for the saved than they were with expanding their roles.

The framers of the Constitution went further, preventing the federal government from supporting all Christian churches equally through taxation. As James Madison argued in 1785: "Who does not see that the same authority which can establish Christianity, in exclusion of all other Religions, may establish with the same ease any particular set of Christians, in exclusion of all other Sects?" (quoted in Frankel 1994, 27). This sentiment lay behind Thomas Jefferson's famous phrase that there should be "a wall of separation between church and state" (Berman 1990, 40).

There was, however, no single state and no single church in the United States, then as now. Rather, there were many different governments and many different ways in which people pursued religious beliefs. The Constitution only affected the powers of the federal government, and prevented it only from passing laws that would infringe upon the free exercise of religion or that would establish a church. It did not forbid officials from acting on their religious beliefs in passing other laws, nor did it keep them from effectively making one set of religions dominant in public discourse.

Nor did the Constitution say that religion was a matter for individuals to decide. As the legal historian Harold Berman argues (1990), for Americans of the 1780s and 1790s, free exercise of religion meant the freedom of religious communities to regulate family and social life, not the freedom of the individual to do as he or she pleased. Such was clearly true for the majority of American Puritans, for whom religious membership was seen as a binding social covenant, but true as well for denominations we now think of as highly individualistic, such as the Unitarians. One Salem Unitarian church even records that in the seventeenth century it flogged and sold into slavery some Quakers who refused to contribute to a new church building! In the late seventeenth and early eighteenth centuries, states aided parochial schools and all public schooling was explicitly intended to further Christianity. Well into the twentieth century, marriage was considered to be religious, and divorce law was derived from English ecclesiastical law (Berman 1990). The authority of the community, embodied in its church, was taken for granted by most citizens of the early Republic, and it is this set of experiences that those arguing for maintaining public religious tradition cite.

Balancing Rights and Tradition in a Pluralistic Nation

In the two centuries since independence the United States has changed from a nation dominated by Protestant, and particularly Puritan, Christians to a nation of diverse major religions, including Catholicism, Judaism, and Islam, and of many citizens not affiliated to a major religion. From a nation where most people thought of religion in terms of community norms as well as private faith, the United States has become a nation where most people think of religion in terms of individual beliefs alone.

In 1800, nearly everyone in the United States belonged to a Protestant denomination; Catholics, Jews, and other faiths taken together amounted to perhaps 2 percent of the population (Hunter 1990). Then came the enormous migrations of European Catholics at midcentury and again at the turn of the twentieth century, along with migrations of Jews and Asians of various religions. By the 1990s, Catholics constituted about 25 percent of the population, and Jews and Mormons each about 2 percent. Protestants of various denominations made up about 56 percent of U.S. residents. And within each of these large categories are more religious-based diversities than before. Whereas once the major divisions among Catholics were their countries of origin (especially among Irish, Italians, and Germans), today the major divisions concern the stands taken on doctrinal issues and on the authority of the pope. The severe cleavages today among fundamentalists, evangelicals, and others within the many Protestant denominations as well as between these denominations is paralleled in the nineteenth century only by the hostility exhibited by most Protestants against Mormons and Adventists. Nor was there an explicit "secular humanism" such as is professed by many today.

The relation between governments and religions has changed as well, but arguments for rights and those for tradition continue to have their strong supporters. Only in the 1940s did the Supreme Court explicitly hold that the Fourteenth Amendment prevented states from enacting laws establishing religion or preventing free exercise. In a 1947 case, *Everson v. Board of Education of Ewing Township,* the Court emphasized

Jefferson's "wall of separation between church and state," and stated that states as well as the United States could not favor one religion over another. (Ironically, this broad doctrine was declared in a case in which the Court upheld a state law that gave state aid for buses used to take children to parochial schools.) The Court distinguished between aid to children and aid to schools, approving the former. In subsequent decisions the Court has upheld laws aimed at granting children equal opportunity, for example, the right for a deaf child to have a sign language interpreter in a parochial school when that right is already granted to public school students. But the Court struck down as illegitimately "advancing religion" state permission for a Hasidic Jewish group to form a public school district that included only their own adherents (Frankel 1994, 96–107).

Despite these decisions, to some degree law and public discourse in the United States continue to give special status to Christian religions. Christian prayers in the White House and Congress are a reminder of the tendency to mix Christian symbols into public life. In 1997, the second inauguration of President Clinton began with a prayer by the evangelical Christian minister Billy Graham.

Public prayer continues to be fought over in the courts. The current law of the land is that school-sponsored prayers violate the establishment clause. But this apparent consensus is tenuous, based as it is on a series of close decisions. For example, in the 1992 case *Lee v. Weisman,* the Supreme Court decided five to four that prayer delivered by a rabbi at a public school graduation was unconstitutional. The majority opinion stressed that any school-sponsored prayer, whether in the classroom or at an assembly, engendered social pressure on those not subscribing to the majority faith. But the dissent argued that graduation prayers were a tradition, the idea of coercive social pressure was fabricated, and that Americans have always thanked God for their blessings.

Some recent decisions have emphasized the argument from historical traditions. A 1984 case, *Lynch v. Donnelly,* upheld the right of a city to display a nativity scene, and in 1983, in *Marsh v. Chambers,* the Supreme Court upheld the right of the Nebraska legislature to pay a chaplain to open sessions with public prayer.

Although today a majority Court opinion would probably not state that "this is a Christian nation," as one did in 1892; nonetheless, judges and politicians from time to time continue to refer to the United States as a Christian nation or Judeo-Christian nation. Moreover, apparently neutral laws, such as laws mandating a "moment of silence" in schools, may be seen as discriminating in practice by stigmatizing students who do not adopt prayerful attitudes or who find the dominant model of "silent prayer" to be in fact a Christian model. Muslims, for example, carry out obligatory worship or ritual prayer (salat) at specific times of the day and in doing so stand, bow, and prostrate themselves—none of which actions can be performed during the "moment of silence." The Supreme Court recognizes this problem in general; in the *Yoder* case (406 U.S. 220) discussed below, the majority stated: "A regulation neutral on its face, in its application nonetheless offends the constitutional requirement for governmental neutrality if it unduly burdens the free exercise of religion."

One contested area concerns whether only beliefs, or beliefs and practices, are protected by the free exercise clause. In 1879, in a decision (*Reynolds v. U.S.*) that upheld a law against the Mormon practice of polygamy, the Court held that religious practices were not themselves protected: while laws "cannot interfere with mere religious belief and opinions, they may with practices" (98 U.S. 166).

But in 1972, in the landmark case *Wisconsin v. Yoder,* the Supreme Court ruled that a state had to prove a compelling interest before it could constitutionally compel a community to obey a state law that conflicted with its religious practices. In that case, an Amish parent had been sued by the State of Wisconsin for violating a law requiring school attendance until age 16. The parent had removed his child from school after finishing eighth grade and claimed that continuing in school would unduly subject the child to the influence of the secular world and would thereby endanger her salvation. The Court found that the state did not show the required compelling interest in this case. Spending the years after eighth grade at home, learning the skills that would serve children best on the farm, was not obviously inferior to continuing on in school. Compelling school attendance would infringe on the Amish religious way of life, so the Court ruled that the law violated the free exercise clause.

Justice Douglas dissented in *Yoder,* noting that the Court did not know the wishes of the children, and that many children do leave the Amish community and are disadvantaged if they do not have the years of high school education required by the state.

Equal Treatment versus Special Religious Rights

Under debate in these and in more recent cases is the extent to which claims based on religious belief or practices merit special judicial consideration. As Rogers Smith (1998; 2007) has argued, these claims have not fared well in recent U.S. Supreme Court decisions. The Christian Right has advanced its arguments for a greater public presence through claims for equal treatment, not special rights.

Two issues galvanized the Christian Right at two stages of its organization: equal access to the radio airwaves in the 1940s and 1950s, and equal tax treatment for private Christian universities (the Bob Jones University case) in the 1970s. In both cases litigants advanced claims that they deserved the same privileges as enjoyed by other groups: privileges enjoyed by liberal Protestant groups to broadcast their religious messages over the public airwaves, and privileges enjoyed by other private colleges to be free of tax obligations. In the 1970 *Walz* decision, the Supreme Court ruled that churches did not have tax exemptions as religious institutions per se, but as part of a broad class of institutions that served the public interest and that included hospitals, libraries, and professional organizations. Furthermore, the nonestablishment clause could be invoked when it appeared that the state was unduly aiding religious groups per se. A series of cases from the 1970s on struck down aid to parochial schools as involving "excessive entanglement" of the state in religious affairs (*Lemon v. Kurzman* 1971), and that "Lemon test" was invoked in subsequent cases as well.

The Christian Right strategy since that time has been to ask only for equal access to services, and equal rights of free speech, and often they have won their cases: for access to school facilities, for example (*Lamb's Chapel* 1993; *Rosenberger* 1995), or for equal opportunities to provide federally commissioned social services, the "charitable choice" argument (not yet ruled on by the U.S. Supreme Court as of early 2007).

Secularism and Public Religion: Three European Variants

*I*n European societies, states have developed a mixture of even-handed regulation of all religions, nominal precedence (or "establishment") of one church, and preferences for or principles of secularist public policy deliberation. These mixtures usually achieve practical even-handedness and general avoidance of religious claims in public. Britain may have an established Church (the Church of England, of course), but politicians generally avoid public discussion of private religious beliefs, and similar statements could be made of the Lutheran-heritage Scandinavian societies. France proclaims itself to be secularist, but actively aids religious private schools by giving them teachers' salaries. Germany, Belgium, Italy, and Spain have mechanisms for publicly recognizing certain religions, but each has developed nonreligious political discourse.

The particular features of each of these mixtures become most easily visible when pushed or tried by minority religions. Let us consider what has happened in three of these states.

French Secularism versus Headscarves in Schools

France, has made state secularism a part of its legal framework. Throughout the nineteenth century, Republican and Catholic factions struggled for control of the schools—and through them, control of the hearts and minds of French children. From that struggle came strong laws preventing the state from granting official recognition to any religion and laws guaranteeing public, secular education to all French children. The French legal doctrine of *laïcité,* perhaps best understood as keeping religion out of public affairs and keeping public officials from displaying their religion, has generally been understood to constrain the state and its employees, but not citizens in their private capacity (Bowen 2007).

French laïcité also has a broader sociopolitical meaning, however, which transcends this legal doctrine. Many French teachers and public officials, particularly on the political left, have inherited a tradition of strong anti-Catholic sentiment that sometimes also is an antireligious sentiment. For them, the French Republic depends on a public sphere that is free of religious messages. French citizens become complete political individuals by being socialized in public institutions, and they retain their citizenship qualities by continuing to interact in such institutions qua citizens—and not as Muslims, Protestants, or Scientologists. They recognize each other as equivalent citizens, indistinguishable on the dimension of their participation in French public life.

The norm of public laïcité leads some teachers and principals of secondary schools to expel girls who come to class wearing headscarves, or some employers in private industry to demand that employees not wear "clearly Islamic" dress. When Muslim schoolgirls began to wear headscarves to school in the late 1980s, some teachers and principals resented the girls' public display of difference, and a number of prominent French intellectuals publicly cried out that the Republic was endangered. Within a few years the highest administrative law body, the Conseil d'État, had arrived at what would be its consistent ruling that nothing in French law prevents schoolchildren from expressing their religious beliefs by wearing garments that imply a religious affiliation, as long as such garments are not "ostentatious" and the children in question neither "proselytize" nor disturb "public order." Indeed, the Conseil d'État ruled that they had the right to engage in religious self-expression in school, and that the law restricted the apparel and the conduct only of teachers and other state employees.

Teachers and principals have continued to expel or isolate children wearing head-scarves and sometimes they have declared strikes to dramatize their position. One such incident occurred in 2002 to 2003, when the teachers in a high school near Lyon threatened to strike if one female student was not expelled. In Lyon and elsewhere, some teachers and principals claimed that the presence of the headscarves was divisive, that it brought broader social tensions, and even the war in Palestine, into the schools. The headscarf issue surfaced in the media again in April 2003, when Muslims attending the annual assembly sponsored by the large Muslim association Union des Organisations Islamiques de France (UOIF) booed the call by the Minister of the Interior to enforce the law requiring women to bare their heads for their identity photos. Newspaper articles in April and May 2003 replayed the arguments first heard in the 1980s, according to which the headscarf was a sign of female submission and a direct attack on the principle of laïcité. In March 2004, after public hearings by two governmental commissions and a continued media campaign against the scarves, France passed a law preventing the wearing of any clothing or signs that clearly displayed the religious affiliation of a student in public school.

Ironically, some women consider wearing the headscarf to be part of breaking with immigrant culture, a way of distinguishing between an Islam learned in France and the insufficiently Islamic traditions of the "old country." As many French observers have noted, when young women choose to wear a head covering, misleadingly called *le voile* ("the veil"), it often signifies a moment of personal growth and transition—such as graduating from school, traveling to another country, beginning work, or making a break with the social norms of their family. Wearing a headscarf rarely is a mark of continuity in family dress but a mark of discovery and self-identification as an individual.

France is fast becoming an openly multicultural and multireligious country, but at this point has chosen to reaffirm its tradition of public laïcité in an effort to bring people together under the umbrella of French values and customs. It is too early to know whether this policy will have the desired effect.

The National Church in Britain

In the European context France is an unusual case. Most other members of the European Union make available some state funding for religious organizations. In some European countries, political parties have links to particular religious denominations.

Britain, for example, has an established church, the Anglican or Episcopal Church, in which all state weddings and funerals take place. Other churches and religious organizations are allowed, and some even receive state support, but they take second place to the Anglican Church.

Some Britons recently have urged that the Church be disestablished, deprived of its official status. Non-Anglicans, including many Muslims and Jews, argue that for all British citizens to enjoy full citizenship, they all must enjoy an equal capacity to shape the public culture. Such an equality implies that the public culture cannot favor one religion over another, as it currently does.

However, some Jewish and Muslim leaders have come out publicly in support of the continuing establishment of the Anglican Church (Modood 1994). They argue that when there is a national religion the followers of that religion feel comfortable about their place in the society and therefore exert less pressure on minority groups to convert or conform. They also argue that Anglicanism is less threatening than secularism to Muslims and Jews, because at least it supports other religions' continued existence. By contrast, secularism contains an anti-Islamic sentiment. These people cite the example of France, where strict secularism makes it more difficult for some people to accept the public religious self-identification by Muslims.

The Crucifix in Bavaria

German attitudes toward public religion are still further away from French secularism than are British ones. Recent controversy in Germany has concerned both the wearing of religious dress in schools and whether the state of Bavaria may make compulsory the display of the crucifix in schools (Caldwell 1996).

In France the normal state of affairs had been, at least in theory, the absence of any religious markers in the classroom, and the signs of religious difference, the Muslim headscarves, introduced into the classroom clashed with secular state officials' expectations. In Germany, and especially in Bavaria, the normal state of affairs was quite different. The state required that all primary school classrooms prominently display a large crucifix.

In 1995, however, the Federal Constitutional Court responded to a suit from a non-Christian ("anthroposophist") family and overturned the Bavarian regulation. The decision set off a storm of protest. The court ruling did not require the crucifixes to be removed, only that schools would not be obliged to hang them. But the furor was intense. Even Chancellor Helmut Kohl objected that the state had an obligation to pass Christian values on to children, and numerous commentators compared the federal court's decision to the Nazis' acts of exchanging crucifixes for swastikas. Some politicians called for disobedience of the court order.

To explain the reaction it helps to consider how these key religious symbols give public solidity to boundaries between "Us" and the "Other." In France, the Other is either Islamic fundamentalism or religion taking over the state. In Germany, it is the denial of Christian values under Nazi and communist rule. In the United States, it is persecution of religious dissenters by a state-backed church.

The place of religion in Germany traces back to the aftermath of religious wars in the seventeenth century. The German lands adopted the principle that a ruler could determine the religion of his subjects, a principle that tolerated princes, not subjects. It provided for shared practices and beliefs throughout the realm.

This principle continues to claim legitimacy. In 1918 Catholic Bavaria demanded protection against the potential persecution of Catholics in a Germany now two-thirds

Protestant. In response, the framers of the Weimar Constitution granted to the German states the right to administer public education. They also gave all registered churches the status of public corporations, to be supported by taxes. These articles were adopted into the 1949 Basic Law, the West German Constitution. The Basic Law continues to be interpreted as the expression of German values that the state should take active steps to promote. The furor over the Bavarian cross decision was thus aimed at a court seen as violating its obligation to promote Christian values.

German attitudes toward religion continue to be shaped by the idea that states could choose between established forms of religion, which meant in practice the Roman Catholic or Lutheran Churches. This historical background has led some Germans to strongly oppose the presence of new religions, or sects such as Scientology. These Germans see Scientology's claims to religious status as a cover for attempts to extract wealth from converts and have led state governments to limit the development of local Scientology branches. By the late 1990s the controversy had reached international proportions, with Scientologists taking out full-page ads in newspapers in the United States and elsewhere to protest German state suppression of religious freedom.

When Religion Underlies Law

So far, we have seen that states that we would think of as secular in fact are engaged in active dialogue, support, and often regulation vis-à-vis organized religious bodies. Now let me turn to the opposite end of the spectrum, societies (or subgroups within larger societies) that wish, and claim, to follow religious law. In Israel, Jewish courts enforce Jewish law, but the Knesset retains the capacity to define the legal conditions of enforcement. (And in North America, Jewish tribunals enjoy a sometimes ambiguous status with respect to civil courts.) In Indonesia, the state runs Islamic courts alongside civil ones, but the legislature and executive also set the ground rules for enforcement. Finally, in India judges make rulings in family law matters on the basis of the religion of the parties, but they have acted to move interpretations of religious law, particularly Hindu and Islamic, toward more gender-equal terms.

In these and other cases we cannot simply say that the state enforces religious law; the state, and specific individuals and groups with state functions, also interpret, modify, and condition the application of religious norms. Religion remains within the confines of a political system, and thus we may consider these states to be secular and, to contain a political sphere with its own autonomous norms and procedures.

Gender and Marriage in Israeli Jewish Law

Although in some respects Moses holds the place in Judaism that Muhammad does in Islam, in fact the lives of the two prophets play very different roles with respect to modern authority and law. Muhammad's life casts a very direct and very specific shadow over daily decisions made by jurists, who base their decisions on his statements and actions. Moses delivered the first five books of the Hebrew Bible to his people as the original Torah, but at that point his life made no additional contributions to Jewish scripture.

The Torah has since had a life of its own, accruing layers upon layers of commentary. Indeed, the term *torah* today can refer to the first five books of the Hebrew Bible, or to the entire Bible, or to both the Bible as written Torah and the "oral Torah," further commandments handed to Moses and embodied today in biblical commentaries.

As we saw in Chapter 12, each commandment in the Torah requires elaboration to make it specific and exceptions to adapt it to changing conditions of life. For example, the commandment to do no work on the Sabbath has required jurists to specify which activities count as work and which do not. The consensus today has it that certain activities, such as carrying an infant or pushing a wheelchair, constitute work when in public but not when in private. Because most Jews consider these particular activities essential even on the Sabbath (when babies and older people also attend worship services), authorities have created nominally private spaces, called *eruv*, within which the activities may still be carried out without violating religious law.

For some Jews, then, understanding Torah and living a religious life requires the interpretive intervention of religious authorities. For certain matters, such as resolving disputes and performing marriages, Jews living in many parts of the world have long had recourse to religious courts. In the Ottoman Empire, Jews had rabbinical courts, empowered to decide matters of marriage and divorce as well as such ritual issues as "carrying on the Sabbath." The courts continued to hold this authority under the British Mandate (1917–1948) and in the post-1948 state of Israel. Israel has continued the Ottoman practice of providing a certain degree of legal autonomy and distinct religious courts to each religious community, including Jews and Muslims.

The place of Jewish law remains contested, however (Edelman 1994). Officially, Israel is a nonconfessional state, meaning that no religion enjoys exclusive state support. The parliament, or Knesset, has final authority over all matters, including religious ones. The law regulating the rabbinical courts, passed in 1953, stipulates that marriage and divorce of Jews will be handled by the courts "in accordance with Jewish law." But who is to interpret Jewish law? Prior to the creation of the Israeli state, political leaders had already committed themselves to granting this authority to Orthodox rabbis, who controlled the courts. In 1947, the executive body preparing for statehood entered into an agreement with an Orthodox body, the Agudah movement, stipulating that the new state would respect the Sabbath, require observance of dietary laws (*kashrut*) in all state institutions, maintain the authority of the rabbinical courts over matters of personal status (especially marriage and divorce), and establish religious schools.

How the remainder of social life would be regulated was left open, and the issue continues to inflame passions on both sides. Many Orthodox Jews see Israel as too secular and try to change social life through direct intervention, some even blocking off streets to traffic during the Sabbath to ensure that Jews follow the law. These men and women see most secular Jews as threatening Israel's distinctive character as a Jewish society. Most of Israel's Jewish citizens indeed consider themselves nonreligious, and they want the freedom to dress as they wish and to drive and visit restaurants and theaters when they wish, including on the Sabbath. They see the Orthodox rabbis as threatening their freedoms. Most of them think that Israel should retain its Jewish character as long as individuals may choose not to observe certain religious rules. What should the character of public life then be? The issue remains subject to debate and, at times, public confrontations.

The same tension emerges over the law to be applied in courts. The Knesset has ruled that the rabbinical courts must decide certain matters, such as the age of marriage, in accord with the statutes passed by the Knesset. Civil courts recognize all marriages conducted outside of Israel if they are in accord with the laws of the land, even if they are not conducted in accord with Jewish law. The rabbinical courts have responded to these pressures by becoming less flexible in their interpretations of religious law, especially on matters of marriage and divorce. Israel has no institutions of civil marriage, and Jews may only be married by an Orthodox rabbi. Jews may not marry non-Jews, nor may they marry people not properly (according to Orthodox rabbis) divorced.

Two resulting problematical questions in Israel (and among Jews in the United States) are: Who is a Jew? and What is divorce? Orthodox authorities accept as Jews only those persons whose maternal lineage (ties through women, starting with one's mother) contains only Jews, or those persons who converted to Judaism under the guidance of an Orthodox rabbi. Thus, many U.S. converts are not recognized as Jews in Israel, and children of Jewish fathers whose mothers either converted or are non-Jews are similarly denied Jewish status for purposes of marriage. But the Israeli government itself recognizes as a Jew anyone sincerely and plausibly identifying himself or herself as a Jew.

This disparity in definition has led to anomalies, such as the treatment of the 35,000 Ethiopian Jews airlifted to Israel in 1984 and 1990. These men and women were granted Israeli citizenship as Jews under the 1950 Law of Return. But the rabbinical courts refused to marry them unless they underwent conversion (and, for the men, recircumcision) on grounds that in the past their ancestors may have married non-Jews. The Ethiopian issue was further complicated by accusations of racism. At one point it was revealed that the blood banks had thrown out all blood donated by the Ethiopians for fear it was tainted with HIV. Finally, the rabbinical courts created a special court to allow Ethiopian Jews to marry among themselves, but still refused to permit them to marry other Jews (Edelman 1994).

Divorce presents additional problems in the gendered nature of Jewish law. Israel recognizes no civil divorce. Jews can obtain a divorce only from the rabbinical court, and the court recognizes divorce only when the husband presents his wife with a document called a *get*. The document, written in a combination of Hebrew and Aramaic, proclaims the husband's act of "releasing" his wife from the marriage. The court must authorize the divorce but cannot deliver the get in the husband's name. (They can imprison a husband if he refuses to grant the divorce but he may still refuse to do so.) If both parties agree to the divorce, then no problem arises. But when the husband refuses to grant it, the wife is unable to remarry. In other countries, including the United States, the Orthodox wife is placed in an anomalous status: she may obtain a civil divorce and legally remarry—and some women do so—but then she is considered by the rabbis to have committed adultery (Breitowitz 1993; Meislin 1981).

Islamic Law in Indonesia

Now I turn to a Muslim society that grants distinct legal rights to citizens on the basis of their religion. Does the claim that Islamic law is based on the Qur'ân and the hadîth (reports of deeds and actions by the Prophet Muhammad) mean that Islamic law is alongside or outside the state? I will argue that, for Indonesia, it is considerations of equity and equality that drive the state and its judges to maintain control over the interpretation of how Islamic law is to be applied. I suggest that this hierarchy of state law over religious law is not unique to Indonesia, but characterizes the workings, if not the explicit policy, of some other countries with Islamic legal systems.

One might expect that some states granting formal autonomy to religious law for some persons would retain their prerogatives to at least modify religious norms, if not overrule them, if they infringed on certain rights. Several sources of normative pressure make such expectation reasonable. International conventions on human rights and women's rights, internal pressures from civil society organizations, and developments within the interpretation of religious law may converge to urge states to adopt such measures. In legally pluralistic states, those that recognize more than one set of legally binding norms applicable to distinct segments of the citizenry, considerations of cross-segment fairness may exert such pressure.

All these sources are in evidence for Indonesia, as described below, but the reforms in Islamic law regarding women's rights in many Muslim-majority societies have meant a partial, de facto convergence of several countries in the way Islamic laws regarding marriage and divorce are applied. Sometimes these reforms are visible in codes, as in the recent case of the reform of the Moroccan code; in other instances they are only discernable through the study of judicial practice, as in Egypt and Iran. My argument is not that equality is thereby achieved, but that a sense that discrimination against women should be at least reduced, if not eliminated, motivates many of these reforms, and that the reforms take place via the state's reserved right to modify how religious law is applied.

Indonesia has an Islamic court system that runs parallel to its system of civil courts (Bowen 2003). Each system hears civil cases in the first instance and on appeal, and allows requests for cassation to be made to the Supreme Court. The Islamic courts only hear cases brought by Muslims. They give legal sanction to marriages and divorces and can hear disputes over inheritance or the division of property upon divorce. The civil courts hear all other types of civil cases and all criminal ones, and also cases involving marriage, divorce, or inheritance brought by non-Muslims. (Special courts also exist for administrative, military, and commercial matters.) The demand for a separate Islamic judiciary was made in part as the right of Muslims to seek a remedy for the discrimination they had suffered at the hands of the Dutch. Islamic judges or tribunals existed in parts of what was then the Dutch East Indies, and in the nineteenth century the Dutch created uniform tribunals on Java and Madura. But in 1937 the government withdrew the rights of those tribunals to hear inheritance disputes, on grounds that Islam was not the source of the "living law" in Indonesia. The 1989 law creating the courts was thus hailed by some as putting an end to this history of discrimination against a religious group.

More broadly, Indonesia grants distinct rights to its citizens depending on their declared religious confession. The state not only grants legal recognition to Islam, along with a small number of other official religions, but also requires that each citizen declare, and indicate on his or her identity card, a recognized religion. (The list was recently extended to include Confucianism.)

If the Islamic courts are limited in jurisdiction to cases involving Muslims, the civil courts not only hear cases involving any and all Indonesians, but also emphasize the multireligious nature of the country and of its justice. I recall the manner in which one chief judge of a local civil court in Aceh asked each witness to state his or her religion (required at the swearing-in). When each responded "Islam", he would say *kebetulan*, "as it happens," in order to make of this simple and routine question a didactic moment, an occasion to remind his audience that in his court one might find Christians or Hindus testifying or litigating as well as Muslims, and that this was the nature of justice in Indonesia.

However, the segmentation of the court system also created problems, in part because it suggested that with respect to family law people could be easily separated into two distinct and sealed communities. Muslims would have their affairs regulated in one court, and those of all other faiths in the other. This idea has two types of difficulties associated with it. First, it creates practical problems whenever a couple or family contains people of different religions, or, more precisely, one or more Muslims and one or more people of another religion, or when a Muslim wishes to marry a non-Muslim. No solution yet exists that would allow marriages of Muslims to non-Muslims to be registered in Indonesia. Secondly, it may reduce the degree to which people consider themselves citizens first and Muslims, or Christians, second.

Convergence of Norms

In most respects, jurists and politicians in Indonesia have worked to develop avenues along which Islamic law can converge with general norms of interreligious tolerance and human rights. These norms date back at least to statements made by the Indonesian Supreme Court in the 1950s that the new "living law" in Indonesia was one in which men and women had equal rights. Efforts to reinterpret Islamic law so as to guarantee equal rights for women are far from complete, but were important in bringing about substantive reform in marriage, divorce, and post-divorce property settlements. These reforms were within the context of Islamic jurisprudence rather than against it.

Divorce provides a good example of how the state could promote Islamic law and at the same time work to limit discrimination against women within Islam. Current Indonesian divorce law for Muslims did not change the Islamic understanding of how a person brings about a divorce. In that understanding, as a religious law expert or an ordinary person might describe it, the acts brought by a man and those brought by a woman are not equivalent. A husband unilaterally repudiates his wife by uttering the *talaq*, which is valid upon utterance. A wife must appeal to a judge to grant an annulment (*fask*). (There are other categories but they are much less frequently applied in Indonesia.)

However, the substantial conditions for granting a divorce are the same in the two cases. In both cases the initiating party must appear before a judge and demonstrate that one of a specified number of reasons for divorce has been met. The reasons are the same whether the action was brought by the husband or by the wife. The judge may then either grant the wife a divorce, or allow the husband to pronounce the divorce formula. The same Indonesian legal terms for "divorce" are used in the two cases, thus masking the underlying Islam-based formal law asymmetry. All property acquired during a marriage, regardless of title, is divided equally between the husband and wife.

Islamic law experts state that these conditions simply limit how God's word is carried out without contravening it. Most make the same judgment concerning current laws on polygamy, which stipulate that a judge must approve a polygamous marriage before it is legal, and that the first wife must approve of the second marriage, although during the early 2000s there has been a sharp public debate concerning polygamy.

This process of convergence allows different advocates to continue to adhere to their respective, conflicting universalistic positions. Advocates of international human rights and women's rights can insist that men and women enjoy just and equitable judgments. They can point to the changes in Islamic legal practices brought about by Indonesian law as measures to combat discrimination against women—although many would press for the abolition of polygamy. Advocates of Islamic rights and duties can insist that Muslims obey God's commands as set out through the Qur'ân and through the words and deeds of the Prophet Muhammad. Indonesian law also meets this standard. In this way, two or more meta-normative claims, claims about the supremacy of one set of norms over another, can coexist.

Indian Courts and Religious Interpretation

India contributes in important ways to our understandings of secularism. India's constitution proclaims it to be a secular state, but the Indian version of secularism gives religion a central role. Moreover, India was politically and legally constructed around compromises intended to keep various minorities, regions, and language groups enthusiastic about the project of forging a nation.

In the domain of law, these compromises produced what we could call a multicultural or multireligious approach to family law. As is the case with Israel, Indonesia, and some other countries, India directs judges to adjudicate cases regarding marriage, divorce, and certain other aspects of family life in accord with the normative frameworks of one's religious or ethnic group. In India, these groups include Hindus, Muslims, Christians, and members of certain tribes. India's legal system also includes community courts, mosque assemblies, and other sources of law, all subject to appeal within the court system. Judges draw on jurisprudence, statutes, international law, the religious traditions of each religion, and other sources.

Indian judges therefore must decide which body of religious law governs the lives of a particular person or family. When judging a Muslim couple, they must determine which legal school (*madhhab*) the couple follows. Most Muslims follow the Hanafi school of Sunni Islam, but some are Shiites and in southern India some are governed by the Shafi'i Sunni school. These differences make a difference in some family law disputes; for example, if a Shia woman initiates divorce proceedings, she may be allowed to keep the wealth given to her at marriage, the dower, whereas if she were Sunni (whether Hanafi or Shafi'i) she could not keep this wealth.

Because judges also draw on broader bodies of religious and international law, they have been able to inflect older religious norms in new directions, and in many instances they have rendered religious laws more mindful of gender equality. For example, they now require that Muslim husbands pay their ex-wives alimony until they remarry, rather than, as the older practice required, only three months of support. India's most famous recent civil case, in 1985, touched on this issue. Judges awarded a woman named Shah Bano "permanent alimony" (until remarriage or death) and, moreover, they castigated Muslims for discrimination against women. The subsequent uproar by some Muslims led the legislature to pass an act that limited the period of post-divorce payment to the traditional three months. However, the wording of the law led some judges to subsequently rule that the ex-husband must pay, within three months, a sum substantial enough to provide for his ex-wife until she might remarry! The Supreme Court subsequently confirmed this interpretation.

What has led India's judges to push religious law, Hindu as well as Muslim, in a direction favoring gender equality? One reason surely lies in the relatively progressive nature of judicial culture, but another is the effect of political competition, as some Muslim leaders found in gender-equal views the most effective retort to Hindu nationalist attacks on Islam.

More broadly, as we saw earlier in this book, India's citizens draw on alternative narratives to think about their nation (as do citizens of most nations), including narratives of Indian secularism and a Hindu India. (Thinking about a Muslim nation was displaced onto Pakistan.) Secularism in India promises to keep the state neutral with respect to religions (and in that respect resembles U.S. secularism). The constitution and the positions of most political parties grant equal citizenship rights to all Indians regardless of religious affiliation. India's national movement, associated with Mahatma Gandhi and Jawaharlal Nehru, proclaimed this vision of India, and Nehru's Congress Party is its main standard-bearer.

Hindu nationalism, by contrast, reaches back to a Hindu past to construct images and stories of India's greatness. It has its counterpart in Islamic nationalism, and portrays the creation of Muslim Pakistan as implying that India ought to embody Hinduism. Because over 80 percent of Indians are Hindu, say the advocates of Hindu unity, they ought to set the agenda for politics and society. Now, India's Hindus do not constitute a single political block. Hindus are sharply divided along local caste lines, and often Muslims and lower-caste Hindus form electoral alliances against upper-caste Hindus. But the call for Hindu unity (Hindutva) is intended precisely to forge an all-Hindu alliance despite these divisions.

For Muslim judges and jurists, finding gender-equal versions of Islam afford the best means to argue that Islamic law can have a place in a secular Indian political system. As with their Indonesian counterparts, the Indian legal experts have found ways to apply Islam while recalibrating to fit global norms of equal justice.

Secularism, Faith, and Toleration

When in the 1660s, John Locke wrote his *Essay on Toleration,* he argued for equal rights of conscience for all Protestants, on grounds that the Sovereign could not know what was in their minds and that in any case dissenting Protestants, those not in the Church of England, did not trouble public order. Catholics, obedient to the Pope, and atheists, whose oaths could not be believed, were not included in this plea. In the United States, our early notions of religious toleration today look similar to Locke's and thus quite narrow. It took special promises by John F. Kennedy that he would not listen to the Pope first and foremost to make possible his election, and we have yet to see a Jewish, much less Muslim, president.

If today, then, societies in Europe and North America are relatively accepting of religious diversity, this acceptance is but the result of a recent and often hard-fought battle for religious toleration. I would argue that it is some form of secularism that best permits and pushes a broadening of religious toleration in all countries, and that we need to see secularism as also permitting religious practice. Secularism need not imply antagonism to religions; understood as the political guarantor of equal treatment and respect, secularism may be and probably is the best way to guarantee freedom of religious beliefs and practices. It is, as I hope I have shown, not inimical to the application of religious law or, to put it more precisely, state law that has been inspired by religious traditions and norms.

This particular set of studies and issues reminds us, once, again, that it is only when we look beneath the surface of slogans and ideologies—French laïcité, Indonesian Islamic law—that we appreciate how, in practice, people interpret and live their ideas of what religion is and should be.

References

Abou El Fadl, Khaled (1994). Islamic law and Muslim minorities: The Juristic discourse on Muslim minorities from the second/eighth to the eleventh/seventeenth centuries. *Islamic Law and Society, 1*(2), 143–187.

Abou El Fadl, Khaled (2001). *Speaking in God's name: Islamic law, authority and women.* Oxford: Oneworld.

Ainsworth, Mary D. S. (1967). *Infancy in Uganda: Infant care and the growth of love.* Baltimore: Johns Hopkins University Press.

Alexander, Jeffrey C. (1982). *The antimonies of classical thought: Marx and Durkheim.* Los Angeles: University of California Press.

Ammerman, Nancy Tatom (1987). *Bible believers: Fundamentalists in the modern world.* New Brunswick, N.J.: Rutgers University Press.

Apter, Andrew (1993). Atinga revisited: Yoruba witchcraft and the cocoa economy, 1950–1951. In Jean Comaroff and John Comaroff (Eds.), *Modernity and its malcontents* (pp. 111–128). Chicago: University of Chicago Press.

Ariès, Philippe (1974). *Western attitudes toward death: From the Middle Ages to the present.* Baltimore: Johns Hopkins University Press.

Atkinson, Jane Monnig (1983). Religions in dialogue: The construction of an Indonesian minority religion. *American Ethnologist, 10,* 684–696.

Atkinson, Jane Monnig (1987). The effectiveness of shamans in an Indonesian ritual. *American Anthropologist, 89,* 342–355.

Atkinson, Jane Monnig (1989). *The art and politics of Wana shamanship.* Los Angeles: University of California Press.

Auslander, Mark (1993). "Open the wombs!": The symbolic politics of modern Ngoni witchfinding. In Jean Comaroff and John Comaroff (Eds.), *Modernity and its malcontents* (pp. 167–192). Chicago: University of Chicago Press.

Babb, Lawrence A. (1983). Destiny and responsibility: Karma in popular Hinduism. In Charles F. Keyes and E. Valentine Daniel (Eds.), *Karma: An anthropological inquiry* (pp. 163–181). Los Angeles: University of California Press.

Babb, Lawrence A. (1986). *Redemptive encounters: Three modern styles in the Hindu tradition.* Los Angeles: University of California Press.

Baldwin, Tom (2007). Creationist museum brings dinosaurs on board Noah's Ark. *The Times,* May 28, 2007.

Barker, John (1993). We are Eklesia: Conversion in Uiaku, Papua New Guinea. In Robert W. Hefner (Ed.). *Conversion to Christianity: Historical and anthropological perspectives on a great transformation* (pp. 199–230). Berkeley: University of California Press.

Barth, Fredrik (1987). *Cosmologies in the making: A generative approach to cultural variation in inner New Guinea.* Cambridge: Cambridge University Press.

Bastian, Misty L. (1993). "Bloodhounds who have no friends": Witchcraft and locality in the Nigerian popular press. In Jean Comaroff and John Comaroff (Eds.), *Modernity and its malcontents* (pp. 129–166). Chicago: University of Chicago Press.

Bateson, Gregory (1958). *Naven* (2nd ed.). Stanford: Stanford University Press.

Bauman, Richard (1983). *Let your words be few: Symbolism of speaking and silence among seventeenth-century Quakers.* Cambridge: Cambridge University Press.

Bax, Mart (1991). Marian apparitions in Medjugorje: Rivaling religious regimes and state-formation in

Yugoslavia. In Eric R. Wolf (Ed.), *Religious regimes and state-formation* (pp. 29–53). Albany: State University of New York Press.

Bayart, Jeans-François. (1989). *L'État en Afrique: la politique du ventre.* Paris: Fayard.

Becker, Penny Edgell (1999). *Congregations in conflict.* Cambridge University Press.

Bell, Diane (1981). "Women's business is hard work: Central Australian aboriginal women's love rituals." *Signs, 7*(2): 314–337.

Berkey, Jonathan Porter (2003). *The formation of Islam: Religion and Society in the Near East, 600–1800.* Cambridge: Cambridge University Press.

Berman, Harold J. (1990). Religious freedom and the challenge of the modern state. In James Davison Hunter and Os Guiness (Eds.), *Articles of faith, articles of peace* (pp. 40–53). Washington, D.C.: The Brookings Institution.

Bloch, Maurice (1982). Death, women and power. In Maurice Bloch and Jonathan Parry (Eds.), *Death and the regeneration of life* (pp. 211–230). Cambridge: Cambridge University Press.

Bloch, Maurice, and Jonathan Parry (1982). Introduction: Death and the regeneration of life. In Maurice Bloch and Jonathan Parry (Eds.), *Death and the regeneration of life* (pp. 1–44). Cambridge: Cambridge University Press.

Boddy, Janice (1989). *Wombs and alien spirits: Women, men, and the Zár cult in Northern Sudan.* Madison: University of Wisconsin Press.

Bohlen, Celestine (1995). Crying Madonna, blood and many, many tears. *New York Times,* April 8, 1995, A4.

Bokser, Baruch M. (1984). *The origins of the Seder.* Los Angeles: University of California Press.

Boon, James A. (1990). *Affinities and extremes.* Chicago: University of Chicago Press.

Bossy, John (1983). The mass as a social institution, 1200–1700. *Past and Present, 100,* 29–61.

Bourdieu, Pierre (1990). *The logic of practice.* (Orig. French 1980) (Richard Nice, Trans.) Stanford: Stanford University Press.

Bourdieu, Pierre (1998). *Practical reason: On the theory of action.* (Orig. French 1994.)

Bowen, John R. (1991). *Sumatran politics and poetics: Gayo history, 1900–1989.* New Haven, Conn.: Yale University Press.

Bowen, John R. (1993). *Muslims through discourse: Religion and ritual in Gayo society.* Princeton, N.J.: Princeton University Press.

Bowen, John R. (1996). The myth of global ethnic conflict. *Journal of Democracy, 7*(4), 3–14.

Bowen, John R. (2003). *Islam, law and equality in Indonesia: An anthropology of public reasoning.* Cambridge: Cambridge University Press.

Bowen, John R. (2007). *Why the French don't like headscarves.* Princeton: Princeton University Press.

Bowlby, John (1980). *Loss: Sadness and depression.* New York: Basic Books.

Boyer, Pascal (2000). Functional origins of religious concepts: Ontological and strategic selection in evolved minds. *Journal of the Royal Anthropological Institute, 6*(2): 195–214.

Boyer, Pascal (2001). *Religion Explained.* New York: Basic Books.

Boyer, Paul, and Stephen Nissenbaum (1974). *Salem possessed: The social origins of witchcraft.* Cambridge, Mass.: Harvard University Press.

Breitowitz, Irving A. (1993). *Between civil and religious law: The plight of the Agunah in American society.* Westport, Conn.: Greenwood Press.

Brison, Karen J. (1992). *Just talk: Gossip, meetings, and power in a Papua New Guinea village.* Los Angeles: University of California Press.

Brown, Diana DeG. (1986). *Umbanda: Religion and politics in urban Brazil.* Ann Arbor, Mich.: UMI Research Press.

Brown, Karen McCarthy (1987). Alourdes: A case study of moral leadership in Haitian vodou. In John Stratton Hawley (Ed.), *Saints and virtues* (pp. 144–167). Los Angeles: University of California Press.

Brown, Peter (1987). The saint as exemplar in late antiquity. In John Stratton Hawley (Ed.), *Saints and virtues* (pp. 3–14). Los Angeles: University of California Press.

Brubaker, Rogers, and David D. Laitin (1998). Ethnic and nationalist violence. *Annual Review of Sociology 24*: 423–452.

Brzezinski, Matthew (1994). Pilgrimage to Poland's holiest shrine losing its political role. *New York Times,* August 30, 1994, A12.

Burns, John F. (1997). Gandhi's ashes rest, but not his message. *New York Times,* January 31, 1997, A1, A8.

Burns, J. Patout (1994). The atmosphere of election: Augustinianism as common sense. *Journal of Early Christian Studies, 2*(3), 325–339.

Bynum, Caroline Walker (1987). *Holy feast and holy fast: The religious significance of food to medieval women.* Los Angeles: University of California Press.

Caldwell, Peter C. (1996). The crucifix and German constitutional culture. *Cultural Anthropology, 11*(2), 259–273.

Cannon, Walter B. (1942). "Voodoo" death. *American Anthropologist, 54,* 169–181.

Casanova, José (1994). *Public religions in the modern world.* Chicago: University of Chicago Press.

Cesari, Jocelyne (1994). *When islam and democracy meet: Muslims in Europe and in the United States.* New York: Palgrave Macmillan.

Cesari, Jocelyne (1998). *Musulmans et républicains: Les jeunes, l'islam et la France.* Brussels: Éditions Complexe.

Chodorow, Nancy (1974). Family structure and feminine personality. In Michelle Z. Rosaldo and Louise Lamphere (Eds.), *Women, culture and society.* Stanford: Stanford University Press.

Christian, William A., Jr. (1984). Religious apparitions and the cold war in southern Europe. In Eric R. Wolf (Ed.), *Religion, power and protest in local communities: The northern shore of the Mediterranean* (pp. 239–266). Berlin: Mouton.

Christian, William A., Jr. (1989). *Person and god in a Spanish valley* (rev. ed.). Princeton, N.J.: Princeton University Press. (Original work published 1972)

Clark, Francis (1967). *Eucharistic sacrifice and the reformation.* Oxford: Basil Blackwell.

Cohn, Norman (1970). *The pursuit of the millennium* (rev. ed.). Oxford: Oxford University Press.

Collier, Jane F., and Michelle Zimbalist Rosaldo (1981). Politics and gender in simple societies. In Sherry B. Ortner and Harriet Whitehead (Eds.), *Sexual meanings* (pp. 275–329). Cambridge: Cambridge University Press.

Comaroff, Jean (1985). *Body of power, spirit of resistance.* Chicago: University of Chicago Press.

Comaroff, Jean, and John Comaroff (1986). "Christianity and colonialism in South Africa." *American Ethnologist, 13*(1): 1–22.

Comaroff, Jean, and John Comaroff (1991). *Of Revelation and revolution: Christianity, colonialism, and consciousness in South Africa.* Chicago: University of Chicago Press.

Comaroff, Jean, and John Comaroff (1997). *Of Revelation and revolution: The dialectics of modernity on a South African frontier.* Chicago: University of Chicago Press.

Conkey, Margaret W., and Sarah H. Williams (1991). Original narratives: The political economy of gender in archeology. In Micaela di Leonardo (Ed.), *Gender at the crossroads of knowledge: Feminist anthropology in the postmodern era* (pp. 102–139). Berkeley: University of California Press.

Conseil européen des fatwâs et de la recherché (2002). *Receuil de fatwas.* Lyon: Tawhid.

Covington, Dennis (1995). *Salvation on sand mountain: Snake handling and redemption in Southern Appalachia.* Reading, Mass.: Addison-Wesley.

Cragg, Kenneth (1980). *Islam from within: Anthology of a religion.* Belmont, Calif.: Wadsworth.

Danforth, Loring M. (1982). *The death rituals of rural Greece.* Princeton, N.J.: Princeton University Press.

Davis, Natalie Zemon (1965). *Society and culture in early modern France.* Stanford: Stanford University Press.

Davis, Winston (1980). *Dojo: Magic and exorcism in modern Japan.* Stanford: Stanford University Press.

Demos, John Putnam (1982). *Entertaining Satan: Witchcraft and the culture of early New England.* Oxford: Oxford University Press.

Doi, L. Takeo (1986). *Amae:* A key concept for understanding Japanese personality structure. In Takie Sugiyama Lebra and William P. Lebra (Eds.), *Japanese culture and behavior* (rev. ed., pp. 121–129). Honolulu: University of Hawaii Press. (Original work published 1962)

Douglas, Mary (1966). The abominations of Leviticus. In Mary Douglas (Ed.), *Purity and danger* (pp. 41–57). London: Routledge & Kegan Paul.

Durkheim, Émile (1995). *The elementary forms of the religious life* (Karen E. Fields, Trans.). New York: The Free Press. (Original work published 1912)

Durkheim, Émile, and Marcel Mauss (1963). *Primitive classification* (Rodney Needhamn, Trans.). Chicago: University of Chicago Press. (Original work published 1903)

Earhart, H. Byron (1982). *Japanese religion: Unity and diversity* (3rd ed.). Belmont, Calif.: Wadsworth.

Eck, Diana L. (1982). *Banaras: City of light.* Princeton, N.J.: Princeton University Press.

Edelman, Martin (1994). *Courts, politics, and culture in Israel.* Charlottesville: University Press of Virginia.

Edwards, David B. (2002). *Before Taliban: Genealogies of the Afghan jihad.* Berkeley: University of California Press.

Eickelman, Dale F. (1976). *Moroccan Islam: Tradition and society in a pilgrimage center.* Austin: University of Texas Press.

Eickelman, Dale F. (1985). *Knowledge and power in Morocco*. Princeton, N.J.: Princeton University Press.

Eickelman, Dale F. (1992). Mass higher education and the religious imagination in contemporary Arab societies. *American Ethnologist 19*(4): 643–655.

Eickelman, Dale F. (1999). Communication and control in the Middle East: Publication and its discontents. In Dale F. Eickelman and Jon Anderson (Eds.), *New media in the Muslim world: The emerging public sphere* (pp. 29–40). Bloomington: Indiana University Press.

Eisenlohr, Patrick (2007). *Little India: Diaspora, time, and ethnolinguistic belonging in Hindu Mauritius*. Berkeley: University of California Press.

Eliade, Mircea (1954). *The myth of the eternal return*. Princeton, N.J.: Princeton University Press. (Original work published 1949)

Engels, Friedrich (1956). *The peasant war in Germany*. Moscow: Progress. (Original work published 1850)

Europol (2007). *EU Terrorism Situation and Trend Report*.

Evans-Pritchard, E. E. (1937). *Witchcraft, oracles and magic among the Azande*. Oxford: Clarendon Press.

Evans-Pritchard, E. E. (1956). *Nuer religion*. Oxford: Clarendon Press.

Fearon, James D., and David D. Laitin (2003). Ethnicity, insurgency, and civil war. *The American Political Science Review, 97*(1), 75–90.

Feeley-Harnik, Gillian (1981). *The Lord's table: Eucharist and passover in early Christianity*. Philadelphia: University of Pennsylvania Press.

Ferguson, R. Brian (1990). "Explaining the War." In J. Hass (Ed.), *The anthropology of war* (pp. 26–55). Cambridge: Cambridge University Press.

Fischer, Michael, and Mehdi Abedi (1990). *Debating Muslims: Cultural dialogues in tradition and postmodernity*. Madison: University of Wisconsin Press.

Flynn, Thomas J., M.D., and Charles B. Fulton, Th.D. (2002). Letter to the editor. *Journal of the American Medical Association, 288*(20), 2541.

Forbes, H. D. (1997). *Ethnic conflict: Commerce, culture, and the contact hypothesis*. New Haven: Yale University Press.

Foucault, Michel (1978). *The history of sexuality: An introduction*. New York: Pantheon Books.

Fox, Richard (1989). *Gandhian utopia: Experiments with culture*. Boston: Beacon Press.

Frankel, Marvin E. (1994). *Faith and freedom: Religious liberty in America*. New York: Hill and Wang.

Fraser, Caroline (1996). Mrs. Eddy builds her empire. *New York Times Book Review,* July 11, 1996, 53–59.

Frazer, James G. (1981). *The golden bough: The roots of religion and folklore*. New York: Avenel Books. (Original work published 1890)

French, Howard W. (1997). The ritual: Disfiguring, hurtful, wildly festive. *New York Times,* January 31, 1997, A4.

Freud, Sigmund (1930). *Civilization and its discontents*. London: Hogarth Press.

Freud, Sigmund (1989). *Totem and taboo*. New York: Norton.

Fuller, C. J. (1992). *The camphor flame: Popular Hinduism and society in India*. Princeton, N.J.: Princeton University Press.

Fuller, C. J. (2003). *The renewal of the priesthood: Modernity and traditionalism in a south indian temple*. Princeton: Princeton University Press.

Gardner, Katy (2002). *Age, narrative and migration: The life course and life histories of Bengali elders*. Oxford: Berg.

Geertz, Clifford (1960). *The religion of Java*. Chicago: University of Chicago Press.

Geertz, Clifford (1966). *Person, time, and conduct in Bali: An essay in cultural analysis*. New Haven, Conn.: Yale University, Southeast Asia Studies, Cultural Report Series No. 14.

Geertz, Clifford (1968). *Islam observed: Religious developments in Morocco and Indonesia*. New Haven, Conn.: Yale University Press.

Gerbrands, Adrian A. (1967). Art and artist in Asmat society. In Michael Rockefeller, *The Asmat of New Guinea*. A. Gerbrands (Ed.) (pp. 11–39). New York: Museum of Primitive Art.

Geschiere, Peter (1997). *The modernity of witchcraft: Politics and the occult in postcolonial Africa (Sorcellerie et politique en Afrique)*. Charlottesville, Va.: University Press of Virginia.

Gill, Sam (1981). *Sacred words: A study of Navajo religion and prayer*. Westport, Conn.: Greenwood Press.

Gill, Sam (1987). *Native American religious action: A performative approach to religion*. Columbia: University of South Carolina Press.

Gilovich, T., Vallone, R., and Tversky, A. (1985). The hot hand in basketball: On the misperception of random sequences. *Cognitive Psychology 17*: 295–314.

Gluckman, Max (1963). Rituals of rebellion in South East Africa. In Max Gluckman (Ed.), *Order and rebellion in tribal Africa* (pp. 110–137). London: Cohen & West.

Gmelch, George (1978). Baseball magic. *Human Nature,* 1(8).

Goheen, Miriam (1996). *Men own the fields, women own the crops.* Madison: University of Wisconsin.

Gold, Ann Grodzins (1988). *Fruitful journeys: The ways of Rajasthani pilgrims.* Los Angeles: University of California Press.

Golomb, Louis (1993). The relativity of magical malevolence in urban Thailand. In C. W. Watson and Roy Ellen (Eds.), *Understanding witchcraft and sorcery in Southeast Asia* (pp. 127–145). Honolulu: University of Hawaii Press.

Gombrich, Richard, and Gananath Obeyesekere (1988). *Buddhism transformed: Religious change in Sri Lanka.* Princeton, N.J.: Princeton University Press.

Goodman, Felicitas D. (1988). *How about demons? Possession and exorcism in the modern world.* Bloomington: Indiana University Press.

Graham, William A. (1987). *Beyond the written word: Oral aspects of scripture in the history of religion.* Cambridge: Cambridge University Press.

Guillermoprieto, Alma (1990). *Samba.* New York: Knopf.

Gujar, Ram Bhoju, and Gold Ann Grodzins (1992). From the research assistant's point of view. *Anthropology and Humanism Quarterly* 17(3), 72–84.

Haberman, Clyde (1988). Shinto is thrust back onto the nationalist stage. *New York Times,* June 7, 1988, A4.

Hall, John R., Philip D. Schuyler, and Sylvaine Trinh (2000). *Apocalypse observed: Religious movements and violence in North America, Europe, and Japan.* London and New York: Routledge.

Hammoudi, Abdellah (1993). *The victim and its masks.* Chicago: University of Chicago Press. (Original work published 1988)

Hardacre, Helen (1989). *Shinto and the state, 1868–1988.* Princeton, N.J.: Princeton University Press.

Harding, Susan Friend (2000). *The Book of Jerry Falwell: Fundamentalist language and politics.* Princeton, N.J.: Princeton University Press.

Harris, Lis (1985). *Holy days.* New York: Collier Books.

Harris, W. S., M. Gowda, and J. W. Kolb, et al. (1999). A randomized, controlled trial of the effects of remote, intercessory prayer on outcomes in patients admitted to the coronary care unit. *Archives of Internal Medicine, 159,* 2273–2278.

Hayden, Cori (2003). *When nature goes public.* Princeton: Princeton University Press

Hefner, Robert W. (1993). World building and the rationality of conversion. In Robert W. Hefner (Ed.), *Conversion to Christianity: Historical and anthropological perspectives on a great transformation* (pp. 3–44). Berkeley: University of California Press.

Helm, J., J. C. Hays, E. Flint, H. G. Koenig, and D. G. Blazer (2000). Effects of private religious activity on mortality of elderly disabled and nondisabled adults. *Journal of Gerontology* (Medical Sciences), 55A, M400–M405.

Herdt, Gilbert H. (1981). *Guardians of the flutes: Idioms of masculinity.* New York: McGraw-Hill.

Herdt, Gilbert H. (1982). Fetish and fantasy in Sambia initiation. In Gilbert H. Herdt (Ed.), *Rituals of manhood: Male initiation in Papua New Guinea* (pp. 44–98). Los Angeles: University of California Press.

Hertz, Robert (1960). *Death and the right hand* (Rodney and Claudia Needham, Trans.). New York: The Free Press. (Original work published 1907)

Hill, Christopher (1961). *The century of revolution, 1603–1714.* New York: W. W. Norton.

Hiltebeitel, Alf (1985). On the handling of the meat, and related matters, in two south Indian buffalo sacrifices. *L'Uomo: Societa Tradizione Sviluppo,* 9(1/2), 171–199.

Hinton, Alexander Laban, ed. (2002). *Annihilating difference: The anthropology of genocide.* Berkeley: University of Califoria Press.

Hirsch, Susan F. (1994). Kadhi's courts as complex sites of resistance: The state, Islam, and gender in postcolonial Kenya. In Mindie Lazarus-Black and Susan F. Hirsch (Eds.), *Contested states: Law, hegemony and resistance* (pp. 207–230). New York: Routledge.

Hume, David (1993). *Dialogues concerning natural religion* and *The natural history of religion.* Oxford: Oxford University Press. (Original works published 1779 and 1757)

Humphrey, Caroline, and James Laidlaw (1994). *The archetypal actions of ritual.* Oxford: Oxford University Press.

Hunter, James Davison (1990). Religious freedom and the challenge of modern pluralism. In James Davison Hunter and Os Guiness (Eds.), *Articles of faith, articles of peace* (pp. 54–73). Washington, D.C.: The Brookings Institution.

Introvigne, Massimo, and Jean-Francois Mayer (2002). Occult masters and the Temple of Doom: The fiery end of the Solar Temple. In D. G. Bromley and J. G. Melton (Eds.), *Cults, religion, and violence* (pp. 170–188). Cambridge: Cambridge University Press.

Jaeger, Werner (1961). *Early Christianity and Greek paideia.* Cambridge, Mass.: Harvard University Press.

James, William (1972). *Varieties of religious experience.* London: Fontana. (Original work published 1901–1902)

Journal of Ethnic and Migration Studies (2004). Special Issue on "Islam, Transnationalism and the Public Sphere in Western Europe," *30*(5).

Juergensmeyer, Mark (2003). *Terror in the mind of god: The global rise of religious violence* (3rd ed.). Berkeley: University of California Press.

Jung, Carl Gustav (1964). *Man and his symbols.* Garden City, N.Y.: Doubleday.

Kalb, Claudia (2003). Faith and healing. *Newsweek,* November 10, 2003, 44–56.

Kammerer, Cornelia Ann (1990). Customs and Christian conversion among Akha highlanders of Burma and Thailand. *American Ethnologist 17*(2), 277–291.

Kapferer, Bruce (1997). *The feast of the sorcerer: Practices of consciousness and power.* Chicago: University of Chicago Press.

Kapferer, Bruce (2003). *Beyond rationalism: Rethinking magic, witchcraft and sorcery.* New York: Bergahn Books.

Kastoryano, Riva (2002). *Negotiating identities: States and immigrants in France and Germany.* Princeton: Princeton University Press.

Katz, Richard (1982). *Boiling energy: Community healing among the Kalahari Kung.* Cambridge, Mass.: Harvard University Press.

Keane, Webb (2007). *Christian moderns: Freedom & fetish in the mission encounter.* Berkeley: University of California Press.

Keesing, Roger M. (1982). *Kwaio religion: The living and the dead in a Solomon Island society.* New York: Columbia University Press.

Kenyon, Susan M. (1995). *Zar* as modernization in contemporary Sudan. *Anthropological Quarterly 68*(2): 107–120.

Kepel, Gilles (1997). *Allah in the west: Islamic movements in America and Europe.* Stanford: Stanford University.

Kepel, Gilles (2002). *Jihad: The trail of political Islam.* Cambridge, Mass.: Harvard University Press.

Kinzer, Stephen (2003). Interest surges in voodoo, and its Queen. *New York Times,* November 20, 2003, A18.

Kipp, Rita Smith, and Susan Rodgers (1987). Introduction: Indonesian religions in society. In Rita Smith Kipp and Susan Rodgers (Eds.), *Indonesian religions in transition* (pp. 1–31). Tucson: University of Arizona Press.

Kluckhohn, Clyde (1967). *Navaho witchcraft.* Boston: Beacon Press. (Original work published 1944)

Knauft, Bruce M. (1985). *Good company and violence: Sorcery and social action in a lowland New Guinea society.* Berkeley: University of California Press.

Koenig, Harold G. (2002). An 83-year-old woman with chronic illness and strong religious beliefs. *Journal of the American Medical Association, 288*(4), 487–493.

Koenig, H. G., et al. (1992). Religious coping and depression in elderly hospitalized medically ill men. *American Journal of Psychiatry, 149,* 1693–1700.

Koenig, H. G., et al. (1997). Attendance at religious services, interleukin-6, and other biological indicators of immune function in older adults. *International Journal of Psychiatry in Medicine, 27,* 233–250.

Korom, Frank J. (2003). *Hosay Trinidad: Muharram Performances in an Indo-Caribbean diaspora.* Philadelphia: University of Pennsylvania Press.

Kraybill, Donald B. (1989). *The riddle of Amish culture.* Baltimore: Johns Hopkins University Press.

Kuruwaip, Abraham (1974). The Asmat bis pole: Its background and meaning. *Irian, 3*(2), 32–78.

Kymlicka, Will (1995). *Multicultural citizenship.* Oxford: Oxford University Press.

La Barre, Weston (1964). The snake-handling cult of the American Southeast. In Ward H. Goodenough (Ed.), *Explorations in cultural anthropology* (pp. 309–333). New York: McGraw-Hill.

Laderman, Carol (1983). *Wives and midwives: Childbirth and nutrition in rural Malaysia.* Los Angeles: University of California Press.

Lafaye, Jacques (1976). *Quetzalcoatl and Guadalupe: The formation of Mexican national consciousness 1531–1813* (Benjamin Keen, Trans.). Chicago: University of Chicago Press.

La Fontaine, J. S. (1985). *Initiation.* Harmondsworth, UK: Penguin.

Landman, Nico (2002). Islam in the Benelux Countries. In Shireen T. Hunter (Ed.), *Islam, Europe's second religion* (pp. 97–120). Westport, CT: Praeger.

Latour, Bruno (1993). *We have never been modern.* Cambridge: Harvard University Press.

Leibovich, Lori (2000). The online religion with shopping, too. *New York Times,* April 6, 2000, D1, D10.

Leishman, Thomas Linton (1958). *Why I am a Christian Scientist.* New York: Thomas Nelson & Sons.

Lester, Rebecca J. (2005). *Jesus in our wombs: Embodying modernity in a Mexican community.* Berkeley: University of California Press.

Lévi-Strauss, Claude (1963a). *Totemism* (Rodney Needham, Trans.). Boston: Beacon Press. (Original work published 1962)

Lévi-Strauss, Claude (1963b). The effectiveness of symbols. In C. Lévi-Strauss, *Structural anthropology* (pp. 180–201). (Claire Jacobson and Brooke Grundfest Schoepf, Trans.). Garden City, N.Y.: Anchor Books. (Original work published 1949)

Lévi-Strauss, Claude (1976). The Story of Asdiwal. In C. Lévi-Strauss, *Structural anthropology* (vol. 2, pp. 146–197). (Monique Layton, Trans.). Chicago: University of Chicago Press. (Original work published 1958)

Lewis, Philip (2002). *Islamic Britain: Religion, politics, and identity among British Muslims* (3rd ed.). London: I. B. Tauris & Co. Ltd.

Lifton, Robert Jay (1986). *The Nazi doctors: Medical killing and the psychology of genocide.* New York: Basic Books.

Lofland, John, and Rodney Stark (1965). Becoming a world-saver: A theory of conversion to a devout perspective. *American Sociological Review, 30*(6), 862–875.

Lukes, Steven (1973). *Émile Durkheim: His life and work.* Harmondsworth, UK: Penguin.

Lutkehaus, Nancy C. (1995). Gender metaphors: Female rituals as cultural models in Manam. In Nancy C. Lutkehaus and Paul B. Roscoe (Eds.), *Gender rituals: Female initiation in Melanesia* (pp. 183–204). New York: Routledge.

MacCormack, Carol, and Marilyn Strathern (1980). *Nature, culture, and gender.* Cambridge: Cambridge University Press.

Mahmood, Saba (2005). *Politics of piety: The Islamic revival and the feminist subject.* Princeton: Princeton University Press.

Malcolm X (1973). *The autobiography of Malcolm X.* Alex Haley (Ed.), New York: Ballantine Books. (Original work published 1964)

Malinowski, Bronislaw (1954). Magic, science, and religion. In B. Malinowski, *Magic, science, and religion and other essays* (pp. 17–92). Garden City, N.Y.: Anchor Books. (Original work published 1926)

Mankekar, Purnima (1999). *Screening culture, viewing politics: An ethnography of television, womanhood, and nation in post-colonial India.* Durham, N.C.: Duke University Press.

Marx, Karl, and Friedrich Engels (1965). *The German ideology.* London: Lawrence & Wishart. (Original work published 1846)

Matory, Lorand J. (2005). *Black Atlantic religion: Tradition, transnationalism, and matriarchy in the Afro-Brazilian Candomblé.* Princeton: Princeton University Press.

Mayer, Ann Elizabeth (1990). The *Sharli'ah*: A methodology or a body of substantive rules? In Nicholas Heer (Ed.), *Islamic law and jurisprudence.* Seattle: University of Washington Press.

McNearney, Kelly (2002). Athletes believe rituals leading to winning games. *www.kusports.com/new/rowingstorypr/105011.*

McPherson, Robert S. (1992). *Sacred land, sacred view: Navajo perceptions of the four corners region.* Salt Lake City: Brigham Young University.

Meigs, Anna (1990). Multiple gender ideologies and statuses. In Peggy Reeves Sanday and Ruth Goodenough (Eds.), *Beyond the second sex.* Philadephia: University of Pennsylvania Press.

Meislin, Bernard J. (1981). Pursuit of the wife's right to a "*Get*" in United States and Canadian courts. *The Jewish Law Annual* (vol. 4). Kinderhook, N.Y.: E. J. Brill.

Metcalf, Barbara Daly (2001). "Traditionalist" Islamic Activism: Deoband, Tablighis, and Talibs. In Craig Calhoun, Paul Price, and Ashley Timmer (Eds.), *Understanding September 11.* New York: The New Press.

Metcalf, Peter (1982). *A Borneo journey into death.* Philadelphia: University of Pennsylvania Press.

Miller, Daniel, and Don Slater (2000). *The Internet: An ethnographic approach.* Oxford: Berg.

Miller, Perry (1956). *Errand into the wilderness.* Cambridge, Mass.: Harvard University Press.

Modood, Tariq (1994). Establishment, multiculturalism, and British citizenship. *Political Quarterly, 65*(1), 53–73.

Momen, Moojan (1985). *An introduction to Shi'i Islam.* New Haven, Conn.: Yale University Press.

Morris, Brian (1987). *Anthropological studies of religion.* Cambridge: Cambridge University Press.

Morrison, Michael (2003). Sports and the Number 13. *www.infoplease.com/spot/superstitions2.html.*

Moruzzi, Norma Claire (1994). A problem with headscarves: Contemporary complexities of political and social identity. *Political Theory, 22*(4), 653–672.

Murphy, Joseph S. (1994). *Working the spirit: Ceremonies of the African diaspora.* Boston: Beacon Press.

Nanda, Meera (2003). *Prophets facing backward: Postmodern critiques of science and Hindu nationalism in India.* New Brunswick, N.J.: Rutgers University Press.

Nations, Marilyn, and Linda-Anne Rebhun (1988). Angels with wet wings can't fly: Maternal sentiments in Brazil and the image of neglect. *Culture, Medicine, and Psychiatry, 12,* 141–200.

Nemeroff, Carol, and Paul Rozin (1992). Sympathetic magical beliefs and kosher dietary practice: The interaction of rules and feelings. *Ethos, 20,* 96–115.

Newberg, Andrew B., Eugene G. D'Aquili, and Vince Rause (2001). *Why God won't go away: Brain science and the biology of belief.* New York: Ballantine Books.

Nolan, Mary Lee, and Sidney Nolan (1989). *Christian pilgrimage in modern Western Europe.* Chapel Hill: The University of North Carolina Press.

Norton, Mary Beth (2003). *In the Devil's share: The Salem Witchcraft Crisis of 1692.* New York: Alfred A. Knopf.

Nuckolls, Charles W. (1998). *Culture: A problem that cannot be solved.* Madison: University of Wisconsin Press.

Obeyesekere, Gananath (1981). *Medusa's hair: An essay on personal symbols and religious experience.* Chicago: University of Chicago Press.

Oe, Kenzaburo (1995). The day the Emperor spoke in human voice. *New York Times Magazine,* May 7, 1995, 103–105.

Ortner, Sherry (1974). Is female to male as nature is to culture? In Michelle Rosaldo and Louise Lamphere, (Eds.), *Woman, culture, and society* (pp. 66–88). Stanford, CA: Stanford University Press.

Ortner, Sherry B. (1996). *Making gender: The politics and erotics of culture.* Boston: Beacon Press.

Ortner, Sherry B., and Harriet Whitehead (1981). *Sexual meanings: The cultural construction of gender and sexuality.* Cambridge: Cambridge University Press.

Palgi, Phyllis, and Henry Abramovitch (1984). Death: A cross-cultural perspective. *Annual Review of Anthropology, 13,* 385–417.

Pargament, K. I., H. G. Koenig, N. Tarakeshwar, and J. Hahn (2001). Religious struggle as a predictor of mortality among medically ill elderly patients: A two-year longitudinal study. *Archives of Internal Medicine, 161,* 1881–1885.

Parsons, Elsie C. (1939). *Pueblo Indian religion* (2 vols.). Chicago: University of Chicago Press.

Peacock, James L., and Ruel W., Jr. Tyson (1989). *Pilgrims of paradox: Calvinism and experience among the primitive Baptists of the Blue Ridge.* Washington, D.C.: Smithsonian Institution Press.

Peletz, Michael G. (1993). Knowledge, power and personal misfortune in a Malay context. In C. W. Watson and Roy Ellen (Eds.), *Understanding witchcraft and sorcery in Southeast Asia* (pp. 149–177). Honolulu: University of Hawaii Press.

Peters, F. E. (1994). *Muhammad and the origins of Islam.* Albany: State University of New York Press.

Peters, Rudolph (1996). *The jihad in classical and modern times.* Princeton, N.J.: Markus Wiener.

Pew Global Attitudes Project (2006). *The Great Divide: How Westerners and Muslims View Each Other,* http://pewglobal.org/reports/display.php?ReportID=253.

Plath, David W. (1964). Where the family of God is the family: The role of the dead in Japanese households. *American Anthropologist, 66,* 300–317.

Pocock, David F. (1973). *Mind, body, and wealth: A study of belief and practice in an Indian village.* Oxford: Blackwell.

Pollack, Andrew (1996). This way to peace of mind: 750 miles and 88 stops. *New York Times,* March 20, 1996, A4.

Pollock, Sheldon (1993). Ramayana and political imagination in India. *Journal of Asian Studies 52*(2): 261–297.

Poole, John Fitz Porter (1982). The ritual forging of identity: Aspects of person and self in Bimin-Kuskusmin male initiation. In Gilbert H. Herdt (Ed.), *Rituals of manhood: Male initiation in Papua New Guinea* (pp. 99–154). Los Angeles: University of California Press.

Povinelli, Elizabeth A. (1993). *Labor's lot: The power, history, and culture of aboriginal action.* Chicago: University of Chicago Press.

Prell, Riv-Ellen (1989). *Prayer and community: The havurah in American Judaism.* Detroit: Wayne State University Press.

Putnam, Robert (2000). *Bowling alone: The collapse and revival of American community.* New York: Simon & Schuster.

Qutb, Sayyid, and International Islamic Federation of Student Organizations (1978). *Milestones.* Beirut, Lebanon: Holy Koran Publishing House.

Radcliffe-Brown, A. R. (1965). Taboo. In Radcliffe-Brown (Ed.), *Structure and function in primitive society* (pp. 133–152). New York: The Free Press. (Original work published 1939)

Ramadan, Tariq (2002). *Dâr ash-shahâda: L'Occident, espace du témoignage.* Lyon: Tawhid.

Reader, Ian (2000). *Religious violence in contemporary Japan: The case of Aum Shinrikyo.* Honolulu: University of Hawaii Press.

Reader, Ian (1991). *Religion in contemporary Japan.* Honolulu: University of Hawaii Press.

Redfield, Robert (1956). *Peasant society and culture.* Chicago: University of Chicago Press.

Regan, Richard J. (1996). *Just war: Principles and cases.* Washington, D.C.: Catholic University Press of America.

Remnick, David (1992). Waiting for the apocalypse in Crown Heights. *The New Yorker,* December 21, pp. 52–57.

Richeport, Madeleine (1985). *Macumba, trance and spirit healing.* Film. New York: Filmmaker's Library.

Riding, Alan (1987). In Brazil, Evangelicals are on the rise. *New York Times,* October 25, 1987, A16.

Robinson, David (1985). *The Holy War of Umar Tal: The Western Sudan in the mid-nineteenth century.* Oxford: Clarendon.

Rogerson, J. W. (1980). Sacrifice in the Old Testament: Problems of method and approach. In M. F. C. Bourdillon and Meyer Fortes (Eds.), *Sacrifice* (pp. 45–59). London: Academic Press.

Rosaldo, Michelle Z. (1974). Woman, culture and society: A theoretical overview. In Michelle Z. Rosaldo and Louise Lamphere (Eds.), *Women, culture and society.* Stanford: Stanford University Press.

Rosaldo, Renato I. (1984). Grief and a headhunter's rage: On the cultural force of emotions. In Edward Bruner (Ed.), *Play, text, and story* (pp. 178–195). Washington, D.C.: American Ethnological Society.

Rosen, Lawrence (1989). *The anthropology of justice.* Cambridge: Cambridge University Press.

de Rosny, Eric (1992). *L'Afrique des guérisons.* Paris: Karthala.

Rothkrug, Lionel (1980). Religious practice and collective perceptions: Hidden homologies in the Renaissance and Reformation. *Historical Reflections, 7*(1).

Roy, Oliver (1994). *The failure of political Islam.* Cambridge, Mass.: Harvard University Press.

Ruthven, Malisa (1984). *Islam in the world.* New York: Oxford University Press.

Sageman, Marc (2004). *Understanding terror networks.* Philadelphia: University of Pennsylvania Press.

Sahlins, Marshall (1985). *Islands of history.* Chicago: University of Chicago Press.

Sanders, Todd (2000). Rains gone bad, women gone mad: Rethinking gender rituals of rebellion and patriarchy. *Journal of the Royal Anthropological Institute* (N.S.) 6: 469–486.

Sanger, David E. (1990). For a job well done, Japanese enshrine the chip. *New York Times,* December 11, 1990, A4.

Saunders, E. Dale (1964). *Buddhism in Japan.* Philadelphia: University of Pennsylvania Press.

Sayle, Murray (1996). Nerve gas and the four noble truths. *The New Yorker,* April 1, 1996.

Schauss, Hayyim (1938). *The Jewish festivals: History and observance.* New York: Schocken Books.

Scheper-Hughes, Nancy (1992). *Death without weeping: The violence of everyday life in Brazil.* Los Angeles: University of California Press.

Schiffauer, Werner (1996). Islamic vision and social reality: The political culture of Sunni Muslims in Germany. In Steven Vertovec and Ceri Peach (Eds.), *Islam in Europe: The politics of religion and community* (pp. 156–176). Houndmills, UK: Palgrave Macmillan.

Schimmel, Annemarie (1973). *Mystical dimensions of Islam.* Chapel Hill: University of North Carolina Press.

Shariati, Dr. Ali (1977). *Hajj.* (Somayyah and Yaser, Trans.). Bedford, Ohio: Free Islamic Literatures.

Sharma, Ursula (1980). *Women, work, and property in Northwest India.* London: Tavistock.

Sharp, Lesley A. (1993). *The Possessed and the dispossessed: Spirits, identity, and power in a Madagascar migrant town.* Berkeley: University of California Press.

Singer, Milton (1964). The social organization of Indian civilization. *Diogène, 45,* 84–119.

Smith, Robert J. (1974). *Ancestor worship in contemporary Japan.* Stanford: Stanford University Press.

Smith, Robert J. (1983). *Japanese society: Tradition, self, and the social order.* Cambridge: Cambridge University Press.

Smith, Rogers M. (1998). "Equal" Treatment? A liberal separationist view. In Stephen V. Monsma and J. Christopher Soper (Eds.), *Equal Treatment of Religion in a Pluralistic Society* (pp. 179–199). Grand Rapids, MI: William B. Eerdmans Publishing Co.

Smith, Rogers M. (2007). Secularism, constitutionalism, and the rise of christian conservatism in the United States. Unpublished manuscript.

Smith, Wilfred Cantwell (1978). *The meaning and end of religion.* San Francisco: Harper & Row. (Original work published 1962)

Soares, Benjamin F. (2003). An African Muslim saint and his followers in France. Unpublished manuscript.

Spencer, Jonathan (2000). *A Sinhala village in a time of trouble: Politics and change in rural Sri Lanka.* Oxford: Oxford University Press.

Stark, Rodney, and Roger Finke (2000). *Acts of faith: Explaining the human side of religion.* Berkeley: University of California Press.

Starrett, Gregory (1998). *Putting Islam to work: Education, politics, and religious transformation in Egypt.* Berkeley: University of California Press.

Steinfels, Peter (1992). The vision that wasn't. Or was it? *New York Times,* September 2, 1992, A14.

Stern, Jessica (2003). *Terror in the name of God: Why religious militants kill.* New York: Ecco.

Stirrat, R. L. (1992). *Power and religiosity in post-colonial setting: Sinhala Catholics in contemporary Sri Lanka.* Cambridge: Cambridge University Press.

Sudarman, Dea (1984). *Asmat.* Jakarta: Penerbit Sinar Harapan.

Svensson, Frances (1979). Liberal democracy and group rights: The legacy of individualism and its impact on American Indian tribes. *Political Studies, 27,* 421–439.

Swain, Tony (1995). Australia. In Tony Swain and Garry Trompf, *The Religions of Oceania* (pp. 19–118). New York: Routledge.

Swallow, D. A. (1982). Ashes and powers: Myth, rite and miracle in an Indian god-man's cult. *Modern Asian Studies, 16*(1), 123–158.

Tabor, James D., and Eugene V. Gallagher (1995). *Why Waco?: Cults and the battle for religious freedom in America.* Los Angeles: University of California Press.

Tambiah, S. J. (1970). *Buddhism and spirit cults in northeast Thailand.* Cambridge: Cambridge University Press.

Tambiah, S. J. (1976). *World conqueror and world renouncer.* Cambridge, Mass.: Harvard University Press.

Tambiah, S. J. (1986). *Sri Lanka: Ethnic fratricide and the dismantling of democracy.* Chicago: University of Chicago Press.

Taylor, Charles (1990). Religion in a free society. In James Davison Hunter and Os Guiness (Eds.), *Articles of faith, articles of peace* (pp. 93–113). Washington, D.C.: The Brookings Institution.

Trillin, Calvin (1994). Drawing the line. *The New Yorker,* December 12, pp. 50–62.

Trompf, Garry (1995). Pacific Islands. In Tony Swain and Garry Trompf, *The religions of Oceania* (pp. 121–222). New York: Routledge.

Turner, Victor (1967). *The forest of symbols: Aspects of Ndembu ritual.* Ithaca: Cornell University Press.

Turner, Victor (1969). *The ritual process: Structure and anti-structure.* Ithaca: Cornell University Press.

Turner, Victor (1974). Pilgrimages as social processes. In *Dramas, fields, and metaphors* (pp. 166–230). Ithaca: Cornell University Press.

Tylor, Edward Burnett (1970). *Primitive culture* (2 vols.). Gloucester, Mass.: Peter Smith. (Original work published 1871)

Urban, Greg (1991). *A discourse-centered approach to culture.* Austin: University of Texas Press.

van Gennep, Arnold (1960). *The rites of passage.* (Monika B. Vizedom and Gabrielle L. Caffee, Trans.). Chicago: University of Chicago Press. (Original work published 1908)

van der Veer, Peter (1994). *Religious nationalisms: Hindus and Muslims in India.* Los Angeles: University of California Press.

Varshney, Ashutosh (2002). *Ethnic conflict and civic life: Hindus and Muslims in India.* New Haven: Yale University Press.

Venel, Nancy (1999). *Musulmanes françaises: Des pratiquantes voiles à l'université.* Paris: L'Harmattan.

Volkman, Toby Alice (1985). *Feasts of honor: Ritual and change in the Toraja highlands.* Urbana: University of Illinois.

Walker, Sheila S. (1990). Everyday and esoteric reality in the Afro-Brazilian Candomblé. *History of Religions, 30,* 103–128.

Warner, Marina (1996). Blood and tears. *The New Yorker,* April 8, pp. 63–69.

Watson, James L. (1982). Of flesh and bones: The management of death pollution in Cantonese society. In Maurice Bloch and Jonathan Parry (Eds.), *Death and the regeneration of life* (pp. 155–186). Cambridge: Cambridge University Press.

Waugh, Earle H. (1977). Muharram rites: Community death and rebirth. In Frank E. Reynolds and Earle H. Waugh (Eds.), *Religious encounters with death* (pp. 200–213). University Park: Penn State University Press.

Webb, Malcolm C. (1965). The abolition of the taboo system in Hawaii. *Journal of the Polynesian Society, 74,* 21–39.

Weber, Max (1958). *The protestant ethic and the spirit of capitalism.* (Talcott Parsons, Trans.). New York: Charles Scribner's Sons. (Original work published 1904–1905)

Weber, Max (1978). *Economy and society* (2 vols.). Los Angeles: University of California Press. (Original work published 1956)

Weiner, Annette B. (1976). *Women of value, men of renown: New perspectives in Trobriand exchange.* Austin: University of Texas Press.

Weisman, Steven R. (1990). Akihito performs his solitary rite. *New York Times,* November 23, 1990, A7.

Werbner, Pnina S. (2003). *Pilgrims of love: Anthropology of a global Sufi Cult.* London: Indiana University Press.

Westermarck, Edward Alexander (1968). *Ritual and belief in Morocco* (2 vols.). New Hyde Park, N.Y.: University Books. (Original work published 1926)

Whitehead, Harriet (1987). Fertility and exchange in New Guinea. In Jane Fishburne Collier and Sylvia Junko Yanagisako (Eds.), *Gender and kinship: Essays toward a unified analysis* (pp. 244–267). Stanford: Stanford University Press.

Wikan, Unni (1990). *Managing turbulent hearts: A Balinese formulation for living.* Chicago: University of Chicago Press.

Wilson, Bryan R. (1961). *Sects and society: A sociological study of three religious groups in Britain.* London: William Heinemann.

Witherspoon, Gary (1977). *Language and art in the Navajo universe.* Ann Arbor: University of Michigan Press.

Wolf, Arthur (1974). Gods, ghosts, and ancestors. In Arthur Wolf (Ed.), *Religion and ritual in Chinese society* (pp. 131–182). Stanford: Stanford University Press.

Wolf, Eric (1958). The virgin of Guadalupe: A Mexican national symbol. *Journal of American Folklore, 71,* 34–39.

Wolff, Alexander (2003). SI Flashback: That old black magic. *Sports Illustrated, 27,* August 2003.

Woodburn, James (1982). Social dimensions of death in four African hunting and gathering societies. In Maurice Bloch and Jonathan Parry (Eds.), *Death and the regeneration of life* (pp. 187–210). Cambridge: Cambridge University Press.

Worsley, Peter (1968). *The trumpet shall sound* (rev. ed.). New York: Schocken Books.

WuDunn, Sheryl (1996). In Japan, a ritual of mourning for abortions. *New York Times,* January 25, 1996, A1, A8.

Wuthnow, Robert (1988). *The restructuring of American religion: Society and faith since World War II.* Princeton, N.J.: Princeton University Press.

Wyman, Leland C. (1970). *Blessingway, with three versions of the myth recorded and translated from the Navajo by Father Berard Haile, O.F.M.* Tucson: University of Arizona Press.

Yahya, Harun (2000). *The creation of the universe.* Scarborough, Canada: Al-Attique.

Zegwaard, Rev. Gerrad A. (1959). Headhunting practices of the Asmat of Netherlands New Guinea. *American Anthropologist, 61,* 1020–1041.

Zimdars-Schwartz, Sandra L. (1991). *Encountering Mary: From La Salette to Medjugorje.* Princeton, N.J.: Princeton University Press.

Index